It's About Time

America's Imprisonment Binge

Fourth Edition

JAMES AUSTIN

National Council on Crime and Delinquency

JOHN IRWIN

Professor Emeritus, San Francisco State University

It's About Time

America's Imprisonment Binge

Fourth Edition

JAMES AUSTIN

National Council on Crime and Delinquency

JOHN IRWIN

Professor Emeritus, San Francisco State University

WADSWORTH
CENGAGE Learning™

Australia • Brazil • Japan • Korea • Mexico • Singapore • Spain • United Kingdom • United States

It's About Time: America's Imprisonment Binge, Fourth Edition
James Austin, John Irwin

Publisher/Executive Editor: Linda Schreiber-Ganster

Acquisitions Editor: Carolyn Henderson Meier

Marketing Manager: Michelle Williams

Marketing Communications Manager: Heather Baxley

Content Project Management: PreMediaGlobal

Art Director: Maria Epes

Manufacturing Planner: Judy Inouye

Rights Acquisition Specialist: Don Schlotman

Production Service: PreMediaGlobal

Cover Designer: Riezebos Holzbaur/Tae Hatayama

Cover Image: © Ted Soqui/Corbis

For product information and technology assistance, contact us at
Cengage Learning Customer & Sales Support, 1-800-354-9706

For permission to use material from this text or product, submit all requests online at **www.cengage.com/permissions**. Further permissions questions can be e-mailed to **permissionrequest@cengage.com**.

Library of Congress Control Number: 2011934201

ISBN-13: 978-0-534-61596-3

ISBN-10: 0-534-61596-1

Wadsworth
20 Davis Drive
Belmont, CA, 94002-3098
USA

Cengage Learning is a leading provider of customized learning solutions with office locations around the globe, including Singapore, the United Kingdom, Australia, Mexico, Brazil, and Japan. Locate your local office at **www.cengage.com/global**.

Cengage Learning products are represented in Canada by Nelson Education, Ltd.

To learn more about Wadsworth, visit **www.cengage.com/wadsworth**.

Purchase any of our products at your local college store or at our preferred online store **www.cengagebrain.com**.

Printed in the United States of America
1 2 3 4 5 6 7 15 14 13 12 11

Contents

■

Preface

WHY THIS BOOK?

Since 1970, John Irwin and I have been witnessing the national tragedy and disgrace of America's imprisonment binge. We, as sociologists/criminologists, have kept in close contact with America's prison systems, including their administrators, staffs, policy makers, and, most of all, clients—the prisoners. During the 1980s, we nervously listened to our political parties (both Republicans and Democrats) and special interest groups advocate their simplistic but appealing message that to solve the crime problem we only needed to escalate the use of imprisonment. We were equally dismayed to witness many of our colleagues pursue government-financed studies that would later justify the "war on crime" agenda. Then, we watched, incredulously, the unparalleled explosion of prison populations.

Our education and experience regarding the relationship between crime and imprisonment had taught us that the ideas that were the conceptual building blocks of the conservative rhetoric on crime and its control were fallacious. The basic tenets of this political agenda can be summarized as follows:

- The War on Poverty, which sought to fight crime through education, job training, and rehabilitation in the 1960s and 1970s, was a total failure.

- Dangerous criminals repeatedly go free because of liberal judges or decisions made by the liberal Supreme Court that help the criminal but not the victim.

- Swift and certain punishment in the form of more and longer prison terms will reduce crime by incapacitating the hardened criminals and making potential lawbreakers think twice before they commit crimes.

- Most inmates are dangerous and cannot be safely placed in the community.

- It will be far cheaper to society in the long run to increase the use of imprisonment.

- Greater use of imprisonment is the most effective way to reduce crime.

To counter this perspective we began conducting research to counter what we view as grossly misleading and often fallacious statements. One of the unique attributes of American democracy is its diversity—in both its citizenry and its ideas. For a democracy to exist, there must be a marketplace of ideas that often compete with one another. The dominant "imprisonment reduces crime" ideology created a stranglehold on criminal justice policy. Studies designed to evaluate the effects of the conservative policy objectively or to look at alternatives were not requested or were denied funding. For these reasons, we felt it important that an alternative perspective be articulated— a perspective that we deeply believe will ultimately become accepted. So, we wrote this book.

We first presented this research in a series of pamphlets in the 1980s—It's About Time, Who Goes to Prison, and Does Imprisonment Reduce Crime?— that was published and distributed by the National Council on Crime and Delinquency (NCCD) over five years. Since then, many others have begun to openly question the wisdom of the massive increase in the use of imprisonment to control crime. Today the mounting costs of constructing and operating prisons coupled with the 2008 great recession have led many states to terminate all prison construction programs. Governors and mayors openly state that they cannot afford to build another jail or prison. Some jurisdictions are actually reducing their prison terms and funding alternatives to prison. Our largest state, California, spurred by its own recession and the intervention of the federal courts, is lowering its prison system by some 40,000 prisoners.

We also take heart that those criminologists who have provided the intellectual fodder for the imprisonment binge now concede that their incapacitation theories were misguided and that we have built too many prisons. Indeed, no credible criminologist supports the notion that the imprisonment binge has, or will in the future have, the largest impact on crime rates. Many other books and articles authored by respected scholars now echo the view that the imprisonment binge has gone on far too long and has reached a point of diminishing returns. But not unlike Robert McNamara's public confession of his failed Vietnam policy, these admissions come far too late after far too much damage has been inflicted on millions of Americans, their families, and their communities. This is especially true for African-American males who have a 30 percent chance of being sent to prison during their life.

CHANGES TO THE 4TH EDITION

In this edition, new and updated national statistics on crime, victimization, and imprisonment rates are provided. There is also detailed information on the size and attributes of not only the prison population but also probation, parole, and jail, as well as their costs. The numerous charts and tables are presented so the reader will have a firm understanding of the size and costs of the entire criminal justice and correctional systems over the past 30 years.

The 4th edition also covers contemporary topics such as the use of confidential informants in the war on drugs, whether prisons can become breeding grounds for terrorism, sex offenders, and whether the new trend toward reentry will help reduce the prison population. In each chapter, current examples of crimes, people, and prison sentences that have been covered by the popular media begin each chapter to show how the criminal justice system responds to a wide variety of offenses and punishes those convicted of their crimes.

ORGANIZATION OF THE TEXT

The ordering of the chapters has been modified to provide a more logical flow of the topics from the point of admission to prison through release. Chapter 1 offers a comprehensive and contemporary overview of the major trends in all forms of incarceration and correctional supervision. Chapter 2 provides quantitative and qualitative portraits of the numbers and types of people being admitted to prison and their crimes. The incarceration of women and children is then discussed. While the number of women being incarcerated has increased at a pace that exceeds men, the incarceration of juveniles has now dropped significantly, which may mean drops in the adult jail and prison populations.

The next four chapters tackle the nature of imprisonment today. Chapter 4 describes the experience of "doing time" in terms of its daily routine and meager offerings of rehabilitative services. The chapter shows that prisons are designed to control prisoners and in many ways serve to diminish their abilities to make it when they are returned to their families and communities.

This perspective flows into Chapter 5 on the correctional industrial treatment complex. Lofty claims have been made about the ability of the prison system to offer effective treatment services. Too often these claims result in people being required to participate in such ineffective services or even worse to remain incarcerated for not participating in such programs. Hoping that prison populations will recede as treatment increases is unfortunately a naïve strategy.

The popularization of "super max" prisons—the harshest form of imprisonment—is then reviewed in Chapter 6. While few prisoners face what is referred to as "administrative segregation," the severe forms of isolation can be devastating. Fortunately, several states are either being forced to or are voluntarily reducing their use of long-term isolation.

In Chapter 7 we discuss the rise of private prisons and whether they can do better in terms of costs and performance than public prisons. While private prisons have thus far only secured a small "market share" of the nearly 2.3 million prison and jail inmates, several states are considering turning over large shares of their prisons to private prison companies.

Chapter 8 shifts our focus back to the release of prisoners and the problems they face once they return to their communities and families. We also examine the latest fad—"prisoner reentry." Recidivism rates have not changed appreciably in the past three decades and part of this trend is the criminogenic effects of parole supervision itself. Several states are now reducing the amount of time spent under parole supervision with good results.

Chapter 9 offers a stimulating discussion of five highly controversial topics that relate to high incarceration rates—the use of confidential informants, prisons as recruitment centers for terrorists, three strikes and you're out laws, the growing number of lifers, and sex offenders.

The last chapter provides a detailed and practical plan to reduce not only the prison population but also the jail, probation, and parole populations. This can be achieved by simply adopting current or past criminal justice policy and sentencing practices that have been shown to be effective in other states. A core principle is that punishment should be proportional to the crime committed. To that end the length of imprisonment needs to be reduced. Only then will the imprisonment binge ease.

ACKNOWLEDGMENTS

Many persons and organizations helped us finish the various editions of this book. Over the course of our research, financial assistance was periodically provided by the Edna McConnell Clark Foundation, the Jessie Ball Dupont Religious, and the Charitable and Educational Fund. More recently, the Open Society Institute and the Rosenbaum Foundation provided funding for research that became the basis for the "Unlocking America" chapter. We also received the support of the National Institute of Justice, the National Institute of Corrections, the Bureau of Justice of Statistics, and the Bureau of Justice Assistance to complete studies and/or access data that are part of the analysis presented in this report. We particularly would like to thank the various administrators who were associated with those agencies at the time: Laurie Robinson, Allen Beck, Jeremy Travis, Nancy Gist, Timothy Murray, Chris Innes, Morris Thigpen, and Larry Solomon.

LaDonna Thompson, Pat Caruso, Chase Riveland, Michael Lane, Harry Singletary, and George Sumner—all of whom were directors of state prison systems at the time of our research—granted us permission and provided us with the necessary resources to conduct our inmate interviews in Michigan, Kentucky, Washington, Nevada, Illinois, and Florida. In all these states, a number of prison guards and administrative staff—too many to mention here—assisted us in compiling data on the inmates and providing access to the inmates.

Suzanne Boyd-Smith Austin, Garry Coventry, and Dana Amaadi Coleman helped with researching and assembling much of the data and editing the new additions to this book.

We want to express our deep appreciation to the numerous prisoners and parolees we have interviewed and met in the course of doing this research. Although they represent a tiny subsample of the millions of Americans who are imprisoned each year, we hope that their life experiences, as represented in this book, will lead to a more enlightened and humane imprisonment policy.

Finally, my good friend and partner in crime, John Irwin, died in 2009. Before his death he actively participated in the writing of this edition of the book, especially the sections on lifers and the final chapter on "Unlocking America." It is my hope that this new edition accurately reflects and carries forward John's values, science, and lifelong contributions to the field of criminology and prison reform.

James Austin
July 4, 2011

1

Our Imprisonment Binge

LEARNING OBJECTIVES

1. Understand the major trends in the growth of the U.S. prison system since the 1970s.

2. Be familiar with the use of rates of incarceration and crime and how they are interrelated with one another.

3. Develop and understand the two key factors that drive prison population increases—admissions and length of stay (LOS)

4. Understand how the rates of incarceration vary by gender and race.

5. Be able to distinguish between prison, parole, probation, and jail systems and their growth since 1970.

6. Develop a historical perspective on the origins of the U.S. prison system and its relationship to economic and political trends.

The United States has 5 percent of the world's population, but 25 percent of the world's prison population—the highest incarceration rate in the world. The United States currently has 7 million people in the criminal justice system and incarcerates more than 2.3 million individuals. The costs are staggering. "We're putting more and more people in jail each year, and yet 70 percent of Americans will tell you that they feel less safe in their communities than they did a year ago,"

Senator James Webb, July 28, 2010 (press release on the establishment of the National Criminal Justice Commission Act of 2010).

AMERICA'S GROWING CORRECTIONAL
INDUSTRIAL COMPLEX

The United States has been engaged in an unprecedented imprisonment binge. In 1970 the nation's entire prison population (federal and state) was 196,429. By 2009 it had reached 1,524,513—a nearly eightfold increase![1] This massive increase is not explained by the increase in the U.S. population, which went from 203 million in 1970 to 307 million by 2009 (a 50 percent increase). The incarceration rate (number of persons in state and federal prison on any given day per 100,000 population) increased 425 percent during the same time period from 96 to 504 (see Figure 1-1). The nation that prides itself as the "land of the free" now imprisons its citizens at a higher incarceration rate than any nation in the world, having surpassed China and Russia.[2] The increase was so great that by 2009, the number of citizens incarcerated in state and federal prisons exceeded or approximated the resident populations of eighteen U.S. states and was larger than all of our major cities with the exceptions of New York, Los Angeles, Chicago, and Houston.[3]

Most Americans are unaware that the adult prison population represents no more than one-fifth of the entire correctional industrial complex. There are another 760,400 people in jail, another 4.2 million on probation, and 819,308 on parole. In total, 7.2 million adults are under some form of correctional supervision.[4] This represents 3.1 percent of the entire U.S. population.

In terms of growth, the rise in prison populations has been accompanied by equally large increases in other forms of correctional supervision. Between 1980 and 2008, the jail populations (facilities that typically house pretrial defendants and offenders sentenced to short jail terms of one year or less) and probation and parole populations grew almost as rapidly as the prison population (Table 1-1).

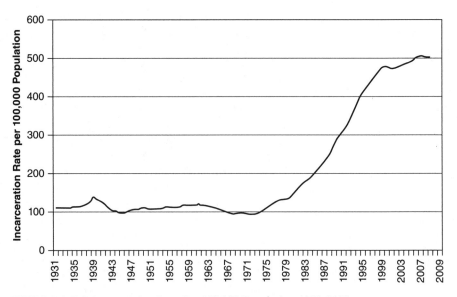

FIGURE 1-1 U.S. Incarceration Rate Per 100,000 Population 1931–2009

Table 1-1 Changes in the Adult Correctional Populations 1980–2009

	1980	2009	% Change 1980 to 2009
Prisons	319,598	1,524,513	+377%
Probation	1,118,097	4,203,967	+276%
Parole	220,438	819,308	+272%
Jails	182,288	760,400	+317%
Total	1,840,400	7,225,800	+293%
U.S. Population	227 million	307 million	+35%
Reported Index Crimes	13.4 million	10.6 million	−20%

SOURCES: U.S. Bureau of the Census website: www.census.gov; U.S. Department of Justice, Bureau of Justice Statistics website: http://bjs.ojp.usdoj.gov/index.cfm?ty=pbdetail&iid=2316.

It should also be noted that more Americans experience jail time than any other form of correctional control. Jails, unlike prisons, are where people are held following their arrest for criminal charges. They also include people who have received sentences of less than a year, people awaiting transfer to state prison, and people who have violated the conditions of probation or parole. In 1994, the U.S. Department of Justice (DOJ) reported 9.8 million admissions to the nation's 3,300-plus jails.[5] In 2008, the DOJ estimated 260,000 admissions per week or 13.5 million per year—an increase of nearly four million from 1994.[6] Assuming that approximately 75 percent of these 13.5 million admissions represent mutually exclusive adults, this means that nearly one of every twenty adults in America goes to jail each year.

Those under the control of the various correctional systems do not represent a cross section of the nation's population. They tend to be young, African-American and Hispanic males who are uneducated, without jobs, or, at best, marginally employed in low-paying jobs. According to the most recent data from the U.S. Department of Justice, there are enormous disparities in incarceration rates by race and ethnicity. Blacks and Hispanics have incarceration rates that are two to six times higher than whites (Tables 1-2 and 1-3).

Finally, one should note the progressive racial attributes of the criminal justice process. It is not possible to assess this phenomenon based on Hispanic origin, but data are available for blacks and whites from the point of arrest through release from prison. As shown in Table 1-4, there is a consistent increase

Table 1-2 Male Incarceration Rates per 100,000 Male Population by Race and Ethnicity, 1990–2008

Year	All	White	Black	Hispanic
1990	564	338	2,234	1,016
2008	952	487	3,161	1,200
% Change	49%	44%	41%	18%

SOURCES: U.S. Department of Justice, Bureau of Justice Statistics, *Prisoners in 1998* (Washington, DC, 1999) and *Prisoners in 2008* (Washington, DC. 2009).

Table 1-3 Female Incarceration Rates per 100,000 Female Population by Race and Ethnicity, 1990–2008

Year	All	White	Black	Hispanic
1990	31	19	117	56
2008	53	50	149	75
% Change	71%	68%	64%	55%

SOURCES: U.S. Department of Justice, Bureau of Justice Statistics, *Prisoners in 1998* (Washington, DC, 1999) and *Prisoners in 2008* (Washington, DC. 2009).

Table 1-4 Racial Proportions of U.S. Residents: Arrests, Convictions, Prisoners, and Length of Stay

Racial Group	U.S. Population	Offender Population	Arrested Population	Convicted Population	Prison or Jail Dispositions	Average Prison Sentence	Average Length of Stay
White	75%	69%	70%	59%	41%	61 mos	26 mos
Black	12%	22%	28%	38%	42%	68 mos	32 mos

SOURCES: Bureau of Justice Statistics. *2006 Victimization Data Tables* (cv0640.cvs); Bureau of Justice Statistics. (2008). *Felony Sentences in State Courts, 2003*. Washington, DC: U.S. Department of Justice; Federal Bureau of Investigation. (2008). *Crime in the United States, 2007*. Washington, DC: U.S. Department of Justice.

Table 1-5 Sentence Length and Time Served in Prison by Race

Offense Group	White		Black	
	Sentence	Time Served	Sentence	Time Served
All Offenses	63 mos	27 mos	69 mos	32 mos
Violent	85 mos	45 mos	95 mos	53 mos
Property	56 mos	22 mos	58 mos	25 mos
Drug	61 mos	19 mos	64 mos	23 mos
Public Order	44 mos	18 mos	45 mos	21 mos

SOURCE: Bureau of Justice Statistics, Corrections Reporting Program 2005.

in the proportion of blacks from the point of arrest through sentencing. It is also noteworthy that the racial differences in sentence length and length of imprisonment persist even when controlling for the nature of the crime the person was convicted of (Table 1-5).

THE COSTS OF THE IMPRISONMENT BINGE

As the size of the correctional complex has skyrocketed, so too has its costs. Annual spending on corrections rose from $9 billion in 1982 to nearly $70 billion as of 2006. While all three components of the criminal justice system (police, the courts, and corrections) have increased substantially, since 1982 corrections has been the faster

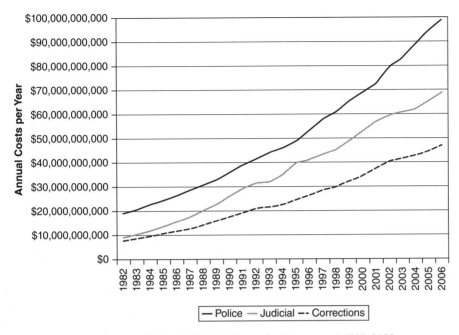

FIGURE 1-2 Annual Costs of Criminal Justice System by Component 1982–2006

growing component (Figure 1-2).[7] Corrections has increased 660 percent versus 503 percent for the courts and 420 percent for police. Spending on the entire criminal justice system has increased from $36 billion per year to $215 billion.

There are 2 million persons directly employed by criminal justice agencies, and this number does not include persons who perform services but are not directly working for these agencies. Over 750,000 people are employed by correctional agencies.[8] In California and New York, the booming prison population has resulted in these two states spending more on prisons than on their university systems.[9]

Significantly, the costs of crimes to victims are far below the costs of criminal justice (see Figure 1-3). In 2006, the total costs of crimes to victims, as reported in the U.S. Department of Justice's National Crime Victim Survey (NCVS), were $18.4 billion based on 25.2 million crimes or about $735 per crime; the majority of crimes had value losses below $100.[10] These costs include economic losses from property theft or damage, cash losses, medical expenses, loss of pay caused by victimization, and other related costs. This figure, however, does not include the reimbursement of such losses by insurance companies or recovery of stolen property by criminal justice agencies. That recovery rate has been estimated at 35 percent, which reduces the direct losses to $12 billion.

The states are just beginning to feel these enormous increases in the cost of imprisonment. The budgetary battles, in which important state services for children, the elderly, the sick, and the poor are gutted to pay for prisons, have already begun. In coming years, great cutbacks in funds for public education, medical services for the poor, highway construction, and other state services will occur unless the imprisonment binge is reversed.

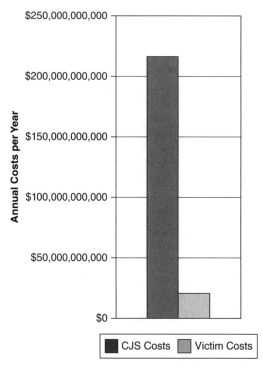

FIGURE 1-3 Comparison of Criminal Justice System Costs and Victim Costs
SOURCE: Bureau of Justice Statistics, NCVS 2006 and Employment and Expenditures 2006.

In California, the percent of the state's general fund that has gone to the state's two major university systems has declined since 1985 from 11 percent to 6 percent. At the same time, the percent of the general fund allocated to California corrections and rehabilitation has increased from 4 percent to 10 percent. This dramatic shift in spending led Governor Schwarzenegger to argue for a constitutional amendment to limit growth in the state's prison budget. Ironically, the same governor has argued against a recent federal court order to reduce the state's prison population due to its unconstitutional conditions.[11]

More generally, the overall share of state budgets that is allocated to higher education has been declining while the share for state prisons has been increasing. Between 1988 and 2008, corrections' spending at the state levels has increased by 303 percent as compared to elementary and secondary education (205%), higher education (125%), transportation (82%), and welfare (9%).[12]

THE POLITICS OF THE FEAR OF CRIME

To fully understand the impetus for the historical population increases in all segments of the adult correctional system, one must have a historical perspective. The most powerful development has been America's growing fear of crime.

Bill Chambliss has documented the well-orchestrated effort by powerful interest groups since the 1960s to make crime the most important issue on the public's mind. Chambliss points out that prior to the 1960s, crime was never cited by the public as a major concern.[13] But beginning in the 1960s and led by a well-funded cartel of conservatives who were greatly concerned about the civil rights and anti-Vietnam movements, a "War on Crime" was formally launched by an increasingly defensive President Lyndon Johnson. Part of the increasing concern regarding crime was fueled by a substantial increase in the major "index" crimes (homicides, assaults, rape, burglary, theft, and arson) reported to police beginning in the late 1960s and early 1970s. Coupled with the assassinations of President Kennedy, Senator Robert Kennedy, Martin Luther King, and major race riots in large cities, such as Los Angeles, Chicago, Detroit, and Washington DC, the public was in no mood for tolerance.

The 1970s began to see a steady buildup of law enforcement resources and harsher sentencing laws. In several states, the indeterminate sentencing laws, which symbolically embraced rehabilitation, were replaced by determinate sentencing laws that were designed to lengthen the period of incarceration. We also saw the early passages in some states on a variety of mandatory prison terms that sought to eliminate probation as a sentencing option. By 1980, the prison population had risen to 315,974. But despite massive increases in the amount of money being spent on law enforcement and corrections and a decline in the FBI Uniform Crime Report (UCR) crime rate, the public continued to believe that crime had been increasing.

Through the 1980s, the fear of crime and drug abuse was elevated each election year by the attention that politicians (both Democrats and Republicans) and the media gave to crime and drug problems. The extreme fluctuations in the public's attitude toward violent crime and drugs can be seen in Figure 1-4. In the 1980s the public was led to believe there was a drug epidemic; this was followed by another concern about violent crime in the early 1990s. But these perceptions do not correlate with actual drug use and violent crime rates.

The first and most blatant example of these tactics was then Republican presidential candidate George Bush's successful effort to erase his opponent's (Michael Dukakis) early lead in the 1987 presidential campaign by blaming the tragic Willie Horton incident on liberal Democratic Party politics. Smarting from this poignant lesson in dirty politics, Democrats have now fully embraced "get tough on crime" policies in an effort to outflank and neutralize what has traditionally been a Republican perspective.

It was under the Democratic-controlled Congress that the now infamous Federal Sentencing Guidelines, which mandated long prison terms for possession of crack cocaine, were adopted in 1984 with bipartisan support.[14] The public has shifted its focus (or more correctly has had its focus shifted by the media) on the subject of violent crime even as the crime rate has declined (see Chapter 6 on crime rate analysis). As we have suggested in an earlier publication:

> Politicians harangue on the street crime problem because it is a safe issue. It is easy to cast in simple terms of good versus evil and no powerful constituency

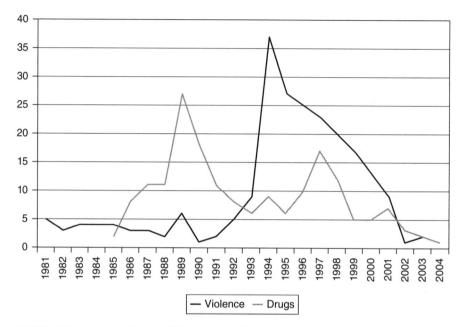

FIGURE 1-4 Changes in Percent Citing Violent Crime and Drugs as Most Important Problem Facing the Country, 1981–2004

is directly offended by a campaign against street crime. Some politicians also use street crime to divert attention away from other pressing social problems—such as the threat of nuclear war, unemployment, high living costs, and the economy—all of which persistently top the list of public concerns. Measures to solve these problems would require changes that would offend powerful interest groups.[15]

The public's concern over drug use has also been used as a political football to justify an ever-increasing imprisonment of drug users. The public's attention on drugs accelerated dramatically at the end of the 1980s, and then declined but rose again in 1997 and 1998 as Republicans and Democrats began to worry about increases in the use of marijuana by high school students.

Marsha Rosenbaum, in her analysis of the nation's early rationale for the War on Drugs, states:

> The Reagan administration initiated a "War on Drugs" in the early 1980s. The Bush administration appointed a "Drug Czar" and recently offered a major plan to remove the "scourge" of drugs from the American landscape. The media have reported on the violence occurring in our inner cities and in cocaine-source nations like Colombia. The public is bombarded with news about drugs, like the drug death of sports figure Len Bias and the confessions of celebrities about personal struggles with substance abuse.[16]

The War on Drugs also spurred a movement toward more punitive sentencing policies for drug offenders. In addition, mandatory drug testing and a reduction in affordable publicly funded drug treatment programs have meant that more and more released felons are being returned to prison for using illegal drugs.

Moreover, because this war was focused on crack cocaine, which was mainly sold and used in inner-city communities, it is increasing the already disproportionately high number of African-American and Hispanic prisoners. For example, in 1926, the first year that the race of prison admissions was recorded on a national basis, only 21 percent of all prison admissions were African American. By 1970, that figure had increased to 39 percent; by 1996, it had further grown to 51 percent. In their steady and unrelenting harangues on the crime and drug problems, politicians argued that steady and dramatic expansion of prison populations is absolutely necessary to maintain a safe society. They said that massive increases in imprisonment are positive signs—indications that the nation is increasingly intolerant of criminals and their antisocial and too often violent behavior. Moreover, they claimed that increasing the use of imprisonment in particular and punishment in general has reduced crime. In 1992, then Attorney General William Barr restated this position well, indicating that the country had a "clear choice": either to build more prisons or to tolerate higher violent crime rates.[17]

By 1990 the prison population had risen to 740,000 with no signs of abating. Under both Democrat and Republican administrations and congresses under the control of both parties, the prison populations continued to rise. It was President Clinton's administration that endorsed the most expensive crime bill. Written in part by then Senator Joe Biden, the bill funded 200,000 police officers and boot camps, along with $10 billion to help pay for prison construction for states willing to pass laws that would require longer prison terms for people convicted of violent crimes. By then the Democratic party had achieved a major political goal—the public would view them as conservative on the crime issue as Republicans.

By 2000 the prison population had doubled yet again reaching 1.3 million. At this time two major criminal justice trends began to emerge. First, while the prison population was continuing to increase, it was increasing at a much slower rate. Indeed, by 2009, twenty-four states reported, albeit slight, declines in their prison populations. The only system that was continuing to increase at a rapid pace was the federal Bureau of Prisons (BOP), which was increasingly being filled by drug offenders arrested by Drug Efforcement Agency (DEA) and local state strike forces and illegal immigrants.

The declining rate of increase ... in the prison population ... was related in part to the continuing decline in the nation's crime rate, which in turn was lowering the arrest rate with the exception of the drug arrest rate, which was continuing to increase (see Figure 1-5). Since prison populations are the next result of admissions times the length of stay (or imprisonment), a decline or lowering of arrest rates usually means a slowing of the prison admission stream. As will be shown in Chapter 2, this indeed was the case; prison admissions from the courts has remained relatively flat over the past five years.

The second major development was the worsening economic picture for local and state government. As noted earlier, the dramatic increase in the operating costs of the criminal justice system and corrections in particular placed increased pressure on the government to lower prison and jail costs. These economic problems

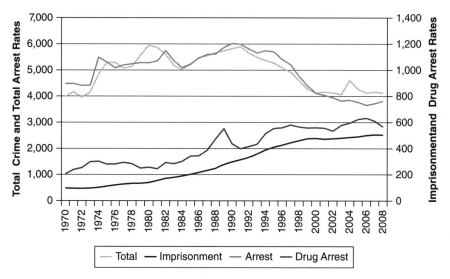

FIGURE 1-5 Crime, Arrest, and Imprisonment Rates 1970–2008

worsened as the 2008 recession hit. The worsening fiscal picture for state and local government agencies has led to a new interest of lowering prison populations as advocated initially by a variety of foundations, organizations, and even the federal government.[18] Known more popularly as "justice reinvestment," the goal is to reallocate prison funds to more crime preventive initiatives. Whether or not justice reinvestment succeeds remains to be seen but there is a glimmer of hope that the imprisonment binge can be reversed.

AMERICA'S HISTORY OF WAREHOUSING PRISONERS

Imprisonment as society's punishment for serious crime has been part of the American social fabric since the founding of this country. In colonial times, before the American Revolution, most felons were fined, whipped, branded, publicly shamed, or banished. A few were executed. The prison, a special location in which to place people for punishment of their crimes, was introduced soon after the revolution, ostensibly as a device to reform offenders. Americans, rejecting what they saw as excessively cruel measures employed in England and in the colonies under English rule, adopted the concept of the "penitentiary," where felons would "be kept in quiet solitude, reflecting penitently on their sins in order that they might cleanse and transform themselves." After several decades of building and running penitentiaries, the states more or less gave up on reformation but continued to use the prison as the main form of punishment for serious crime.

During the nineteenth century, prisons became extremely cruel places in which convicts were kept under control through brutal forms of corporal

punishment and were frequently used as cheap labor. Around 1900, federal legislation and emerging union power forced most convicted labor out of the public
sector. For the next fifty years, prisons were "big houses"—fortress-like institutions
where prisoners did little more than "time." After World War II, many states
returned to the reformative goal, with some new social scientific embellishments.
Prisoners were to be "rehabilitated" through new scientific methods. This era
lasted until evidence mounted that rehabilitative efforts were making no
difference—that is, prisoners who were involved in treatment programs returned
to prison at the same rate as those who were not.[19] This persistent finding of
"no difference" convinced social scientists and then criminal justice policy makers
that rehabilitation had been a mistake.[20] The social scientists argued that under
rehabilitation, sentences were increased and many inhumane programs and routines were practiced.[21] Government policy makers believed that rehabilitation
had been an expensive failure that led to higher crime rates. At this time, the general society entered a punitive period (1975) that continues today. Rehabilitation
was abandoned, and now felons are sent to prison to receive their "just desserts"
and to be deterred from committing crimes in the future.

In examining this history of shifting rationales for imprisonment, we clearly
see that none of them accounts for our persistent and almost exclusive reliance
on prison as the appropriate response to serious crime. What it does explain is
the American people's strong desire to banish from their midst any population
of people who are threatening, bothersome, and repulsive. As David Rothman
points out in *The Discovery of the Asylum*, this is what was done from the outset
with the insane, the feeble-minded, the poor, wayward children, and felons.[22]
We continue to do it with the elderly poor, troublesome insane, street rabble,
and felons.[23] The pattern is particularly clear in the latest upsurge in the use of
prisons, which followed a period (1965–1970) during which there was considerable interest in finding other forms of punishment and actual success in significantly lowering prison populations.

By the 1980s many unsettling developments made Americans more fearful,
conservative, and mean-spirited. The aforementioned perception of steady
increases in crime was one contributing factor. But more fundamental were the
growing nationwide economic difficulties. Currently, high unemployment, deval-
uation of the housing market, and a decline in real wages for a significant proportion of the middle class has caused great uncertainty about our economic future.
Also, the proliferation of a materialistic, isolated, and highly technical culture,
ostentatious parvenus, and the expansion of an underclass perceived as menacing,
further diminishes our quality of life.

These disturbing developments began in the 1980s and have been aggravated
by the perception that, because of global, unmanageable economic processes, our
society's economic problems are insoluble. For example, between 1980 and
2009, the number of persons living in poverty rose from 29 to 43.6 million
(50% increase).[24] Over 20 million children live in poverty. Today only one in
four Americans believe the "American Dream" is attainable for them.[25]

How did these disturbing trends emerge? Part of the explanation lies in fundamental shifts in the distribution of wealth, as first documented by Kevin Phillips

in his book *The Politics of Rich and Poor*.[26] Phillips, using a wide variety of official data, argued that the government's economic policies of the past decade have improved the economic status of the rich at the expense of the lower and middle classes. He identified some of the more striking economic trends during the 1980s:

- Between 1979 and 1987, earnings for male high school graduates with one to five years of work experience declined by 18 percent.

- Between 1981 and 1987, the nation lost over 1 million manufacturing jobs.

- Between 1977 and 1988, the average after-tax family income of the lowest 10 percent, in current dollars, fell from $3,528 to $3,157 (a 10.5% decline). Conversely, the income of the top 10 percent increased from $70,459 to $89,783 (a 24.4% increase), and the incomes of the top 1 percent increased from $174,498 to $303,900 (a 74% increase).

- Between 1981 and 1988, the total compensation of chief executives increased from $373,000 to $773,000 (an increase of 107%), and the number of millionaires and billionaires increased by more than 250 percent.[27]

- In 1987, the income of the typical African-American family ($18,098) equaled just 56.1 percent of the typical white family's income, the lowest comparative ratio since the 1960s.

Despite these trends, the middle and upper class were enjoying the prosperity of a booming U.S. economy fueled in part by the dramatic increase in housing values, which were being driven by what we now know was a fraudulent financial and credit market. Eventually, the dramatic crash in world economies in 2008 delivered a powerful and sobering message—we as a country were living well beyond our means. Even worse, while some were prospering in the 1990s and the early 2000s, many Americans were not benefiting and are in worse shape today. In economic terms, the United States has now become a more fragmented and segregated society. In particular, the number of those Americans who were uneducated and raised in impoverished conditions has continued to grow, thus justifying the need to further expand the correctional system to control and manage that population. As Phillips forecast more than a decade ago:

> For women, young people, and minorities the effect of economic polarization during the 1980's was largely negative. The nation as a whole also suffered as unemployable young people drove up the crime rate and expanded the drug trade. Broken families and unwed teenage mothers promised further welfare generations and expense. And none of it augured well for the future skills level and competitiveness of the U.S. work force.[28]

More recently, R. Wilkinson and K. Pickett found considerable evidence that high rates of incarceration, violence, and mental illness in the United States are associated with the increased levels of inequality documented earlier by Phillips. These findings persist not only when compared to other countries but also within the United States. This means that states that have higher levels of income inequality have higher rates of imprisonment, and homicides, and mental illness (see Figures 1-6 and 1-7).[29]

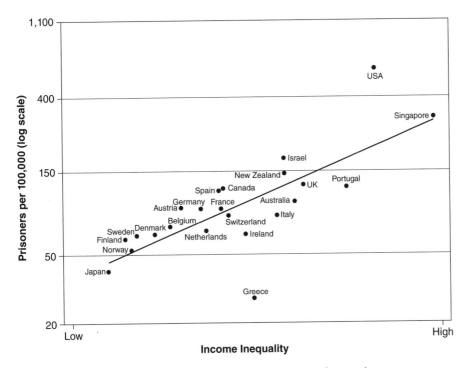

FIGURE 1-6 Rates of Imprisonment are Higher in More Unequal Countries

SOURCE: Wilkinson & Pickett, The Spirit Level (2009)

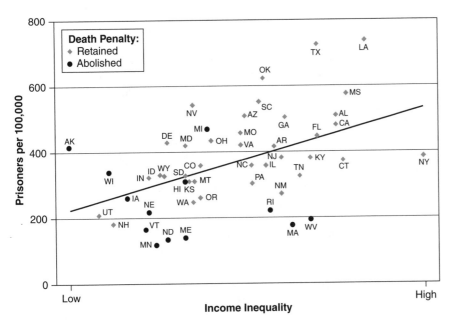

FIGURE 1-7 Rates of Imprisonment are Higher in More Unequal US States

SOURCE: Wilkinson & Pickett, The Spirit Level (2009)

Our society now faces an enormous public policy dilemma. On the one hand, we are expending a greater portion of our public dollars on incarcerating, punishing, treating, and controlling persons who are primarily from the lower economic classes in an effort to reduce crime. On the other hand, we have set in motion economic policies that will serve to widen the gap between the rich and the poor, producing yet another generation of impoverished youths who will end up under the control of the correctional system. By escalating the size of the correctional system, we are also increasing the tax burden and diverting billions of dollars from those very public services (education, health, transportation, and economic development) that would reduce poverty, unemployment, crime, drug abuse, and mental illness.

Although we have become more punitive than at any other time in our history, the public still believes that we have been overly soft on crime; they continue to support the election of politicians, prosecutors, and judges who say they want to "get tough" on crime, even in the face of declining crime rates and a declining standard of living. Edward Luttwak, in his analysis of the impact of U.S. economics on the middle class, argued a decade ago that the growing insecurity of the middle class would translate into an almost "insatiable demand" for even more punitive sentencing practices:

> The insecure majority does not realize that the economy too can be subject to the will of the majority ... so it vents its anger and resentment by punishing, restricting, and prohibiting everything it can. The most blatant symptom is the insatiable demand for tougher criminal laws, longer prison terms, mandatory life sentences for repeat offenders, more and prompter executions, and harsher forms of detention (including, of late, chain gangs). Politicians, including President Clinton, have heard the people, and the result is a mass of new federal and state legislation that will greatly add to the staggering number of Americans already behind bars.[30]

In many ways, our current situation is similar to that of eighteenth-century England, which was passing through even more unsettling changes than we are today and was faced with unprecedented crime waves in its new, crowded, filthy, polluted, slum-encircled, rabble-ridden cities.[31] After experimenting with extraordinary punishments, particularly wholesale hanging and the use of prison barges, England turned to banishment as its primary penal measure. An important difference between eighteenth-century England and modern-day America, however, is that the world offered England locations to which it could send its felons—first America, and then Australia. Between 1787 and 1868, hundreds of thousands of convicts (over 100,000 in the first fleet) were transported to Australia.

America has had to construct its locations of banishment within its borders. This it is doing at a feverish pace. As was done in eighteenth-century England, we have even tried using barges in New York City. Although we lack an Australia where we can set up prison colonies, we are increasingly building huge mega-prison settlements in isolated rural locations where land is cheap and recession-starved communities are anxious for the economic benefits that a major prison will bring.

WHAT HAS BEEN ACCOMPLISHED BY THE IMPRISONMENT BINGE?

Americans wanted several things accomplished by their support of our expensive imprisonment practices. Above all, they wanted to feel safer in their homes, in their neighborhoods, on the street, and in any public place. For this reason, they wanted menacing "street criminals" removed and placed in prison. They were also angry at criminals, particularly the types highlighted in the media and by politicians. Moreover, they wanted apprehended criminals punished harshly so that other potential or active criminals will think twice before committing a crime in the future. But ironically, they also wanted prisoners in prison to be given treatment and services that will result in their rehabilitation. For example, as the prison populations were escalating, a 1996 national survey by Sam Houston University found that rehabilitation was the most important goal of prison. A similar finding was identified by the Public Agenda Foundation.[32]

Given the public perception of the crime problem at that time, these were reasonable goals. But was the public view correct? Were persons sent to prison being given appropriate punishment for their crimes? Were large numbers of potential criminals deterred by imprisonment? Were prisoners having their chances of returning to crime reduced by any program or activity that occur in our new prisons? The evidence suggests otherwise.

UCR crime rates did not begin to decline until the mid 1990s. But the question is what are the principle causes of this decline? This question is discussed in greater detail in Chapter 10. But Figure 1-8, which compares the official UCR

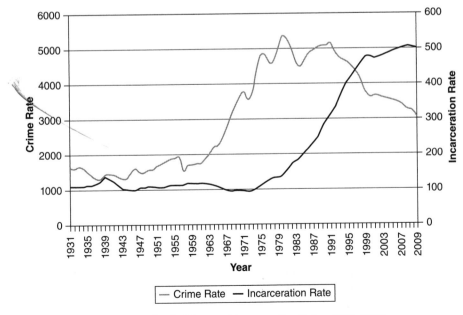

FIGURE 1-8 Comparison of U.S. Crime and Incarceration Rates, 1931–2009

crime rate to the incarceration rate for the same time period, offers some initial insights and raises some questions. First, for many years the incarceration and crime rates were quite similar. In essence this means that the United States enjoyed both a relatively low crime and incarceration rate. So it's true that for many decades the United States did not require a huge prison system to keep crime rates low. This raises the question of why crime rates climbed so dramatically in the 1970s and early 1980s.

Second, the dramatic increase in the crime rate was not caused by a dramatic drop in the incarceration rate. Beginning in the early 1960s, the crime rate began to escalate even as the incarceration rate remained stable. In other words, the crime rate did not start to increase in reaction to a lowering of the incarceration rate. It was not until 1975 that the incarceration rate began to rise for the reasons noted earlier.

Third, although crime rates have declined significantly since 1995, most of these decreases cannot be directly linked to the imprisonment binge. The most recent estimates by William Spelman is that no more than 25 percent of the drop in the crime rate was due to higher incarceration rates.[33] Such estimates may exaggerate the impact on crime rates as they do not account for the substantial increase in the probation population, which is another form of control and has the largest number of people under its jurisdiction. But the 25 percent estimate means that the majority of the drop in crime rates is due to factors other than increased incarceration rates, such as demographic changes, the increased presence of police, lower numbers of people on welfare, and other factors.

Finally, the U.S. crime rate is now what it was in the late 1960s when our national incarceration rate was only 100 per 100,000 population. It raises the question of whether we really need such a high incarceration rate when (1) most of the drop in the crime rate is not due to a higher incarceration rate, and (2) we were able in the past to have much lower crime and incarceration rates.

Ironically, despite the drop in UCR crime rates, a 2007 report by the Gallup Poll finds that a majority of Americans believe that national crime rates have been *increasing*.[34] For now, suffice it to say that Americans perceptions on crime and the scientific findings show that our crime problem has not been solved and the reductions in crime that have been achieved are only marginally related to an increased use of incarceration.

These facts indicate we are wasting large sums of money on a system that has diminishing returns. This view is growing in popularity with some of our more conservative policy thinkers. For example, Supreme Court Justice Anthony Kennedy said, "Our resources are misspent, our punishments too severe, our sentences too long." Renown criminologist James Q. Wilson has also taken a stand on this position: "lengthening time served beyond some point will, like increasing the proportion of convicted criminals sent to prison, encounter diminishing marginal returns."[35] Similarly, former incarceration advocates, such as Professor DiIulio and former U.S. attorney general Edward Meese, are calling for a repeal of mandatory minimum sentencing and are challenging the wisdom of a massive imprisonment policy.[36] Put differently, if incarceration ever had a public safety benefit, it has apparently run its course.

A GLIMMER OF HOPE

Despite the massive increases in all forms of imprisonment and correctional supervision, there are some trends that suggest the United States is beginning to change its thirty-year imprisonment binge. As of 2009, there were twenty-four states that lowered their prison populations, led by New York, which had gone from 73,000 to 59,000 state prisoners. In Mississippi, the state overturned its "truth in sentencing" laws on drug crimes purposely to lower the prison systems. The federal court has intervened in California and has ordered that its crowded prison system be reduced by 40,000 over the next three years. There is an increasing number of studies that have been published showing the limits and counterproductive aspects of imprisonment for those imprisoned, their families, and our communities. Recent polls conducted by Gallup and the PEW Charitable Trust show broad public support for the use of alternatives to incarceration and reductions in the period of imprisonment for large segments of the current prison population. Perhaps more striking is the persistent finding that the public believes attacking "social problems" is the most effective way to lower crime in the future.[37]

We also know that several states have very low incarceration rates (Figure 1-9). This means that for many jurisdictions we have already achieved the goal of low

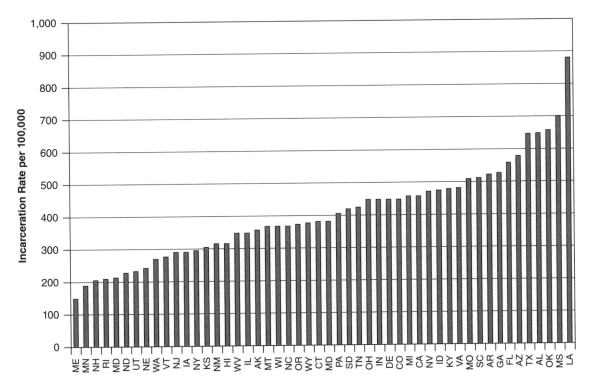

FIGURE 1-9 Incarceration Rates by State, 2009

SOURCE: Bureau of Justice Statistics, Prisoners in 2009.

incarceration rates. The reason(s) why some states have incarceration rates that are onehalf or more than the national average is complex. Certainly a major reason is that crime rates are lower in those states than the high incarceration rates. But whatever the reason, it should be clear that it is not higher incarceration rates that produce low crime rates but other socioeconomic factors that produce a better educated, more fully employed, and better adjusted society. As will be shown throughout the book, higher incarceration rates can serve to reduce the establishment of a more equitable society.

The remainder of the book provides data and analysis on a variety of topics including who goes to prison, how they are released, the use of super-max and private prisons, the effectiveness of rehabilitation and treatment, and the emerging focus on prison reentry. All of this information is then used to present the final chapter: a strategic plan to significantly reduce not only the prisons but their parole and probation populations to the levels that existed a mere twenty years ago.[38] What is interesting is that more and more states are now adopting these reforms and are beginning to unlock America.

NOTES

1. U.S. Department of Justice, Bureau of Justice Statistics website accessed October 21, 2010. http://bjs.ojp.usdoj.gov/index.cfm?ty=pbdetail&iid=2272.

2. King's College, London, International Centre for Prison Studies, *Prison Brief—Highest to Lowest Rates* accessed 2010. http://www.kcl.ac.uk/depsta/rel/icps/world brief.

3. U.S. Census Bureau website accessed October 21, 2010. www.census.gov.

4. U.S. Department of Justice, Bureau of Justice Statistics Correctional Surveys (The Annual Probation Survey, National Prisoner Statistics Program, Annual Survey of Jails, and Annual Parole Survey) as presented in *Correctional Populations in the United States, Prisoners in 2008*, and *Probation and Parole in the United States, 2008.*

5. U.S. Department of Justice, Bureau of Justice Statistics, *Jails and Jail Inmates 1993–1994* (Washington, DC: U.S. Government Printing Office, 1994).

6. U.S. Department of Justice, Bureau of Justice Statistics, *Jails Inmates at Midyear 2008.* (Washington, DC: U.S. Government Printing Office, March 2009).

7. Bureau of Justice Statistics website accessed October 21, 2010. http://www.ojp.gov/bjs/glance/tables/exptyptab.htm.

8. Bureau of Justice Statistics website accessed October 21, 2010. http://bjs.ojp.usdoj.gov/index.cfm?ty=tp&tid=5.

9. Justice Policy Institute, *Class Dismissed: Higher Education vs. Corrections During the Wilson Years* (September 1998); and *New York State of Mind? Higher Education vs. Prison Funding in the Empire State, 1988–1998* (Washington, DC: Justice Policy Institute, December 1998).

10. U.S. Department of Justice, Bureau of Justice Statistics accessed August 2008. *Criminal Victimization in the United States, 2006. Statistical Tables.* Table 82.

11. www.lao.ca.gov/reports/2010/edu/educ_prisons/educ_prisons_012610.aspx.

12. Pew Center on the States, *One in 31: The Long Reach of American Corrections* (Washington, DC: Pew Charitable Trusts) March 2009.

13. William J. Chambliss, *Power, Politics, and Crime* (Boulder, CO: Westview Press, 1999).

14. U.S. Department of Justice website http://www.justice.gov/opa/documents/United_States_v_Booker_Fact_Sheet.pdf.

15. John Irwin and James Austin, *It's About Time* (San Francisco: National Council on Crime and Delinquency, 1987).

16. Marsha Rosenbaum, *Just Say What?* (San Francisco: National Council on Crime and Delinquency, 1989), p. 1.

17. William P. Barr. "Expanding Capacity for Serious Offenders." Attorney General's Summit on Corrections, Ritz Carlton Hotel, McLean, VA, April 27, 1992.

18. The original origins of the justice reinvestment was initiated by the Open Institute Foundation and the Council of State Government (CSG). See the CSG website that describes the program at http://www.justicereinvestment.org/about.

19. The issue of whether rehabilitation is effective is controversial and will be taken up in Chapters 2 and 6.

20. In the late 1960s, a series of studies and reviews began to indicate that most of the "treatment" programs practiced in the 1950s and 1960s had no impact on recidivism. This was particularly true of the programs based on personality disorder theories. Even though a small number of programs, particularly those that pursued a learning or cognitive approach, seemed to show some reduction in recidivism, a general consensus formed at this time said that "nothing worked." See particularly Robert Martinson, "What Works? Questions and Answers About Prison Reform," *Public Interest* 35 (April 1974): 22–54; and Douglas Lipton, Robert Martinson, and Judith Wilks, *The Effectiveness of Correctional Treatment: A Survey of Treatment Evaluation Studies* (New York: Praeger, 1975). Recently James Austin commented on the claim that some programs work, observing that well-designed and well-administered treatment programs are the exception, not the rule.

21. These criticisms of rehabilitation on the part of social scientists and "liberal" prison reformers were first stated in the American Friends Service Committee, *The Struggle for Justice* (New York: Hill & Wang, 1971), which was followed by a series of books criticizing rehabilitation.

22. David Rothman, *The Discovery of the Asylum* (Boston: Little, Brown, 1971).

23. In his study of the county jail, *The Jail* (Berkeley: University of California Press, 1985), John Irwin discovered that it was intended as a device to help manage society's rabble—disorganized and disreputable people.

24. http://www.census.gov/hhes/www/poverty/data/incpovhlth/2009/tables.htmlmillion.

25. http://thehill.com/house-polls/thehill-poll-week-3/124935-only-1-in-4-see-american-dream-as-attainable.

26. Kevin Phillips, *The Politics of Rich and Poor* (New York: Random House, 1991).

27. Ibid.

28. Ibid., p. 208.

29. R. Wilkinson and K. Pickett, *The Spirit Level: Why More Equal Societies Almost Always Do Better.* Allen Lane, 2009.

30. Edward Luttwak, "The Middle-Class Backlash," *Harper's* 292 (January 1996): pp. 15–16.

31. England was also experiencing its own drug problem, that of "killer gin." See Robert Hughes, *The Fatal Shore* (New York: Random House, 1988), Chapter 2, for an excellent discussion of threats from crime, urban mobs, or the "dangerous classes" in England, which led to an expansion of transportation as a remedy.

32. An early study by John Doble of the Public Agenda Foundation found that besides wanting criminals punished and incapacitated, Americans believe that criminals are produced by remedial circumstances and want prisons to rehabilitate prisoners into peaceful, productive citizens. See *Crime and Punishment: The Public's View* (New York: Edna McConnell Clark Foundation, 1987). Also see Survey Research Program (College of Criminal Justice, Sam Houston State University, 1996).

33. William Spelman, "The Limited Importance of Prison Expansion," in *The Crime Drop in America*, ed. Alfred Blumstein, revised edition (New York: Cambridge University Press, 2006), pp. 97–129.

34. Lydia Saad, "Perceptions of Crime Problem Remain Curiously Negative." Gallup Poll, accessed October 22, 2007. www.gallup.com/poll/102262/ perceptions-crime-problem-remain-curiously-negative.aspx.

35. James Q. Wilson, "Crime and Public Policy" in *Crime*, eds. James Q. Wilson and Joan Petersilia (Oakland, CA: ICS Press, 1995), pp 489–507.

36. Jacob Sullum, "Prison Conversion: After Studying Non-Violent Drug Offenders, A Criminologist Who Once Said 'Let 'Em Rot' Now Says 'Let 'Em Go'," August/September 1999. Reasonline, http://www.reason.com.

37. The Gallup Organization, Inc., The Gallup Poll, accessed Aug. 2, 2007. http//www.galluppoll/.

38. This plan is now being supported by the U.S. Department of Justice's National Institute of Corrections as part of its effort to reform and reduce local and state adult correctional systems.

2

■

Who Goes to Prison?

LEARNING OBJECTIVES

1. Develop an understanding between the attributes of people who are sent to prison versus the daily prison population.

2. Review the most current national data on the numbers and attributes of the people sent to prison each year.

3. Understand the difference between quantitative and qualitative/ethnographic forms of analysis as it pertains to prisoner attributes.

4. Understand how changes in the length of stay (LOS) in prison has a large impact on prison population.

5. Develop an understanding of the lifestyles of people sent to prison each year.

PUBLIC MISPERCEPTIONS ABOUT WHO GOES TO PRISON

The public reacts to crime with fear and panic, because they have been led to believe by the media and public officials that thousands of vicious, intractable street criminals menace innocent citizens. Actually, they have two slightly different images of the new street criminal. The "softer" version is that of a person who persists in committing property crimes even after repeated opportunities to live an honest life and after being arrested many times and serving numerous jail and prison sentences. The "harder" version is that of a violent criminal, equally intractable, who goes about his or her predatory crimes with no regard for other humans. When he (usually a male) snatches purses from old ladies, he bashes them in the head, because he enjoys hurting people. When he robs a mom-and-pop grocery store, he executes his victims with a sneer on his face. Most Americans still believe that millions of these two slightly different types of street criminals stalk our streets; raid our homes; rape, assault, and murder innocent citizens; and generally menace and vilify our society.

But as shown below, it does not take much today to be sentenced to prison. While these cases may not be the "typical" prisoner, they do show that the threshold for being sentenced to prison for relatively minor criminal behavior has been lowered. In addition to these types of low-level convictions, hundreds of thousands of people are being sent to prison each year, not for being convicted of a felony crime but for not complying with the bureaucratic rules associated with probation and parole supervision, such as not reporting to one's parole or probation officer, not paying supervision fees, and not reporting for drug treatment.

The emergence of criminology as a science in the nineteenth century had served to debunk the "evil person" theory of crime and instead attributed the crime problem to social and economic conditions. But recently, many researchers, perhaps swayed by the general conservative shift or lured by government incentives in the form of grants, jobs, and recognition, have resurrected old theories of the "criminal type" (now most often labeled the "career criminal") and have searched for methods to identify such people.

This trend started in 1970, when Marvin E. Wolfgang, Robert M. Figlio, and Thorsten Sellin examined the arrest records of all youths born in Philadelphia in 1945 and discovered that 6 percent of the youth in that "birth cohort" accounted for more than half of all the arrests or police contacts of the entire cohort. The idea that a few criminals commit most of the crime evolved from this study—along with the hope that there was some way to identify these persons before they embarked on their criminal careers.[1]

"Offenders"	Prior Record	Crime	Description	Sentence
Elisa Kelly and George Robinson Mother and Stepfather	None	Nine counts of contributing to the delinquency of a minor	Hosting drinking party for son's nine friends at parent's home	Original sentence of 8 years—later reduced to 27 months
Cecilia Ruiz Single parent—two children ages 6 and 8	None	Forgery	Deleting a DUI conviction from the county DUI database	42 months
Jessica Hall Unemployed mother of three children with Marine husband serving in Iraq	None	Throwing a missile at an occupied vehicle	Threw a cup of McDonald's coffee at another car that cut her off while driving	24 months
Lewis "Scooter" Libby	None	Four counts of perjury	Provided false testimony to U.S. Attorney	30 months—commuted by President Bush
Stephen May	None	Child molestation	Inappropriately touched two girls and a boy; there was no sexual activity or penetration	75 years
Genarlow Wilson	None	Aggravated child molestation	17-year-old male had consensual oral sex with 15-year-old girl at a party that was videotaped.	10 years—resentenced to two years by Georgia Supreme Court

SOURCE: *Unlocking America: Why and How to Reduce America's Prison Population*, November 2007 (Washington, DC: JFA Institute), p. 2.

In the early 1980s, Peter Greenwood and his colleagues at the Rand Corporation set out to identify "high-rate" offenders in samples of incarcerated burglars and robbers in Texas, Michigan, and California. Greenwood and Alan Abrahamse asked these prisoners how much crime they had committed in the months before incarceration. Ten percent of their sample stood out from the rest in the number of crimes they reported, and a set of characteristics distinguished this subgroup of high-rate offenders from the other robbers and burglars. Even though Greenwood and his associate at Rand Corporation, Susan Turner, discovered later that persons identified by these same characteristics actually did *not* continue to commit crimes of the type and at the rate expected of high-rate offenders (a finding that caused Greenwood to recant his earlier claims), the idea of the high-rate offender or career criminal had taken hold. Even today, the concept of the career criminal continues to drive America's imprisonment binge.[2] This has been exemplified by the passage of many laws, such as truth in sentencing, mandatory prison, life without the possibility of parole, and three strikes and you're out—all of which serve to send more people to prison for a longer period of time.

In a series of longitudinal studies, Alfred Blumstein, along with various coauthors, examined forty-one different "criminal careers," which they offer as a category independent of that of career criminal.[3] (All persons who are arrested have a criminal career even if they commit one crime, which would constitute their entire criminal career.) Blumstein and his colleagues located subgroups of male offenders who, instead of maturing out of crime like the vast majority of offenders, continued to commit crime at the same rate throughout a relatively extended criminal career, that is, until they were past 35 years of age. Blumstein abstained from calling these people either high-rate offenders (actually, the frequency with which they committed crimes was relatively low) or career criminals. He recognized instead that the idea of a career criminal implies that certain individuals have significant differences from other offenders and these differences, whatever they are, propel them toward a career in crime. This is particularly essential in employing the concept of career criminal in criminal justice decisions, because there must be some way to distinguish career criminals early in their careers from the majority of offenders who do not persist in crime.

Blumstein's "persisters," it turned out, were not identified until they were far along on their criminal careers, and he and his associates could not locate "background" characteristics that separated them from many other male offenders who had less enduring criminal careers. In estimating the effect of Blumstein's articles, however, David Greenberg points out that there is a tendency for "laypersons to oversimplify, misunderstand, or lose sight of distinctions and qualifications criminologists make" and to see in these studies the positive identification of the career criminal. And this misperception definitely occurred, particularly among criminal justice policy makers. Characterizing the search as fruitless, Michael Gottfredson and Travis Hirschi noted:

> On March 26, 1982, 14 leading members of the criminology community in the United States met in Washington, D.C. to discuss the future of criminal justice research in this country. The priority area for future research listed first by this panel was "criminal careers." … Four years later the criminal career notion so dominates discussion of criminal justice policy and so controls

expenditure of federal research funds that it may now be said that criminal justice research in this country is indeed centrally planned.[4]

Fear of crime and these new images of the criminal have encouraged politicians and judges to change sentencing laws and practices, a practice that has multiplied prison populations. Popular images and the social scientists' ideas about contemporary criminals are not accurate. Most of these popular images of crime and criminals are shaped by the media, and media depiction consists mostly of selective attention on sensational crimes, politicians' rhetoric, and studies of career criminals funded by the federal government.

In these studies, social scientists have formed most of their ideas "in armchairs" (or now, more accurately, at computer desks), using evidence that is unreliable and skimpy—police arrest records, prison files, and convicts' penciled-in answers to questionnaires—which they study to discover the elusive traits of the career criminal. Very few of these criminologists have spent any significant time observing or talking to their subjects, the prisoners, something that is absolutely necessary to develop an accurate understanding of offenders' motives and criminal practices.

To discover who is actually going to prison, the extent of their criminal involvement, the seriousness of their crimes, and the "danger" they pose to society, we pursued a broad research methodology. In addition to examining the official records, we have conducted lengthy interviews of persons sentenced to prison. This is not to say that we ignored the records and available statistics, but we went beyond the so-called hard data and sought a more accurate and comprehensive understanding of a complex social issue.

NATIONAL TRENDS ON PRISON ADMISSIONS

There are three basic ways that you can be sent to a state or federal prison. First, you can be convicted of a felony-level crime and be sent directly to prison.[5] Second, you can be convicted of a felony-level crime, but sentenced to a term of probation in lieu of a prison term. Should you fail to complete the probation term for any of a variety of reasons (for example, you are convicted of another crime, fail to meet the terms of probation supervision, and so on), your probation status can be revoked by the judge, and you can be sentenced to prison. Third, if paroled from prison, you can be readmitted to prison as a parole violator if you fail to complete the conditions of parole supervision or if you are rearrested and convicted for a new felony.

In 2009, the last year that aggregate national-level data are available, it was reported that there were an estimated 674,707 admissions to state prisons with another 56,153 sent to the federal prison system (see Table 2-1). As shown in the table, most of the state and federal admissions were new court commitments, which means that they were not under parole supervision at the time they were convicted and sentenced to prison. About one-third are parole violations, but bear in mind that embedded in the parole violation figure are people who have been convicted of a new felony while on parole supervision.

Table 2-1 State and Federal Prison Admissions, 2009

Correctional System	Number	%
Total State Prison Admissions	**674,707**	**100%**
New Court Commitments	422,910	67%
Parole Violators	247,449	33%
Total Federal Prison Releases	**56,153**	**100%**
Conditional/Parole Releases	51,524	92%
Unconditional Releases	4,628	8%

SOURCE: U.S. Department of Justice, Bureau of Justice Statistics, *Prisoners in 2009* (December, 2010).

Table 2-2 The Number of People Going to State Prison, 1990, 2000, 2005, 2008, and 2009

Year	State Prison Population	State Prison Admissions	% New Commitments	% Parole Violators
1990	689,577	460,739	70%	30%
2000	1,100,850	581,487	63%	37%
2005	1,340,311	676,952	62%	38%
2008	1,408,479	690,954	62%	38%
2009	1,405,622	674,707	67%	33%
% Change	104%	49%	−10%	+17%

SOURCE: U.S. Department of Justice, Bureau of Justice Statistics, *Special Report. Truth in Sentencing in State Prisons* (January 1999); U.S. Department of Justice, Bureau of Justice Statistics, *Prisoners in 2008* (June 30, 2010).

Although the number of admissions has increased by 49 percent since 1990, the state prison population has more than doubled (Table 2-2). The larger increase in the prison population, as compared to prison admissions, has occurred for one major reason—the length of stay (or LOS) in prison. Specifically, the LOS in prison has increased from 21 months in 1988 to 29 months by 2006.[6] While this increase in LOS may seem minimal, it has a dramatic impact on the size of the prison population.

All correctional populations are the result of two key factors: admissions and length of stay (or LOS). A correctional population is the function of the following formula:

(Admissions × Length of Stay) = Correctional Population

As either, or both, of these two population-drivers change, so too will the resulting correctional population. Using the current number of 674,707 admissions each year, you can see that for each reduction or increase in the LOS by just one month will increase or lower the prison population by nearly 60,000 inmates (674,707/12 = 56,226).

Another major trend shown in Table 2-2, alluded to in Chapter 1, is that the number of new admissions began to decline in 2009. Why this is occurring is the subject of great interest and speculation. An important reason is the dramatic reduction in the crime rate, which in turn is reducing the arrest rate. But another reason is that national state prison data are largely driven by California, which accounts for nearly 20 percent of all state prison admissions (129,904 in 2009). In 2008, California reported 140,827 admissions. The major reason for the decline was a drop of about 10,000 parole violators for the state. If California is removed from the analysis, there is a decline but at a much smaller level.[7] The bottom line is that the historic increases in prison admissions seem to have ended and may even be starting to decline albeit at a small pace.

It should be noted that the 29-month LOS figure does not include the estimated 5 to 6 months one waits in jail before being transferred to the state prison or the amount of time parole violators spend in jail and prison until they are released again. Nor do the data include the growing number of prisoners who have been sentenced to life. In 2006, approximately 1 percent of all prison sentences were life sentences.[8] Because these inmates must die in prison, it will be many years before the effects of these sentences are factored into the national release data, which would then increase the average LOS statistics.

Another misperception of the public is that most persons convicted for serious crimes are infrequently imprisoned. Using national data, we can see that this perception is profoundly inaccurate (Table 2-3). Contrary to popular perceptions, the vast majority of all offenders who are convicted of a felony are incarcerated, with 69 percent sentenced to prison or jail. *The most frequent disposition for all crimes is*

Table 2-3 Percent of Court Dispositions for Felony Cases in 2006

Most Serious Conviction Offense	Total Incarceration	Prison	Jail	Probation	Other
All Offenses	69%	41%	28%	27%	4%
Violent Offenses	**77**	**54**	**23**	**20**	**3**
Murder/Manslaughter	95	93	2	3	2
Sexual Assault	81	64	18	16	3
Robbery	85	71	14	13	2
Aggravated Assault	72	43	30	25	3
Other Violent	70	39	30	26	4
Property Offenses	**67**	**38**	**29**	**29**	**4**
Burglary	73	49	24	24	3
Larceny	69	34	34	28	3
Motor Vehicle Theft	83	42	41	15	2
Fraud/Forgery	59	32	27	35	6
Drug Offenses	**65**	**38**	**28**	**30**	**4**
Possession	63	33	31	33	4
Trafficking	67	41	26	29	4
Weapon Offenses	**73**	**45**	**28**	**25**	**2**
Other Specified Offenses	**70**	**36**	**34**	**27**	**3**

SOURCE: Bureau of Justice Statistics, *Felony Sentences In State Courts, 2006,* (December 30, 2009), Statistical tables: http://bjs.ojp.usdoj.gov/index.cfm?ty=pbdetail&iid=2152.

Table 2-4 Type of Offense for 2006 Prison Admissions: New Court Commitments and Parole Revocations

	New Court Commitments	Parole Revocations
Violent Offenses	27.6%	23.2%
Homicide	2.8	1.5
Kidnapping	0.6	0.5
Rape	1.5	0.9
Other Sexual Assault	4.6	3
Robbery	6.9	7.1
Assault	9.5	8.8
Other Violent	1.6	1.5
Property Offenses	27.6	33.3
Burglary	9.8	12.3
Larceny	6.6	7.6
Motor Vehicle Theft	2.6	5.5
Arson	0.4	0.3
Fraud	5.3	4
Stolen Property	1.7	2.8
Other Property	1.2	0.9
Drug Offenses	30.6	32.6
Possession	8.8	9.7
Trafficking	13	14.6
Unspecified Drug	8.8	8.3
Public-Order Offenses	13.7	10.2
Weapons	3.8	4
DWI	4.4	2.1
Other Public-Order	5.5	4.1
Other Offenses	0.5	0.6

SOURCE: U.S. Department of Justice, Bureau of Justice Statistics, *National Corrections Reporting Program* (May 2010).

state prison. For those convicted of the most serious crimes, the rates are even higher, with three out of four convictions resulting in prison or jail.

These data also mean that most people sentenced to prison were admitted for either nonviolent crimes or no crimes at all (technical parole violators). As shown in Table 2-4, the vast majority (about 75%) has been sentenced for property, drug, or public order crimes. But these data provide very little information on such important items as the number of prior prison terms or prior felony convictions.

About 30 percent of all prison sentences are for drug crimes, with one-third being for simple possession. By contrast, in 1960, the proportion of prison admissions for drug crimes was only 5 percent; in 1981, the percentage was only 9 percent (Figure 2-1).[9] It is also no coincidence that as the proportion of prison admissions for drug crimes has increased, so have the proportions of nonwhites being sent to prison. Since 1960, this proportion has increased from 32 percent to 50 percent.

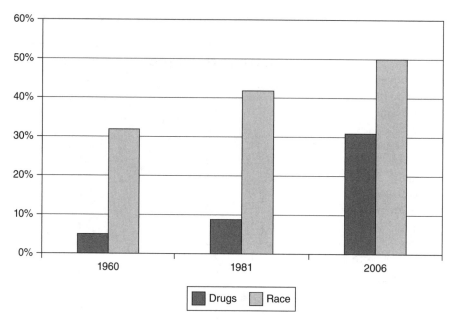

FIGURE 2-1 Percent of State Prison Admissions by Drugs and Race

Finally, we should note that the vast majority of prison admissions are people who were on probation and parole but failed to complete those forms of community supervision. We have already noted that about one-third of the prison admissions are people who fail parole after being released from prison. But there is another large group of people who fail to complete probation and are sent to prison for one of two reasons. One group is probationers who are convicted of another felony crime while on probation and are sentenced to prison for the new crime. The second group is probationers who fail to adhere to the rules of probation and are arrested but not convicted of a new felony crime.

There are no direct national statistics on how many probation violators are being sent to prison. The Bureau of Justice Statistics (BJS) does report on the number of probation terminations and the percentage of terminations that were revoked and were re-incarcerated. In 2009, there were 2.3 probation terminations; 65 percent of these successfully completed probation. At the same time, 16 percent were revoked and were incarcerated. That rate would mean that some 375,000 probationers were re-incarcerated, which would be over 50 percent of the 675,000 prison admissions. However, we cannot assume that all of these re-incarcerations would represent people being sent to prison. Some portion may reflect people who are detained at the local jail level for their revocation hearing and are then reinstated on probation supervision.

There are data from selected states that are more precise and give us a better idea of what portion of the prison admission stream are probation violators. In Kentucky, 53 percent of the prison admissions are probation or parole violators. In California, over 60 percent of the prison admissions are parole violators. Data

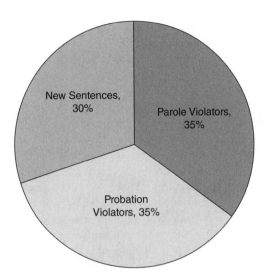

FIGURE 2-2 Estimated Percent of New Prison Admissions by Reason for Prison Admission

from other states like Texas, Nevada, and Michigan suggest that as much as one-half of the new court commitments are probation violators. Thus, the majority (estimated at 70%) of the prison admission stream consists of either probation or parole violators (Figure 2-2). As the probation and parole populations increase, there will be a growing number of these people sent to prison. In essence, the entire correctional system is feeding on its own high rates of failure.

All of these statistics suggest that a significant number of people are being sentenced to prison for relatively minor crimes. This is not to say that there are not offenders who are highly dangerous and need to be incarcerated for long periods of time. But what proportion of these half-million prisoners are truly dangerous and require long-term confinement? To answer this question requires a more detailed analysis of who goes to prison.

A CLOSER LOOK AT WHO GOES TO PRISON

Quantitative data are unable to paint a complete picture of the criminal lifestyles or the types of crimes committed by the present prison population. The only way to better understand who is going to prison is to examine their social and criminal backgrounds prior to being sent to prison. In the social sciences, such analysis is referred to as ethnographic studies. Such studies of prisoners in general and prison admissions in particular are extremely rare. Due to funding restrictions and the advent of high powered computers and statistical software packages, few criminologists ever spend any substantial time in correctional facilities. Rarely do they spend time talking to or observing prisoners. Virtually all of the major criminology journals consist of reports that are quantitative studies.

To counter this trend, the authors first conducted an ethnographic study of newly admitted prisoners in the early 1990s. The study consisted of interviewing and reviewing 154 males who were sentenced to prison in three states (Washington, Nevada, and Illinois).[10] While the numbers may seem small, they were randomly selected from the entire list of all prison admissions at the time of the study. Although these cases were drawn from studies conducted in the early 1990s, they continue to be reflective of inmates who continue to be incarcerated and remain incarcerated, due to the recently enacted sentencing reforms discussed earlier. We emphasize intake population because most studies of prison populations are designed to answer the question "Who is in prison at a particular time?" Surveys of the daily inmate population provide a distorted picture of who is going to prison because those prisoners with longer sentences, usually sentenced for more serious crimes, "stack up" in the prison population and are overrepresented in one-day surveys.

The states selected for the study varied in their sentencing structures, population sizes, rates of imprisonment, and lengths of imprisonment at the time of our research. Illinois uses a determinate sentencing structure in which release occurs after a prisoner serves a significant proportion of the original sentence. Although a parole board exists, it has no authority to grant a release. Although Illinois's determinate sentencing law eliminated discretionary release by the parole board, the vast majority of inmates must serve some period of parole supervision.

Washington adopted sentencing guidelines with the specific goal of increasing lengths of stay for inmates convicted of violent crimes. Because Washington eliminated parole as part of its sentencing guidelines reform act, very few inmates were released to parole, and thus very few violators returned to prison. Nevada uses an indeterminate sentencing scheme that allows inmates to be released by a parole board after serving approximately 20 percent of the original sentence.

We interviewed these persons in lengthy open interviews; we covered their social histories, criminal activities in the period before the current arrest, and the full circumstances of their arrests. The information gathered from the interviews was verified and augmented by the arrest records along with police and probation office reports.[11]

HOW SERIOUS ARE THEIR CRIMES?

An essential part of the public conception of street crime is that growing numbers of people are engaged in very serious crime. To evaluate the severity of the crimes committed by inmates in our samples, we used an objective measure of seriousness from the public's perspective based on data gathered in 1980 by the Center for Studies in Criminology and Criminal Law at the University of Pennsylvania. In the center's survey of crime seriousness, a national survey asked 52,000 Americans to assign a numerical score to a short description of 204 criminal acts, which reflected the respondents' perceptions of the crimes' seriousness. For example, two of the acts described were "A person, using force, steals property worth $10 from outside a building" and "A person, using force, robs a victim of $1,000.

No physical harm occurs." The center reduced these raw scores into "ratio scores," which indicated the relative severity of each crime.

We observed that if the acts involved minor injury, the threat of injury, theft over $1,000, the use of a weapon, use of heroin, or the selling of marijuana, they received a score of more than 5 on the center's scale. We labeled these "moderate" crimes. If they involved theft of over $10,000, serious injury, attempted murder, sales of heroin, or the smuggling of narcotics, they received a score of more than 10. We considered these "serious" crimes. If they involved rape, manslaughter, homicide, a child victim, or kidnapping, they received a score of more than 15. We labeled these "very serious" crimes. Crimes that lacked any of these characteristics received a score of less than 5. We called these "petty" crimes. Two such acts from the survey were: "A person breaks into a department store and steals merchandise worth $10" and "A person smokes marijuana."

We sorted the crimes of our sample into the categories "petty," "moderate," "serious," and "very serious" according to these characteristics. Figure 2-3 summarizes the results of this distribution. In this figure, we have adjusted our stratified samples so that they reflect the offense distribution for the nation.[12] About half of the crimes for which persons are sent to prison (53%) fall into the petty category. This finding is wholly consistent with the BJS prison admissions and inmate classification studies that have repeatedly found that most prisoners are committed to prison for nonviolent property or drug crimes, with the result that the majority (50 to 70%) are classified as minimum-custody inmates.

The distribution on crime seriousness was somewhat different in the three states. Washington, which has the lowest rate of incarceration of the three states, also had the lowest proportion of petty felonies (31%) and the highest proportion

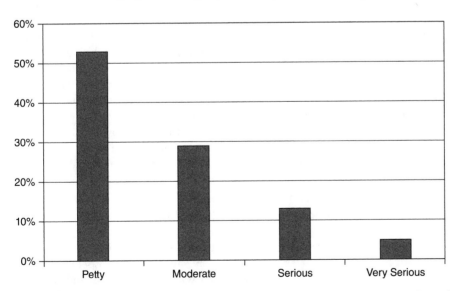

FIGURE 2-3 Severity of Crime Committed by New Prison Admission in Illinois, Nevada, and Washington State

(30%) of serious crimes. This is to be expected, as Washington had enacted sentencing guidelines that purposely restrict the use of prison for nonviolent and property crimes. Illinois, which had a medium rate, did not differ very much from the total sample. Nevada, which had the highest rate of the three states and the highest rate in the nation, predictably had the lowest proportion of serious (5%) and very serious crimes (4%). These different patterns between the three states also verified the validity of the sampling methods.

These findings show that over half of the people being sent to prison in these three very diverse states are being sent for petty crimes, which are crimes with no aggravating features—that is, no significant amount of money, no injury, or any other feature that would cause ordinary citizens to view the crime as particularly serious. The following are narrative descriptions of three typical petty crimes from our sample.

George, a 17-year-old black youth, was arrested for possession of a stolen vehicle. He had been kicked out of school in the ninth grade. Since then, he had worked at a couple of jobs—a small soul food restaurant and a small garage fixing cars. He had not been working for a while. He had been arrested a few times before, once for curfew, another for shoplifting. A couple of months before this arrest, he was arrested for "busting a car window." "A man tried to hit me with his car, and I swung at him and broke his window. I got three months' supervision." On the current arrest he was caught inside a car trying to steal the radio. "They said I busted the window, but it weren't locked. He [the policeman] took the screwdriver I was using and put it in the lock and said I was stealing the car." He was sentenced to three years in prison.

Jimmy, a 26-year-old black man, dropped out of high school in the tenth grade. He worked at several unskilled jobs as a teenager but started getting into trouble when he was 17. After several arrests, he was sent to prison for aggravated assault against a relative. He served three years and then another year and a half for violation of parole. He had been out for two months when he was arrested this time. He was living with his grandmother, "trying to stay out of trouble." He was not able to find a job and was living on general assistance. He was caught in an abandoned school where he and some other young men were looking for junk metal that they intended to sell for "some loose change." The school had been abandoned for six years, and local people had been stealing from it repeatedly. He received seven years for burglary.

Edmond was a 50-year-old white carpenter who worked in Florida in the winter and Seattle in the summer. He had been arrested once 22 years before for receiving stolen property. He was passing through Las Vegas on his way to Seattle and said he found a billfold with $100 on a bar where he was drinking and gambling. The owner, who suspected him of taking it, turned him in. He was charged with grand larceny and received three years.

Twenty-nine percent of our sample fell into the "moderate" severity category, but many of these were aggravated because the charges involved possession or sales of heroin or cocaine. Most of our sample's heroin or cocaine crimes involved only very small amounts of the drugs, and the persons, if they were dealers, were small-fry, as the following cases indicate.

Luis, a 29-year-old Puerto Rican raised in Chicago, had never been arrested before. He had been a member of Latin gangs but in recent years had less and less contact with them. He used cocaine occasionally and hung around with a lot of guys who dealt cocaine. He was riding with a friend on a motorcycle, and the police pulled them over because they were not wearing helmets. The police found a packet of cocaine on his friend and several on the ground around them. He and his friend were charged with possession of cocaine. Luis was sentenced to three years.

Felix had been in trouble on the West Side of Chicago since he was 10 years old. He had dropped out of school in the eighth grade and was arrested several times before he was 18. He had served three prison terms since then. At 26, he was living at home with his mother, "taking little side jobs," and hustling a little. He said he wanted "an average job and to go home after it and enjoy life." On the present arrest, he was riding with his girlfriend, and the police stopped them. The police said they had a report that a man and a woman were selling drugs out of a car in that neighborhood. They found one bag of cocaine (0.5 grams) on his girlfriend's side of the car and arrested him. He was sentenced to two years.

Robberies were considered at least moderate crimes because the public, officials, and criminologists invariably view robbery as a serious crime and a violent crime (government agencies that compile statistics on crimes always place robbery in their "violent" category). In actuality, however, many robberies differ from the public's perception of them. The following accounts, for example, do not seem to fit the image, and many citizens, perhaps a majority, would not consider them serious or violent crimes.

Darryl was a 21-year-old black man raised on the South Side of Chicago in housing projects. He had dropped out of school in the tenth grade and had been working on and off at minimum-wage jobs. He had been arrested three times for minor crimes (battery, disorderly conduct, and marijuana) and had no convictions. In this case, he had gone to a neighborhood drug dealer to borrow some money on his girlfriend's watch because his "brother was coming to town and I wanted to have some money to do things with him." The dealer offered him $60 but only gave him $20, telling him that he would give him $40 later. Darryl did not see the dealer for two weeks, and when he finally encountered him and asked him for the money, the dealer said he did not have any and offered Darryl drugs. When he was showing him the drugs, Darryl saw the watch and grabbed for it. They fought and the drug dealer was "whipping" him. Darryl's brother jumped in and helped him. Then the dealer gave Darryl the watch. Three days later, the police came to his apartment and arrested him for robbery and assault. He was bailed out and later went to a jury trial. The jury found him not guilty on aggravated assault and was hung on the robbery. However, Darryl had run from the court while they were deliberating. He later turned himself in, bail was set at $150,000, and the public defender talked him into pleading guilty to robbery. He was sentenced to prison for three years.

Richard graduated from high school in Seattle and went into the armed services. After being discharged, he went to cosmetology school and worked for 13 years as a cosmetologist. Three years ago he began learning a new trade and worked part-time in a print shop. He had started using marijuana and heroin in high school. When he was working as a cosmetologist, he and his wife "got into coke, heavy." He had several arrests for driving while under the influence and one for child molesting. "That was a mistake. I was drunk and high and I just got carried away with this young girl." After this last arrest, he and his wife decided to change their lives and quit all drugs. "I became responsible and became manager of Super Cuts. But after a while, I got bored and started hanging around with my old friends. They were freebasing and pretty soon I was back into drugs heavy. I left my wife and moved in with a friend. I couldn't believe that I had let my life get so fucked up again, so I went into a drug program, but I didn't get along with the director. After three weeks I tried coke again. And I was right back into the same lifestyle. I needed money, so I decided to rob some stores. I robbed the same store three times, a convenience store like 7-Eleven. I got about $50 each time. I tucked a BB gun in my belt and went in, showed the clerk the gun in my belt, and asked for the money. In court the clerk said I was polite." He was sentenced to five years.

About 18 percent of the sample fell into the "serious" and some "very serious" crime ratings in our samples. Two were very serious armed robberies (they involved larger amounts of money and people were threatened during the robberies). There were seven first-degree homicides (2% of our adjusted samples), and three were gang-related. The following is one:

Parnell, a 20-year-old member of the Disciples, had dropped out of school and hung around with his neighborhood branch of the gang since he was 15. He had never held a job and was arrested fourteen or fifteen times for activities related to "gang banging," mostly possession of weapons.[13] He was arrested once for robbery when he was 17. "The guy I was walking with strong-armed some guy. But I wasn't into robbing, just gang banging." The night of the murder, he and some of his gang were at a skating rink, which was the location of many altercations between rival gangs. His group saw a guy from another gang who they thought had robbed one of their buddies. They chased him, and one of them beat him with a baseball bat. He died a week later. Parnell was the only one convicted because "I was the only one a witness identified." He received twenty-five years.

Two of the homicides occurred during drug robberies. This is one of them:

Anthony, a 24-year-old black man, was sent to prison when he was 17 for aggravated battery. "Some guy broke out the windows of a neighbor of mine. I went to court, and after the court a fight broke out and they arrested all of us." After serving eighteen months, he completed two years in community college and had been working for five years as a roofer. He says he was living a clean life in the suburbs of Chicago—working, playing basketball, and taking care of his common-law wife and her son. "They said I went to this house, kicked in the door, and demanded drugs and money, and then shot the man. The woman in the house identified me. The police had received an anonymous phone call and they arrested me. They said I searched the house, but they didn't find any fingerprints. The description she gave the police didn't fit me."

In two of the homicide cases, people were convicted of killing their girl-friends. In one, a 33-year-old Cuban man who had never been in trouble before and who had worked steadily was convicted of killing his girlfriend:

It was an accident. I was fighting with my girlfriend. She bothered me a lot. I had a son with her, and she was wanting me to leave my wife. We had been drinking and we got into a fight. I hit her with my fist and killed her.

Most of the serious crimes (53%) were sex crimes. These ranged from child molesting to rape, and most were acts committed against family members or close associates. These are serious crimes, but it should be noted again that most of them depart from the popular images of crime and criminals in which a menacing stranger is the perpetrator. The other serious crimes were robberies (17%), attempted murders (8%), manslaughters (12%), and drug charges (10%). Several of the robberies and drug crimes do approach the popular image: that is, they involved larger amounts of money, threats or injuries to victims, or larger amounts of cocaine or heroin.

PATTERNS OF CRIME

The concept of a career criminal is now entrenched in criminal justice—a dramatic rethinking of policy and practice. In the United States, legislators, judges, and prosecutors have passed laws to extend sentences, have recommended or have granted longer sentences, because they hold this belief in the prevalence of high-rate offenders. The habitual offender and three strikes laws are examples of this.(See Chapter 9 for a full discussion of these laws and their impact on prison populations). To test the validity of the "career criminal" viewpoint, we focused on patterns of offending among our surveyed convicts. We discovered five distinct patterns—"into crime," "crime episode," "one-shot crime," "being around crime," and "dereliction"—that are defined and summarized here. Figure 2-4 indicates the proportion of our sample that corresponds to each crime pattern.

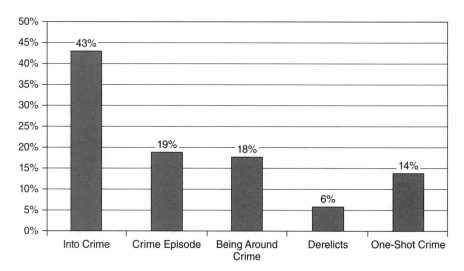

FIGURE 2-4 Criminal Pattern of Prison Admissions in Illinois, Nevada, and Washington State

Into Crime (43%)

Persons into crime call themselves "thieves," "hustlers," "dope fiends," or "gang bangers," which they understand as identities within particular criminal systems. They also follow the patterns of crime consistent with these identities and criminal systems—that is, they attempt to steal large amounts of money through burglaries and robberies; they "hustle" on the streets, making money any way they can; they maintain drug habits by selling drugs and stealing; or they hang out with their fellow "homeboys," wear their gang's colors, steal, and fight with other gangs. Parnell, described earlier, was a gang banger into crime. Bertram, a thief, and Donald, a dope fiend, were all into crime:

> Bertram says he "started a life of crime" when he was in high school. When he was 17, every weekday he and older friends walked from their neighborhood on the South Side of Chicago to Hyde Park, a middle-class racially mixed neighborhood, and burglarized some houses. They took TVs, jewelry, and any other thing they could sell. "It was like a job." They were caught in one house and arrested. Bertram was sentenced to three years in prison. When he got out of prison, his brother and sisters were living alone, and his younger brother was selling cocaine. Bertram stopped him, but he had to supply them with money. So he started burglarizing houses and trucks on the West Side at night. Then he and his "rappies" pulled sixteen armed robberies of gas stations and convenience stores.

> In one week, he says, they made $7,000 apiece. After the last robbery, they were pulled over by the police, who found guns in their car. He received a ten-year sentence.

> Donald started using heroin and cocaine when he was 19. He was convicted of burglary when he was 25 and served six months in the county jail. He was

convicted of possession of drugs when he was 29 and received a year in the state prison. As soon as he got out, he was arrested again for burglary and served four years. He says he did not want to go back to drugs, but he met a friend right after getting out and got high with him. He was quickly addicted and stealing again. He says he was pulling one or two burglaries a day. He could not sell drugs because the police knew him too well. In his last arrest, he was caught trying to pry open a door of a construction business and was convicted of two attempted burglaries. At 33, he says he wants to stop using drugs, but he does not know how. He says he is getting tired.

Since they were committing crimes regularly, it is accurate to view the 43 percent of our sample who were into crime as high-rate offenders. Of these high-rate offenders, more than half (57%) had served a prior prison sentence, and 32 percent a juvenile sentence. However, most of the active offenders (59%) were convicted of petty crimes. All of our data strongly suggest that, rather than being vicious predators, most were disorganized, unskilled, undisciplined petty criminals who very seldom engaged in violence or made any significant amount of money from their criminal acts.

Crime Episode (19%)

These inmates had engaged in a crime episode or spree. Many had committed crimes in some earlier period; some had even been into crime. Unlike the "into crime" group, these offenders had less severe histories of prior incarcerations, either as adults (33% had a prior prison term) or as juveniles (26% had a prior record). But for an extended period, perhaps after a jail or prison sentence, they had lived a relatively conventional life.

Joe joined a Latin gang when he was 13. By his 18th year he had been arrested three times in activities with his "homeboys" (the Latin Kings). For the last, a residential burglary, he served a county jail sentence and was placed on probation for two years. After that, he pulled back from gang banging but was still hanging around with some of his old friends. "We hung around the corner drinking, but we didn't think of ourselves as a gang. We thought of ourselves as an organization. We tried to protect all the old people, to stop the blacks from robbing them." He was working steadily at the Golden Grain packinghouse making $7 an hour. "I was going to work there the rest of my life." He had a car and a girlfriend, and they were buying furniture—a bedroom set. The crime he was convicted of occurred early on a Sunday morning. He had been partying at a house with his friend—"smoking, drinking, and snorting." Someone borrowed his car and did not bring it back to the house. He was angry about this. A friend gave him a ride home, and on the way, he said, "Someone said, 'Let's go rob someone.' I guess I said, 'Let's go, I'll do it.' I don't remember much about it. A white guy was stabbed in the stomach and neck. For all I know, the other guy in the car did it. It was stupid. I blacked out from the time I got home until the police came." He received six years for attempted murder.

Richard was one of the few black students in his high school in Montana and the star football player. He was also selling drugs. "I scored five touchdowns on Friday and was busted on Monday. I was hanging around white kids trying to prove myself. They wouldn't let me play football after that." His father put him out of the house, so he left for Oklahoma with some friends. He returned to Montana but could not find a job. He began hanging around some of the black guys who were "going to discos and being cool." He was arrested for a house burglary and received two years' probation. He went to California with a friend who was in the air force. He joined the army, got married, and had two kids. He had broken up with his wife by the time he was discharged from the army. He stayed in Fort Lewis, Washington, and worked part-time in construction, living across the street from a corner where drugs were being sold. "One night I walked over there, and a guy asked me if I wanted to make some money. So I started selling drugs. I sold to the police. They wanted me to set up my supplier, so I went back to the corner, but the word had got out, so the other dealers told me to get out of town." He went back to California and went back to his wife. They both used cocaine heavily. He turned himself into a drug program, but she continued to use cocaine. He went back to the house and found her in bed with another man. He kicked the man out and took his son. He was charged with kidnapping his child and served two years in a California prison. He was transferred to Washington upon release and charged with unlawful delivery of drugs for the earlier arrest. He received fifteen months.

Being Around Crime (18%)

About one-fifth (18%) of our sample were "corner boys," men who were raised and lived in lower-class neighborhoods in which street crime is a prominent feature. Many in these neighborhoods, particularly young males, regularly commit crimes. Most other young males avoid regular participation in crime but accept it as a normal feature of life around them. Many of the males, particularly younger ones, though they avoid regular involvement in crime and do not think of themselves as criminals, are at risk of being arrested because they are on the streets for many hours and police regularly patrol these neighborhoods looking for street criminals. When confronted by police, these corner boys also frequently exhibit macho behavior that provokes hostile reactions from the police. Finally, corner boys are often present at crimes being committed by friends or relatives, and, under special circumstances—such as when they are in the company of more criminally oriented acquaintances, saving face in front of peers, intoxicated, or trying to take advantage of an opportunity for financial gain—they are drawn into the commission of a crime.

Once arrested, their corner boy or lower-class identity makes it very likely that police, district attorneys, and judges will treat these young men as if they were more criminally involved than they actually were. Sixty-eight percent of our corner boys were convicted of petty crimes. Only a small minority had adult prior terms (8%) and/or juvenile terms (15%). The cases of Darryl and Robert described in the section on crime seriousness are examples of this pattern. The following are two more examples:

> Maurice is an 18-year-old black youth raised on the South Side of Chicago. He was in the Disciples from ages 12 to 16, but he dropped out. "My grandmother told me to get out of the gang. They hate it when you pull out, so they were right at my door waiting for me." He dropped out of high school in the tenth grade. He had gotten into a little trouble before—some fights and the theft of a moped, for which he received two years' probation. "A guy let me ride it. I didn't know he had stole it." At the time of this arrest, he was staying off the streets. "I had a girlfriend with two kids. She lived with her father. I would go over to her house and stay all day. We'd sit around and watch TV, clean the house, help with the kids." On the day of this arrest, he was going to his grandmother's to get something and a policeman who worked in that area stopped to question him. "There's a guy around there that looks like me. He would get into a few things. The police asked what was I doing over there. I wrestled with him and his gun fell out of his holster. I kicked it and ran. They got me later. They found out I didn't do nothing so they charged me with taking his gun." He received five years for disarming a police officer.

> Eddie is a 32-year-old black man who was raised in Little Rock, Arkansas. His mother supported the family of six kids. She worked as a cook in a motel, and they lived in a housing project. He quit school in the ninth grade and went to work as a busboy in the motel. He worked there for seven years, ending up as a cook. He got married in Little Rock to a woman with a daughter. They moved to Seattle, where he worked at several jobs, the last one as a supervisor of a janitorial crew in a federal building. Years before, the police had arrested him in an apartment he managed. The charge was dismissed. This was his only prior arrest. In Seattle he spent a lot of time playing basketball. He was on a team sponsored by the Mormons. He was the top player and scored 36 points in one game. He started hanging around one of the other players who was using a lot of cocaine. Eddie says he "sort of took this guy under his wing." He started using cocaine with him. His wife objected to this, so Eddie stopped. He says he was trying to get his friend to stop also. One night he took his friend to his friend's apartment to collect some money from his roommate. Eddie stayed in the car. The friend and the roommate got into a fight over the money, and the friend ended up stabbing the roommate. The roommate accused both of them of robbing him, and Eddie was arrested for robbery. He was released on his own recognizance, but after a week the supervisor said she did not want to supervise him. He was held in the county jail for five months, and finally he pled guilty. The public defender told him since he had admitted being there he would not be able to win a trial. "I decided I was going ahead and get it over with and get on with my life." He received five years for robbery.

Dereliction (6%)

These men had completely lost the capacity to live in organized society. Some had teetered on the edge of physical survival. All had been incarcerated a lot in early life, and most used drugs and alcohol, usually from their early teens. Though they tried to avoid committing serious crimes (to avoid returning to prison), they occasionally robbed, burgled, or committed some other felony (for example, arson, assault, sexual deviations) and were arrested. Though their crimes were invariably very petty, their repulsive disreputability and former records resulted in imprisonment. This small group had the highest prior prison record (91%), with 71 percent incarcerated as juveniles.[14] The following are two examples of their crimes and lifestyles:

Leonard is a 32-year-old black who grew up on the South Side of Chicago. His father died when he was small, and his mother raised seven children on welfare. He dropped out of school in the ninth grade and never had a steady job. He was a Disciple until his early 20s. He started to drink heavily when he was a teenager. He was first arrested when he was 15 and again when he was 17. Both times he was sent to youth institutions. He was arrested for robbery and auto theft as an adult and served two prison terms. He lived with his mother and says all he did was drink. Three years ago it was discovered that he had cirrhosis of the liver. Two years before this imprisonment, he and a friend robbed another black man on the street. This man lived in the neighborhood and knew them. His friend had a stick, and they were charged with robbery. Leonard received probation, but he quit reporting, and they arrested him and sentenced him to five years.

Charles and his three sisters were raised by his nurse mother on the South Side of Chicago. He "got to drinking and smoking reefer at about 10." He was hanging around with the "bad kids" and not going to school. He started getting into trouble with the police, and then "they started harassing me." He was in a small local gang, and they got into a lot of fights. Later he joined the Gangster Disciples, a splinter group of the Disciples. He has never held a steady job. He was arrested when he was 16 for not going to school and was sent to a boys' school. He ran away and was sent to another youth institution. When he was 17, he was arrested for robbery and was sent to Stateville (Illinois State Prison) for six months. When he was 22, he was convicted of another robbery and sent back to prison for five years. For the last five years, he has been a derelict. He stays high or drunk most of the time. "I been stealing petty things, anything you can take from a store. I quit robbery. Made a believer out of me. I been 'carrying a stick'" [had no residence and slept anywhere he could]. Some days before this arrest, he went to the house of a girlfriend and a man came to the door. "I asked him for my girlfriend, and he said, 'Fuck you, punk.' I went to his car and hit it with a water-meter cover I picked up off the street. He came after me with a hatchet and hit me in the head. I went to the hospital, and when I got out, I went over and smashed his car. Then a week later, I started a fire in a old building next to his house. My old girlfriend told them who did it. I was drunk at the time." He received four years for attempted arson.

One-Shot Crime (14%)

A significant number of our sample (14%) had never been involved in serious crime before the current arrest. Something about the crime—its seriousness or an associated mandatory sentence—resulted in their receiving a prison sentence. The following are two of these crimes.

Jose was born in Puerto Rico, and his father sent for him to come to Massachusetts when Jose was 10. He quit high school when he was a junior. He joined the army when he was 20 "to get a GED" and was discharged three years later. He worked as a baker for the next ten years for Nabisco. He quit this job to help a friend run a grocery store. Then he worked for five years with Sanco, until the firm moved to Philadelphia in 1983, four years before. He had not found a steady job since. He had been married for twenty years and had four daughters. At 46 he had no steady job and was drinking a lot. He had a friend who dealt in cocaine. A narcotics under-cover officer who had been trying to set up his friend repeatedly asked Jose to buy some cocaine for him. He finally did and was arrested. He was out on bail for two and a half years before sentencing, but the sentence was mandatory.

Donald was raised on a farm in Iowa. Two years after graduating from high school, he went into business for himself, leasing livestock. At 30, he changed businesses and had been selling mobile home running gear ever since. He was married for ten years but separated five years before. He had been arrested for failure to pay child support, but nothing else. He was drinking heavily in the last year of his marriage but had about quit drinking. All he was doing was "work[ing] my ass off in my business. I have been working seven days a week. Most of the time I am on the road with two helpers, delivering mobile home running gear." Three years ago, he and two employees were making a delivery with a large truck and trailer. After dinner, they picked up a six-pack, and a little later they stopped on the side of the road in a rural area of Illinois to urinate. He and one of the employees got back into the cab of the truck. He says he thought the other employee, a 16-year-old (who had told Donald he was 18) was also in the cab, but he was not, and he was run over by the truck when Donald pulled out onto the highway. "He might have been trying to get on the trailer and fell under the wheels." They accused him of being drunk, although he says he only had a couple of beers. "They never ran a test on me, and the officer who arrested me testified that I didn't have alcohol on my breath." Donald was convicted of reckless homicide and sent to prison for a year.

MORE RECENT PORTRAITS

One might argue that these descriptions of people being sent to prison are outdated and no longer accurate. While we were not able to conduct another multistate study, we were able to develop case studies of people who were readmitted to prison for violating parole by committing new crimes in the state of Michigan. These are people who are part of the one-third of prison admissions who are parole violators. The methodology used was to randomly select cases of prisoners returning to prison as parole violators after completing a reentry program. While most people who entered the program succeeded, these are the ones failed. One would have hoped they had "learned" their lessons and no longer were attracted to criminal conduct, but what emerges are people who are very unsophisticated in their criminal careers and continue to engage in petty criminal conduct.

Caught In The Act   Kevin and his young cousin decided to go shopping. They started their spree in broad daylight by driving into a Target parking lot. They got out of their truck and proceeded to check car doors to find those that were unlocked. They didn't know they were being watched by the bank teller across the street, who had immediately called the police. The patrol officers arrived just in time to see the duo leaving Target's parking lot; they followed the victim's truck into their next location, the Home Depot parking lot. They were apprehended there as police found a stolen purse in their vehicle.

All of the victim's possessions were returned to her that day. Kevin blamed his younger cousin for the plan. The young boy had to write a letter to apologize to the victim, submit to a drug test, a curfew, counseling, and twenty hours of probation. Kevin was sentenced on a second-degree home invasion charge carrying two to fifteen years; the assault, resisting arrest, and obstructing a police officer carried a one- to two-year sentence.

Groundhog's Day   Michael loved stealing cars; unfortunately, he loved to steal them from the Shelbyville Garage on Tenth St. Michael's M.O. was the same as it was back in 2007; steal a car or a bike, get to the Shelbyville Garage, kick in the door panel, steal all the quarters from the register for gas money, take all the car keys from the wall rack, and pick a car to take for a ride. Based on a full confession to State Trooper Clute of the Michigan State Police, 2007 was just the beginning. In 2008, Michael returned to the garage by stealing a Chrysler to get him there, kicked in the door panel, stealing the quarters for gas, and taking an 1999 Olds Alero. On March 5, 2009, Michael returned to the Shelbyville Garage on a bike he stole from his neighbor's backyard. Same scenario: kick in panel, take quarters, take keys, take car. This time he took a Ford Mustang for a ride, but he returned it because it was a little too fast for him to handle. He exchanged the Mustang for a Chevy Impala and returned later to take a Pontiac Bonneville for a drive, until the head gasket blew.

Ironically, Michael was stopped by the police as he was walking down the street. He had six sets of car keys, three were to the cars reported stolen. He also carried his collection of trophies: the visor from the Impala, the CD player from the Mustang, and a victim's checkbook. Michael's voluntary comment to the police was "You know who I am, just arrest me, the keys are in my front pocket."

Michael was charged with breaking and entering a building and unlawfully driving away motor vehicles and a Habitual 4th offense (meaning his 4th felony conviction). Michael committed his first and second felonies while on parole. The garage owner stated that he is out over $2500 for replacing door panels and keys and getting the cars cleaned after Michael's joy rides. He said that the first time he felt sorry for Michael, but after the second and then a third time, his empathy was gone. Based on a defendant's statement, Michael remains proud of his astute car stealing and driving abilities. The interviewer stated that he does not appear to have any remorse.

Crime Pays?   In October 2008, Shane entered a Kroger store to pick up a purse. He decided to grab the purse of an 82-year-old woman as she turned away from her cart to pick up a donut. Shane realized he was seen by an employee and ran out the store Another Kroger employee chased him on foot, but he lost the suspect.

The victim said she was going to purchase some donuts and did not want to get her purse sticky. Though visibly shaken, she said she had credit cards and $5 worth of coins in a change purse. She also stated that she "might" have had $300 in cash from her Obama stimulus check.

Shane, highly intoxicated, was apprehended with a blood alcohol content (BAC) of 0.116 percent on a bike. Shane told the police they had the wrong guy and then attempted to flee. The officer had a hold on his sweatshirt, so Shane did not get far. The officer stated that Shane continued to try to run away, with no luck. Shane was taken to the ground and handcuffed, yet still refused to give his name.

Shane was interviewed by the sheriff department's detective and confessed everything. He planned to go into Kroger's and steal some drinks and a purse; he had a "get away" bike waiting outside. He then went to the liquor store, bought a bottle of vodka, and got about $7 out of the purse and ditched it. Shane cooperated and showed the detective where he had dumped the purse. The purse was recovered with its contents, except for the $300 stimulus money.

Shane was on parole at the time of the crime and was charged with three counts of retail fraud with mandatory consecutive sentencing, and he pleaded "no contest." In the meanwhile, the victim stated that she got her purse and its contents back.

When the Bartender Doesn't Like You   Police responded to a call from a bartender at a local pub indicating that one of his patrons was in possession of cocaine. The defendant, Mr. McNeil, was sitting in his green Buick, still in the parking lot, when police arrived. Mr. McNeil was unaware that standing outside the bar was a large group of bar patrons pointing him out to the police. The officers pulled behind him, blocked him with their patrol car, and approached to investigate. The officers told him to get out of the car; McNeil complied with a search and was asked a few questions, the last being "What's this in your pocket?" McNeil responded, "Some drugs, it means nothing."

McNeil continued to respond honestly to the officers. What kind of drug? Crack. Why did he have the drugs? I'm a piece of shit. Was he selling the drugs? No, but he could. He had people who would buy it and then confessed that he had sold a gram or two at the bar, just tonight. McNeil also stated to the officers that he occasionally smokes crack, but had not in about two weeks.

In a further search of his parked car, the officers found an open beer and a digital scale with white residue. The officers interviewed the bar's doorman who stated he saw McNeil holding a bag of what looked like cocaine, then observed him trying to sell to two women at the bar, who he says declined the offer. The bouncer did his job and bounced him, as the bartender called the police.

McNeil had time to leave the scene, but instead he got in his car, sat there for awhile, then drove it to the parking lot exit. He then decided to park his car again and sit for awhile. A field test of the substance found on McNeil was cocaine, and he was arrested and transported to the Kent County Correctional Facility where he was charged with possession with intent to deliver crack cocaine and possession of open intoxicants in a motor vehicle.

McNeil later stated that he did not remember selling any drugs or saying any of the statements that got him arrested. All he remembered of the night was being put in the cop car and that nothing he said made sense.

Stop, it's the Bike Police!   Anthony was on parole. He was walking down Benjamin Street in front of the elementary school, when he saw a car with its window down and a purse in it. Anthony also saw an opportunity to supply his drug habit. Twenty minutes later, just a block or so away, the police responded to a call from a resident of Benjamin Street that a man was in their backyard rummaging through a purse.

A bicycle patrol officer saw Anthony who fit the description of the backyard purse rummager. The officer yelled, "Stop! Police!" and pedaled toward Anthony. Anthony ran through a park and jumped over a fence. The officer left his bike at the fence and pursued Anthony on foot. They physically collided during the chase and both fell to the ground. After a brief struggle, Anthony was searched and was found with the contents of the purse, a cell phone, and a driver's license.

Anthony was taken into custody and charged with unarmed robbery and home invasion in the second degree. All of the victim's possessions were returned. At the time of this case, Anthony had three children on the way, from three different women. He also had no motivation to seek employment or stop his drug use. Anthony stated that he was hoping to be sentenced to jail time, so that he can think and prepare himself for his kids. He pled guilty to larceny from a motor vehicle.

The High Cost of Gas   A home owner called the police to report that his garage was on fire. The owner also stated that two white males had taken off southbound on bikes and he thinks they have something to do with it. Two officers were dispatched to canvass the area, but with no luck in locating the suspects.

The firemen dispatched to the scene found flames shooting out of a gas tank of a lawn mower in the garage. Only the fumes were ignited, all the gas had been siphoned. After further investigation and interviews, two names came up as suspects. A witness stated that he saw both Mr. Sopha and Mr. Craven exiting the garage, then the flames shooting out of the garage. After being caught, not far from the scene, they both gave statements implicating each other for the gas caper.

Both defendants were charged with attempted larceny in a building and arson of personal property under $200. One was on parole and has received consecutive sentences. The only damage to the victim was a melted and deformed gas tank, but he wasn't out any money as the lawn mower still worked.

The Happy Pizza Robbery A delivery driver for Happy's Pizza called the police because he had been robbed. The driver arrived at the Gunn residence to deliver a large pizza and was approached by Mr. Gunn and another man. Mr. Gunn handed the driver cash and the other man was handed the pizza. The driver, quickly realizing that the $50 bill he was handed was counterfeit, demanded to be paid with real money. With each man having a hold on the pizza box, a tug of war ensued between the driver and Mr. Gunn. During the struggle, the driver pulled out his cell phone and tried to take pictures of the two robbers; they both fled, leaving the pizza box behind.

The pizza box was taken into evidence and tested by the lab. Mr. Gunn's fingerprints were found all over the pizza box. After being shown Mr. Gunn's last mug shot, the driver positively identified him as his assailant. There was no monetary loss to the victim or Happy's Pizza.

Mr. Gunn was arrested, and, with this offense being Mr. Gunn's fourth felony conviction, the sentence agreement was for one to five years with mandatory consecutive sentences. Still a juvenile and on parole, his parole officer said that Mr. Gunn, at only nineteen years of age, has one of the most extensive criminal records he had ever seen at such a young age. He also stated that Mr. Gunn has a poor attitude and mumbles when he talks so that you have to keep asking him to repeat himself. With an extensive juvenile record and over ten felony convictions, it seems as though Mr. Gunn does keep repeating himself.

Watching You, Watching Me Early in the evening, a police officer observed three males walking down the street. The officer's partner noticed that one of the men, Mr. Jones, looked right in their direction and grabbed his right hip. Before the patrol officers could even slow down, Mr. Jones turned and then took off running. The officers did what officers do, they pursued him. They watched as he threw a handgun under the front porch of a house on the corner. One officer retrieved the discarded .45 caliber handgun loaded with live rounds. Mr. Jones was caught and arrested shortly thereafter. In a full confession, Mr. Jones admitted to having an unregistered, loaded gun while on parole, but that he needed it for his personal protection.

SUMMARY

Most people being sent to prison today are very different from the image of Willie Horton that fuels the public's fear of crime. Most crimes are much pettier than the popular images promoted by those who sensationalize the crime issue. More than half of the people sent to prison committed crimes that lacked any of the features the public believes compose a serious crime.

Other recent research supports our findings. The original Rand Corporation studies on career criminals, which greatly influences the current imprisonment binge, actually found that the vast majority of newly admitted inmates were low-rate offenders involved in petty crimes. When these same researchers studied people they labeled as "high-rate" and "predatory" offenders, their findings were similar to ours: that most in this group committed very unskilled and unprofitable crimes. As Greenwood and Turner note, many high-rate offenders "appeared to have taken foolish risks for very modest potential gains.... a much larger proportion of [career criminals] are not particularly successful at crime, but they periodically return to it because they are not good at anything else."[15]

Research reveals that the popular conception of criminal careers is a distortion of reality. The majority of people sent to prison were not following criminal careers. Most were sent to prison for petty crimes, and their dedication to criminal behavior did not appear to be as firm as the popular image suggests. In fact, the majority of them, as well as the majority of those following other patterns of crime (for example, one-shot, crime episodes, being around crime, or dereliction), indicate that many wanted to stop violating the law and were preparing themselves for conventional careers while they were in prison. Instead of a large, menacing horde of dangerous criminals, our inner cities actually contain many young men, mostly nonwhite, who become involved in unskilled, petty crime because there are no other avenues to a viable, satisfying conventional life. The majority have not finished high school, have no marketable job skills, have never been employed steadily, and were not working at the time of arrest. But these are the very same people we are spending tens of billions of dollars a year by imprisoning them.

What is the public's view on this? For a number of years, studies have discovered that when respondents are given scenarios that are closer to the actual crimes of most people sent to prison, the majority recommend some punishment other than imprisonment. A national poll taken by the Wirthlin Group in 1991 found that four of five Americans favored a non-prison sentence for offenders who are not dangerous. A 1991 California poll found that three-fourths of Californians felt that the state should find ways of punishing offenders that are less expensive than prison. In Alabama and Delaware, a focus-group analysis conducted by the Public Agenda Foundation found that when citizens were given detailed data about the crimes committed and the relative costs of various sanctions available to the courts, the public strongly supported non-prison sentences for inmates convicted of nonviolent crimes (who represent the vast majority of prisoners).[16] More recently, the PEW completed a poll in 2010 and found that 86 percent of the public agrees that;

"We have too many low-risk, non-violent offenders in prison. We need alternatives to incarceration that cost less and save our expensive prison space for violent and career criminals."[17]

The same poll found that the public believes 22 percent of the people currently in prison in the U.S. could be released from prison and would not pose a threat to overall public safety.

Collectively, these polls show that a majority of citizens would not recommend imprisonment for many people being sent to prison, especially if they knew more about the offenders' crimes and life circumstances and if they posed little threat to public safety.

NOTES

1. Marvin E. Wolfgang, Robert M. Figlio, and Thorsten Sellin, *Delinquency in a Birth Cohort* (Chicago: University of Chicago Press, 1972).

2. Peter Greenwood and Alan Abrahamse, *Selective Incapacitation* (Santa Monica, CA: Rand Corporation, 1982).

3. Peter Greenwood and Susan Turner, *Selective Incapacitation Revisited: Why the High-Rate Offenders Are Hard to Predict* (Santa Monica, CA: Rand Corporation, 1987).

4. See Alfred Blumstein, Jacqueline Cohen, and David P. Farrington, "Criminal Career Research: Its Value for Criminology," *Criminology* 26, 1, 1988): 1–35, for a summary of their work on criminal careers.

5. Michael Gottfredson and Travis Hirschi, "The True Value of Lambda Would Appear to Be Zero: An Essay on Career Criminals, Criminal Careers, Selective Incapacitation, Cohort Studies, and Related Topics," *Criminology* 24, 2 (1986): 213.

6. In most states, only people convicted of felony-level crimes are sentenced to state prison. Those convicted of misdemeanor crimes generally receive a sentence of less than twelve months, and they serve that time in a county jail.

7. Bureau of Justice Statistics, *National Corrections Reporting Program*, May 25, 2010, ncrp0608.csv.

8. U.S. Department of Justice, Bureau of Justice Statistics, *Felony Sentences in State Courts, 2006.* (December 2009).

9. U.S. Department of Justice, Bureau of Justice Statistics, *Historical Corrections Statistics in the United States, 1850–1984* (Washington, DC: U.S. Government Printing Office, December 1986). U.S. Department of Justice, Bureau of Justice Statistics (December 2010); *Prisoners in 2009* (Washington, DC: Bureau of Justice Statistics).

10. The main reason for choosing these states was access. We wanted to include California, but the then-director of corrections refused our request. Among those states we had access to, we selected these three on the grounds that they represented a spread on several variables—urban/rural, small population/large population, West/Midwest, and particularly on rates on incarceration.

11. Each selected inmate was informed of the purpose of the interview and told that participation was voluntary. Only three inmates refused to participate. In those instances in which an inmate declined to participate, that inmate's name was replaced with another from the same crime category list. Each person was visited twice, and twenty-five persons were selected each time. This was done to spread the sampling over a longer time period and thereby to avoid any particular skewing of the samples by temporal variables. Also, we mistakenly selected and interviewed four persons over the fifty total in Washington. We left them in our study because we eventually adjusted our stratified sample

so that our percentages of different time categories—for instance, robbery, violent crimes, other theft, drug-related crimes, sex crimes, and miscellaneous crimes—corresponded to national percentages. Consequently, the four extra interviews did not introduce any distortion.

12. It will be recalled that our original samples were stratified so that each crime category had an equivalent number of prisoners to be interviewed. Given that the vast majority of persons admitted are convicted of property and, increasingly, drug crimes, our samples had disproportionate numbers of violent crimes and robberies and needed to be statistically adjusted to reflect a true intake population. This was done by reweighing the sampled cases consistent with their observed proportions in the national admission data. For example, offenders convicted of robbery represent 11 percent of prison admissions as compared to the 20 percent representation in our sample. To make our sample nationally representative of robbers, we reweighted the robbery cases by a factor of 0.55 so that they constitute 11 percent of the adjusted sample.

13. *Gang banging* is the term gang members use for engaging in gang violence against other gangs and more generally for belonging to a gang and participating in gang activities.

14. The number of these cases is so small (six) that little can be made of these descriptive statistics.

15. Peter Greenwood and Susan Turner, *Selective Incapacitation Revisited: Why High-Rate Offenders Are Hard to Predict* (Los Angeles: Rand Corporation, 1987), p. 36.

16. See *Americans Behind Bars* (New York: Edna McConnell Clark Foundation, March 1992); and John Doble and Josh Klein, *Punishing Criminals: The Public's View: An Alabama Survey* (New York: Edna McConnell Clark Foundation, 1989).

17. The Pew Center on the States. *Public Attitudes on Crime and Punishment.* (September 2010, Washington, DC: The Pew Charitable Trusts).

3

■

The Imprisonment of Children and Women

LEARNING OBJECTIVES

1. To understand the history and unique attributes of the juvenile court and detention system.
2. To become familiar with key juvenile court concepts, such as status offenses, waivers to adult courts, and the Juvenile Justice and Delinquency Prevention Act.
3. Develop knowledge in juvenile arrest and incarceration trends.
4. Become familiar with the size and trends in the number of women being incarcerated.
5. Understand the key differences in the attributes of women who are imprisoned versus men.

70 Youths Sue Former Judges in Detention Kickback Case

More than 70 juveniles and their families filed a class-action lawsuit Thursday against two former judges who pleaded guilty this month in a scheme that involved their taking kickbacks to put young offenders in privately run detention centers. The suit contends that before resigning last year, the judges "used kids as commodities that could be traded for cash," placing an "indelible stain" on the juvenile justice system of Luzerne County in northeastern Pennsylvania. The suit, filed in the Federal District Court in Scranton by the Juvenile Law Center, seeks to have all profits that the detention centers earned from the scheme placed in a fund that would compensate the youths for their emotional distress.

New York Times, February 26, 2009

Why Are the Scott Sisters of Mississippi Serving Life Sentences for Petty Theft?

Gladys and Jamie Scott are finally free after over 16 years in prison. Making a complete mockery out of our criminal justice system, their life sentences for a robbery of $11 as young adults tinged with Old South racism. After dozens of advocacy groups took on their cause, Republican Mississippi Governor Haley Barbour has just suspended their life sentences. In 1993, the two black women reportedly took part in an $11 robbery. For that crime, in which no one was harmed, you'd think that the sisters would've avoided hard time. Instead, the Scott sisters, who had no priors, were ordered to serve two consecutive life sentences. That's right, back-to-back life sentences for petty theft. The Scotts, who were 19 and 21 when the robbery occurred, have been incarcerated for 16 years. Meanwhile, three male acquaintances also convicted in the robbery are free after serving just a couple of years in prison. The men reportedly received lighter sentences in exchange for providing the prosecution with incriminating information against the Scotts.

Alex Dibranco, January 4, 2011 http://humanrights.change.org/blog/view/why_ are_the_scott_sisters_of_mississippi_serving_life_sentences_for_petty_theft.

INTRODUCTION

I n the study of crime and punishment, there are no two more important demographic variables than age and gender. The vast majority of all crimes are committed by younger males—generally between the ages of 15 and 24. Similarly, this same demographic group has the highest rates of being arrested and imprisoned. Because juvenile crime (typically defined as crimes committed by youth under the age of 18) has always been of concern given that so many of our youth become involved in criminal activities, it is important to understand how we as a society treat those youth who are arrested and punished for a wide variety of delinquent activities. For women, the issue is just the opposite. Given that such a smaller proportion of females become involved in serious crime (as opposed to males), for what reasons are they being incarcerated? As will be shown in this chapter, while juveniles and women make up a small proportion of the adult prison and jail populations, there have been significant increases in the use of imprisonment for both populations although there are some important positive trends that suggest a change in policy.

THE CHILDREN'S IMPRISONMENT BINGE

The History of the Juvenile Correctional System

The development of a distinct justice system specifically tailored to recognize the many mitigating factors associated with juvenile crime is generally recognized as one of the most progressive developments in the evolution of criminal justice in the United States. Until this century, no formal differentiation had been made in society's response to crimes committed by juveniles versus crimes committed by adults. Beginning in Illinois in 1899, juvenile court systems were instituted throughout the United States to provide greater emphasis on the welfare and rehabilitation of youth in the justice system. Specialized detention centers, training schools, and youth centers were developed to confine and treat delinquent youth apart from adult offenders. These facilities were intended to provide a structured, rehabilitative environment where the individual educational, psychological, and vocational needs of youthful offenders could be effectively addressed. Although system crowding and funding shortfalls have frequently compromised the achievement of these objectives in many jurisdictions, the goals of the juvenile court system have remained focused on protecting the welfare of youthful offenders.

This vision of a distinct justice system for juveniles focused upon treatment has come under attack in recent years. Beginning in the late 1980s, communities around the nation began to experience dramatically increased rates of juveniles being arrested for criminal and noncriminal acts. Unlike adults, there is a class of behavior known as "status offenses," which means that only people who have a status of "juvenile" can be arrested and incarcerated for certain offenses. These status offenses are behaviors such as "running away," "truancy," "curfew violations," and being "incorrigible."

The FBI's Uniform Crime Index does not allow criminologists to separate reported crimes by age or gender of the person committing the crime. The only national indicator of juvenile crime is the number being arrested each year. As shown in Figure 3-1, both the overall and violent juvenile arrest rates began to increase in 1985 and continued to escalate until the mid-1990s. This trend has reversed itself to the extent that the arrest rate is what it was in 1980.

The increasing incidence and severity of violent crimes committed by juveniles after 1985 led many to question the efficacy of the juvenile court system and to call for a harsher response to juvenile crime. Juvenile delinquency, at least for more serious offenses, has come to be viewed more as a criminal rather than a behavioral problem, resulting in a substantial shift in public responses to the management of juvenile offenders. Researchers have noted this shift in trends toward more arrests, longer periods of incarceration, fewer opportunities for rehabilitation, and most significantly, in the increasing transfer of juveniles to the adult criminal justice system.

Related to this harsher punishment trend has been a shift in the informal handling of youth arrested by police. In 1972, the FBI reported that 45 percent of the youth arrested were "handled within the department and released" without a

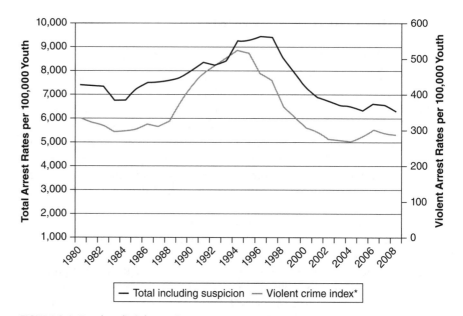

FIGURE 3-1 Total and Violent Crime Arrest Rates 1980–2008

SOURCE: National Center for Juvenile Justice (October 31, 2009). Juvenile Arrest Rates by Offense, Sex, and Race.

referral to either the juvenile court (51%) or referred to the adult court (only 1%). By 2009, only 22 percent of the juvenile arrests were being handled informally and 67 percent were being referred to the juvenile court. More significantly, 9 percent of the cases were being referred to adult courts.[1]

Such a shift toward harsher punishments toward juveniles led to the increasing numbers of juveniles in adult correctional facilities despite the decline in the number of juveniles arrested for violent crimes. Concerned that the juvenile justice system may be ill-equipped to handle youth charged with serious crimes and that the juvenile court may be too lenient in its ability to punish and control such youth, many states initiated the process of amending their criminal codes so that youth charged with certain crimes can be waived into the adult court, where they are tried and sentenced as adults. All states now have the authority to try some juveniles as adults in criminal court under a number of mechanisms and circumstances (usually determined by the youth's age and type of crime committed).[2] Subsequent to conviction, youth who are charged as adults are often held in an adult correctional facility (either a jail or prison).

For example, in 2010, the Baltimore city jail held over 110 juveniles charged as adults and awaiting trial. The unit they lived in is a self-contained cell block within the jail, which is required by federal law under the Juvenile Justice and Delinquency Prevention Act (JJDPA) that was originally passed by Congress in 1973. Similarly, the New York City jail holds hundreds of youth in an adolescent housing unit at Rikers Island who are also separated from adult inmates. These units must provide educational services each day, as if the youth were attending a public school system as required by the JJDPA.

Trends in the Number of Youth Confined

Most youth are housed in facilities that are designed to hold only youthful offenders. Generally, these facilities are separated into two major categories—detention facilities and secure placement or "commitment" facilities. The former are similar to jails where youth that have been arrested are detained until the court either releases or adjudicates (another term for being found guilty) and then sentences them (disposition). Many of the secure placement or commitment facilities are like adult prisons with cell blocks or large dormitories where youth are incarcerated until they are paroled or reach the age of adulthood. In some states, a youth can remain in a secure facility until they reach the age of 21.

The first comprehensive survey of these facilities was conducted in 1975 as part of the JJDPA legislation. Prior to 1975, Children in Custody (CIC) surveys only covered public operated facilities. But since a significant percentage of the secure placement facilities are operated by private companies, the CIC was expanded to cover those facilities as well.

As shown in Figure 3-2, the number of youth incarcerated increased steadily until 2000 when it reached 108,802. Since then, the number of youth housed in these juvenile jails and prisons has steadily declined. As of 2008, the total number

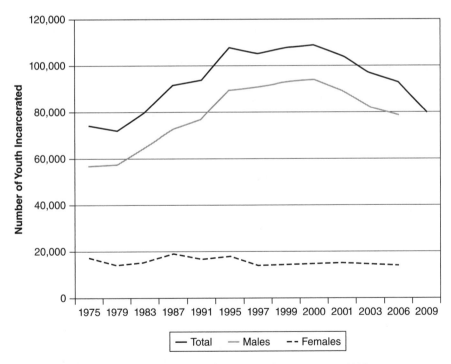

FIGURE 3-2 Number of Incarcerated Youth On Any Given Day 1975–2008

SOURCES: 1975 to 1995 data drawn from Bradford Smith, "Children in Custody: 20-Year Trends in Juvenile Detention, Correctional, and Shelter Facilities," *Crime and Delinquency*, (1998): 44 (4): 526–544. All subsequent years provided by Melissa Sickmund, T. J. Sladky, and Wei Kang (2008) "Census of Juveniles in Residential Placement Databook." Online. Available: http://www.ojjdp.ncjrs.gov/ojstatbb/cjrp/.

of youth in these facilities was 79,000, which is 26 percent lower than the number reported in 2000 (108,802 juveniles). The decline was not as steep as the decline in juvenile arrest rates as noted earlier, which dropped 33 percent. In 2006, the last year that detailed demographic data exist, the vast majority of these youth are males aged 15 and higher with a significant number over age 17 (Table 3-1). This young adult population occurs in those states where youth can be incarcerated beyond the age of 18.

Another noteworthy attribute is that most of the youth are either charged or convicted of nonviolent crimes with over 15,000 incarcerated for public order

Table 3-1 Juvenile Correctional Facilities Population Profile, 2006

Attribute	Total	Male	Female
Total	92,854	78,911	13,943
Age			
12 & younger	1,207	1,011	196
13 years	3,424	2,714	710
14 years	9,127	7,329	1,798
15 years	17,574	14,424	3,150
16 years	24,646	20,769	3,877
17 years	23,761	20,588	3,173
18 & older	13,115	12,076	1,039
Type of Offense			
Person	31,704	27,680	4,024
Property	23,177	20,400	2,777
Drugs	7,996	6,989	1,007
Public Order	9,944	8,714	1,230
Status Offenses	4,717	2,766	1,951
Race			
White	32,494	26,464	6,031
Black	37,337	32,541	4,796
Hispanic	19,027	16,738	2,289
Other	3,995	3,168	827
Incarceration Rates			
White	170	270	65
Black	767	1,317	200
Hispanic	326	560	80
	Committed-Sentenced	Detained	Diversion
Placement Status	64,558	26,344	1,865
	Total	Public	Private
Facility Type	92,093	63,502	28,426

SOURCE: www.ojjdp.gov/ojstatbb/corrections/qa08210.asp?qaDate=2006.

and status offenses. Like the adult jail and prison systems, most of the youth are minorities with Black males having the astronomical rates of incarceration (1,317 per 100,000 Black youth). Most are sentenced, with a sizeable number in privately operated facilities.

Despite the decline in the juvenile arrests and juvenile correctional facility populations, the number housed in adult facilities has increased. This has occurred even though Congress attempted to eliminate this practice. Since 1985, there has been a sharp increase in the number of persons under age 18 housed in local jails (from 1,736 to 7,220). The vast majority (5,847 or 76%) of youth in local jails are there because they are being held as adults, meaning that they have been "waived" from the juvenile court and are being charged as adults in adult courts.

Youth housed in state prisons increased sharply and reached a peak in 1995. According to the last national study on the number of juveniles housed in state prisons, between 1985 and 1997, the number of youth admitted to state prisons had doubled from 3,400 to 7,400.[3] Significantly, 40 percent of these juveniles were convicted of nonviolent crimes. There was a large racial disparity in the data with about 60 percent of the admissions being Black. Overall, 75 percent of the admissions were minorities. At that time the Bureau of Justice Statistics (BJS) estimated that approximately 5,400 youth were in state public and private prisons as compared to 2,300 in 1985. The most recent data from BJS shows that the number has declined significantly. According to the BJS, there are now only 2,778 juveniles in state prisons, which is an approximate 50 percent decline. Most of the decline occurred between 1995 and 2002. Since then, the number has remained constant although there has been a slight increase through 2008 (Table 3-2).

"Adult Crime, Adult Time"—Waivers to Adult Court

A major reason for the increases in youth being held in local jails, as noted in the previous section, has been the adoption of laws that allow youth charged with

Table 3-2 Juveniles in Adult Jails and State Prisons, 1983–2008

Year	Jails	Prison	Total
1985	1,629	NA	NA
1990	2,301	3,600	5,901
1995	7,800	5,309	13,109
2000	7,615	3,896	11,511
2005	6,759	2,208	8,967
2008	7,220	2,717	9,937

SOURCES: U.S. Department of Justice, Bureau of Justice Statistics, *Sourcebook of Criminal Justice Statistics 2009* (Washington, DC: Office of Justice Programs), 2010. Table 6.39 2009, and *Jail Inmates At Midyear 2009 – Statistical Tables*, Table 6.

felony-level crimes to be waived to adult courts and to be tried as adults. During the past decade, most states have adopted legislation that allows youth to be transferred from the juvenile court to the adult court to be tried as adults. Usually these laws target very serious crimes and allow the age of jurisdiction to be lowered. Relative to the issue of juveniles in adult correctional facilities, these laws often become the basis for a juvenile to be housed in a jail (if charged and awaiting court disposition) or within a prison if the juvenile has been convicted and sentenced.

A striking example of this practice is the case of Nathaniel Abraham who was tried in Michigan's court after being charged with murder at the age of 11. He is believed to be the youngest defendant to ever be tried as an adult for first-degree murder. This was possible in Michigan, because they had passed legislation that set no age limit for waiving juvenile offenders to the adult court. As Governor Engler stated to the media in response to the case, "adult crime, adult time."[4]

More recently is the case of Genarlow Wilson. Genarlow was convicted in 2005 in Georgia for having oral sex with a consenting 15-year-old girl when he was 17. He was sentenced as an adult to 10 years. He was eventually released from prison in 2007 after spending more than two years behind bars for a teen sex conviction. The release only occurred after his case was reviewed by the Georgia Supreme Court and ordered him to be released, ruling 4–3 that his sentence was cruel and unusual punishment.[5]

Forty-four of the fifty-one state legislatures (including the District of Columbia) made substantive changes to their laws targeting juveniles who commit violent or serious crimes between 1992 and 1996. All but ten states adopted or modified laws making it easier to prosecute juveniles in criminal court. Nearly half of the states (twenty-four) added crimes to the list of excluded offenses, and thirty-six states and the District of Columbia excluded certain categories of juveniles from juvenile court jurisdiction. The list of offenses considered serious enough for transfer as young as age 14 included murder, aggravated assault, armed robbery, and rape; but the list also included less serious and violent offenses, such as aggravated stalking, lewd and lascivious assault or other acts in the presence of a child, violation of drug laws near a school or park, sodomy, and oral copulation. Since 1992, thirteen states and the District of Columbia have added or modified statutes that provide for a mandatory minimum period of incarceration for juveniles adjudicated delinquent for certain serious and violent crimes.

A legal method used to try a youth as an adult is accomplished by lowering the age of jurisdiction. For example, seven states (Georgia, Illinois, Louisiana, Massachusetts, Michigan, South Carolina, and Texas) set their age of jurisdiction at 16, while New York, Connecticut, and North Carolina have lowered the age to 15 years. Missouri lowered the age for transfer to criminal court to 12 years of age for any felony.

In all but two states (Nebraska and New York), a juvenile court judge can waive jurisdiction over a case and transfer youth to the adult court for certain crimes and at certain age limits. The number of juvenile court cases transferred to criminal court increased from approximately 7,200 in 1985 to a high of nearly 12,300 in 1994. The numbers then declined to approximately 10,000 by 1996.[6]

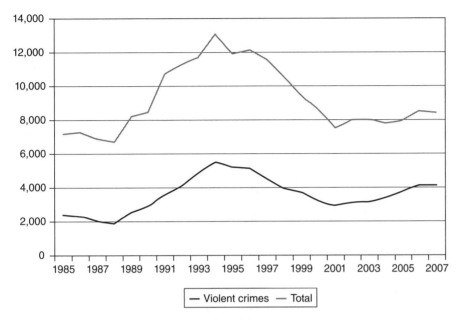

FIGURE 3-3 Number of Juveniles Waived to Adult Courts 1985–2007
SOURCE: Office of Juvenile Justice and Delinquency Prevention website. http://www.ncjrs.gov/pdffiles1/ojjdp/230167.pdf.

Although the legal basis for waiver varies from state to state, the clear trend across the country is to rapidly expand the use of waivers.[7] This is being accomplished by casting wider nets in criteria for waiver by lowering the age of adult jurisdiction or by adding to the list of applicable crimes, and by adopting more procedures by which youth can be transferred to adult court (for example, either through the discretion of the prosecutor or through legislative mandate). Currently, waiver provisions are often applied to nonviolent offenders, and in some states, running away from a juvenile institution is grounds for prosecution in adult courts. Although crimes against the person is now the most frequent offense related to the waiver, the majority of cases are charged with property, drugs, and public order offenses (see Figure 3-3). Similar to other juvenile arrest and correctional populations, the numbers are declining in concert with the declining number of arrests for serious and all other types of crimes.

Conditions of Confinement

One of the concerns regarding the jailing of kids is their safety in such facilities. For example, one study found that the juvenile suicide rate in jails is five times higher than the rate in the general youth population and eight times higher than the rate for adolescents in juvenile detention facilities.[8] In a later study, juveniles were more likely to be violently victimized in adult prisons than in juvenile correctional facilities.[9] Although property crime victimization rates are about the same for the two groups (over half of the inmates), 37 percent of the juveniles in training schools versus 47 percent of juvenile prison inmates suffer violent victimization, including violence at the hands of staff. Sexual assault is five times more likely in prison, beatings by staff nearly twice as likely, and attacks with weapons almost 50 percent more common.

These data suggested that placing juveniles in adult prisons and jails posed unique problems for the adult corrections system, including development of treatment and reintegrative services and protection from adult predatory inmates.

It was for these reasons that Congress passed the JJDPA in 1973. In 1980, the act was amended by Congress to require states to remove all juveniles from jails within a five-year period. However, as noted above, thousands of juveniles remain in adult facilities throughout the United States.

Further, there are many problems with the juvenile correctional facilities where most of the youth are incarcerated. The Civil Rights of Institutionalized Persons Act (CRIPA) was enacted by Congress in 1980 to help eliminate unlawful conditions of confinement for detained and incarcerated youth. CRIPA gives the Civil Rights Division of the U.S. Department of Justice (DOJ) the power to bring actions against state or local governments for violating the civil rights of persons institutionalized in publicly operated facilities. Since then there have been over one hundred investigations of such allegations in over sixteen states. The entire state juvenile correctional systems in Georgia, Louisiana, Mississippi, California, and Maryland have been forced by the DOJ to significantly improve the conditions of confinement in all of their facilities. The DOJ is currently monitoring conditions in sixty facilities. Table 3-3 is a list of the settlements and court decisions that have been reached thus far. Suffice it to say that many of the nation's juvenile correctional facilities are not meeting the basic mental health and medical care conditions and basic protection from harm conditions.

One of the major problems with these facilities is that they fail to protect youth from being assaulted by staff or other youth. In particular is the incidence of rape and sexual assault. A recent report from the Department of Justice's Bureau of Justice Statistics (BJS) finds that youth in juvenile corrections facilities are sexually abused at alarming rates and are victimized significantly more often than adult inmates. Almost one in eight of the detained youth who participated in the survey reported sexual abuse at their current facility during the previous year. The study is based on a survey given to 9,198 youth detainees in 195 facilities from all fifty states and the District of Columbia. The BJS report also included these findings:

1. 80 percent of the reported abuse was perpetrated by a member of the facility's staff.

2. 95 percent of youth who alleged abuse by staff reported at least one female perpetrator.

3. Victimized youth usually endured repeated sexual abuse, often more than ten times, and frequently by multiple perpetrators.

4. 65 percent of youth who had previously been sexually assaulted at another facility also reported having been sexually abused in the facility they are currently housed in.

5. Youth with a sexual orientation other than heterosexual reported being sexually abused by another inmate at a rate more than ten times higher than that of youth who identified as heterosexual.[10]

Table 3-3 Juvenile Correctional Facilities Settlements and Court Decisions

United States v. State of New York (Juvenile Facilities) (Settlement Agreement) (7/14/10)

United States v. State of Texas, Evins Regional Juvenile Center (Compliance Report) (11/05/08)

Los Angeles Probation Camps (L.A. Camps) (10/31/08)

United States v. State of Oklahoma, L.A. Rader Center (09/09/08)

United States v. State of Maryland (Second Amended Settlement Agreement Regarding Conditions at Three Juvenile Justice Facilities) (06/23/08)

United States v. State of Ohio (Ohio Juveniles) (06/24/08)

Settlement Agreement between the United States Department of Justice and the Marion Superior Court Concerning the Marion Superior Court Juvenile Detention Center (4/09/08) See also, Complaint (4/09/08)

United States v. State of Texas, Evins Regional Juvenile Center (Order) See also, U.S. v. State of Texas (Evins Complaint) (2/01/08)

First Amendment to Memorandum of Agreement between the United States of America and the County of Los Angeles, and Los Angeles County Office of Education (L.A. Halls) (8/01/07)

United States v. The State of Maryland, the Baltimore City Juvenile Justice Center and *United States v. The State of Maryland* (Complaint) (5/22/07)

United States v. State of Indiana, the Logansport Intake/Diagnostic Facility and the South Bend Juvenile Correctional Facility (02/08/06)

United States v. State of Hawai'i, the Hawai'i Youth Correctional Facility (Memorandum of Agreement) (02/07/06)

United States v. State of Maryland (Rule 41 Settlement Agreement concerning the Cheltenham and Hickey Youth Facilities) (06/29/05)

United States v. Mississippi (Consent Decree concerning the Oakley and Columbia Training Schools) (05/04/05)

United States v. Mississippi (Rule 41 Settlement Agreement concerning the Oakley and Columbia Training Schools) (05/04/05)

Memorandum of Understanding between the State of Michigan (W.J. Maxey Training School) and the United States Department of Justice (01/05/05)

Memorandum of Agreement Between the United States Department of Justice and the State of Arizona Concerning Adobe Mountain School, Black Canyon School, and Catalina Mountain School (09/15/04)

Agreement Between the United States, Los Angeles County and The Los Angeles County Office of Education (L.A. Halls) (08/24/04)

Memorandum of Understanding by and between the United States and the State of Nevada (02/23/04)

United States v. Louisiana (2004 Agreement) (12/31/03)

United States v. State of Arkansas, the Arkansas Division of Youth Services, and the Arkansas Department of Human Services and U.S. v. Arkansas (Complaint)

United States v. Louisiana (2003 Agreement) (01/17/03)

United States v. Louisiana (Jena Agreement) (04/13/00) (Closed 02/12/01)

United States v. Georgia (03/18/98)

SOURCE: U.S. Department Civil Rights Division web site: http://www.justice.gov/crt/about/spl/findsettle.php.

THE IMPRISONMENT BINGE OF WOMEN

Beyond the unprecedented growth of the total prison and jail population and the increased incarceration of juveniles, there is another hidden crisis—the growing incarceration of women. Between 1983 and 2009, the number of women in the nation's state and federal prisons increased by 504 percent compared to a 279 percent increase in the number of men in prison. By the end of 2009, the women prisoner population reached nearly 115,000. And there are another 93,199 women in jail for a total of over nearly 210,000 incarcerated women on any given day. Just like the prison population, the female jail population increased at twice the rate of the male population (Table 3-4).

Although the image most commonly evoked by the word prisoner is that of a minority male, the reality is that the faces of prisoners also increasingly belong to women, especially women of color. When Marc Mauer and Tracy Huling of the Sentencing Project released their historic 1995 report "Young Black Americans and the Criminal Justice System," the finding that gained the most national attention was that one in three young black men, nationally, was under some form of criminal justice control. However, the same study revealed another equally striking finding: that due to the war on drugs legislation and other factors, "African American women have experienced the greatest increase in criminal justice supervision."[11] And as shown in Table 3-4 that 1995 trend has continued to the present.

More striking is the fact that the female prison population is far less dangerous than the male population. As shown in Table 3-5, incarcerated women are far less likely to be convicted of a violent crime (largely due to low incidents of rape and sexual assault) and far more likely to be convicted of property and drug

Table 3-4 Jail and Prison Populations by Gender, 1983–2009

Year	Jail		Prison	
	Males	**Females**	**Males**	**Females**
1983	206,163	15,652	396,021	19,020
1985	235,909	19,077	479,359	23,148
1990	365,821	37,198	729,840	44,079
1995	448,000	51,300	1,057,406	68,468
2000	543,120	70,414	1,298,027	93,234
2005	646,807	93,963	1,420,303	107,626
2009	667,201	93,199	1,502,499	114,797
% Change	224%	495%	279%	504%

SOURCES: U.S. Department of Justice, Bureau of Justice Statistics, *Sourcebook of Criminal Justice Statistics, 1997* (Washington, DC: Office of Justice Programs, 1999), Table 6.35; U.S. Department of Justice, Bureau of Justice Statistics, *Prisoners in 1998* (Washington, DC: Office of Justice Programs, 1999); U.S. Department of Justice, Bureau of Justice Statistics, *Prisoners in 2009* (Washington, DC: Office of Justice Programs, 2010); U.S. Department of Justice, Bureau of Justice Statistics, *Jails at Midyear 2009, Statistical Tables* (Washington, DC: Office of Justice Programs, 2010).

Table 3-5 Current Offense of 2008 State Prison Population and Recidivism Rate by Gender

Offense	Male	Female
Violent	54%	36%
Murder	13%	12%
Manslaughter	1%	1%
Rape	5%	1%
Other sexual assault	8%	2%
Robbery	14%	9%
Assault	10%	9%
Other violent	3%	3%
Property	18%	29%
Burglary	9%	7%
Larceny	3%	8%
Motor vehicle theft	2%	2%
Fraud	2%	10%
Other property	2%	2%
Drug	18%	27%
Public-order	9%	7%
Other/unspecified	1%	1%
1994 Return-to-Prison Recidivism Rate	53%	39%

crimes. In terms of recidivism rates, the male three-year return to prison rate is 14 percent higher than it is for females.

Descriptions of the Female Inmate

Lorraine Fowler describes the "typical" female inmate as follows: probably minority, aged 25 to 29, unmarried but has one to three children, a likely victim of sexual abuse as a child, a victim of physical abuse, has current alcohol and drug abuse problems, has had multiple arrests, first arrested around 15, a high school dropout, on welfare, has low skills, and has held mainly low-wage jobs.[12] A study in Indiana described female inmates as having very high needs for educational programs, job training, health and mental health counseling; as having drug problems and job problems; and as having poor parenting skills and continued responsibility for children.[13]

1. Current Offense and Prior Record As noted above, women have less violence in their current or prior criminal record than men and are more generally convicted of minor crimes. They have fewer prior convictions than men, usually for minor or nonviolent crimes—for example, fraud, larceny, theft, or drug offenses. Although national data suggest an increasing number of women are charged with serious crimes, they are generally accessories and not the instigator or leader.[14]

Furthermore, many of women's violent crimes occur in a specific long-term relationship and are unlikely to generalize to the public at large. Mary Morash, citing 1991 BJS statistics, notes that more female offenders relative to male offenders were incarcerated for killing a family member, spouse, or other close intimate (25 percent versus 6 percent).[15]

2. Institutional Conduct   Women's institutional behavior appears substantially better than that of male inmates.[16] They exhibit less escape or escape attempts, less violence, and about half as many formal misbehavior reports as males. Put differently, there has never been a major riot at a female prison. Females "almost uniformly" pose lower institutional risks as indicated by lower severity of current crimes, lower criminal histories, lower levels of disciplinary infractions, and lower escape activities. Most disciplinary infractions by women tend to be nonviolent (for example, refusal to obey an order, unauthorized possession of money, and so on).

In contrast, male infractions involve more fights and assaults. Correctional staff describes female inmates as being more socially adjusted and positive in their attitudes than males.[17] Peggy Burke and Linda Adams found that many correctional staff felt that women were more sensitive, more demanding, needed more daily attention, were more concerned with personal problems, and had higher expectations that staff listen and care about their problems. While less violent and risky, staff felt that females were "more trouble" than male prisoners.[18]

3. Children and Family Relationships   An intense need that primarily characterizes women inmates is the maintenance of bonding with children and family. Austin described this need as the foremost difficulty women inmates' experience, with many of them hoping to resume their maternal role following release. Considerable stress and anxiety occur among female inmates if this bond is threatened. The staff have noted that this anxiety has a very negative impact on women's adjustment to incarceration.

A majority of female inmates have children, most have primary responsibility for child rearing, and most have legal custody. Morash reported that about 66 percent of women in prison had children under 18 years of age. Austin reported slightly different statistics—but reached the same general conclusions. More than 80 percent of female inmates had at least one child and close to 70 percent had children under 18 years of age. More recently, the BJS reported that among female state prisoners, two-thirds are mothers of a minor child.[19]

Additionally, the effects of the increasing incarceration of women are reaching into the next generation. Their children are routinely left without a parent, without a coordinated system of care, and without the supports guaranteed to other children in America by the Federal Adoption Assistance and Child Welfare Act (PL 96-272, a federal law mandating services primarily to promote the preservation of families). While the traumatic effects on children of losing their mothers to prison or jail have been well documented, the children themselves have remained largely invisible. They have not yet become part of the equation when policy makers evaluate the costs of incarcerating women.

4. Medical and Mental Health Needs   The medical needs of female inmates include several special issues: pregnancy, abortions, birth control, birth, child custody, and so on. Classification is crucial in detecting these needs and referring the female inmate for appropriate care. Female inmates overall have a higher demand for both medical and psychiatric services than males. Nearly three-quarters (73.1%) of women in state prisons in 2005 had a mental health problem compared to 55 percent of men in prison. Nearly one in four women are diagnosed with a mental illness and 12 percent of women in jails have severe psychiatric disorders; fewer than 25 percent of them receive mental health services.[20] A failure to properly assess or adequately treat such needs would have a disparate impact on the welfare of the female inmate.

5. Vocational, Educational, and Economic Needs   Women inmates have more severe social, educational, and economic risk factors than male inmates. The few statistical reports of the early 1990s suggest that most women inmates are uneducated, unskilled, poor, unemployed, or hold minimum-wage jobs; that about 20 percent have not attained functional literacy; and that about 60 percent are on public assistance.[21] Unfortunately, alleviating these social needs is not prioritized in prisons and jails, and such problems are ignored or not addressed due to lack of resources. This low priority regarding rehabilitation has been vigorously attacked. Burke and Adams, for example, criticize the low emphasis on "habitation" relative to security.[22] Fowler argues that cost-effective solutions in corrections must emphasize prevention by placing a higher emphasis on alleviating social needs.[23]

Abuse of Women Inmates

Finally, there have been increasing reports of female inmates (and staff as well) being sexually abused by male guards. As reported by the Washington Post in 1999, Amnesty International released a study of the level of abuse occurring in the nation's jails and prisons.[24] Abuse occurs because many guards working in female prisons are males. In federal prisons, approximately 70 percent of the guards working in female prisons are male, while in Canada only 9 percent are male. When performing normal activities, male guards are allowed to touch a prisoner's breasts and genitals during routine pat downs and strip searches, and they can watch women as they shower and dress. There have even been reports of selling women inmates to male inmates for sex. Some of the examples cited in the Amnesty International study, as reported by *The Washington Post*, are as follows:

> A female prisoner was raped and impregnated by a guard at a Washington state prison. The Federal Bureau of Prisons agreed to pay $500,000 to settle a lawsuit filed by three female inmates who said they had been sexually abused

at the Federal Detention Center in Pleasanton, California. One of the women, Robin Lucas, stated she was housed in a men's facility where she was attacked by a male inmate who was allowed in her cell by the staff. When she complained, she claims the guard retaliated by allowing three men in her cell; she was handcuffed, beaten, and raped.

Florence Krell committed suicide by hanging herself after she had written numerous letters to her mother and a judge complaining about mistreatment, including being observed by male guards when she was left naked in her cell. In 1994, a federal judge ruled that the D.C. Department of Corrections had violated the constitutional rights of thirteen female inmates by allowing male guards to fondle and rape them.

In the Arlington County jail, based on its own internal investigation, found that female inmates were being sexually abused by male guards over a six-month period. Currently, there are twelve states where it is not a crime for guards to have sex with an inmate.[25]

These and other atrocities have led many to recommend that male guards be removed completely from prisons that house women. Although such a personnel policy may not pass constitutional muster, it is clear that if left unattended, this dark side of the prison experience will emotionally scar thousands of women who are exposed to such repugnant behavior.

NOTES

1. Sourcebook of criminal justice statistics online (2010), http://www.albany.edu/sourcebook/pdf/t4262009, Table 4.26. 2009.

2. Melissa Sickmund, *How Juveniles Get to Criminal Court* (Washington, DC: U.S. Department of Justice, Office of Juvenile Justice and Delinquency Prevention, May 1994).

3. K. J. Strom, 2000 *Profile of State Prisoners Under Age 18*, Bureau of Justice Statistics. NCJ 176989. Washington, DC: U.S. Department of Justice.

4. "13-Year-Old Convicted in Shooting," *The Washington Post*, November 17, 1999, p. A3.

5. http://articles.cnn.com/2007-10-26/us/wilson.freed_1_conviction-genar low-wilson-unusual-punishment?_s=PM:US.

6. Anne Stahl, "Delinquency Cases Judicially Waived to Criminal Court, 1987–1996."

Office of Juvenile Justice and Delinquency Prevention Briefing Book (July 1, 1999).

7. P. Torbet, R. Gable, H. Hurst, I. Montgomery, L. Szymanski, and D. Thomas, *State Responses to Serious and Violent Juvenile Crime* (Washington, DC: U.S. Department of Justice, Office of Juvenile Justice and Delinquency Prevention, 1996).

8. Community Research Center, *Juvenile Suicides in Adult Jails* (Washington, DC: U.S. Department of Justice, Office of Juvenile Justice and Delinquency Prevention, Juvenile Justice Transfer Series, 1980).

9. M. Forst, J. Fagan, and T. S. Vivona, "Youth in Prisons and State Training Schools," Juvenile and Family Court Journal 39 (1989): 1–14.

10. U.S. Department of Justice, Bureau of Justice Statistics (2010), *Sexual Victimization in Juvenile Facilities Reported by*

Youth, 2008–09 (Washington, DC: U.S. Department of Justice).

11. Marc Maurer and Tracy Huling, *Young Black Americans and the Criminal Justice System* (Washington, DC: The Sentencing Project, 1995).

12. Lorraine T. Fowler, "What Classification for Women?" in *Classification: A Tool for Managing Today's Offenders* (American Correctional Association, 1993).

13. James Austin, *Women Classification Study—Indiana Department of Corrections* (San Francisco, CA: National Council on Crime and Delinquency, 1993).

14. Charlotte Nesbitt, *The Female Offender in the 1990's Is Getting an Overdose of Parity* (Longmont, CO: U.S. Department of Justice, National Institute of Corrections Information Center, Unpublished paper, 1994).

15. Mary Morash, *Identifying Effective Strategies for Managing Female Offenders* (Longmont, CO: U.S. Department of Justice, National Institute of Corrections Information Center, 1992).

16. James Austin, *Women Classification Study*; Nesbitt, *The Female Offender*; Jack Alexander and Elaine Humphrey, *Initial Security Classification Guidelines for Females* (Longmont, CO: NY State Department of Correctional Services, National Institute of Corrections Information Center, 1988).

17. Nesbitt, *The Female Offender*.

18. Peggy Burke and Linda Adams, *Classification for Women Offenders in State Correctional Facilities: A Handbook for Practitioners* (Washington, DC: National Institute of Corrections, 1991).

19. Christopher J. Mumola, *Incarcerated Parents and Their Children*, Bureau of Justice Statistics, August 2000.

20. The Sentencing Project (May 2007). *Women in the Criminal Justice System: Briefing Sheets*. Washington, DC: The Sentencing Project.

21. Nesbitt, *The Female Offender*.

22. Burke and Adams, *Classification*.

23. Lorraine T. Fowler, "What Classification for Women?" in *Classification: A Tool for Managing Today's Offenders* (American Correctional Association, 1993).

24. Amnesty International. *United States of America, Rights for All. "Not part of my sentence". Violation of the Human Rights of Women In Custody*. (New York, NY: Amnesty International, 1999).

25. "Abuse of Female Prisoners in U.S. Is Routine, Rights Report Says," *The Washington Post*, March 4, 1999, p. A11.

4

■

Doing Time

LEARNING OBJECTIVES

1. Develop an understanding of the conditions in prisons and how they vary throughout the United States.

2. Become familiar with the rates of violence and rape in correctional facilities.

3. Understand the past and current history on prison litigation.

4. Present findings on prison routines to confront idleness and the threat of violence.

5. Understand modern techniques now being used to manage the expanding prison population.

WAREHOUSING PRISONERS

About 1.5 million prisoners and another 768,000 jailed inmates are housed on any given day in approximately 1,600 state and federal prisons and about 3,400 jails. State prisons can best be described as warehouses where they are increasingly deprived, restricted, isolated, and consequently embittered and alienated from conventional worlds and where less and less is being done to prepare them for their eventual release.[1] As a result, most convicts are rendered incapable of returning to even a meager conventional life after prison. Because most will be released within two years, we should be deeply concerned about what happens to them during their incarceration. In particular, what has been the nature of their prison and jail experience?

Prisons have been called warehouses for decades, but in earlier periods the label was misleading. In most prisons in the first half of the twentieth century, prisoners were involved in complex prison societies; they performed all the essential tasks to operate the prison.[2] They cooked and served the meals, washed the clothing, fixed the plumbing, electrical wiring, and appliances, painted the buildings, tended the boiler, landscaped the grounds, delivered most of the medical services, and kept all the records. They worked in prison industries, making "jute" clothes, furniture, license plates, or other commodities consumed by the state. The prison staff oversaw all of these activities and kept track of the convicts, but convicts supplied most of the labor.[3]

In addition, convicts played all the sports possible within limits imposed by the physical plant: baseball, football, basketball (when there was a court), handball (there was always a wall for this), boxing, tennis (occasionally there was a court), and even marbles. They carried on the favorite convict pastime, "shucking and jiving"—that is, telling stories about their and others' exploits, mostly in crime, drugs, and sex. They "wheeled and dealed"; they smuggled food from the kitchen and ran sandwich and other food businesses; they made prison brew—pruno—that required sugar, yeast, fruit, and some place to stash it during fermentation (a stash was easy to locate, because prunes were such smelly stuff); or they bought or sold any contraband that they could steal, smuggle in, or manufacture: food, coffee, stingers (to heat water with), special clothing items, radios, phonographs, typewriters, paper, illegal drugs, and even nutmeg (gives one a cheap high when several spoonfuls are swallowed). Some participated in the special prison sexual life with its "punks," "queens," and "jockers."

Collectively, prisoners developed their own self-contained society, with a pronounced stratification system, a strong convict value system, unique patterns of speech and bodily gestures, and an array of social roles: "right guys," "politicians," "crazies," "regulars," "punks," "queens," "stool pigeons," and "hoosiers." Importantly, their participation in this world, with its own powerful value system, the convict code, gave them a sense of pride and dignity. It was them against what they perceived as a cruel prison system of a corrupt society.

The prison administration tolerated, even encouraged, most of the convict activities and their social organization, because these features promoted a high degree of order within the prison. Rarely did the administration have to intervene to maintain control over the inmates. The convicts ran the prison and kept the peace. There was not much emphasis on "reformation" or "rehabilitation," and most inmates left prison without having improved or acquired skills for living a conventional life. In the 1940s and 1950s, the return-to-prison rates ranged from 30 to 45 percent, which is basically what it is today.[4] However, society was more accepting of the ex-convict then than it is now.

THE DEVELOPMENT OF THE
CONTEMPORARY PRISON

Immediately after World War II, many state prison systems adopted the rehabilitative ideal and attempted to change their "big house" prisons into "correctional institutions."[5] In the "big houses" like Stateville, Illinois, and Jackson, Michigan, tough authoritarian wardens watched over populations of prisoners who, for the most part, did their time immersed in the prison society as just described. In correctional institutions (which became the new name for prisons), offenders were imprisoned not for punishment, but for rehabilitation. During the 1950s and 1960s, prisoners were sentenced under "indeterminate" sentence systems that granted prison and parole board officials considerable discretion over when an inmate was to be released. Inmates were expected to be involved in a variety of treatment programs and were released when parole boards decided the inmate had responded to treatment. However, a variety of factors, particularly the lack of sufficient funds, undermined the delivery of rehabilitation and, consequently, the rehabilitation model never was implemented as designed.

The Demise of Rehabilitation

The whole concept of treatment presumed that inmates had deficiencies that could be treated within a prison environment. By the late 1960s and early 1970s, many observers of the rehabilitative penal system began to question this assumption. Specifically, a number of questionable, discriminatory and even illegal practices were being carried on in the name of rehabilitation and through the margins of discretion given to prison administrators within the indeterminate sentence system.[6] Adding to the growing criticism of the rehabilitation model, criminologists, who had conducted or reviewed the studies, found that prison-based rehabilitative efforts in prison did not work as well as they had hoped.[7] In general, they found that prisoners who participated in a wide range of rehabilitative programs were rearrested at the same rate as those who did not. Even when programs were found to be "effective," they only reduced the recidivism rate by 5 to 10 percent from that of inmates who did not participate in such programs.

Consequently, in the early 1970s, "liberal" reformers sought to abolish indeterminate sentence systems and replace them with the short and uniform sentences known as "determinate" sentencing. Unlike indeterminate sentences when a person was sentenced to a minimum and maximum sentence and parole boards have broad discretion on when a person would be released, a determinate sentence consisted of a single sentence with the requirement that a prisoner must serve some percentage of the sentence. Unlike indeterminate sentencing, the prisoner would be automatically released after serving the required percentage of the sentence, unless one had been a disciplinary problem.

In the mid 1970s, as these efforts were beginning to produce some changes in sentencing statutes and policies across the country, conservatives took up the issue of criminal justice and also called for an end to not only the indeterminate sentence systems, but all prison rehabilitation. Unlike the liberal-minded reformers, however, conservatives objected to rehabilitation and indeterminate sentencing because inmates were being released too quickly, only to prey again on the public, so they insisted.

As the divergent efforts of liberals and conservative critics both sought to eliminate indeterminate sentencing for different reasons during the late 1970s, public fear of crime rose significantly, and conservatives had their way. Most states instituted sentencing and parole policies that made sentences more uniform and considerably longer (mandatory minimum prison laws) for many crimes (for example, residential burglaries, crimes involving the use of guns or violence, drunk driving, sex crimes, and/or criminals with prior convictions—habitual offenders).[8] In addition, most of the states that shifted their emphasis from rehabilitation to punishment reduced funding for rehabilitative programs, including education and vocational training.

Reduction in prison programs has been fueled by politicians who create an artificial view for the public of prisons being akin to luxury hotels. Former Massachusetts Governor William Weld, a moderate Republican, told then-Attorney General William Barr's Summit on Corrections that life in prison should be "akin to a walk through the fires of hell."[9] Michigan State Representative Mike Goshka, during a debate on prison conditions, said: "Prisoners have it too easy now. They got color TVs, weight-lifting equipment, libraries.... We need to return to the concept that prison is not fun."[10] In 1998, then-governor of California Pete Wilson ordered his department of corrections to revoke numerous privileges, including weight-lifting equipment. Wilson explained that "prisoners are there to be punished, and hopefully rehabilitated.... They're not there to be entertained and catered to."[11]

Prison Crowding

As the conservative sentencing agenda took hold, prison populations began to escalate. Although prison construction had proceeded rapidly, it still did not keep up with the prisoner population explosion, discussed in Chapter 1. By 1994, only nine states were operating their prisons below their bed capacities, and of these nine states, two were below 90 percent of their bed capacities. About 50,000 prisoners (about 5% of the entire prison system) were being held in local jails because of prison crowding.[12] These statistics mean that to accommodate the excessive inmate population, cells built to hold one inmate had to be converted to double occupancy cells. Many prisoners were being held in new, quickly constructed prisons that had only the bare facilities and infrastructure required to house and maintain prisoners on a long-term basis. Similarly, classrooms, gymnasiums, and recreation rooms were converted to dormitories, thus increasing inmate idleness and reducing the level of security and safety for staff and inmates.

These short-term efforts to expand the capacity of existing prisons were not sufficient to meet the growing need for more prisons. Consequently, most states embarked on record-level prison construction programs. Between 1990 and

2000, the bed capacity of the country's state prison system more than doubled from 580,362 to 1,151,222.[13] Between 2000 and 2005, only another 61,354 were added as the funding stream began to dry up.[14]

As prison populations have stabilized and even declined since 2007, what seemed like a never-ending demand for more prison capacity has waned. Instead of trying to build more prisons, states are now starting to close facilities. For example, since 2008, Michigan has closed eight prisons, as its prison population has declined by about 5,000 prisoners.[15] Illinois constructed a new prison but is unable to open it due to a lack of demand and budget issues. Today, the state is trying to sell the facility to the federal government to house suspected and known terrorists held at Guantanamo, Cuba.[16]

With respect to the rapid increase of prison construction over the past two decades, states adopted two strategies for siting new prisons. One approach focused on expanding the capacity of existing prisons by appending new prisons to existing sites. The only requirements were open space adjacent to the current prison and water and sewage systems sufficient to handle the additional prison and staff populations. This strategy was popular because it bypassed the problem of siting prisons in communities where they were not welcomed and resulted in the emergence of mega-prisons where 5,000 to 10,000 prisoners can be accommodated at a single site.

The second strategy has prompted many states to return to an old tradition of placing most new prisons in remote areas, far from urban centers.[17] There are three main reasons to do this: (1) land is cheaper and more available in remote areas; (2) most urban and suburban populations do not want prisons in their midst; and (3) many rural communities that are experiencing financial difficulties welcome the economic benefits of a prison that would provide employment and tax revenues. Building prisons in remote areas also leads to other consequences. Since the vast majority of prisoners come from cities, this means that relatives and friends visit prisoners at much greater expense and much less frequently (if at all). Also, fewer organizations—such as schools, churches, unions, businesses, and voluntary support groups—are available to offer services to prisoners. These circumstances have greatly increased the isolation and deprivation of prisoners.

The third and relatively new approach is to contract out inmates to other states or to "speculative" prisons constructed and operated by private prison companies. As of 2009, there were nearly 130,000 state and federal inmates housed in private prisons. Some of these inmates were housed in private facilities outside of their states. For example, Hawaii and Alaska have about 1,600 inmates each in private prisons outside of their home states. California is the largest state to ship its inmates to other states (10,000 people so housed) in a desperate attempt to reduce its crowding situation . The other category, as referenced earlier, is the use of local jails to house sentenced inmates (approximately 87,000). Louisiana with 50 percent and Kentucky with 35 percent lead the nation in this practice of housing their inmates in local jails.[18] This option is quite undesirable given that jails are ill-equipped to hold long-term inmates. They frequently do not have the level of programming, recreational space, or a medical or mental health service that is required by the inmates as determined by national health care standards. Such standards are promulgated by the National Commission on Correctional Health Care. The primary beneficiary of this practice is local government as it creates many local jobs that otherwise would not exist.

The bottom line is that crowding is now an accepted way of operating a prison system. There are few lawsuits being filed that challenge the crowding situation. Legislators and other policy makers are reluctant to spend even more money to alleviate the crowding condition unless it becomes intolerable or a major disturbance occurs. With crowding, there is an associated decline in access to programs and increased tension that can often result in increasing levels of violence and death.

Racial Skewing

As noted in Chapter 1, the number of Black and Hispanic prisoners continues to grow. In 1923, the first year that the racial makeup of the nation's prison system was counted, 31 percent of the inmates were black. By 2009, that figure had reached 41 percent Black, with another 22 percent of Hispanic origin.[19]

A major reason for the continual increase in racial skewing of the prison population stems from the fact that most convicts come from inner-city, lower-class populations. Increasingly, the urban lower class is made up of Blacks and Hispanics, as the middle and upper classes (of all races) flee the urban centers to seek a better way of life in America's suburbs. The young males in these lower-class ethnic groups have extremely high rates of unemployment, in some cases close to 50 percent. While idle, they often become involved in the social worlds of deviance and crime, such as using and dealing crack cocaine that offend and threaten the classes above them, and they are arrested and incarcerated at an astounding rate. As noted in Chapter 1, Black and Hispanic males have from three to eight times the rate of incarceration Whites.

Before the 1950s, Black and White prisoners were segregated into separate prisons in the South and into separate sections of prisons in other parts of the country. The convict societies in the East, Midwest, and West, were dominated by White prisoners, who were a majority, were racially prejudiced, and enforced "Jim Crow" segregation patterns. When formal segregation was ended by the 1960s, the growing numbers of non-White prisoners began asserting themselves, sometimes violently, in prison social affairs. The solidarity of prisoner society was shattered, and prisoners divided into hostile factions, mostly based on race and location of residence before prison. A small, but significant, faction of the current inmate population consists of murderous racial gangs that have dramatically altered the traditional prison world.[20]

The practice of racially segregating inmates has continued in some major prison systems. In 2005, the Supreme Court in *Johnson v. California,* No. 03-636, struck down the formal policy of the California Department of Corrections and Rehabilitation (CDCR) of racially segregating all inmates for the first 60 days of their admission to the prison system or whenever they were transferred to a new facility for another 60 days. It was also discovered that haircuts were being made according to the race of the inmate. It is also common for inmates to be housed according to their gang membership, which is often a proxy for race. As noted in the court case, Oklahoma and Texas are state prison systems that formerly took race into account in making initial housing decisions. According to a recent assessment of racial segregation in state prisons, the practice is not formally endorsed but occurs on a more informal basis in many states.[21]

Court Intervention

In the early 1960s, Black Muslim prisoners in Illinois won a case on their right to follow practices related to their religion (the First Amendment guarantees freedom of religion). Their successful litigation and a few subsequent cases expanded the remedies available to prisoners under a writ of habeas corpus and removed procedural obstacles to filing such writs in federal courts, thereby ending the court's "hands-off" policy toward prisoners grieving their treatment in prison.[22] More and more prisoners, inspired and aided by the protest movements of the late 1960s and early 1970s, sought remedy for their treatment, and increasingly, the courts intervened into the management of prisons. In particular, they were able to also challenge violations of the Eighth Amendment (cruel and unusual punishment) and the Fifth and Fourteenth Amendments (due process issues). In the late 1970s, the ACLU's Prison Law Project filed a case in Alabama arguing that the "totality" of conditions in the state's prison system constituted cruel and unusual punishment (*Newman v. Alabama*). The federal court heard the case, held for the complainants, and oversaw the correction of the unconstitutional conditions. Other "in-total" cases have followed.

By 1998, thirty-five states, plus the District of Columbia, Puerto Rico, and the Virgin Islands were under court order or consent decree to either limit prison crowding and/or improve conditions in either the entire prison system or a specific facility.[23] However, the passage of the Prison Litigation Reform Act (PLRA) by Congress in 1996 greatly altered the direction and scope of prison litigation. In effect, the PLRA requires there be a burden of proof by the litigants that the contested conditions of confinement violate the inmate's constitutional rights. Essentially, the PLRA makes it far more difficult to use litigation as a means for correcting deficient prison conditions. In effect, the courts have moved from "hands off" to active intervention in the management of prisons.

As a result of the PLRA, the number of state and federal facilities operating under consent decrees to limit the size of their inmate population has declined from 145 in 2000 to 44 by 2005. Similarly, facilities under court order or consent decrees for specific conditions of confinement (generally referred to as health care, medical care, or protection from harm issues) have declined from 320 to 218. Nonetheless, in California, the nation's largest state prison system in 2011, a three-judge federal court found that the provision of medical and mental health services violated the constitutional rights of the inmate popualtion. The unconstitutional conditions were linked by the court to the massive level of overcrowding that has existed in the system for many years. The court then ordered the the state to lower its 170,000 inmate population by about 40,000 over a two-year period.[24] So despite the reduction of federal court intervention in the affairs of state prisons, California stands out as a stark reminder that the conditions of confinement in many correctional facilities remain, at best, problematic.

Table 4-1 lists those facilities that have been recently investigated by the U.S. Department of Justice's Civil Rights Division for possible civil rights violations. In many of these cases, the violations have to do with access to mental health, medical services, and use of force issues. This list of current investigations is ongoing and changes from year to year. These investigations are largely based on information the civil rights division receives from individuals and organizations or

Table 4-1 Current Listing of Civil Rights of Institutionalized Persons Act Investigations Jails and Prisons Investigations Regarding Civil Rights Violations by the U.S. Department of Justice, Civil Rights Division

Lake County Indiana Jail (12/17/09)

Westchester County Jail, Valhalla, New York (11/19/09)

Orleans Parish Prison System, New Orleans, Louisiana (9/11/09)

Erie County Holding Center and the Erie County Correctional Facility in Buffalo, New York (07/15/09)

Harris County Jail in Houston, Texas (06/04/09)

Mobile County Metro Jail, Mobile, Alabama (01/15/09)

Oklahoma County Jail and Jail Annex, Oklahoma (07/31/08)

Cook County Jail in Chicago, Illinois (07/11/08)

Worcester County Jail and House of Correction in West Boylston, Massachusetts (04/29/08)

King County Correctional Facility in Seattle, Washington (11/13/07)

Wilson County Jail, Tennessee (8/30/07)

Oahu Community Correctional Center, Honolulu, Hawaii (3/14/07)

Delaware Correctional Centers; Howard R. Young Correctional Institution; Sussex Correctional Institution; John L. Webb Correctional Facility; and Delores J. Baylor Women's Correctional Institution (12/29/06)

Dallas County Jail, Dallas, Texas (12/08/06)

Sebastian County Adult Detention Center in Fort Smith, Arkansas (05/09/06)

Taycheedah Correctional Institution, Wisconsin (05/01/06)

Grant County Detention Center, Kentucky (05/18/05)

McPherson and Grimes Correctional Units in Newport, Arkansas (11/25/03)

Garfield County Jail and Garfield County Work Center in Enid, Oklahoma (04/17/03)

LeFlore County Jail in Poteau, Oklahoma (04/17/03)

Patrick County Jail (Virginia) (03/06/03)

Santa Fe County Adult Detention Center (Formerly the Santa Fe County Correctional Facility) (New Mexico) (03/06/03)

Wicomico County Detention Center in Salisbury, Maryland (09/09/02)

Baltimore City Detention Center (8/13/02)

Shelby County Jail in Memphis, Tennessee (6/27/01)

Wyoming State Penitentiary (06/29/99)

Correctional Facilities of the Commonwealth of the Northern Mariana Islands (08/05/98)

investigations made by news organizations. So it must be construed that in many other prisons the conditions of confinement are deficient in their handling and care of inmates, but it does not reach the attention of the federal government. For example, the California case noted above was litigated over a number of years by the Prison Law Project, a nonprofit organization with no federal funding or support. Had the Prison Law Project not existed, the deplorable conditions and massive overcrowding that has existed in California might never have been litigated by the U.S. Department of Justice. Another massive overcrowding situation exists in the Federal Bureau of Prisons (BOP), which is operating at 136 percent capacity as of 2009. The U.S. Civil Rights Division cannot (or will not) litigate the BOP, as it is part of the same U.S. Department of Justice.

Breakdown of Administrative Solidarity

As mentioned earlier, the "big houses" before World War II were traditionally run by an authoritarian warden. White rural males, often raised in the small towns near the prison, filled the ranks below this figure of authority. A formal, military-style hierarchy and an informal, "good ol' boy" social organization, with its special guard culture, produced a great deal of solidarity among administration and staff.[25]

As states embraced the rehabilitation concept, along with the need to hire more staff for the rapidly expanding prison population, many treatment-oriented administrators and staff were hired or advanced in prison agencies. As noted earlier, during this time, prisons tried the rehabilitation model. The terms penitentiary and prison were replaced with correctional center or correctional facility. Guards became "correctional officers," and "departments of prisons" were renamed "departments of rehabilitation and corrections." Staff with college degrees in the social sciences and a "treatment" orientation were hired to work in "program services" or "clinical services." These new staff were also expected to participate in all major operational decision making and were assigned to classification, program, and disciplinary committees at each prison. The influx of college-educated personnel, with a non-security orientation, drove a wedge between the new staff and the old guard who believed in punishment and maintenance of order. Furthermore, several court rulings on employment hiring practices that had excluded minorities and women resulted in the hiring of more and more nonwhite and female guards.

For example, the U.S. Civil Rights Division sued both the Florida Department of Corrections and the Parish of Orleans (New Orleans) because both agencies were restricting women from applying for many guard positions, arguing that these jobs posed a unique threat to the safety of women employees if assigned to these positions.[26] In Seattle, minority officers sued their employer, claiming that they were being harassed by white officers who were attempting to drive them out of the workforce.[27]

As the size of the correctional system workforce increased, it was organized into increasingly powerful labor unions and professional organizations (such as the American Correctional Association and the American Probation and Parole Association) that had become very active in pursuing the interests of their rank and file. Consequently, the top administration has lost a considerable amount of control over its employees, who are now divided along many lines: race, gender, union versus management, and rural versus urban. The prison administration has belatedly followed the path of other government organizations in moving from a more homogeneous, informal social organization to a formal and professionalized bureaucracy.[28]

Administrative Confusion

Presently, prison administrators lack a vision to give their task purpose and direction. Rehabilitation, an early guiding principle of modern penology has fallen into disrepute. For administrators, its replacement—punishment—converts simply to maintaining order in the prisons. Given the rapidly expanding prison populations, the new problems of keeping prisoners under control and a more politically active labor force, prison administrators have their hands full dealing with the day-to-day exigencies of running a crowded, unstable, conflict-ridden prison system. In effect, they have evolved from captains of ships to bureaucrats. To cope, they increasingly turn to formal procedures, rules, standards, and use of force to manage the inmate population.[29]

Guards have taken the new emphasis on imprisonment for punishment as a mandate to employ excessively firm, even extreme, force to keep prisoners in line. The term "excessive use of force" refers to situations where correctional staff resort to the use of chemical agents, such as tear gas, taser guns, and pepper spray to temporarily "neutralize" an inmate. Once controlled, inmates can be placed in "mechanical restraints," such as a restraint chair, leg irons, handcuffs, and other devices.

These situations often occur in the high-security or super-max units that are discussed in greater detail in the following chapter. Typically, an inmate, for any number of reasons, may be refusing to leave his or her cell. In such a situation, a "cell extraction" will occur, where a team of officers, with special training in cell extraction, forces its way into the cell and uses all of the methods and techniques discussed previously to remove the inmate. These events are often videotaped to ensure the extraction is done according to the department's standards. The following is an example of a typical cell extraction.

> At approximately 1710 hours, Inmate Smith refused to relinquish his tray following the evening meal. After numerous unsuccessful attempts were made by the unit officers and sergeants to retrieve the tray, permission was given by the administrative officer of the day to extract Smith from his cell. At approximately 1730 hours, Sergeant Wilson incapacitated Smith with a taser round, and he was placed in mechanical restraints (handcuffs and leg irons) by an extraction team. Smith was treated by medical staff for minor abrasions and rehoused. There were no injuries to staff. Smith was written up on a 115 and charged with violation of D.R. 300(c), Force and Violence.[30]

A more recent version of a cell extraction in New York's Sing Sing prison was captured by Ted Conover's classic investigative book on being a prison guard.

> The cell extraction officers stood one in front of the other, the second and third holding on to the officer in front of him and the lead officer carrying a see-through riot shield. On a signal, they started moving forward in step, like a locomotive gaining speed. "Open 101!" someone shouted. Another officer pulled open the cell door, and they went in on one another's heels. The shield was used to force Duncan (the inmate) into the back corner of the cell. It was hopeless for him, I knew—like going into battle with a rhino. Three minutes and many thuds later, the team emerged with the inmate in handcuffs and leg restraints.[31]

The news of such actions spread quickly in the prisons. If viewed as "unfair" or "excessive" by the prisoners, these actions will serve to further widen the gap of hostility, hate, and violence between guards and prisoners.

THE MODERN BUREAUCRATIC PRISON

The trends noted here have forced states to move from what James Jacobs calls a "patriarchal organization, based on traditional authority, to a rational-legal bureaucracy."[32] This new management style requires a more centralized approach for managing prisons that takes authority and discretion away from the wardens and individual prisons. Directors of corrections now oversee a vast, corporate-like conglomerate of prisons, work release centers, and parole units supported by increasingly sophisticated accounting and computerized information systems. Many of the senior staff who work in the corporate headquarters have no experience in running prisons, but have expertise in budgeting, report writing, public relations, information systems, and planning. It is not uncommon to have a director of corrections who has no experience in the field but has served in other areas of state government. The primary mission of the new corrections agency is not to question the status quo but to manage these huge agencies with minimal negative press that could embarrass the current governor.

In order for the agency to function effectively, the lines of authority, as well as the procedures, prescriptions, or guidelines for all practices, are formalized in detailed written rules and regulations appearing in elaborate manuals. An extensive and professionalized training program is needed to keep staff abreast of the most recent changes in an increasingly complex array of administrative regulations and procedures imposed by the central office. Routine audits are conducted by central office staff to ensure compliance. In effect, wardens and other key figures in the prison—unlike the formerly powerful captain—no longer have the autonomy and wide discretion they once possessed. They must now answer to the central command and do things according to the book.

As the workforce has become increasingly professionalized with staff who profess to possess special expertise in the area of "corrections," salaries and status have increased correspondingly. According to the Bureau of Labor Statistics, in 2009 there were an estimated 450,000 people employed as correctional officers. Their average salary is $42,600, but ranges from $26,000 to $65,000. Southern states have the lowest salaries with California having the highest average salary of nearly $67,000.[33] In addition to the basic salary, many guards earn overtime, which can total tens of thousands of dollars more each year. Their retirement coverage entitles correctional officers to retire at age 50, after twenty years of service, or, at any age with twenty-five years of service and generous medical care benefits, both while employed and after retirement. However, large numbers of guards are poorly educated and poorly paid. This is especially true in jurisdictions where unions are less intrusive and a large number of unemployed people reside. Few of these guards have gone beyond a high school education, and about 15 percent of the workforce resigns or retires each year.[34] But despite the lack of formal education and training and by virtue of their work experience alone, the guards claim a specialized discipline of prison operations and have built a protective wall of esoteric knowledge to justify their actions.[35]

Prior to the 1980s, wardens and line staff relied mostly on informal and "subjective" systems of control to manage their prisoner populations. In most states, prisoner leaders were given power through various informal arrangements, and these inmates maintained order in the prison. In many states, these prisoners were "right guys" or "politicians" who were given special privileges in return for keeping other prisoners in line. In some Southern states, such as Texas and Arkansas, convict "barn bosses" were given the right to control prisoners through intimidation and violence, including homicide. The informal prison social system effectively controlled by "right guys" and "politicians," who were almost always White, disappeared when prisoner populations became increasingly Black, Hispanic, and militant. By 1980, most states were required, by court intervention, to eliminate these convict boss systems.[36]

Replacing the informal inmate system has resulted in the development of more modern and formal decision-making procedures that are designed to reduce the discretion of wardens and their security staff. Bureaucratic professional administrations now attempt to control prisoners through increasingly formal and rational systems. These central office prison officials have promulgated more extensive and restrictive formal procedures and rules governing prisoner behavior and have made greater use of prison classification and new formal incentives, such as time off for participation in work programs and compliance with prison regulations.

These new techniques are based on ostensibly valid scientific methods and knowledge. For example, "classification" of prisoners for the purpose of assignment to particular prisons, to the custody levels they are to be held in, and to "programs," such as educational or vocational training programs, now involves much less discretion and individual judgment than was previously exercised by captains, lieutenants, and guards. Prior to 1980, newly admitted prisoners went through a diagnostic process at the state's reception center. Based on an interview with a classification officer or staff person, the newly admitted prisoner was transferred to a prison based on geography (where the inmate was from), gender, and age (younger inmates were grouped together to "protect" them from older and more sophisticated inmates). For example, in Illinois, younger inmates from Chicago were housed at Pontiac prison, while older prisoners from Chicago were assigned to Joliet and Stateville prisons. If you were an older prisoner from St. Louis, you would be assigned to the state's southern prison (Menard).

Although the policy formation and decision-making procedures are now more centralized, they are also much more subject to outside influences. The intervention of the courts, as described earlier, has meant that many procedures are either court-mandated or developed within court-mandated guidelines. In many states, for example, the courts have ordered that minimal due process procedures be followed in all disciplinary actions and that objective classification systems be implemented. All states must conform to statutes or case law that guarantee certain prisoner rights.

Today, most prison systems use objective scoring systems to assign prisoners to prisons that match their custody levels (minimum, medium, close, and maximum custody). Reviews of their designated custody levels are monitored and adjusted based on the inmate's conduct and time remaining to serve. Modern information systems are designed to keep better track of prisoners and ensure that inappropriate mixing of certain inmates does not occur. All of this work is organized at the central office level to enhance efficiencies and to reduce the often subjective influence of wardens at the local prison level.

Administrators use three forms of classification—external, internal and high security classification systems. The external classification is used to assign prisoners to a custody level (usually minimum, medium or maximum custody that in turn is used to assign them to either a minimum, medium, or maximum security prison. In many states, the committee or classification unit relies heavily on a quantified, "objective," scoring system based on a prisoner's past criminal record, current conviction and sentence length, escape history, and social factors, such as age, marital status, and employment history. After the inmate has been in custody for a certain period of time, he or she is reclassified on a different instrument that places greater emphasis on the inmate's record of institutional misconduct.

One of the positive results of using these new objective classification systems is learning that a large percentage of prisoners are minimum custody. Minimum custody generally means that the inmates have no history of violence, have no prior or very few prior convictions, are not management problems, and pose little risk to public safety. According to the National Institute of Corrections, approximately 35 percent of the state prison population is in minimum or lower custody.[37]

Once the inmate arrives at a facility, a second classification system (internal), often less objective and structured, determines which programs the inmate can participate in and assigns the inmate to a housing unit. Typically, the new bureaucratized prisons have several different sections, such as protective custody and honor cell blocks, to which a prisoner may be assigned. A prisoner's custody level also determines what range of jobs is available to him or her. For example, minimum-custody prisoners, even at a maximum-security prison, are usually allowed to leave the walled or fenced prison compound to attend to various work assignments including: landscaping, working in staff houses on the prison grounds, assisting at the front gate, and the like.

The third classification system is applied to prisoners who are seen as a threat to the prison's social order. These prisoners are assigned, through another classification process, to highly secure units where—except for two or three two-hour exercise periods a week, restricted visits, and occasional official business (for example, talking to their lawyers)—they remain locked in their cells, twenty-four hours a day. In most states, assignment to the "administrative segregation," "super-max," or "lockup" units (the common general names for these units), includes some limited due process, mandated by state or federal courts. The next chapter discusses in greater detail these high-security units.

THE PRISONER EXPERIENCE

What is it like to do time in today's massive prison system? There is one thing that is clear—there exists a wide variety of prison facilities and prison populations, both among states and within a specific state. In the smaller populated states, like Vermont, North Dakota, and Maine, the entire prison system consists of only a handful of facilities, with a single and often aging main prison where most of the inmates are incarcerated. It is common in these states for the warden and his senior staff to know most of the inmates by name, the circumstances surrounding their crime, and family background, especially those who are serving longer sentences. The staff are also "long-termers" who will serve 25 to 40 years as an employee. It is common for many of the same family to be employed at the prison either as a guard or in some support service function.

On the other extreme are large prison systems like California, Texas, Florida, and the Federal Bureau of Prisons (BOP), where each system operates fifty or more facilities, some of which house over 10,000 inmates. Here the relationship between staff and inmates is virtually nonexistent as the constant flow of inmates and staff make it impossible to forge any kind of personal experience. These mega prison systems operate like large cities with vast acreage, prison complexes, transportation systems, and large warehouses to store food, equipment, and supplies.

Inmates in state and federal prisons must presently cope with an extremely aggravating and threatening set of conditions, brought on by crowding, racial conflict, new practices stemming from the punitive penological philosophy, and bureaucratic policies. The worst of these features is the potential for prisoner-to-prisoner violence. The other key dimension is idleness and boredom that dominants much of the prison experience today.

Idleness and Boredom

Perhaps the overriding attribute of doing time is the lack of any structured or meaningful activity. Table 4-2 shows the typical weekday schedule for most inmates in the general population. For most prisoners, the typical day consists of being fed early in the morning followed by being out of the cell for either a work assignment or, if they are lucky, having a paid job in the prison industries. Some are able to attend some educational program, but the largest segment of the prison population has no meaningful work or program assignment. They may remain in their cells or dorms all day with the exception of going to the yard for an hour or two for unstructured recreational activity. Typically, this just consists of walking the yard with what few friends the prisoner might have. Lunch and dinner are served early (11 A.M. and 4 P.M.) to accommodate the work shift for the staff. In most prisons, inmates are placed back in their housing units for the evening count and will remain there for the rest of the night.

Inmate counts are made repeatedly by security at the beginning of each eight-hour shift, which further interrupts the opportunity to run training programs in a meaningful manner. Weekends are even worse as there are no structured programs or work assignments, as the staff levels are reduced. This same routine is repeated over and over again until one's sentence is served.

As shown in Table 4-3, large proportions of the state prisoner population spend their time doing basically nothing but watching television, reading newspapers, magazines, and being fed three meals a day. Visits are infrequent. The primary means for communicating with family and friends is via collect phone calls, which are the most expensive type of call for the prisoner's family.

Violence

As prison populations have become much more racially heterogeneous and divided, the old prison leaders have lost their control over prisoners. Racial hatred often leads to violence. Prison gangs attempt to control prison rackets, protect their members, pursue vendettas against their enemies, and earn prestige

Table 4-2 Typical Daily Schedule for General Population Prisoner

Time	Activity
5:00–6:00 A.M.	Wake up and personal hygiene
6:00–7:00 A.M.	Breakfast—dining hall, cell, or housing unit
7:00–8:00 A.M.	Back to housing unit for count
8:00–11:00 A.M.	Work assignment, attend program, or outside cell recreation
11:00–12:00 P.M.	Lunch—dining hall, cell, or housing unit
12:00–3:00 P.M.	Work assignment, program, or outside cell recreation
3:00–4:00 P.M.	Back to housing unit for count
4:00–5:30 P.M.	Dinner
5:30–10:00 P.M.	Housing unit downtime—television, cards, phone calls
10:00 P.M.	Lights out and repeated counts

Table 4-3 Self-Reported Prisoner Responses to National Survey Questions on Inmate Activity

Prisoner Activity	Response
Exercised Past 24 hours?	55%
Hours Exercised?	1 to 2 hours
Watched TV?	65%
Read Newspapers, Magazines, Books?	74%
Attended Religious Activity?	57%
Received Phone Call Past Week?	55%
Visit Past Month?	30%
No Work Assignment?	40%
Not Being Paid for Work?	63%

SOURCE: Survey Of Inmates in State Correctional Facilities, 2004.
U.S. Department of Justice, Bureau of Justice Statistics.

as "tough" convicts by menacing all other prisoners. Although most prisoners are not involved in these criminal activities while incarcerated, there is a constant threat that violence may erupt over the most trivial episode or event.

In general, most prisons and prisoners are not exposed to violence, as most inmates are assigned to minimum and medium custody. In 2007, there were 3,388 prisoners who died in custody. Of this number, about 3,000 were illness related and 57 were homicides. Based on what is reported on a national level, that translates into a homicide rate of about 4 per 100,000 inmates. This rate is about the same as the nation's homicide rate. Given that prison populations consist of a primarily young male population, with a disproportionate number of known offenders, the overall rate is quite low. However, in the high-security units, where most of this violence occurs, violent acts occur on a regular basis.

In the 1970s and 1980s, assaults and homicides in most high-security prisons became so common that the possibility of being attacked or killed has loomed as the major concern of offenders incarcerated in these prisons or those anticipating going to one. Looking at California, where the new prison violence started, prisoner homicides increased dramatically after 1970 and ranged from 10 to 36 per year.[38] Figure 4–1 shows that major incidents, which includes inmate-on-staff and staff-on-staff assaults, stayed high until the late 1980s and then dropped, although there has been a recent upturn in the number of homicides and assaults.

> I've been on the yard watching people get shot, watching people die. You know how hard it is coming out with tears in your eyes knowing that you're going to get hit, knowing that someone is going to physically hurt you, or try to kill you.... Eighty-two, 83, 84, people were dropping like flies, people getting stuck. After two or three years of that, it's hard. People on the outside say, ah, that doesn't happen. You weren't there, man.[39]

Since prisoners must constantly prepare themselves to cope with this possibility, what they actually do will be discussed later.

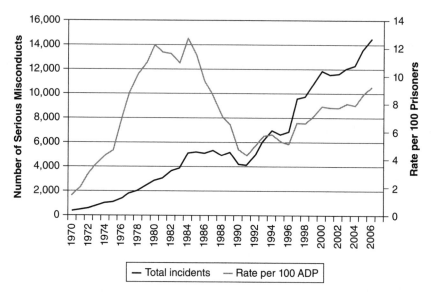

FIGURE 4-1 Number and Rate Per 100 Inmate Population Serious Incidents in California prisons 1970–2006

SOURCE: California Department of Corrections, Annual Reports 1970–2006.

Prison Rape

Much has been made in the media and in prison folklore on the extent of prison rape. Some studies have estimated that as many as 20 percent of the prisoner population is raped or sexually assaulted each year. To address this issue, the U.S. Congress established the Prison Rape Elimination Act in 2003. Part of the legislation required the U.S. Department of Justice to determine the extent of rape and other forms of sexual assault that were occurring in the prisons, jails, and juvenile facilities. To address that issue, a sophisticated survey was administered to samples of the incarcerated populations asking them if they had been raped or sexually assaulted in the past twelve months or since being admitted to prison. The results showed that 4 percent of the prisoners had been raped as compared to 3 percent of the jail inmates. Nationwide, these percentages suggest that approximately 88,500 adults held in prisons and jails at the time of the survey had been sexually assaulted.[40]

An earlier study of official reports of sexual assault in the Texas prison system found that each year 500 to 600 prisoner-on-prisoner sexual assaults were reported by prisoners and staff in Texas. This number of incidents produced a 3.95 rate per 1,000 prisoner population per year. This is almost four times the national average for the states of 1.05. Texas also had one of the lowest substantiation of claims of being raped (less than 3%). Like other systems, these incidents tend to occur in facilities that use cell blocks rather than dormitories where predatory prisoners can shield the rapes from staff. While not a common experience of most prisoners, it occurs with sufficient frequency to be a disturbing aspect of doing time, especially if staff are not concerned about it.[41]

Restricted Freedom

Because of prisoner rights' statutes and court rulings over the last twenty years, inmates may now receive any publication that may be legally sent through the mail (except those likely to incite violence); correspond and receive visits from many more persons than in earlier eras; enter into contracts, including marriage; receive conjugal visits (when eligible); have a partial due process hearing when they receive punishment within the prison; and are protected from systematic physical brutality delivered by the administration (or their agents, such as the convict bosses). However, only the last of these has substantially improved the prisoner's situation.

Much more important to prisoners is that they have lost much of their physical mobility and access to prison facilities and resources. In earlier years, when prisoners were not working, they were usually allowed to wander relatively freely around the prison facilities: in and out of their cell block to the yard, gym, library, canteen, and other sections of the prison, such as the school facilities. Now, most maximum- and medium-security prisoners may only make use of these areas and facilities during short designated periods. Most of the time during the day and night, prisoners are either at their work or school assignments or are restricted to their cell blocks or cells.

Reduced Resources and Contacts

As a consequence of the redefinition of prisons as locations for punishment (instead of rehabilitation), crowding and the new quickly constructed remote prisons, the resources prisoners may use to accomplish a variety of goals—education, vocational training, and recreation—has dramatically decreased. The states that have expanded their prison populations are driven by punitive sentiments and are usually fiscally conservative. Consequently, the proportion of money for programs and features, other than those promoting security, has been reduced. Moreover, the remote location of the new prisons has meant that most of the services and support, voluntarily offered to prisoners from churches, prisoner support organizations, family, and other individuals, have diminished greatly.

In preceding decades, particularly during the rehabilitative era (1950 to 1965), prison administrators greatly encouraged betterment activities, and they supplied the resources and programs for accomplishing this. Educational opportunities, for example, expanded during this period. By the early 1970s, prisoners could receive a high school education in most prisons and some college credit in many. In addition, most prisons offered a wide variety of vocational training programs. Many forms of counseling were also available.

That is not the case today. Table 4-3 indicates that only a small percentage of the inmate population is involved in meaningful prison activities. About one-fourth of them are idle. Those few who have prison work jobs often do low-skill maintenance jobs requiring them to only push a broom occasionally or pick up trash. Very few are in low-paying prison industry programs, vocational training, or education programs. What emerges is a picture of prison life that has minimal program opportunities and considerable idleness.

Lack of Education and Vocational Training

One of the major problems facing inmates is the lack of access to educational services. Even though most inmates do not have a high school diploma or basic literacy skills, only 30 percent of the current prisoner population has received any form of formal educational services. The dominant form of educational services that is provided is for high school or GED preparation courses with about 20 percent of inmates receiving such services. According to the U.S. Department of Justice, only 7 percent of all inmates report having attended some form of college while incarcerated. In general, the vast majority of prisoners receive no formal educational services.[42] In California, the nation's largest and most expensive prison system, about 18 percent of released inmates had received some form of educational services.[43]

New York provides an example of the limited amount of educational services available to inmates. New York's prison system is one of the nation's largest systems with an inmate population of about 58,000 people in 2011. With respect to academic opportunities, the state standards proclaim:

> [The] objective of correctional education in its broadest sense should be the socialization of the inmates.... The objective of this program shall be the return of these inmates to society with a more wholesome attitude toward living, with a desire to conduct themselves as good citizens and with the skills and knowledge which will give them a reasonable chance to maintain themselves and their dependents through honest labor. (New York Corrections Law, Section 136)

To meet that standard, the department has concentrated its academic resources on assisting inmates who have limited basic education skills. According to the department, most of the inmates are functioning below the eighth-grade level. Consequently, most of the department's educational services are limited to Adult Basic Education (ABE), pre-GED, and GED curricula. At one time California had a robust college program with over 1,000 inmates receiving college-level degrees and certificates. Today that number has been reduced by 50 percent. The decline in college education within the department of corrections is directly due to funding cutbacks at both the federal and state levels. Presently, there is virtually no opportunity for inmates to participate in college-level coursework while incarcerated. This is especially troubling given the recent passage of numerous sentencing laws that have greatly extended the length of incarceration for many inmates who could benefit from an advanced curriculum.

Arbitrary Disciplinary Punishment

As mentioned, prison staff must follow a partial due process system in disciplining prisoners. However, prisoners view the due process disciplinary procedure as a sham and much more arbitrary than it was in preceding decades. The "judge" or "judges" at these hearings are prison officials who are far from impartial. In fact, they are often close associates of the people who bring the charges against the prisoner. Moreover, their primary goal is maintaining order in the prison, not delivering fair, legal, and impartial decisions. In addition, much of the evidence used against the prisoner is hearsay and anonymous, often a "note dropped"—that is, an anonymous letter from a prisoner, sent to the administration through special mechanisms for this purpose. For example, a prisoner at San Quentin was placed in the "hole" (solitary confinement) for participating in a cell burning:

> When I was in the honor block, someone "dropped a note" on me and accused me of being the "point" for a cell burning. I had nothing to do with it, but I couldn't convince 'em in the hearing. I offered to take a lie detector test. They put me in Max B, and I wrote an appeal. After a few weeks, a guy came from Sacramento. Eventually, he arranged for a lie detector test and I passed it. They still left me in the hole for the rest of my sentence.[44]

"Chickenshit Rules"

In earlier eras, prisoners enjoyed considerable freedom to embellish their drab and monotonous prison life. For example, they decorated the walls of their cells, altered their prison clothing, acquired various pieces of furniture—such as rugs, chairs, and bookshelves—and kept birds and other small pets in their cells. These special touches enriched their lives with considerable comfort and individuality, which is very important in a world so marked by monotony.

The centralization of authority and the formulation of rules and regulations have resulted in a much more stringent and uniform prison routine that has mostly eliminated these special features and privileges. Dannie Martin, an ex-prisoner at Lompoc, a federal maximum-security prison, writes about the "gulag mentality" of the BOP's Lompoc prison:

> As the saying goes, it's the little things that make a house a home. To those of us who face the mind-killing boredom of long prison sentences, small changes take on large significance in this our home-away-from-home. Among the small things that matter most to us here are our routines and perks and possessions. They help to personalize this cold world.
>
> A few years ago—in what convicts now call the good old days—there were said to be two kinds of wardens: those who lean toward punishment and those who believe in rehabilitation. These days, it seems there is only one kind. But the different ways they choose to do their punishing make a great difference to us, the punished.
>
> The warden here at Lompoc from 1982 until 1987 was Robert Christiansen. We who lived here during his tenure called him "Defoliating Bob." He earned that nickname upon his arrival by chainsawing a row of stately and beautiful old eucalyptus trees in our "backyard," trees that for fifty years or more had served as a windbreak about 150 yards from the prison perimeter. Our cell-block view apartments had lost another amenity.

Not long after cutting down the trees, the warden poisoned all the squirrels that convicts enjoyed feeding near the prison fences, then mounted a genocidal war against the cats and raccoons that roamed the prison grounds. He also managed to curtail most of the small liberties enjoyed by the convict population. Before his arrival, we had been permitted to wear our own clothes. Now we were to wear strictly tucked-in and buttoned-up government issue. And our recreational opportunities and food went from bad to worse.

He did away with little niceties like Christmas packages from home and unrestricted telephone access. As he made these changes, he was busy installing electronic grill gates in the hallway so that the prison could be sectioned off in case of emergency. Sheet-metal plates went up over windows with an outside view.

Defoliating Bob retired last year. One of the first official acts of our new warden, R. H. Rison, was to close down our recreation yard until noon every weekday. Those of us who work on night jobs and ran and exercised in the mornings now sit in gloomy cell blocks watching the sun shine through the window bars.

No sooner did the warden close the yard than we lost our chairs, and that hurt. For as long as most of us can remember, we've had our own chairs in the TV rooms as well as in our cells. There's little enough in here for man to call his own, and over the years these chairs have been modified and customized to an amazing degree—legs bent to suit the occupant, armrests glued on, pads knitted for comfort. And the final personal touch is always the printing of a name on the back.

A couple months ago, the guards came one day with no warning and confiscated all our chairs. Each of us was issued a gray-metal folding chair, along with a memorandum from the new warden stating that anyone writing on or otherwise defacing these chairs would be subject to disciplinary action.[45]

More recent studies affirm this phenomenon. In a 2011 study of the Illinois prison system, it was found that approximately 11,000 official rule violations were recorded each year. The vast majority (80%) of those violations were for "insolence," "failure to obey a direct order," "unauthorized movement," and "violation of general rules" like failure to maintain a clean cell. These violations often result in being placed in disciplinary segregation for many weeks.

In Georgia, similar findings were noted in a 2010 study (see Table 4-4). In that state, there are over 50,000 tickets written on inmates each year. By far the most frequent offense is failure to follow instructions—another version of failure to obey a direct order.

COPING WITH VIOLENCE

Because racial and gang violence has become increasingly prevalent in some prisons, prisoners in such situations must follow a strategy of doing time that reduces the stress of being robbed, raped, assaulted, or killed by other prisoners.

Table 4-4 Most Frequent Disciplinary Tickets Written in 2010 Georgia Department of Corrections

Primary Charge	Number	Percent
Failure To Follow Instructions	20,026	35%
Insubordination	5,568	10%
Unauthorized Absence	3,682	6%
Exposure/Exhibition	3,359	6%
Possession Of Contraband	2,866	5%
Smoking In Restricted Area	2,383	4%
Under Influence Of Drugs	2,011	4%
Unauthorized Presence	1,978	4%
Possession Of Cell Phone	1,493	3%
Injury To Inmate/Oneself	1,422	3%
Verbal/Gesture Threatening	1,120	2%
Total	57,015	100%

SOURCE: Georgia Department of Corrections, 2010.

Gang Banging

Since the 1970s, many prisoners, if they are eligible, affiliate with a gang or clique for protection. Younger prisoners, who were members of gangs on the outside or who graduated from youth prisons where they were members of gangs, are automatically eligible. Other potential recruits have to prove themselves.[46] Gang affiliates are either core members or associates. The core members hang around fellow gang members and are very active in the gang's pursuits: robbing other prisoners, dealing drugs, controlling some of the prison homosexuals, and carrying on murderous feuds with other gangs, particularly those of other races. The potential recruits, though they do not participate in the day-to-day activities, remain ready to be called on when some large display of force or some other form of assistance, such as smuggling drugs from one location to another or hiding weapons, is needed. In return, they have the gang's protection and may circulate much more freely in the prison public places and enjoy some of the fruits of the gang's illegal economic activities.

Prison administrators have responded to the gangs by attempting to identify the leaders and core members and place them in the administrative segregation or "super-max" units. In many prisons, those suspected gang members remain in lockup units for many years. For example, the official policy for inmates identified as being active gang members in Texas is to place them in the administrative segregation unit until they complete their sentences. This strategy, however, has not completely stopped gang activities, and assaults and murders of other prisoners and guards continue to occur in the special segregation units.[47] Moreover, unidentified and new gang members carry on the activities in the "mainline" (the general prison population). In addition, new prisoners from the same neighborhoods or towns, perhaps members of outside gangs, establish new prison gangs or cliques and continue to racketeer and do violence in the mainline.

Locking Up

Those who are being pressured to join a gang for protection but who want no part of it often have only one remaining option—requesting to be locked up in protective custody (PC). As noted earlier, about 2 to 3 percent of the prison population is classified as in PC. These inmates are physically separated from the mainline population and are viewed as weak or "punks" because they cannot "make it." Often, inmates who are overtly homosexual, convicted of child molestation, or are snitches, find their way to PC. There are also inmates who just want to do their time, but the gangs, who are in control, will not allow it to happen.

Such was the case in the Pontiac Correctional Center in Illinois a few years ago. The major gangs had gained control of the housing units by not allowing inmates of different gangs to be housed in certain cells. Since work and program assignments were associated with housing units, the gangs had gained control of them as well. Only after a lawsuit was filed did the department agree to take certain corrective actions to reassert its authority in determining where inmates were housed and which programs they would participate in. As these reforms occurred, the number of inmates in PC declined.[48]

Retired Convicts

A few older prisoners who have spent many years in prisons and have earned good reputations as being tough—usually through their affiliation with one of the gangs—can retire from gangbanging and circulate freely in the prison with immunity from gang attack. Edward Bunker, in his novel about San Quentin in the 1970s, has accurately depicted this prison pattern:

> So, although Earl was at home, it was in the way that the jungle animal is at home—cautiously. He had no enemies here who posed a threat, at least none that he knew, though some might have been threats if he didn't have the affection of the most influential members of the most powerful white gang and friendship with the leaders of the most powerful Chicano gang.[49]

Withdrawal

The vast majority, particularly prisoners who are serving their first prison sentences and have not been involved in gangs on the outside, shy away from most prisoners and settings where masses of prisoners congregate and withdraw into small orbits or virtual isolation. Although they need not go to PC and they may occasionally buy from the racketeers, place bets, or trade commodities on a small scale with other unaffiliated prisoners, they stay out of the large-scale economic activities and dissociate themselves from the violent cliques and gangs. They stick to a few friends who they have met in the cell blocks, at work, on the outside (homeboys), in other prisons, or through shared interests. Either alone or with their few trusted friends, they go to work and/or attend school or meetings of various clubs and formal organizations that the prison administration allows to exist in the prison. Otherwise, they stay in their cells.[50]

CRIPPLED

The fragmenting of prisoner society, the general physical and social isolation of prisoners, the increased use of segregation, and the elevated level of deprivation, fear, and distress, act as socially and psychologically impairing forces on most prisoners.[51] For decades, students of the prison have recognized that the combined factors of being isolated from outside society, subjected to a reduced and deprived routine, and acculturated into a unique "convict" belief and value system that works to "prisonize" men and women—that is, convert them into persons equipped to live in prison and ill-equipped to live outside.[52] It was this insidious process of prisonization that innovative penologists tried to avoid when they planned the "community corrections" approach in the late 1960s.[53]

Prisoner administrators and other policy makers have now completely abandoned the goal of reducing prisoners' isolation from outside society. They build prisons in the remotest regions of the state with only security in mind and further reduce contacts with outside organizations and individuals through their custody-oriented policies. These practices, along with greatly diminished rehabilitative resources, are producing prisoners who have deteriorated in prison, and when they return to the outside, they are much less well-equipped to live a conventional life than they were when they entered prison.

Inmates enter prison poorly educated, vocationally unskilled, and often suffering from serious physical and psychological problems. Most, particularly at the beginning of their sentences, want to better themselves while in prison and improve their chances of living some form of rewarding, viable, conventional life when they are released:

> I want to go to school and get a trade. Then when I get out I want to have my kids with me, have a good job so I can support them. I want to get the drugs out of my life. [Black drug addict, 28, convicted of armed robbery and episodically involved in crime]

> I think I will pass up getting involved in the gangs in prison. I'm going to go to school and get me a trade. I want a nice job, paying pretty good, something to keep me busy instead of running the streets. [Black ex-gang banger, 29, episodically involved in crime and convicted of armed robbery]

> I'm going to go to school and get a job. I'm going to try to get into electronics. I want a job I won't get laid off on. As long as I have a job, I don't

get into trouble. When I get laid off, I get into trouble. [18-year-old corner boy who was "around crime" and convicted of possession of cocaine with the intent to deliver]

When I get out I'm going to try to find a job. If I can't find a job, I'll do what I have to do to survive. But I won't do anything violent. I might get a license to sell something. That way you keep some change in your pocket. [Black petty drug dealer, 26, who was "into crime" and convicted of possession of cocaine]

As these statements indicate, many prisoners intended to take care of serious health problems, participate in drug or alcohol programs to deal with their addictions, and, in general, take advantage of whatever resources exist to better themselves. But as indicated earlier, these resources for change are less available in today's prisons.

ALIENATED

The general society has always held convicts in some contempt, but in earlier decades there was a greater willingness to forget their past and, once they had served their time, "give them another chance." In the 1960s, a large outpouring of sympathy was expressed for convicts, and substantial progress was made in reducing the barriers blocking ex-convicts' reemergence into conventional society.[54] For a short period, ex-prisoners were folk heroes; many strutted around, loudly proclaiming and capitalizing on their ex-convict status. This period ended by the late 1970s, and once again, the convict and ex-convict became a widely hated and feared pariah. In recent years, whenever an ex-convict is in the news, the media usually focuses negatively on that status. Politicians harp on criminal acts committed by released prisoners. Legislators and policy makers, usually with dramatic public display, have passed laws or established policies against hiring ex-convicts for a growing number of jobs. Consequently, most prisoners are acutely aware that they are among society's leading pariahs, and this awareness has greatly increased their alienation from conventional society.

Finally, in earlier decades most prisoners were somewhat psychologically buttressed by the convict identity. The prisoner society, with its solidarity underpinned by a special worldview and code of ethics, not only promoted peace, but also greatly bolstered prisoners' self-esteem. Though they were society's outcasts and "losers," they took pride in being "right guys," "regulars," or "real convicts." They endured the deprivation of imprisonment, itself a matter for pride, and responded to their degradation by turning the conventional status system upside down. They viewed average citizens as "squares" whose behavior was petty, corrupt, weak, and hypocritical; they felt particular contempt for society's representatives to whom they were closest—the guards and prison administrators. Most convicts sincerely believed that they were more honorable than squares.

Some prisoners also feel contempt for their counterparts as well. A former politically active prisoner, about to be released after serving twenty years, addressed a prerelease class: "If I catch any convict coming around my neighborhood after I'm released, I'm calling the cops, because I know he is up to no good."

Partly as a reaction to their negative image, some prisoners become outlaws: "These are mainly persons who present themselves as 'convicts' in the prison and participate in the rapacious, violent activities of gangs. The outlaw scorns the disapproval of society, reveals no mercy or compassion for others, and remains ready to use violence to protect himself or achieve his ends." An archetypical outlaw, Jack Abbott, describes the type:

> The model we emulate is a fanatically defiant and alienated individual who cannot imagine what forgiveness is, or mercy or tolerance, because he has no *experience* of such values. His emotions do not know what such values are, but *imagines* them as so many "weaknesses" precisely because the unprincipled offender appears to escape punishment through such "weaknesses" on the part of society.[55]

Most prisoners, however, just as they have withdrawn from most prison activities, attempt to disassociate themselves from the convict identity. But their experience of being held in contempt and having no supporting counter values is profoundly detrimental. Mainly, it completes their full alienation. This social malady has several separate components: a sense of powerlessness, the expectation that one's behavior will not succeed in bringing about the outcomes one seeks; meaninglessness, the lack of a sense of what one ought to believe; normalessness, the expectation that socially unapproved behaviors are required to achieve given goals; detachment, the disassociation from the central beliefs and values of the society; and self-estrangement, the experience of oneself as alien and unworthy.[56] All of these aspects of alienation are cultivated in the contemporary prison milieu, making fully alienated convicts incapable of normal participation in conventional activities. They skulk in and around the edges and crannies of society (like the homeless), unexpectedly lash out at others, escape into drug addiction, or succumb to psychosis or suicide.

The disturbing truth is that growing numbers of prisoners are leaving our prisons socially crippled and profoundly alienated. Moreover, they understand that they will be returning to a society that views them as despicable pariahs. They are also aware that they will have more difficulty finding employment than formerly, and consequently, their expectations are understandably low.

NOTES

1. Local jails are even less equipped to provide services to prisoners. Whereas the state and federal prisons may be incarcerated months and years, most of the nearly 13 million people who are admitted and released from local jails

spend either a few hours or days in jail before being released on bail or their own recognizance.

2. Starting with Donald Clemmer's *The Prison Community* (New York: Holt, Rinehart, 1958), social scientists produced an extensive literature on prisoner society as it existed from the 1930s through the 1960s. A few of the studies are Graham Sykes, *The Society of Captives* (Princeton, NJ: Princeton University Press, 1958); Rose Giallombardo, *The Society of Women* (New York: Wiley, 1966); David Ward and Gene Kassebaum, *Women's Prison* (Chicago: Aldine, 1965); John Irwin, *The Felon* (Upper Saddle River, NJ: Prentice-Hall, 1970); and James Jacobs, *Stateville* (Chicago: University of Chicago Press, 1977).

3. The increase of staff supervision is evidenced by the inmate-to-staff ratios, which ranged from one officer per nine inmates to eleven inmates from 1926 through 1940. After 1945, however, the ratio continued to shrink until it reached its lowest level of 2.92 inmates per staff by 1979. See Margaret Werner Cahalan, *Historical Corrections Statistics in the United States, 1850–1984* (Washington, DC: Bureau of Justice Statistics, 1986). Today the inmate-to-staff ratio is 3.3. See Census of State and Federal Correctional Facilities, 2005. (October 2008). Washington, DC: Bureau of Justice Statistics, Table 5.

4. See Daniel Glaser, *The Effectiveness of a Prison and Parole System* (Indianapolis, IN: Bobbs-Merrill, 1964), Chapter 1, for a summary of failure rates of released prisoners. The author estimates that in the 1950s and earlier, the rate was about 40 percent. Ironically, the 40 percent return-to-prison rate has remained much the same since then. The most recent national recidivism rate published by the Bureau of Justice lists the three-year return-to-prison rate at 40 percent (see Recidivism of Prisoners released in 1994. (July 2002). Washington, DC: Bureau of Justice Statistics, U.S. Department of Justice.

5. See John Irwin, *Prisons in Turmoil* (Boston: Little, Brown, 1980), for a more complete analysis of this shift.

6. The recognition of potential and actual abuses under the rehabilitative ideal began with Francis Allen's *The Borderland of Criminal Justice: Essays in Law and Criminology* (Chicago: University of Chicago Press, 1964). The criticism of rehabilitative routines culminated in *The Struggle for Justice,* written by a "working party" for the American Friends Service Committee, 1971. This book was followed by a series of works in which the "justice model" was offered as an alternative to the rehabilitative judicial and penological systems. See Norval Morris, *The Future of Imprisonment* (Chicago: University of Chicago Press, 1974); Andrew von Hirsch, *Doing Justice: The Choice of Punishments* (New York: Hill & Wang, 1976); and David Fogel, *We Are the Living Proof: The Justice Model for Corrections* (Cincinnati, OH: Anderson, 1975).

7. As mentioned earlier, a consensus that rehabilitation did not work was reached in the early 1970s. Since then, many people have reexamined the reports on treatment attempts, particularly those that were planned and implemented after the late 1960s, and have argued that many programs do work. Even Robert Martinson, the author of the article "What Works? Questions and Answers About Prison Reform," *Public Interest* 35 (April 1974): 22–54, and coauthor with Douglas Lipton and Judith Wilks of *The Effectiveness of Correctional Treatment: A Survey of Treatment Evaluation Studies* (New York: Praeger, 1975), the culminating criticisms of treatment effectiveness, retracted his hard position in a later review of the literature: "New Findings, New Views: A Note of Caution Regarding Sentencing Reform," *Hofstra Law Review* 7 (1979): 243–258. See also Francis T. Cullen and Paul Gendreau, "The Effectiveness of Correctional Rehabilitation: Reconsidering the 'Nothing Works' Debate," in Lynn Goodstein and Doris McKenzie (eds.), *The American Prison: Issues in Research and Policy* (New York: Plenum, 1989). In general, what Martinson, Cullen, Gendreau, and others have found in reexamining the treatment literature is that programs that emphasize learning or

"cognitive" rather than medical or emotional disturbance models can reduce recidivism. As noted in Chapter 9, there are a number of criticisms one can make regarding the potential of a treatment approach to reduce crime. First, the vast majority of crimes are not committed by persons released from prison; consequently, the success or lack of success of prison-based treatment programs and/or punishment will have little impact on crime rates in general. Second, most correctional treatment programs are not well administered, target the wrong clientele, and are too small to have any impact on crime rates or public safety. Third, factors that will undoubtedly serve to reduce the likelihood of maintaining a criminal lifestyle are age, absence of a juvenile career, no history of violence, no evidence of drug use or abuse, the ability to secure employment and enter a meaningful relationship or marriage. Treatment and punishment will have only moderate effects on crime rates.

8. For a discussion of this "cooptation," see David Greenberg and Drew Humphries, "The Cooptation of Fixed Sentencing Reform," *Crime and Delinquency* 26 (1980): 206–225.

9. Cited in Ken McGinnis, "Make 'Em Break Rocks," in John P. May and Khalid R. Pitts (eds.), *Building Violence: How America's Rush to Incarcerate Creates More Violence* (Thousand Oaks, CA: Sage Publications, 1999).

10. Ibid.

11. Ibid.

12. See U.S. Department of Justice, Bureau of Justice Statistics, *Prisoners in 1994* (Washington, DC: U.S. Government Printing Office, December 1995).

13. U.S. Department of Justice, Bureau of Justice Statistics, *Prisoners in 2000* (Washington, DC: U.S. Government Printing Office, August 2001); and U.S. Department of Justice, Bureau of Justice Statistics, *Census of State and Federal Correctional Facilities, 1990* (Washington, DC: U.S. Government Printing Office, 1992).

14. U.S. Department of Justice, Bureau of Justice Statistics, *Prisoners in 2009* (Washington, DC: U.S. Government Printing Office, December 2010).

15. Michigan Department of Corrections. *2009 Statistical Report* (Lansing: Michigan Department of Corrections, 2010, p. C–16).

16. http://www.politico.com/news/stories/1210/46743.html.

17. This was the practice from about 1850 to 1950, when prisons were seen as places for banishment. However, during the rehabilitative era, during which more general sympathy existed for prisoners, there was some tendency to build new prisons closer to cities. In the late 1960s, progressive penologists recommended that all prisoners should be held close to urban centers. The idea of "community correctional centers" was advanced, though never actually realized (see Irwin, *Prisons in Turmoil,* Chapter 6).

18. *Prisoners in 2009.*

19. For a number of years, Marc Mauer has been documenting the growing number of incarcerated Blacks and Hispanics. His most recent book, *The Race to Incarcerate* (New York: New Press, 1999), provides comprehensive documentation of this tragic trend. Also see Cahalan, *Historical Corrections Statistics;* and *Prisoners in 2009.*

20. See Leo Carrol, *Hacks, Blacks, and Others* (Lexington, MA: Lexington Books, 1974); Jacobs, *Stateville;* and Irwin, *Prisons in Turmoil,* for discussions of the conflict between racial groups in prison.

21. C. R. Trulson, J. W. Marquart, C. Hemmens, & L. Carroll, "Racial Desegregation in Prisons," *Prison Journal* 88, 2, June 2008: 270–299.

22. See Irwin, *Prisons in Turmoil,* pp. 100–106; Jacobs, *Stateville,* Chapter 5; and Ben Crouch and James Marquart, *An Appeal to Justice* (Austin: University of Texas Press, 1989), see Chapters 1 and 8 for discussions of these changes.

23. Darlene Grant and Steve Martin, *Should Prison Reform Litigation Be Curtailed?* (San Francisco: National Council on Crime and Delinquency, 1996).

24. *Coleman, Plato, et al., vs. Schwarzenegger.* August 4, 2010.

25. See Jacobs, *Stateville,* and Crouch and Marquart, *Appeal to Justice,* for descriptions of the emergence of bureaucratic regimens.

26. *United States v. State of Florida: Florida Department of Corrections,* No. TCA 86-7330, N.D. Fla.; and *United States v. The Parish of Orleans Criminal Sheriff's Office.*

27. *(Hammer v. King County).*

28. Jacobs *(Stateville)* and Crouch and Marquart *(Appeal to Justice)* trace these shifts in their books on Stateville and the Texas prison systems.

29. The study by John DiIulio, *Governing Prisons,* has this confusion as its underlying theme.

30. Reported in Robert Schultz, *"Life in SHU": An Ethnographic Study of Pelican Bay State Prison,* M.A. thesis, Humboldt State University, April 1991, p. 90.

31. T. Conover, *New Jack: Guarding Sing Sing.* (New York: Vintage Books, 2001), p. 133.

32. Jacobs, *Stateville,* p. 73.

33. www.bls.gov/oes/current/oes333012 .htm#nat.

34. Criminal Justice Institute, *The Corrections Yearbook, 2002.*

35. See Jacobs, *Stateville,* and Crouch and Marquart, *Appeal to Justice,* for descriptions of the emergence of bureaucratic regimens.

36. See Crouch and Marquart, *Appeal to Justice,* for a description of the court's elimination of the convict boss system in Texas. Also see Thomas Murton and J. Hyams, *Accomplices to the Crime: The Arkansas Prison System* (New York: Grove, 1969), for a description of Thomas Murton's confrontation with the convict boss system in Arkansas.

37. James, Austin and Patricia Hardyman. (2004) Objective Prison Classification: A Guide for Correctional Agencies. Washington, DC: U.S. Department of Justice, National Institute of Corrections, US DOJ.

38. Data on prisoner fatalities were obtained from Offender Information Services Branch, California Department of Corrections, *Inmate Incidents in Institutions: Calendar Year 1998* (Sacramento, CA: May 1999).

39. Quoted in Schultz, *"Life in SHU,"* p. 95.

40. Allen J. Beck, Ph.D. and Paige M. Harrison, *Sexual Victimization in Prisons and Jails Reported By Inmates, 2008–09,* August 26, 2010. NCJ 231169.

41. J. Austin, T. Fabelo, A. Gunter, and K. McGinnis, *Sexual Violence in the Texas Prison System* (Washington, DC: JFA Institute, April 2006).

42. Survey of inmates in state correctional facilities, 2004.

43. California Department on Corrections and Rehabilitation (2006). *Expert Panel on Adult Offender and Recidivism Reduction Programming: Report to the California State Legislature.* Sacramento, CA: CDCR, 2006), p. 55.

44. Interview, San Francisco, 1981.

45. Dannie Martin, "The Gulag Mentality," *San Francisco Chronicle,* Sunday Punch Section, June 19, 1989, p. 5.

46. To be eligible, prospective gang members must be of the same race and sometimes from the same city, town, or neighborhood. They must also have the respect of the other members. To gain this, they must present the persona of a tough convict who is willing to use violence to protect himself and his associates. The prospective members may already have earned this reputation outside or in other prisons. If not, they must earn respect, perhaps by assaulting someone of another race or gang.

47. www.tdcj.state.tx.us/cid/Pamphlet-Narr%20Form-09-07.pdf.

48. See James Austin and Jim Aiken, "Final Report on Pontiac Classification System," *Inmates A, B, C and D v. Illinois Department of Corrections* Consent Decree, 1996.

49. Edward Bunker, *No Beast So Fierce* (New York: Norton, 1973).

50. In a study of prisons in Ontario, Canada, Edward Zamble and Frank J. Porporino found that more than 40 percent of the prisoners interviewed "stay on their own," and another almost 40 percent confine their socialization to a "few

friends." The percentage who stay on their own increased to more than 50 percent by the time they had served sixteen months. Over the span of this study, the percentage who spent the majority of their optional time in their cell increased from 19.8 to 28.6. We must note that these are Canadian prisons, and the violence and other pressures are probably not as acute as they are in the United States. See *Coping, Behavior, and Adaptation in Prison Inmates* (New York: Springer, 1988), p. 117.

51. In their study of Ontario prisoners, Zamble and Porporino did not find that prisoners reported either increases in depression, anger, anxiety, guilt feelings, boredom, and loneliness or increases in depression or anxiety, as measured by standard tests of these variables. The same absence of increases in psychological "symptoms" or indicators of emotional problems have been found in many other studies (see Zamble and Porporino, *Coping,* for a summary of these findings). However, they were measuring different aspects of the "personality" than those addressed here. We are not suggesting that prisoners are becoming emotionally ill but that they are being converted into a distinct personality type—a prisoner—who may not be anxiety-ridden, depressed, guilt-ridden, or even extremely angry. Rather, the prisoner becomes withdrawn, suspicious, untrusting, and socially unskilled. Zamble and Porporino did find that prisoners withdraw more as they serve their sentence.

52. Donald Clemmer introduced the concept in his seminal study of the prison, *The Prison Community*. Dozens of studies since his have further examined this class of detrimental aspects of imprisonment.

53. See the President's Commission on Law Enforcement and Administration of Justice, Task Force Report: Corrections (Washington, DC: U.S. Government Printing Office, 1967); and Irwin, Prisons in Turmoil, Chapter 6.

54. One of the authors, John Irwin, an ex-convict, took great advantage of these changes, finished college, and became a college professor.

55. Jack Abbott, *In the Belly of the Beast* (New York: Random House, 1981), p. 13.

56. See Melvin Seeman, "On the Meaning of Alienation," *American Journal of Sociology* 24 (1944): 783–891.

5

■

The Correctional Treatment
Industrial Complex

"... if Washington successfully implements a moderately-
to-aggressive portfolio of evidenced based options,
a significant level of future prison construction can be
avoided, tax payers can save about two billion dollars
and crime rates can be reduced."
Aos, et al., *Evidence-Based Public Policy Options to Reduce Future
Prison Construction, Criminal Justice Costs and Crime Rates*. 2008, p. 1.

"Let me be clear: this Administration shares your belief in
the power of evidence-based research to help address
some of our nation's most significant challenges. President
Obama has renewed our nation's commitment to
rely on science in the development of public policy.
He understands, as do I, that sound judgment
derives from solid evidence."

*Attorney General Eric Holder, June 15, 2009, National Institute
of Justice, 2009 Annual Conference*

INTRODUCTION

As suggested above, many people believe that the key to turning around
the imprisonment binge is to reduce recidivism through rehabilitation. In
other words, we must redirect our focus on treating inmates rather than
punishing them. Prisoners are seen as problematic but possibly salvageable if

sufficient levels of treatment services can be delivered to them while they are incarcerated. This perspective has led to a resurgence of the rehabilitative ideal and with it an emerging offender treatment industrial complex.[1]

The rehabilitation movement is being led by drug treatment advocates who see much of the crime problem as linked to drug use. To them the best hope for reducing crime and incarceration is to greatly expand the availability of drug treatment services. This has led to the rapid expansion of such innovative programs as drug courts, boot camps, and residential substance abuse programs. All of these programs were initially funded by the federal government in the 1990s and were promised to reduce recidivism and prison costs. The latter goal is achieved by either diverting prison-bound offenders to alternative programs or reducing the likelihood that inmates will be readmitted to prison as parole violators or with a new sentence. Very few, if any, programs are designed to reduce the inmate's length of stay.

As we now know, this movement has had virtually no impact on the number of people incarcerated. Indeed, the size of the nation's prison and jail populations has continued to rise. This chapter examines why drug (and other treatment) programs have not had an impact on correctional populations. In particular, two widely touted "alternatives to incarceration" (boot camps and prison-based drug treatment) claim to be effective in reducing crime, reducing the use of imprisonment, and reducing costs. But first, we will present an overview of the factors that are known to be associated with criminal behavior. For a treatment program to be effective, it should incorporate factors known to suppress or influence criminal behavior.

In evaluating these two types of programs and any other program or policy, there are two fundamental criteria that such programs must meet. Obviously, there must be a reasonable expectation that the treatment being administered to the inmate will have a significant and long-lasting impact on the inmate. Programs that show short-term and/or minimal impact on the offender should not be viewed as effective. For example, a program that demonstrates an initial 5 to 10 percent reduction in a recidivism rate of 40 percent (as compared to a control population) may be statistically significant (based on the number of cases analyzed) but will have little substantive significance, especially if the differences between the experimental and control populations narrow over time.

Second, there must be evidence that the treatment program can be successfully applied to a large proportion of the inmate population. In other words, what is the potential market share of the prison population for this program? Having a program that works successfully with only 1 percent of the inmate population is simply not impacting a significant share of the inmate population to produce real cost savings. Even a pilot program must hold the promise of being expanded so that a large proportion of the inmate population can be "exposed" to the treatment.

Lack of a significant "market share" can happen for a number of reasons. First, the eligibility criteria may be so restrictive that only a very small segment of the prison population can even be considered eligible for the program.

Second, programs that seek to divert so-called "prison-bound" inmates often end up selecting "probation-bound" inmates, thus widening rather than reducing the net of criminal justice control.[2] Third, programs that have a high dropout or in-program failure rate result in too few inmates successfully completing the program. Although the "successful" graduates often have very low recidivism rates, by not including the program failures, which may be substantial, the impact results are unfairly skewed in favor of the "treatment" group.

Before we look at prison-based programs, we should note that the lack of a significant market share is apparent. As shown in Table 5-1, the number of inmates in educational, vocational training and other programs is relatively small. This is especially significant given the educational, employment, and substance needs of these same prisoners. Most were either drinking or under the influence of illegal drugs at the time of the crime, have a sub-par education, and a high unemployment rate. The fact that most inmates are not participating in these rehabilitative programs is instructive. This finding is consistent with the program participation data presented in Chapter 4 (Doing Time). Programs have been touted as highly successful, reducing recidivism and costs, but actually they have had little impact as so few inmates are part of these programs. Why is this so? We will focus on that question throughout this chapter.

Table 5-1 Numbers of State Prisoners in Vocational, Education and other Programs, 2004

Services	% of Prisoners
Vocational Programs	9%
Basic Education to Ninth Grade	2%
GED/High School Classes	19%
College Classes	7%
Employment Counseling	9%
Parenting/Childrearing Classes	10%
Prerelease Programs	5%
Life Skills/Community Adjustment	24%
Inmate Self-Help Programs	7%
Religious Studies	31%
Drug Treatment Programs	14%
Key Attribute at Time of Crime	
Under Influence of Drugs at Time of Arrest?	32%
Drinking at Time of Offense?	37%
Unemployed at Admission?	32%
Less than High School Education?	80%

SOURCE: Survey of Inmates in State and Federal Correctional Facilities, Prisoners, 2004, ICPSR 4572, U.S. Department of Justice, Bureau of Justice Statistics.

FACTORS RELATED TO CRIMINAL BEHAVIOR

Considerable research has been conducted by criminologists that show that criminal careers for both adults and juveniles do not follow a predictable and stable pattern. For example, most youth (especially males) commit delinquent acts during their adolescent years, but they cease their criminal activities as they pass into adulthood. Similarly, many adult offenders have not had extensive juvenile careers but become involved in serious criminal activity when they reached adulthood. However, they are highly unlikely to continue their criminal behaviors indefinitely. Rather, there are many factors that will collectively impinge upon the individual and will impact the likelihood of the initiation and duration of a criminal career.

Gender and Age

Of all the factors that impact criminal behavior, sex and age are by far the most important and powerful. Young males commit the vast majority of crimes. Based on the Uniform Crime Reports (UCR) data, approximately 60 percent of all arrests are for persons under age 30.[3] Thereafter, the rate of offending declines dramatically—youthful offenders "burn out" and are no longer high-risk cases. There are, of course, exceptions to this generalization, but they tend to be adults with extensive juvenile and adult criminal histories who are unable or unwilling to pursue any form of legitimate lifestyles.

The fact that most active criminals are youthful is especially relevant to the ability of rehabilitative programs to have a significant impact on individual recidivism rates and overall crime rates. As reported in Chapter 8, the average age of released prisoners and parolees is in the 32- to 35-year range and the average age will likely increase as segments of the prison population are required to serve longer sentences. About two thirds of the daily prison population is 30 years or older.[4] The contrast between those who commit crimes (ages 15 to 25) and those who are incarcerated suggests that many prisoners are well beyond their peak years of criminal behavior and should be viewed as low risk due to what is known as maturation effects.

Married with Children

Another major life event that reduces offenders' probability of continuing their criminal behavior relates to their ability to maintain a stable and supportive marriage.[5] It must be emphasized that it is not marriage, per se, but the nature of that relationship as it serves to solidify the other key life events of job stability, drug abuse, drinking, and residency. Clearly there are many examples where marriage has actually encouraged rather than diminished criminal behavior. But, in general, offenders who are able to become involved in a common-law or legal relationship are less likely to continue criminal careers than those who do not.[6]

Job Stability

Beginning with the pioneering work of Rushe and Kirchheimer in 1939, criminologists have long noted the relationship of employment to crime.[7] On a structural level, many studies have found that within capitalistic societies, incarceration rates increase as unemployment increases. On a more individual level, we know that prisoners have very high rates of unemployment that is related to their criminal behavior—if nothing more than for basic economic needs. Consequently, the ability of an ex-offender to maintain any form of stable employment that generates sufficient income to survive economically, coupled with marriage and the aging process, will significantly reduce that person's criminal tendencies. Having a job means one can get a credit card, a phone service, a car, an apartment, go shopping, eat out, go to the movies, and travel. These are the symbolic activities and attributes of the middle-class lifestyle that many Americans strive to realize.[8] Even a little "dose" of economic independence can have a significant impact on offenders released from prison. Berk and Rauma in California found that providing even a very modest level of economic assistance to released prisoners greatly reduced their rates of recidivism as compared to a control group that did not receive such assistance.[9]

Drugs

Research also shows a strong association between alcohol, illegal drug abuse, and involvement in crime. Simply stated, people arrested or reporting to have committed serious crimes tend to have higher rates of recent alcohol and drug use than people who are not involved in such criminal activities. Between 50 to 80 percent of adults arrested test positive for drug use at the time of arrest. As will be reported later in this chapter, it has been estimated that approximately 70 percent of the inmate population has some type of drug use or abuse history. However, it is also true that a much larger number of people who regularly use alcohol and illicit drugs do not become involved in criminal activities (other than possession, use, or the purchasing of illegal drugs).

According to the National Institute of Drug Abuse (NIDA), approximately one-half of all Americans will use an illegal drug during their lifetime. Another 118 million Americans have admitted to using illicit drugs since age 12, and these numbers are not declining (Table 5-2). Most of the illegal drug use is linked to marijuana. Over 11 percent (or approximately 28 million) of Americans have used illicit drugs in the past year, and 6.7 percent (or 15 million) have used these drugs in the past thirty days (Table 5-3).

Despite these large numbers of drug users (which, by the way, exclude people who are incarcerated), only 1.6 million of them are arrested each year, with the vast majority being arrests for possession (1.3 million).[10] What these data suggest is that alcohol and/or drug use alone is not a necessary or sufficient condition for one to commit a crime. Rather, some of the other factors, in combination with drug use, can serve to greatly increase the probability of criminality.

Societal and Economic Structures

Related to these individual offender considerations are the more macro-level and structural influences on crime rates. This perspective on the causes of crime rates focuses on social and economic forces that produce social stress, which in turn is associated with variations in crime rates. We have already taken note of the statistical

Table 5-2 Lifetime Estimates of Illegal Drug Use by Americans Age 12+ (in 1,000)

Drug Types	2002	2009
U.S. Population	288,028	307,006
% Any Illegal Drug Use	46%	47%
ILLICIT DRUGS—ALL	108,255	118,705
Marijuana	94,946	104,446
Cocaine	33,910	36,599
Crack	8,402	8,359
Heroin	3,668	3,683
Hallucinogens	34,314	37,256
Ecstasy	10,150	14,234
Psychotherapeutics	47,958	51,771
Pain Relievers	29,611	35,046
Methamphetamine	15,365	12,837
Illicit (Other Than Marijuana)	70,300	75,780
Alcohol	195,452	208,545
Tobacco	171,838	174,119

SOURCE: NIDA. http://www.drugwarfacts.org/cms/Drug_Usage.

Table 5-3 Estimates of Illegal Drug Use by Americans Age 12+ (in 1,000) 2008

Substance	Ever Used	Used in Past Year	Used in Past Month
Marijuana	102.4 million 41.0%	25.8 million 10.3%	15.0 million 6.1%
Cocaine	36.8 million 14.7%	5.3 million 2.1%	1.9 million 0.7%
Crack	8.5 million 3.4%	1.1 million 0.4%	359,000 0.1%
Heroin	3.8 million 1.5%	453,000 0.2%	213,000 0.1%

SOURCE: Substance Abuse and Mental Health Services Administration. (2009). Results from the 2008 National Survey on Drug Use and Health: National Findings (Office of Applied Studies, NSDUH Series H-36, HHS Publication No. SMA 09-4434). Rockville, MD.

relationship between unemploymentand high incarceration rates first stipulated by Rushe and Kirchheimer. Linsky and Strauss have developed a more elaborate and comprehensive explanation designed to explain why similarly situated states had very dissimilar crime rates.[11] They found that the following social and economic factors reflect social stress and that states with higher rates of social stress have higher rates of violent crimes, mental illness, and suicide. The indicators they found to be predictive of these three forms of social illnesses were:

1. Business failures
2. Unemployment claims

3. Workers on strike

4. Personal bankruptcies

5. Mortgage foreclosures

6. Divorces

7. Abortions

8. Illegitimate births

9. Infant deaths

10. Fetal deaths

11. Disaster assistance

12. State residency of less than five years

13. New houses authorized

14. New welfare cases

15. High school dropout rates

The Criminogenic Effects of Incarceration

There have been numerous studies of the relative effects of incarceration on individual offenders. Sampson and Laub, in their pioneering study of 880 juveniles from adolescence through adulthood, found that both the number of incarcerations and the length of incarceration had no direct impact on one's criminal career.[12] They went on to note that incarcerations actually have a deleterious effect on recidivism, as they severely disrupt all efforts to maintain one's relationship or bonds with the offender's family and to secure stable employment.

On a more macro level, Linsky and Strauss did not find an association between incarceration rates and crime rates. In fact, there is a well-established positive correlation that states with high incarceration rates tend to have higher crime rates. Similar to Sampson and Laub, this study concludes that high rates of incarceration may contribute to high levels of social stress and thus increase crime rates in both the individuals experiencing incarceration and the society in general.[13]

There has been less analysis that examines the extent to which probation versus prison has an impact on individual recidivism or, to a larger extent, on a state's crime rate. This is not to say that there has been little research on a wide variety of intermediate sanctions, such as boot camps, intensive supervision, electronic monitoring, and halfway houses. This research, as summarized by Sherman et al., found that most of these intermediate sanctions have little positive impact on recidivism rates.[14] However, some of these programs can be cost-effective if they are used in lieu of incarceration.

One often-neglected study by Petersilia and Turner compared a group of felons who were sentenced to probation with a statistically matched group of offenders who were sentenced to prison.[15] As shown in Table 5-4, the probationers had substantially lower recidivism rates regardless of the measure used.

Table 5-4 Two-Year Recidivism Rates for California Prisoners and Probationers

Recidivism Measure	Probationers	Prisoners
Rearrested	63%	72%
Returned to Jail or Prison	31%	47%
Returned to Prison	19%	28%

SOURCE: J. Petersilia & S. Turner (1986). *Prison versus Probation in California: Implications for Crime and Offender Recidivism.* Santa Monica, CA: RAND.

This study as well as other research led Daniel Nagin to conclude that imprisonment as compared to probation for similarly situated people is "criminogenic." Nagin points out that this finding should not be surprising given the nature of imprisonment and the socioeconomic status of most people who are imprisoned.

> Compared to non-custodial sanctions, the experience of incarceration has a null or somewhat criminogenic impact on future criminal involvement.... There is little evidence that increases in the severity of punishment yield large general deterrent effects.[16]

Michael Tonry, in a recent comprehensive review of the deterrent effects of incarceration, made the following summary comment:

> That prisons make people worse has been a commonplace observation for two centuries. As long as there have been prisons people have known they are criminogenic.[17]

> Most people sent to prison are socially and economically disadvantaged, majorities are or have been alcohol or drug dependent, and most lack strong private systems of familial or social support. Most offenders, following release, are stigmatized, and often are explicitly handicapped by laws precluding many kinds of employment.[18]

WHAT DOES WORK?

There has been a major debate among criminologists on whether treatment works for juvenile and adult offenders. It began with the now-famous publication by the late Robert Martinson that left the unfortunate impression that "nothing works."[19] Martinson's historic publication was based on a review of existing evaluations of prison treatment programs—one of the first "meta-analyses" that attempts to summarize the findings of numerous experimental and quasi-experimental studies of rehabilitation programs. This pioneering work has been followed by several other major meta-analyses, all of which have concluded that under certain conditions, some treatment interventions can have a significant impact on recidivism rates.[20]

The most recent and highly touted meta-analysis has been produced by the Washington State Institute on Public Policy (WSIPP).[21] The WSIPP has reviewed 291 treatment programs and has reached the conclusion that a massive increase in all sorts of effective and evidence-based treatment programs will significantly reduce recidivism and costs. Its conclusion that Washington State would save over $2 billion through treatment is striking.[22]

However, there are some important caveats to be noted. More specifically, the WSIPP reports that 42 percent of the evaluated programs, including jail diversion programs, domestic violence programs, faith-based, psychotherapy or behavior therapy for sex offenders, boot camps, electronic monitoring, and restorative justice programs, *had no impact* on recidivism. Of the 167 effective programs, only one-fourth were prison-based treatment programs. Of these programs, the reduction in recidivism rates generally ranged from 4 to 10 percent. The recidivism reduction results found here are similar to those found in other major evaluations of "what works" (or "doesn't work").[23] Notably, many other programs do not reduce recidivism and may actually increase rates of failure.[24]

One other finding by the WSIPP was that the programs with the highest rates of improvement—intensive supervision: treatment-oriented programs (21.9%) and cognitive-behavioral treatment in the community for sex offenders (31.2%) were community-based programs.[25] Indeed, as a general rule, programs work better when offered in community settings, and results are weakened when the programs are operated in confinement settings. In addition, programs work when applied to people classified as "high risk"; they typically backfire when applied to those who are at lower risk of recidivism.

Many have disagreed with some of the WSIPP and other meta-analysis findings. Put simply, they argue that the meta-analyses methods are suspect and overstate the merits of rehabilitation. Richard Berk points out that meta-analyses may be useful in terms of providing descriptive information on the collective effects of treatment interventions, but they should not be used to make sweeping statements about causality or the overall power of the intervention.[26] There are substantial problems in meta-analysis, such as how the studies are selected, the assumption that they represent the types of programs that exist in the real world, and the mixing of studies using random assignments with those that do not.

In particular, the studies cited by these meta-analyses have tended to use small sample sizes (under 250 cases for experimental and control groups), and the differences between the control and experimental subjects in their recidivism rates have been minimal (5 to 10 percentage points) in many of the studies (this issue is discussed in greater detail at the end of the chapter). Furthermore, the recommended conditions necessary for treatment to succeed have been difficult to define or to replicate in other sites. This is known as "external validity," which questions whether the results at one location (like Chicago) can be replicated in another (like Seattle).

For example, Palmer's summary of these studies concluded that only 25 to 35 percent of all the programs he reviewed showed significant positive results, with about 10 percent of the studies reporting significant positive results for the controls (nontreatment offenders). For the remaining 55 to 65 percent of the studies, two-thirds showed some positive results for the experimental cases, as opposed to one-third for controls. These data provide both optimism for the pro-treatment advocates and affirmation for the critics.

Well-designed and -administered correctional treatment programs are more frequently the exception rather than the rule. The so-called "program integrity" factor is often weak and may well explain the absence of strong treatment effects for many treatment programs. Correctional agencies are often ill equipped to design and implement effective treatment programs. Our belief is that most agencies do not actually believe that effective treatment is possible or that it is part of their agency mission. For example, a survey of prison wardens indicated that only 25 percent of their inmates were amenable to treatment. The wardens also stated that involving inmates in rehabilitation programs was not a high organizational priority. Conversely, they also believed that such programs have an important place in a prison setting.[27]

More recently, an evaluation of a community correctional system in Ohio found that the majority of programs did not adhere to what is referred to as "principles of effective intervention," meaning that services were not delivered or targeted properly to those people who had the greatest need for them. Such programs also showed either no or a negative effect on recidivism.[28]

In summary, it is difficult to find alternatives to incarceration that have been implemented properly, have undergone a rigorous impact evaluation, have demonstrated significant effects on reducing recidivism, and have served to either divert offenders from prison or reduce their lengths of stay.

What follows is a more careful assessment of several well-publicized rehabilitative programs that have all failed to produce significant and sustained effects on recidivism rates.

BOOT CAMPS

The Argument for Boot Camps

The first boot camps emerged in the early 1980s. They were advertised as a means of reducing the high rate of recidivism among offenders and for reducing prison crowding. Often categorized as an intermediate sanction, boot camps were designed to punish and treat juvenile and adult offenders convicted of less serious nonviolent crimes for relatively short periods of time. In confining offenders for shorter periods, it was hoped that boot camps would simultaneously reduce the length of stay for those incarcerated and reduce recidivism. In so doing, the costs of imprisonment would be reduced by inmates' spending a shorter period of time in custody and not returning to prison once released. Over the next decade, the boot camps phenomenon expanded from adult male prisons to include local jails, juveniles, and women.

The well-publicized images of a typical boot camp have generated a tremendous level of popular appeal. The sight of inmates being forced to rise early in the predawn night, to adhere to a rigorous regime of physical exercise led by a mean and dog-faced drill instructor, and to march up and down the prison yard in precisely choreographed drill ceremonies has much allure for the general public. These images not only reflect the desired infliction of pain upon criminal offenders—pain that is often found wanting in traditional prisons—but also have the utilitarian effect of developing character and discipline among the prisoners—characteristics associated with the good and law-abiding, which are almost invariably lacking in the young men and women who find themselves confined in correctional facilities.

Research on Boot Camps

Impact While in the Boot Camp Program   Some evaluations have examined the impact of boot camps on offender adjustments while institutionalized.[29] In general, these studies indicate that boot camps—as compared to traditional prisons—seem to result in more positive adjustments of inmates to institutionalization. These studies are consistent in finding that boot camp offenders tend to develop more prosocial attitudes and more favorable reactions to the correctional environment than do offenders incarcerated in more traditional correctional facilities.

For instance, MacKenzie's multisite evaluation of eight state-level adult boot camps found that, across all sites, inmates who went through the boot camp programs developed more positive attitudes toward their prison experience over time and displayed more prosocial attitudes than did comparison samples of inmates incarcerated in conventional settings. Some studies also suggest that boot camp participants witness significant increases in a number of desirable short-term outcomes, such as improved self-esteem and improved scores on standardized measures of educational achievement.[30]

It remains unclear, however, whether these effects are attributable to anything unique about a military-style boot camp. For instance, these findings may be simply the result of the boot camp participants being directly and intensely supervised by professional staff, suggesting these effects may extend to a variety of treatment-oriented, and not just boot camp, programs.[31] Some of these findings may also be an artifact of initial surveys being conducted after boot camp inductions have taken place, which may result in decreased pretest scores on the measures of adjustment administered. But in general, it does appear that offenders do respond favorably to well-administered and intense counseling and educational services.

We cannot leave this topic without also noting some of the dangers and atrocities that have occurred in boot camps. In these programs, staff can easily take advantage of their authority over their inmates and use excessive force against them. A number of incidents have occurred in boot camps where staff have physically and verbally abused youthful offenders to the point that the programs had to be terminated. One recent incident occurred in Maryland where guards were found to routinely punch, kick, and slam juveniles to the ground during their twenty weeks of boot camp programming. According to media reports, these physical abuses occurred when the youth arrived at the camp shackled and in handcuffs. The abuses were so great that an FBI investigation was launched.[32] Similar abuses were found in Georgia and Florida (where a youth was beaten to death).[33]

Impact of Boot Camps on Recidivism   The area of greatest concern has been the effectiveness of boot camps in reducing offender recidivism. A number of studies of both adult and juvenile boot camps have been completed with very similar results.

MacKenzie's multisite evaluation of eight adult correctional boot camps has been the most important research in this area.[34] This multifaceted study of eight state-level adult boot camps generally found that boot camps do not appear to be reducing offender recidivism rates. It was found that the boot camp experience did not result in a reduction in recidivism in five states. In three states, boot camp participants who successfully completed the program had lower recidivism rates than comparable inmates who served longer prison terms in conventional prisons on at least one measure of recidivism (re-arrest, re-conviction or return to prison).

The three state boot camp programs that appeared somewhat successful in positively impacting offender recidivism rates had some common characteristics. First, post-release, intensive supervision of boot campers was a program component in all three states, while prison releasees in those states were not generally as intensively supervised upon release from prison. Second, the institutional phase of these programs tended to be longer, to contain a stronger rehabilitative focus, and to generate lower in-program dropout rates than the other boot camp programs examined. Other apparently unsuccessful programs also shared some of these characteristics, so it is unclear how these program characteristics influenced failure rates. The analyses could not disentangle the effects of particular program features (for example, intensive supervision), although the authors do suggest that it is quite unlikely that the military boot camp atmosphere alone had much impact on program participants.

The negative results have been reported for those few evaluations that utilized experimental and control populations. These include the California Youth Authority's internal evaluation of its LEAD boot camp program and the Office of Juvenile Justice and Delinquency Prevention's sponsored evaluation of juvenile boot camps in Cleveland, Mobile, and Denver. These studies found that although youth improved while in the boot camp with respect to educational achievement and prosocial values, there were no statistical differences between experimental and control groups in terms of reoffending once they left the boot camp.[35]

A recent boot camp study showed little difference in the early evaluation findings with one important exception. The Michigan Department of Corrections has been operating boot camp programs for several years. An evaluation completed in 2010 showed that the program provided a wide array of cognitive restructuring and substance abuse treatment programs. Interviews with the participants showed a very positive attitude toward the 90-day program in terms of the professionalism of the staff and the quality of services. Such services were not widely available to other prisoners. Further, the average prison term was reduced from 24 months to 8 months. Despite these positive program features, the boot camp participants showed only a slightly lower (less than 5%) recidivism rate compared to a statistically matched control group. Because the length of stay had been reduce by an average of 16 months, the programs were saving about $50 million per year.[36]

In summary, both adult and juvenile boot camps have not succeeded in reducing recidivism or in reducing crowding. There are only a few cases where costs may have been reduced if the program was able to reduce the expected length of stay. The positive gains realized by offenders while assigned to a boot camp appear to diminish once the offender is released to the community. A major challenge for the "next generation" of boot camps will be developing effective aftercare components that will sustain the gains realized in the institutional phase of the program. Furthermore, most boot camps are relatively small in size and have problems operating at full capacity. Unless a larger pool of incarcerated offenders is made eligible for these programs, they cannot function as a viable means for controlling prison crowding or reducing the costs of the correctional system.

PRISON-BASED DRUG TREATMENT

The Argument for Drug Treatment

The past few years have also witnessed a growing interest in the possible impact of drug treatment for inmates in jail and prison as an effective crime-control strategy. This interest has been fueled, in part, by the dramatic growth of inmates incarcerated for drug crimes and the high percentage of inmates who were using either alcohol or drugs at the time of the crime or have a history of drug abuse. This movement is much larger than the boot camp fad discussed. There is no question that drug treatment can be extremely successful and useful for specific individuals. What is new is the promise that most of the serious crime in the country could be virtually eliminated through a massive expansion of prison drug treatment. Because such a proposal would require a considerable initial investment by taxpayers (as shown in the following text, nearly $8 billion per year would be required), it demands close scrutiny.

Perhaps the leading organization in support of drug treatment for offenders is the National Center on Addiction and Substance Abuse (CASA). In a report released in 2010, CASA estimated that approximately 85 percent of the 1.4 million people incarcerated in state and federal prisons (or 1.2 million) in 2006 were "substance involved," meaning they met one of the following three conditions:

1. Had a history of using illicit drugs regularly;

2. Met medical criteria for a substance abuse disorder; or

3. Were under the influence of alcohol or drugs at the time the crime was committed.[37]

The report goes on to claim that by placing these inmates in effective drug treatment programs while incarcerated, the likelihood of them continuing their criminal careers will be greatly reduced. Specifically, the report states the following:

> The benefit of keeping one inmate substance and crime free and employed is therefore $90,953 in savings from expected reduction in crime costs ($6,100), arrest and prosecution costs ($9,000), incarceration costs ($25,144), health care costs ($5,937), and economic benefits ($44,772). If we treated all 1.3 million inmates with untreated substance use disorders and spent the $12.6 billion necessary to do so, we would break even within a year post release if only 10.7 percent of those treated remained substance and crime free and employed: $12.6 billion/$90,953 = 138,200, 10.7 percent of the 1.3 million who received treatment and aftercare.[38]

This sounds almost too good to be true. And a careful review of the assumptions underpinning these numbers show it's not true. It assumes that each untreated prisoner will commit an average of 100 crimes per year, which is based on a single study of California offenders. It is also argued that each successfully treated inmate will secure employment at an annual salary of $21,400, which will produce $44,722 in economic benefits (see Table 5-5). Given this enormous cost-benefit ratio, the CASA report claims that only 10 percent of the inmates entering drug treatment have to succeed for the programs to be justified.

To test the merits and feasibility of the plan, three central components or assumptions of strategy need to be examined. First, there are the two interrelated assumptions that (1) most inmates are drug abusers, and (2) they commit a large number of crimes per year, primarily because of their drug use. Putting aside the thorny issue that inmates' criminal behavior may well predate their drug use,

Table 5-5 Theoretical Cost-Effectiveness of Prison Drug Treatment

Cost/Savings Factors	Estimated Cost/Savings
Drug Treatment Costs	
Residential Prison Drug Treatment	$3,778
Post-Release Aftercare	$5,967
Total Costs	**$9,745**
Savings to Society	
Avoid 100 Crimes Per Year at $50 Per Crime	$5,000
Avoid 2 Arrests/Prosecutions at $3,638 Each	$7,276
Avoid 1 year of State Prison	$25,144
Avoid Health Care and Substance Abuse Treatment	$5,937
Economic Benefits (at $29,849 Salary Times 1.5 Escalator)	$44,772
Total Savings	88,129
Net Savings Per Successful Treatment	**$78,384**

SOURCE: National Center on Addiction and Substance Abuse (CASA).

how realistic is the claim that most inmates are substance abusers who, if not incarcerated, would be committing such a large proportion of the crime occurring in the United States? There is no question that the use of drugs (especially alcohol) is related either directly or indirectly to inmates' current legal problems. The questions are (1) how serious is this addiction and (2) how much crime are these inmates engaged in?

Second, it is assumed that a sufficiently large market exists for expanding drug treatment within prisons. There is little disagreement that in many states the amount of drug treatment made available to inmates represents a small proportion of the inmate population. However, in order for cost savings to be realized at levels that would result in significant reductions in recidivism and the associated averted costs for law enforcement, the courts, and corrections, large numbers of the inmates must successfully complete both the residential drug treatment and the aftercare components. Of particular concern are the number of inmates who, for a variety of reasons related to prison operations and security concerns, cannot be assigned to a treatment program and the number of inmates who will fail to complete the program (dropout rates).

The third critical assumption is that treatment will have a dramatic effect on most participants in reducing their high rates of drug use and associated high rates of criminal behavior. In other words, a body of scientific evidence using experimental designs must exist showing that treatment works. Directly related to this assumption is the requirement that inmates selected for treatment are high-rate drug users with high rates of criminal activity (100 crimes per year). If a drug treatment program selects inmates who are low-rate offenders, the cost benefits of the program collapse. If prisons and jails contain significant numbers of low-rate offenders who, upon release from prison, will either cease or reduce their criminal activities regardless of treatment, then treating these inmates will not be cost-beneficial. The questions remain: (1) how many inmates have a severe drug addiction problem and are career criminals and (2) how many of these inmates can we reasonably expect to successfully treat?

The Drug Offender Crime Rate Assumption   One of the major assumptions underpinning the argument to greatly expand residential drug treatment in prisons is that most inmates (70 to 80%) are drug abusers who, if left untreated, will commit large amounts of crime (100 per year). These are large numbers that suggest that most of the crime being committed each year in the United States can be directly traced to untreated inmates who are released to the streets each year.

Using CASA's estimates of prevalence and frequency, one can evaluate the validity of this assumption. As shown in Table 5-6, there were approximately 685,000 prisoners released from state and federal prisons in 2009. Assume that 85 percent of these prisoners have a drug problem. Of this group, 89 percent did not receive any treatment and are committing an average of 100 crimes per year. Multiplying the number of releases times the 100 crimes per year figure produces a total of 51.9 million crimes per year attributed to these untreated state prisoners.

Table 5-6 Projected Amount of Crime Being Committed by Released Prisoners with Drug Problems, 2009

Factor	Estimates
A. Number of Prisoners Released in 2009 (DOJ)	685,500
B. Percent with Drug Problems, 85% (CASA)	582,675
C. Percent Who Did Not Receive Professional Treatment, 89%	518,581
D. Rate of Crimes Committed Per Year by Drug Offenders (CASA)	100 per year
E. Total Crimes Committed by Released Prisoners (C × D)	51.9 million
F. Total Crimes Reported to Police 2009 (FBI)	10.6 million
G. Total Crimes Reported by Victimization Surveys 2009 (DOJ)	20.0 million

Clearly, there is something *very wrong* with these estimates. The 51.9 million number is more than *four times* the total amount of serious crimes reported to police and *twice* the number of all crimes reported on the National Crime Victimization Survey (NCVS victimization surveys. Moreover, these numbers do not include the nearly 14 million inmates released from jail each year nor the nearly 5 million adults on probation or parole. What these data show is that most prisoners and jail inmates released each year cannot be committing 100 crimes per year. A significant number of inmates will either cease or reduce their rate of offending regardless of whether they have been exposed to drug treatment. The next two sections address two other erroneous assumptions on the efficacy of drug treatment.

The Number of Inmates Who Can Be Treated Assumption   The CASA estimate that approximately 1.2 million inmates would benefit from drug treatment is based upon data from several U.S. Department of Justice surveys in which inmates were interviewed regarding their drug use patterns. Offenders who self-reported to interviewers that they either were regular users of drugs, were under the influence of drugs at the time of their arrests, were convicted of drug crimes, or had prior criminal histories for drug offenses were identified as being in need of drug treatment. It is important to note that the type of treatment being advocated was the therapeutic community (TC) model in which inmates nearing the end of their prison terms are admitted to an intensive treatment program for six to twelve months.[39]

However, a closer analysis of the jail and inmate population suggests that the number of inmates who could be reasonably admitted to a TC is far smaller than 1.2 million. More directly, this estimate fails to take into account those aspects of prison operations and security that would preclude most inmates from participating in an intense drug treatment program regardless of their "need" for such treatment. Here are some of the major factors that would preclude participation in TC-type programs (see Table 5-7):

1. As indicated by CASA, approximately 15 percent of the inmates do not require drug treatment, as they have no drug/alcohol addiction problems.

Table 5-7 How Many Inmates Can Participate In and Benefit From In-Prison Drug Treatment Programs?

Drug Treatment Eligibility Factors	Number	%
Inmate Population as of 2008		
Jails	785,556	34%
State Prison	1,320,582	57%
Federal Prison	198,414	9%
Total Inmates	**2,304,552**	**100%**
Drug Treatment Exclusionary Factors	**Remaining Inmates**	
Have no drug treatment needs: 15 percent of total population	1,959,552	85%
Pretrial and short-term jail inmates: 75 percent of remaining jail population	1,458,760	63%
Inmates in high-security/special management units: 15 percent of remaining total population	1,239,946	54%
Full-time participants in programs/work assignments: 25 percent of state and federal inmate populations	860,197	37%
Short-term sentenced inmates (less than 6 months to serve): 25 percent of state and federal prison populations	654,420	28%
Unwilling to participate: 25 percent of remaining pool	490,815	21%
Program failures: 35 percent of drug treatment pool	319,030	14%
Program recidivists: 25 percent of remaining drug treatment pool	239,272	10%

2. Most (about 75%) of the 785,000 jail inmates are in pretrial status and will spend no more than a few days in custody on relatively minor charges before being released on bail or having their charges dropped. Those who stay in jail have very serious charges pending, and they cannot enter treatment until their cases are resolved by the court. Only a very small number are in jail long enough to even begin a treatment program that requires nine to twelve months to complete. One can assume that no more than 25 percent of the jail inmates could participate in such a TC program.

3. Approximately 15 percent of the prisoners are either high-security risks, have severe mental health and/or medical problems, or are serving short sentences and will be released before a nine- to twelve-month treatment program can begin.

4. Another group will not or cannot participate in treatment because they are working full-time and making money in a prison industries program, learning a vocational skill, getting a high school degree, or simply learning to read and write. We assumed that at least 25 percent of the state and federal inmates are in this group.

5. Finally, of those who might benefit from drug treatment, a significant number simply do not want to participate. Our research shows that 25 percent of all

inmates screened for drug treatment do not enter a program because they are uninterested or unmotivated.

Unless it is being suggested that drug treatment will be coercive, the numbers expected simply will not materialize. These data show that the true drug treatment eligibility pool for the prison and jail systems will be about 20 percent. And these estimates do not include the fact that significant numbers of program participants will either fail to complete the program or will not benefit from the treatment. Using the results of published reports, one can assume that approximately 35 percent of the inmates admitted to treatment will fail to complete the program and that another 25 percent will recidivate. With these assumptions, the total number of inmates who will benefit from drug treatment is about 10 percent of the total inmate population.

The Impact of Drug Treatment Assumptions   There is a growing body of research on the effectiveness of drug treatment for incarcerated offenders. One of the most frequently cited summaries of the research literature on the effectiveness of drug treatment programs is a report published by the National Institute of Justice (NIJ) entitled "The Effectiveness of Treatment for Drug Abusers Under Criminal Justice Supervision."[40] In the 1995 NIJ report, Lipton lists seven model drug treatment programs for inmates in prison and jail settings. Lipton's review focused on the TC model in which inmates must be within a year of their release date and the treatment should last from nine to twelve months and have a strong aftercare component. For all of the programs evaluated, the inmates had volunteered to participate. *Note:* A complete listing of each study is contained in endnote.[41]

In general, Lipton's report is quite favorable with respect to the ability of treatment to reduce recidivism and drug use. His summary of the research literature shows that inmates who have participated in the referenced programs and have completed all phases of treatment have very low rates of recidivism and continued drug use. Clearly, inmates who stay in treatment are far less likely to continue their criminal careers. However, despite these positive findings, there are a number of issues that must be noted before we determine that a drug treatment strategy is able to have a dramatic impact on crime rates and criminal justice costs.

1. *TC-type programs are small in terms of the numbers of inmates in the programs.* The model programs cited by the drug treatment proponents tend to be relatively small, with bed capacities at 300 or less.

2. *There is a considerable level of in-program failure in many programs.* Researchers have consistently found that the dropout rate for TC programs ranges from 30 to 60 percent.

3. *The evaluations have not used randomized experimental designs.* In order to truly measure the effects of any treatment program, the best methodology is to implement an experimental design in which inmates screened as eligible for the program are randomly assigned to the treatment and non-treatment conditions. To date no such evaluations have been completed.

4. *Most of the studies show marginal differences between experimental and control groups when the recidivism rates are calculated properly.* The Stay'n Out female evaluation showed a difference of only 6 percent between the treatment group and a matched control group. Some studies inappropriately fail to include the program failures in calculating the program's success rate. By discounting these failures, the researchers are distorting the true effects of the program's impact. The success rate of most drug treatment programs with program failures included is considerably more modest than that of programs excluding the failures from the calculations.

A Better Understanding of the Limits of Treatment Effects

The finding of modest marginal effects of drug treatment programs applies to all other prison-based treatment programs. We noted at the beginning of the chapter that the differences between experimental and control groups are "marginal" (at best in the range of 5 to 10 percent. Many criminologists provide misleading or incomplete conclusions regarding the effectiveness of such programs. This bias has led policy makers who are not trained in the nuances of research methods to wrongfully assume that (1) treatment has a significant impact on people and (2) large numbers of prisoners will benefit from treatment if so provided. A basic problem is how impact results are presented. There are three ways to present differences between experimental and control groups. Absolute risk (AR) reduction is the simple difference between experimental and control groups on their outcome variables. For example, if a reentry program has a 30 percent recidivism rate while the randomly selected control group has a 40 percent recidivism rate, the absolute rate reduction is 10 percent. This should be the preferred standard for stating results.

A relative rate (RR) reduction is the percentage change in the control rate reduction. So, in the example of the reentry program, the RR reduction statistic will artificially increase the treatment effects from 10 percent to 25 percent. What the RR is actually saying is that a 10 percent reduction is a 25 percent improvement in the 40 percent recidivism rate. Some will wrongfully conclude that the 25 percent reduction will lower the 40 percent recidivism rate to 15 percent.

Researchers should also show what is known as the "Number Needed to Treat" (NNT) estimate. This statistic is used to estimate how many people need to be treated in order for one person to benefit from the treatment. The NNT is calculated by taking the inverse of the absolute rate reduction. So, in the example of the 10 percent reduction of our model reentry program, the NNT is 10 (100 divided by 10), meaning that 10 people have to unnecessarily go through the reentry program in order to prevent one person from recidivating.

All of the meta-analyses referred to earlier in the chapter do not use these three statistics, which will exaggerate the effectiveness of treatment. One such example can be seen in another widely touted treatment program referred to as cognitive restructuring. The earlier referenced WSIPP meta-analysis report cites cognitive restructuring as a successful and effective intervention.[42] The prison-based adult cognitive programs are described as being conducted in small groups (10 to 15 people) and exposing them to 40 to 60 hours of "treatment." The WSIPP conclusion is that such programs produce a 6.3 percent reduction in the number of adults being reconvicted of a new felony charge. But the 6.3 percent is the RR while the AR is 4 percent. Further, based on the 4 percent AR, one can estimate that NNT is 25, meaning that an agency will need to unnecessarily treat twenty-five prisoners in these small groups to prevent one prisoner from recidivating (see Table 5-8).

A more straightforward analysis is presented in Table 5-9. In this scenario, it is assumed that, based on the CASA data, 21 percent of the prison releases (685,000 per year) are exposed to one of the WSIPP recommended programs. Of this number, 65 percent complete the program and then show a 10 percent reduction in their recidivism rate compared to those who do not complete or participate in the program. Based on these assumptions, the overall results are quite modest. There is only a 1 percent reduction in prison admissions, a 1 percent reduction in the nation's prison population.

Table 5-8 Recalculation of the Treatment Effects of Adult Cognitive Treatment in Prisons and in Communities

Experimental Control Population Effects	Rate
Experimental Recidivism: New Felony Conviction	59%
Control Recidivism: New Felony Conviction	63%
Absolute Rate Reduction (AR)	4%
Relative Rate Reduction (RR)	6.3%
Number Needed to Treat (NNT) In Order to Prevent One Recidivist	25
Net Cost Savings Per Participant	$10,299
Incurred Program Cost (based on conversation with DOC official)	$105
Averted Crime Victim Direct Costs (based on Miller et al.)	$4,726
Averted Pain and Suffering Costs (based on civil cases that did not occur)	$5,658
Adjusted Averted Pain and Suffering Costs	$0

Table 5-9 Estimated Overall Prison-Based Treatment System Effects

All Releases	685,000
Exposed to Treatment: 21 percent	143,850
Complete Treatment: 65 percent	93,503
Reduction in Return to Prison: 7.5 percent reduction	7,013
Percent Reduction in Admissions	1%
Bed Savings: 30 Months Length of Stay	$17,532
Percent of Total 1.5 Million Prison Population	1%

SUMMARY

There is no question that providing meaningful work, education, and self-development programs to prisoners promotes more humane and safer prisons. Basic housing, employment, medical and mental health services are lacking for most prisoners as well as those being released. And there is a growing body of research, as noted below, that prisoners who take advantage of well-administered rehabilitative services and complete the programs are more likely to succeed in achieving satisfying conventional lives after prison than persons who do not receive these services. But efforts to expand treatment services will not be sufficient to reduce prison populations.

Ultimately, the purpose of treatment and rehabilitation—and the criteria for assessing their usefulness and efficacy—should not be a major reduction in recidivism, much less reducing the size of the prison population. These are unreasonable burdens to place on programs that are, by their very nature, limited. Unreasonable expectations will inevitably go unfulfilled. The danger of relying on drug treatment and programs to solve America's imprisonment crisis is that when recidivism isn't reduced, imprisonment will be regarded as the only viable answer to the crime problem.

In light of the external factors related to criminal careers, as noted in this chapter, it is clear that among various forms of rehabilitation programs, the interventions that better equip an individual to secure meaningful employment in today's increasingly competitive economy will be the most successful. Conversely, program interventions that are based simply on counseling, drug treatment, or cognitive learning, and do not provide basic enhancements in the offender's ability to perform basic tasks—essential for any form of employment—will not be successful. Furthermore, the private and public sector must recognize the need to provide employment opportunities for this segment of the population.

Based on many studies, the following conclusions can be made regarding the impact of treatment and punishment on crime rates and individual offenders:

1. The vast majority of crimes are not committed by persons released from prison. Consequently, the success or lack of success of prison-based treatment programs and/or punishment will have little impact on crime rates in general.

2. Under certain circumstances, treatment of offenders can have only modest results. Positive results will be strongest for programs that provide for long-term aftercare and serve to increase the offender's ability to secure employment and develop a stable family situation.

3. However, it is also true that under certain circumstances, treatment of offenders can have negative results. Furthermore, change (positive and negative) can also occur and often does occur based on other factors that have nothing to do with treatment (for example, maturation, random events, and so on).

4. Most correctional treatment programs are not well administered, target the wrong clientele, and are too small to have any impact on crime rates or public safety.

5. It is extremely rare to find a well-administered treatment program that has been properly evaluated and has demonstrated dramatic treatment effects.

We do not advocate the abolition of treatment within prisons. These programs can and do play a very important role in turning some lives around and, more importantly, humanizing the prison experience. For this reason alone, the use of rehabilitation and treatment programs that serve to make a more humane and less costly correctional system is warranted and should be expanded. But, in a strange and twisted way, the need for treatment has also served to justify the use of incarceration. No matter how well intentioned, imprisonment in the name of treatment should be strongly resisted.

NOTES

1. See D. A. Andrews, Ivan Zinger, Robert D. Hoge, James Bonta, Paul Gendreau, and Francis T. Cullen, "Does Correctional Treatment Work? A Clinically Relevant and Psychologically Informed Meta-Analysis," *Criminology* 28, 3 (1990): 369–404; and Don Gendreau and Peter Ross, "Revivification of Rehabilitation: Evidence from the 1980s," *Justice Quarterly* 4, 3 (1987): 349–407.

2. See James Austin and Barry Krisberg, "The Unmet Promise of Alternatives to Incarceration," *Crime and Delinquency* 28, 3 (1983): 374–409.

3. Federal Bureau of Investigation, *Age-Specific Arrest Rates and Race Specific Rates for Selected Offenses* (Washington, DC: U.S. Department of Justice, 2009); Travis Hirschi and Michael Gottfredson, "Age and the Explanation of Crime," *American Journal of Sociology* 89 (1983): 552–584; Robert J. Sampson and John H. Laub, *Crime in the Making: Pathways and Turning Points Through Life* (Cambridge, MA: Harvard University Press, 1993).

4. U.S. Department of Justice, Bureau of Justice Statistics, *Prisoners in 2009*, Bulletin NCJ 231675 (Washington, DC: U.S. Department of Justice, December 2010, p. 27. Appendix Table 13: p. 28. Appendix Table 15.

5. Sampson and Laub, *Crime in the Making*.

6. T.C.N. Gibbens, "Borstal Boys After 25 Years," *British Journal of Criminology* 24 (1984): 49–62; B. J. Knight, S. G. Osborn, and D. West, "Early Marriage and Criminal Tendency in Males," *British Journal of Criminology* 17 (1977): 348–360; Alicia Rand, "Transitional Life Events and Desistance from Delinquency and Crime," in Marvin Wolfgang, Terrence Thornberry, and Robert M. Figlio (eds.), *From Boy to Man: From Delinquency to Crime* (Chicago: University of Chicago Press, 1987), pp. 134–162.

7. For an excellent review and current study of the Rushe/Kirchheimer unemployment-imprisonment relationship, see Raymond Michalowski and Susan M. Carlson, "Unemployment, Imprisonment, and Social Structures of Accumulation: Historical Contingency in the Rushe-Kirchheimer Hypothesis," *Criminology* 37, 2 (May 1999): 1–250.

8. John Braithwaite, *Crime, Shame, and Reintegration* (Cambridge: Cambridge University Press, 1989); Robert D. Crutchfield, "Labor Stratification and Violent Crime," *Social Forces* 68 (1989): 489–512; Sampson and Laub, *Crime in the Making;* Neal Shover, *Aging Criminals* (Beverly Hills, CA: Sage Publications, 1985).

9. Richard Berk and David Rauma, "Remuneration and Recidivism: The Long-Term Impact of Unemployment Compensation on Ex-Offenders," *Journal of Quantitative Criminology* 3, 1 (1987): 3–27.

10. Office of National Drug Control Policy, *Drug Data Summary* (Washington,

DC: April 1999) *Crime in the United States, 2009*. (Washington, DC: U.S. Department of Justice, Federal Bureau of Investigation).

11. Arnold S. Linsky and Murray Strauss, *Social Stress in the United States* (Dover, MA: Auburn House, 1986).

12. Sampson and Laub, *Crime in the Making*.

13. Arnold S. Linsk and Murray Strauss, *Social Stress in the United States* (Dover, MA: Auburn House, 1986).

14. L. Sherman, D. Gottfredson, D. MacKenzie, J. Eck, P. Reuter, & S. Bushway, (1997). *Preventing Crime: What Works, What Doesn't, What's Promising*. A Report to the United States Congress by the National Institute of Justice. Washington, DC: National Institute of Justice.

15. J., Petersilia & S. Turner, *Prison Versus Probation in California: Implications For Crime and Offender Recidivism*. Santa Monica, CA: RAND, 1986.

16. D. Nagin, "Imprisonment and Crime Control: Building Evidence-Based Policy" in R. Rosenfeld, K. Quiner, and C. Garcia (eds.), *Contemporary Issues in Criminological Theory and Research: The Role of Social Institutions*. (Belmont, CA: Wadsworth, 2010), p. 310.

17. M. Tonry, "Less Imprisonment Less Crime: A Reply to Nagin", in R. Rosenfeld, K. Quiner, and C. Garcia (eds.), *Contemporary Issues in Criminological Theory and Research: The Role of Social Institutions*. Belmont, CA: Wadsworth, 2010) p. 319.

18. Tonry, "Less Imprisonment" p. 322.

19. Robert Martinson, "What Works?— Questions and Answers About Prison Reform," *Public Interest* 35 (1974): 22–54.

20. D. A. Andrews et al., "Does Correctional Treatment Work?"; William Davidson, L. Gottschalk, L. Gensheimer, & J. Mayer, *Interventions with Juvenile Delinquents: A Meta-Analysis of Treatment Efficacy* (Washington, DC: National Institute of Juvenile Justice and Delinquency Prevention, 1984); C. Garrett, "Effects of Residential Treatment on Adjudicated Delinquents: A Meta-Analysis," *Journal of Research in Crime and Delinquency* 22

(1985): 287–308; Don Gendreau and Peter Ross, "Revivification of Rehabilitation"; R. Gottschalk, William Davidson, L. Gensheimer, & J. Mayer, " Community-Based Interventions," in H. Quay (ed.)., *Handbook of Juvenile Delinquency* (New York: Wiley, 1987); Martin Lipsey, *The Efficacy of Intervention for Juvenile Delinquency*, paper presented at the American Society of Criminology (1989); Ted Palmer, *The Re-Emergence of Correctional Intervention* (Newbury Park, CA: Sage Publications, 1992); Aos, Maa Miller, and Elizabeth Drake. *Evidence-Based Public Policy Options to Reduce Future Prison Construction, Criminal Justice Costs and Crime Rates* (Olympia: Washington State Institute for Public Policy, 2006)

21. Steve Aos, Marna Miller, and Elizabeth Drake, *Evidence-Based Adult Corrections Programs: What Works and What Does Not* (Olympia: Washington State Institute for Public Policy, 2006). Only 20 percent of the evaluations used random assignment procedures to create treatment and control groups. The other studies used "matching techniques" to approximate the attributes of the "treatment" group, which is less rigorous.

22. Aos et al., *Evidence-Based Public Policy Options*, 2008, p. 1.

23. See Brandon C. Welsh and David P. Farrington, eds. *Preventing Crime: What Works for Children, Offenders, Victims, and Places* (New York: Springer, 2006). See also an unpublished meta-analysis: Ojmarrh Mitchell, David B. Wilson, and Doris L. MacKenzie, "The Effectiveness of Incarceration-Based Drug Treatment on Criminal Behavior," which is a meta-analysis of in-prison treatment programs for drugs. The authors conclude that some of the programs reduce recidivism, typically from about 35 percent to 28 percent.

24. Donald A. Andrews, "Principles of effective correctional programs," in Laurence L. Motiuk and Ralph C. Serin, (eds.), *Compendium 2000 on Effective Correctional Programming*. (Ottawa, ON: Correctional Service Canada, 2001); Sherman, *Preventing Crime: What Works, What Doesn't*.

25. Aos, Miller, and Drake, op. cit. The more successful in-prison programs have been those that provide substantial services after release; these are few and far between. See Paul Gendreau and Robert Ross, "Effective Correctional Treatment: Bibliography for Cynics," *Crime and Delinquency* 25 (1979): 463–489; Frances T. Cullen and Karen I. Gilbert, *Reaffirming Rehabilitation*. (Cincinnati, OH: Anderson, 1982).

26. Richard Berk (2007). "Statistical Inference and Meta Analysis," *Journal of Experimental Criminology* 3, 2 (2007): 237–270.

27. Francis T. Cullin, Edward J. Latessa, Velmer S. Burton, Jr., and Lucien X. Lombardo, "The Correctional Orientation of Prison Wardens: Is the Rehabilitative Ideal Supported?" *Criminology* 31, 1 (1993): 69–92.

28. C. T. Lowenkamp, E. J. Latessa, and P. Smith, (2006). "Does Correctional Quality Really Matter? The Importance of Adhering to the Principles of Effective Intervention," *Criminology and Public Policy*, 5, (2006): 201–220.

29. D. L. MacKenzie and J. W. Shaw, "Inmate Adjustment and Change During Shock Incarceration: The Impact of Correctional Boot Camp Programs," *Justice Quarterly* 7 (1990): 125–150; and D. L. MacKenzie and C. Souryal, *Inmate Attitude Change During Incarceration: A Comparison of Boot Camp and Traditional Prison* (University of Maryland: Part II, Final Report to National Institute of Justice, 1992).

30. James Austin, Michael Jones, and Melissa Bolyard, "The Growing Use of Jail Boot Camps: The Current State of the Art," in *Research in Brief* (National Institute of Justice, October 1993); James Austin, Michael Jones, and Melissa Bolyard, *Assessing the Impact of a County Operated Boot Camp: Evaluation of the Los Angeles County Regimented Inmate Diversion Program* (National Council on Crime and Delinquency 1993); Little Hoover Commission, "Boot Camps: An Evolving Alternative to Traditional Prison," (Sacramento, CA: Little Hoover Commission, 1995).

31. R. C. McCorkle, "Correctional Boot Camps and Change in Attitude: Is All This Shouting Necessary?" *Justice Quarterly* 12, 2 (1995): 365–375.

32. "Juvenile Justice Chief, Aides Ousted Over Boot Camp Violence," *The Sun*, December 16, 1999, pp. 1, 18a.

33. S. J. Listwan, C. L. Jonson, F. T. Cullen, and E. J. Latessa. (2008). "Cracks in the Penal Harm Movement: Evidence from the Field." *Criminology & Public Policy*, 7, 3, (2008); 429.

34. MacKenzie and Souryal, *Inmate Attitude Change*.

35. See J. Bottcher, T. Isorena, and M. Belnas, *Lead: A Boot Camp and Intensive Parole Program: An Impact Evaluation: Second Year Findings* (State of California, Department of the Youth Authority, Research Division, 1996); M. Peters, *Evaluation of the Impact of Boot Camps for Juvenile Offenders: Denver Interim Report* (Washington, DC: U.S. Department of Justice, Office of Juvenile Justice and Delinquency Prevention, 1996); M. Peters, *Evaluation of the Impact of Boot Camps for Juvenile Offenders: Cleveland Interim Report* (Washington, DC: U.S. Department of Justice, Office of Juvenile Justice and Delinquency Prevention, 1996); M. Peters, *Evaluation of the Impact of Boot Camps for Juvenile Offenders: Mobile Interim Report* (Washington, DC: U.S. Department of Justice, Office of Juvenile Justice and Delinquency Prevention, 1996).

36. J. Austin, G. Chapman, and A. Bhati, *Michigan Department of Corrections, Special Alternative Incarceration Program, Second Year Process and Impact Evaluation*, Final Report. (Washington, DC: JFA Institute, 2010).

37. National Center on Addiction and Substance Abuse (CASA), *Behind Bars II: Substance Abuse and America's Prison Population* (New York: Columbia University, 2010).

38. National Center on Addiction and Substance Abuse (CASA), *Behind Bars II: Substance Abuse*, p. 96.

39. Douglas S. Lipton, *The Effectiveness of Treatment for Drug Abusers Under Criminal Justice Supervision* (Washington, DC: U.S. Department of Justice, 1995).

40. Lipton, *Effectiveness of Treatment*.

41. The various studies referred to in this table are as follows:

California Department of Corrections (CDC) Office of Substance Abuse Programs, *Overview of Substance Abuse Programs* (Sacramento: California Department of Corrections, 1997).

Fabelo, Tony, "Why It Is Prudent Not to Expand the Correctional Substance Abuse Treatment Initiative," *Bulletin from the Executive Director*, No. 16 (Austin, TX: Criminal Justice Policy Council, 1995).

Federal Bureau of Prisons (FBP), U.S. Department of Justice, *New Research Reveals Federal Inmate Drug Treatment Programs Reduce Recidivism and Future Drug Use* (Washington, DC: U.S. Department of Justice, TRIAD Press Release, 1998).

Field, G., "Oregon Prison Drug Treatment Programs," in C. G. Leukefeld and F. M. Tims (eds.), *Drug Abuse Treatment in Prisons and Jails* (Washington, DC: U.S. Government Printing Office, 1992), pp. 142–155.

Field, G., "A Study of the Effects of Intensive Treatment on Reducing the Criminal Recidivism of Addicted Offenders," *Federal Probation* 48 (1989): 50–55.

Inciardi, J. A., "The Therapeutic Community: An Effective Model for Corrections-Based Drug Abuse Treatment," in K. C. Haas, and G. P. Alpert (eds.), *The Dilemmas of Punishment* (Prospect Heights, IL: Waveland Press, 1995), pp. 406–417.

Lipton, Douglas S., *The Effectiveness of Treatment for Drug Abusers Under Criminal Justice Supervision* (Washington, DC: U.S. Department of Justice, 1995).

Lockwood, D., Inciardi, J. A., and Surratt, H., "CREST Outreach Center: A Model for Blending Treatment and Corrections," in J. A. Inciardi, B. Fletcher, P. Delany, and A. Horton, (eds.), *The Effectiveness of Innovative Approaches in the Treatment of Drug Abuse* (Westport, CT: Greenwood Press, 1995).

Martin, S. S., Butzin, C. A., and Inciardi, J. A., "Assessment of a Multi-Stage Therapeutic Community for Drug Involved Offenders," *Journal of Psychoactive Drugs* 27, 1(1995): 109–116.

Pellissier, B., and McCarthy, D., "Evaluation of the Federal Bureau of Prisons Drug Treatment Programs," in C. G. Leukefeld, and F. M. Tims (eds.), *Drug Abuse Treatment in Prisons and Jails* (Washington, DC: U.S. Government Printing Office, 1992), pp. 261–278.

Pelissier, B., Rhodes, W., Gaes, G., Camp, S., O'Neill, J., Wallace, S., and Saylor, W., *Alternative Solutions to the Problem of Selection Bias in an Analysis of Federal Residential Drug Treatment Programs* (Washington, DC: Federal Bureau of Prisons, 1998).

Wexler, H. K., *Amity/Prison TC: One Year Outcome Results*, unpublished report to NDRI, from Lipton, D. S., *Effectiveness of Treatment* (Washington, DC: U.S. Department of Justice, 1995).

Wexler, H. K., Falkin, G. P., and Lipton, D. S., "Outcome Evaluation of a Prison Therapeutic Community for Substance Abuse Treatment," *Criminal Justice and Behavior* 17, 1 (1990): 71–92.

42. Mark Lipsey (2008) employs the same tactic in his meta-analysis of juvenile prevention programs.

6

■

The Rise and Fall of Supermax

LEARNING OBJECTIVES

1. To understand what constitutes a supermax and the number of people assigned to them as well as trends over time.

2. To understand the distinction between administrative segregation, disciplinary segregation, protective custody, and the general population.

3. To understand the historical reasons that led up to the use of supermax facilities.

36. The Committee remains concerned about the extremely harsh regime imposed on detainees in (U.S.) "supermaximum prisons." The Committee is concerned about the prolonged isolation periods detainees are subjected to, the effect such treatment has on their mental health, and that its purpose may be retribution, in which case it would constitute cruel, inhuman or degrading treatment or punishment (art. 16).

The State party should review the regime imposed on detainees in "supermaximum prisons," in particular the practice of prolonged isolation.

Source: United Nations, Committee Against Torture, 36th session, May 19, 2006, Consideration of Reports Submitted by States Parties Under Article 19 of The Convention, Conclusions And Recommendations Of The Committee Against Torture, United States of America.

32. The Committee reiterates its concern that conditions in some (U.S.) maximum security prisons are incompatible with the obligation contained in article 10 (1) of the Covenant to treat detainees with humanity and respect for the inherent dignity of the human person. It is particularly concerned by

the practice in some such institutions to hold detainees in prolonged cellular confinement, and to allow them out-of-cell recreation for only five hours per week, in general conditions of strict regimentation in a depersonalized environment. It is also concerned that such treatment cannot be reconciled with the requirement in article 10 (3) that the penitentiary system shall comprise treatment the essential aim of which shall be the reformation and social rehabilitation of prisoners. It also expresses concern about the reported high numbers of severely mentally ill persons in these prisons, as well as in regular U.S. jails.

The State party should scrutinize conditions of detention in prisons, in particular in maximum security prisons, with a view to guaranteeing that persons deprived of their liberty be treated in accordance with the requirements of article 10 of the Covenant and the United Nations Standard Minimum Rules for the Treatment of Prisoners.

Source: Human Rights Committee, 87th Session, July 28, 2006, Consideration of Reports Submitted by States Parties Under Article 40 of the Covenant, Concluding Observations Of The Human Rights Committee, United States of America.

SEGREGATION AND SUPERMAX

Within a prison system, inmates are housed according to a classification system that separates inmates according to the likelihood of their attempting to escape, to assault staff and inmates, or to commit other serious prison infractions (for example, possession of a weapon, contraband, and so on). The vast majority of inmates are placed in the so-called "general population." These inmates are allowed to "program," meaning that they can participate in most inmate programs and work assignments. However, a small but highly visible proportion of the population are viewed as so dangerous and disruptive that they must be assigned to a special control unit, usually referred to as "administrative segregation," "the hole," "maximum-security," "control," or "lockup" housing units, that is, "Supermax."

These "supermax" units were in response to what many perceived as unmanageable prisons; departments of correction turned increasingly to long-term segregation or lockdown as the way to manage the rising rates of violence and misbehavior. Sections of prisons and even entire newly constructed facilities were dedicated to isolated confinement. The "super-maximum security" prison emerged.[1] Prisoners in segregation, or isolated confinement (the term employed here), were presumably "the worst of the worst" and had to be separated from the general population if there was to be peace and smooth operations in the prisons.

The most recent national estimates for inmates housed in the administrative segregation units as well as those in disciplinary segregation and protective custody range from 3 to 10 percent of the entire prison population with the overall average being about 5 percent. Based on the current national prison count of 1.6 million, that would mean that about 80,000 to 90,000 prisoners are assigned to these extremely restrictive prisons on any given day (Table 6-1).

Table 6-1 U.S. Administrative Segregation and Protective Custody Populations

Special Inmate Population	Estimated Number	% of All Inmates
Administrative Segregation	32,000	1 to 3%
Disciplinary Segregation	32,000	1 to 3%
Protective Custody	24,000	1 to 2%
Total Segregated Population	88,000	3 to 8%

SOURCE: James Austin and Ken McGinnis. (2004) *Classification of High-Risk and Special Management Inmates: A National Assessment of Current Practices*. Washington, DC: National Institute of Corrections. Association of State Correctional Administrators, 2010.

These segregation categories have different meanings and consequences for prisoners. Prisoners in disciplinary segregation have been found guilty of a serious rule violation and have been sentenced to segregation for a specific time period. Upon completion of their "seg" time, they are released to the general population There are also inmates in disciplinary segregation who are awaiting the outcome of an investigation.

Protective custody (PC) inmates have been admitted to a segregated unit for their own protection from other inmates. They cannot "make it" in general population because they are labeled as "snitches" or are simply too weak to survive without protection. They will remain there until they feel they can make it in the general population or until they complete their sentences.

The PC units are designed to be less punitive than administrative segregation or disciplinary segregation units. In these units, inmates are granted a considerable amount of freedom with respect to being out of their cells, during recreation time, participating in self-help programs, and even holding paid work assignments. They are allowed to have reading materials, radios, and perhaps even televisions (all paid for by the inmates) in their cells. In many units, these inmates will have cell mates rather than being single celled.

The most severe conditions are for prisoners placed in administrative segregation. Unlike the disciplinary segregation status, persons placed in "ad seg" will remain there for an indeterminate amount of time. In many ad seg units, there are prisoners who have been in custody for over ten years with no prospect of being released to the general population. The ad seg units are designed to be highly controlled and punitive. The prisoners will remain in these units until prison officials feel it is safe to release them once again. For these inmates, there is no known release date from these extremely punitive units. Some will never return to the general population and will remain locked down until they finish their entire sentence or die while imprisoned.

In these units, prison administrators have total physical control over all aspects of the inmate's behavior. Inmates assigned to such housing areas spend 23 to 24 hours a day in their single, 60×80-sq.-foot, high-security barren cells with minimal (if any) access to educational, religious, or other self-help programs. The amount of reading material is extremely limited and controlled as well as basic amenities (toothpaste, shaving cream, plastic razor). The front of the cell is often closed with a solid-steel-plate door with a slot to send food, mail, and other items provided by the prison. When an inmate is removed for a shower, a visit, or for recreation, he or she must kneel down with his or her back to the door and place both hands through the slot in the cell door so they can be handcuffed.

Most important, being locked up in segregation means that prisoners lose access to most programs and activities, which in most prisons are extensive: schooling, vocational training, movies, libraries, and recreational activities. When allowed out for "recreation," inmates are escorted to small, self-contained razor-wired recreation and exercise "cages" with no more than two or three inmates allowed at a time out on the yard. They are cut off from socializing with other prisoners during work, during meals, on the yard, and in the day rooms from engaging in literally dozens or hundreds of games, hustles, rackets, and other cooperative enterprises that prisoners undertake. They cannot talk to each other through the barred fronts of their cells or even play games, such as chess, on the walkway directly in front of their cells. For all intents and purposes, prisoners in lockup units are cut off from the general, relatively full social life of the prison world.

In general, these facilities and units represent the most extreme forms of punishment in a state's prison system. This trend should concern us greatly because it has many undesirable consequences for prison systems, for prisoners who experience long periods of lockup, and for the society that must receive most of these prisoners back when they are released.

HISTORY OF ADMINISTRATIVE SEGREGATION

The concept of administrative segregation grew out of the practice of solitary confinement, which prison administrators began using in the nineteenth century along with many other methods (such as flogging, water torture, shackling prisoners to cell walls) to punish particularly troublesome prisoners. By the beginning of the twentieth century, prison authorities had eliminated most of the other cruel forms of punishment but continued to confine prisoners in "solitary," or the "hole," as the major form of punishment for rule breaking. In his 1940 study of a "prison community," Donald Clemmer describes solitary confinement:

> The 24 solitary cells are in a small building known as the yard office. It is set off by itself and is heavily barred and isolated. The cells themselves contain no furniture. The one window is small, and the iron bars of the door have another wooden door which keeps the light from entering. The cells are cold in winter and hot in summer. The inmate is given one blanket and must sleep on a wooden slab raised about two inches from the cement flooring. One piece of bread and a necessary amount of water is allowed each day.[2]

During the first half of the twentieth century, all walled prisons had solitaries or "holes." Some, such as the tin sweat boxes in southern work camps or the "dungeon" in San Quentin, were extremely cruel places. The cells studied by Clemmer at the Illinois Menard maximum-security prison were about average. During this time, many prisons also had cells set aside for segregation of prisoners—such as persons who persistently broke the rules, "open" homosexuals, and persons who needed protection from others—who the administration believed could not be allowed to circulate freely among other prisoners (protective custody). Unlike solitary confinement, inmates could be held in segregation for long periods of time, sometimes years. When one of the authors of this book—James Austin—was first employed by the Illinois Department of Corrections in 1990, one inmate at the Joliet prison had been in administrative segregation ("the hole") for ten years.

By the 1950s, the old system of social order based on a convict code and a few prisoner leaders was breaking down, and new problems of disorder among prisoners developed. Consequently, states began developing new forms of administrative segregation to control an increasingly disruptive inmate population. Many states that had adopted the rehabilitative philosophy of penology—such as California, Illinois, New York, New Jersey, Wisconsin, Washington, and Minnesota—were able to gain conformity for a few years (1950 to 1955) through the indeterminate sentencing system. Using the margins of sentencing discretion contained in the indeterminate sentencing system, along with systems of "good-time" credits, inmates could reduce their time in prison, and prison officials and parole boards could threaten prisoners with longer lengths of stay if they did not conform. However, a small percentage of the prisoners were not responsive either to these sentencing incentives or to the threat of being placed in the "hole." In particular, youthful leaders of well-organized street gangs who had received lengthy prison terms for violent crimes began to assume a greater presence in maximum-security prisons. Prison administrators then expanded the use of administrative segregation to manage this growing and difficult-to-manage population.

By 1970, California had established so-called high-security "adjustment centers" (ACs) at its major maximum-security prisons of San Quentin, Folsom, and Soledad.[3] In Illinois, special program units (SPUs) were established at Joliet, Stateville, and Pontiac prisons in 1972. Other states soon followed in their efforts to isolate and control the most disruptive or potentially disruptive segments of the inmate population. When these first adjustment centers failed to reduce the turmoil and violence, more sections of several prisons were converted into new segregation units (for example, "segregated housing units" and "management control units").

Because the official purpose of segregation units was not punishment, the prison administrators initially planned the units' physical structure and routines so that they would not have any special punitive aspects. When segregation first began, the cells in segregation units were different than those in solitary units. They usually had the same furnishings as mainline cells—a bunk, mattress, toilet, washbowl, and sometimes a small desk. Moreover, the prisoners were not intentionally denied other basic privileges beyond those that were impractical to provide to them because they were restricted to their cells for virtually the entire day. Lockup prisoners could receive and keep about the same range of materials and commodities as mainline prisoners. They were either allowed TV sets in their cells, or they could watch a TV mounted in the unit. Their mail was not restricted. They received and kept books (although their access to the prison library was and is greatly restricted because of their lockup status).

These prisoners were somewhat protected from hostilities and assaults that were increasingly occurring among mainline prisoners. What they sacrificed for this increase in safety, however, was tremendous. Moreover, hostility and violence eventually became more intense in the lockup units than in the "mainline" general population.

TURMOIL IN LOCKUP

During the 1970s and early 1980s, the segregation units became extremely tumultuous and violent. This atmosphere was partly a result of the administrative practice of concentrating the most recalcitrant prisoners in the system to a situation of relatively severe deprivation. Many of them had not conformed to the rules in the much less restrictive mainline and were even less willing to do so in segregation.

Prison administrators began locking up suspected members of organizations believed to be a threat to order in the prison. Suspected leaders of the Black Muslims were the first to be segregated, followed by members of other Black religious and political organizations, such as the Black Panther Party. When organizations of other prisoners—Chicanos, Whites, and Puerto Ricans—appeared, the suspected leaders were assigned to segregation. In the 1970s, gangs of prisoners of the same race, involved in rackets and violence toward other gangs and individual prisoners, became the main concern of prison administrations, and all suspected leaders and many suspected members were isolated in the lockup units.

Making matters worse, several prisoners believed they had been unfairly placed and held in the segregation units. Placement was an administrative decision by a "classification committee" that involved minimal due process and, at best, a pro forma appearance by the inmate at the classification hearing. When Illinois began using its SPUs in 1972, for example, hundreds of inmates were "reclassified" for the Joliet SPU during a single weekend. Inmates were "heard" in hearings that lasted less than a minute.

Once assigned to these segregation units, prisoners' "cases" were reviewed again in a cursory manner. Frequently, the classification committee based its decision on hearsay information, such as that supplied by informers, sometimes anonymously, or on suspicions, such as those expressed in memos from staff who reported that they had witnessed prisoners engaging in acts that suggested the prisoners had been involved in some prohibited behavior. Even if an inmate had not been involved in any disciplinary actions, he or she could remain in the units simply because of staff suspicions.

For these reasons, lockup units became centers of turmoil. Prisoners engaged each other and guards in constant verbal attacks. A prisoner describes his experiences on entering one of the first adjustment centers in California:

> [We] were transferred to Soledad Correctional Facility from "X" Prison. We were placed in the Max Row section, O wing. Immediately entering the

sally-port area of this section, I could hear inmates shouting and making remarks such as, "Nigger is a scum low-down dog," etc. I couldn't believe my ears at first because I knew that if I could hear these things the officers beside me could too, and I started wondering what was going on. Then I fixed my eyes on the wing sergeant and I began to see the clear picture of why those inmates didn't care if the officials heard them instigating racial conflict. The sergeant was, and still is, Mr. M., a known prejudiced character toward Blacks. I was placed in a cell, and since that moment up 'till now, I have had no peace of mind. The white inmates make it a 24-hour job of cursing black inmates just for kicks, and the officials harass us with consistency also.[4]

Racial hostilities ran high in these units since they were filled with inmates representing most of the prison gangs. In Illinois, the dominant prison gangs—such as the Black P. Stone Rangers, the Black Disciples, the Vice Lords, and the Latin Kings—were constantly warring with one another for control. In California, the Aryan Brotherhood, the Black Guerrilla Family, the Mexican Mafia, and the La Nuestra Familia were strongly committed to attacking members of rival groups. When the opportunity presented itself—such as when members of opposing groups were released together to the exercise yard—prisoners fought, knifed, and killed each other. In 1970, a fight between several white and black prisoners housed in Soledad's O Wing broke out as soon as the Blacks and Whites in the section were released together to the exercise yard. A gun tower guard fired at the prisoners and killed three black prisoners.

Prisoners often broke up their cell furnishings—the beds, cabinets, and toilets. On these occasions, water ran out of the cells down the tiers onto the floors. Often the floors in the cells were littered with trash thrown from cells and water running out of cells. To regain order, the staff would shoot tear gas into the units and use "stun guns" or "tasers" to subdue inmates. In return, prisoners in lockup units constantly taunted and vilified their guards. They regularly threw any liquid material, sometimes urine and feces, on passing guards, and occasionally they assaulted and/or murdered them.

Not surprisingly, as these conditions worsened in adjustment centers, guards grew more hostile toward the prisoners. They were deeply offended and angered by the revolutionary rhetoric delivered by some of the more politically oriented prisoners, in which guards ("pigs" or "the police") were excoriated. For example, George Jackson, who was held in adjustment centers for most of his twenty years in California prisons, wrote in 1970:

The great majority of Soledad pigs are southern migrants who do not want to work in the fields and farms of the area, who can't sell cars or insurance, and who couldn't tolerate the discipline of the army. And, of course, prisons attract sadists. Pigs come here to feed on the garbage heap for two reasons really, the first half because they can do no other work, frustrated men are soon to develop sadistic mannerisms; and the second half, sadists out front, suffering under the restraints placed upon them by an equally sadistic, vindictive society. The sadist knows that to practice his religion upon the society at large will bring down upon his head their sadistic reaction.[5]

The guards' hatred deepened when lockup prisoners increased their verbal taunts, began throwing objects and liquid on them, and occasionally succeeded in murdering them. Guards occasionally responded by punishing and harassing prisoners in every way they could. They delivered their own taunts and vilification, occasionally beat prisoners, and frequently shortened, disrupted, or denied privileges, such as correspondence, exercise, and visits that lockup prisoners were supposed to receive. Evidence of these practices was obtained in 1975 by the federal district court investigating the conditions in lockup units:

> Two guards who used to work in the AC testified in support of plaintiffs' allegations that guards have beaten, threatened, and harassed plaintiffs and other first tier AC prisoners, that prisoner reports are at times altered, and that AC guards have a stereotyped view of plaintiffs and treat them in a dehumanizing fashion.[6]

Some guards entered into the conflicts between prisoner factions by aiding one group of prisoners against others or "setting up" individual prisoners. Occasionally, this was done in a routine fashion. For example, a white prisoner who was identified as being affiliated with the Aryan Brotherhood describes his setup by a black guard:

> This black guard was escorting me back to my cell in Max B [a section of the Adjustment Center] and he stopped and handcuffed me to the rail on the row housing black prisoners and said he would be right back. Then he went and unlocked the row to let all the black dudes out to exercise. As they passed by me, they kicked me, spit on me and punched me. Then he came back and put me in my cell.[7]

Sometimes guards set prisoners up to be killed and even participated in the homicides. In the fighting and killings in the Soledad adjustment center yard, in which three black prisoners were shot to death, a Salinas, California, jury found that eight Soledad staff members had willfully and unjustifiably conspired to kill the three prisoners. The staff had released prisoners who were expected to begin fighting. The gun tower guard, who some prisoners reported was leaning out of his tower aiming at the prisoners when the fight began, fired five shots and hit the three black prisoners in the middle of their torsos. Afterward, the guards took over 30 minutes to carry one mortally wounded prisoner to the hospital even though it was adjacent to the adjustment center.[8]

The "staging" of fights with inmates in high-security prisons has again surfaced in the California prison system. At the notorious Corcoran facility, a federal investigation has been launched by the FBI and the U.S. Department of Justice into allegations that guards would purposely put inmates from rival gangs in the same recreation yard and place bets on who would survive. In one such incident, an inmate was shot to death by a guard who claims he fired to break off the staged fight.

Guards and the administration steadily reduced the old privileges of the adjustment centers until the distinction between the former punitive solitary units and the nonpunitive adjustment centers had all but disappeared. A psychiatrist appointed by the Northern California federal district court to examine the adjustment center unit in San Quentin in 1980, comments on the conditions:

> When I walked through Security Housing Unit 2 at San Quentin and heard constant angry screaming and saw garbage flung angrily from so many cells, I felt like I was in a pre-1793 mental asylum, and the excessive security itself was creating the madness. While the mainline playing fields at San Quentin are large and grassy, the various security units are small and paved. Prisoners are not allowed any furniture (desks, chairs, etc.) and are prevented by regulations from even draping their cells with blankets to improve insulation against cold winds. Deprived of most acceptable human means of expressing self, prisoners are left with a meager token of wall decorations.[9]

Instead of having locations where prisoners were incapacitated and pacified in a controlled but humane setting, the lockup units became the most dangerous (for both prisoners and staff), punitive, and deleterious settings in American prisons. Robert Slater, who worked at San Quentin as a psychiatrist between 1982 and 1984, describes the violence in that prison's adjustment center:

> Periodically, bursts of gunfire serve as unpleasant reminders of where we are. Occasionally, a prisoner is killed, maimed, or blinded by gunshot. Crude but effective spears, bombs, hot or corrosive liquids can, and are, hurled through the bars in either direction. In the summer of 1984, during a particularly violent period, the authorities in one of the lockup units brought together a Mexican leader and a Black leader, asking them to walk the tiers together to help cool things down. They agreed to do this. While walking the tiers, a Mexican inmate threw a knife through the bars to the Mexican leader, who proceeded to kill the Black leader.[10]

THE MOVE TO SUPERMAX PRISONS

The apparent failure of administrative segregation units to pacify prisoners and restore order to the prisons during the 1970s and early 1980s did not cause penologists to abandon the policy of concentrating troublesome prisoners in permanent lockup units. What they have done instead is to construct new "maxi-maxi" prisons in which they have attempted to eliminate the features believed to have caused the breakdown of order.

The Federal Bureau of Prisons (BOP) first attempted this goal when it took over Alcatraz Island, the site of an old army prison, and opened a small, maximum-security federal prison in 1934. Alcatraz was intended to house the most "desperate criminals" (for example, "Machine Gun" Kelly, Al Capone) and the bureau's most troublesome prisoners. By the early 1960s, the feds, particularly the attorney general Robert Kennedy, considered the "Rock," which housed only 275 prisoners, an expensive failure and closed it in 1963. Its prisoners were dispersed among other federal prisons, mostly Atlanta and Leavenworth, the two most secure prisons next to Alcatraz.

At this time, the BOP was constructing a new small prison at Marion, Illinois, as an experiment in behavior modification. The prison had a range of units with varying degrees of security. About 350 prisoners were supposed to work their way through the levels, increasing their privileges by demonstrating good conduct. In 1973, however, the BOP returned to the policy of concentrating its troublesome prisoners in one place and began transferring them to Marion's "control unit."[11] The feds continued to send more troublesome prisoners to Marion and reclassified it in 1979 as their only "Level 6" (highest-security) penitentiary, designated for prisoners who (1) threatened or injured other inmates or staff; (2) possessed deadly weapons or dangerous drugs; (3) disrupted "the orderly operation of a prison"; or (4) escaped or attempted to escape when the attempt involved injury, threat of life, or use of deadly weapons. Since its complete conversion to a prison for problem inmates, Marion has experienced difficulties very similar to those in California's lockup units. Through the 1970s, tensions, hostilities, violence, and disruptions increased. In the early 1980s, the unrest reached new heights. From February 1980 to June 1983, there were fifty-four serious prisoner-on-prisoner assaults, eight prisoners were killed, and there were twenty-eight serious assaults on the staff.

The turmoil escalated further in the summer and autumn of 1983. In July, two prisoners took two officers hostage in the disciplinary segregation unit; one officer was stabbed. In the following week, two inmates attacked two officers escorting prisoners from the dining hall. Prisoner-to-prisoner violence increased in this period, and most of the time the prison was placed on complete "lockdown" status. On September 5th, a prisoner assaulted an officer with a mop wringer and a chair. On October 10, an officer was assaulted when he tried to break up an attack by prisoners on another prisoner. On October 22, when three officers were moving a prisoner housed in the control unit, the prisoner stopped to talk to another inmate in a cell, then turned to face the officers, his handcuffs unlocked and a knife in his hands. He succeeded in murdering one officer.

That evening another prisoner was being escorted by three officers from one section of the prison to the recreation cage. He too stopped in front of another prisoner's cell and turned around with his handcuffs removed and a knife in his hands. He succeeded in stabbing all three officers, one fatally. The turmoil in the prison continued for another month. Prisoners started fires, threw trash out of their cells, and continued to assault other prisoners and staff. Repeated searches produced weapons, handcuff keys, lock picks, hacksaw blades, heroin, and drug paraphernalia.

The BOP finally instituted new severe control procedures. David Ward and Allen Breed, who conducted a study of Marion for the U.S. House of Representatives, describe the clampdown:

> New custodial procedures were implemented. All correctional officers were
> issued riot batons and instructed to carry them at all times. A special

operations squad, known as "The A Team," arrived from Leavenworth and groups of Marion officers began to receive training in techniques of conducting forced cell moves and controlling resistant inmates. These officers were outfitted with helmets, riot control equipment and special uniforms. A new directive ordered that before any inmate left his cell he was to place his hands behind his back near the food tray slot in the cell door so that handcuffs could be placed on his wrists and leg irons on his ankles. No inmate was to be moved from his cell for any reason without a supervisor and three officers acting as an escort. Digital rectal searches were ordered for all inmates entering and leaving the Control Unit along with strip searches of inmates before and after visits with the attorneys.[12]

Because Marion had not been designed to hold the most troublesome prisoners, many of its features, such as open cell fronts, turned out to present problems to the staff in their attempts to maintain complete control over recalcitrant prisoners. Many states are building new maxi-maxi prisons designed specifically to hold recalcitrants. In general, these prisons are built to hold prisoners in small, secure, self-contained units. Ward and Breed, in commenting on the inadequacy of Marion's design, describe this type of prison:

> New generation prisons are generally comprised of six to eight physically separated units within a secure perimeter. Each unit of some 40–50 inmates, all in individual cells, contains dining and laundry areas, counseling offices, indoor game rooms, a wire enclosed outdoor recreation yard and a work area. The physical design of inmate rooms calls for only one or two levels on the outdoor side(s) of the unit to facilitate, from secure control "bubbles," easy and continuous staff surveillance of all areas in which inmates interact with each other and with staff.[13]

In addition, the cells in new maxi-maxi prisons usually have solid doors with a shatterproof glass window and an opening through which prisoners can be fed or handcuffed without opening the door. The basic idea is that prisoners, while being held in small secure units and unable to congregate or communicate with each other, can be delivered all essential services (for example, food and medical services). This would avoid the problems administrators encounter when they "lock down" an older prison, which greatly disrupts the delivery of essential services to prisoners. In addition, when prisoners in the new maxi-maxi prisons are kept in their cells, they cannot throw things, yell to each other, or assault guards, as is the case in older prisons, even in the segregation units. In 1994, the BOP opened a new Supermax prison in Florence, Colorado, which was referred to as "Alcatraz of the Rockies."

Other states began to follow the lead of the BOP. By 1997 fifteen states had constructed new supermax facilities; another seven states constructed a separate unit within a larger prison. Among the leading major states that constructed brand-new separate facilities were Virginia, Ohio, Illinois, Nevada, New Mexico, Wisconsin, Texas, and Minnesota. Among these states, California is the clear leader in the construction and use of supermaxes. It has built four new maxi-maxi prisons with a total capacity of 12,000. Within these maximum security prisons are the special housing units or SHUs. And "special" they are.

All have "units" or "pods" that cluster around a control center from which heavily armed guards look down on the units twenty-four hours a day. The cells have fully sealed front doors to restrict objects being thrown by inmates at the staff. Each unit typically has a small day room and an adjacent exercise yard.

The Pelican Bay facility, the last of the four to open, is located in an extremely remote area of northern California. Built in 1990 at a cost of $278 million, it was designed to hold 2,080 maximum-security inmates, but it soon became overcrowded with an inmate population of 3,250. Within the prison itself, the segregated housing unit has the capacity for 1,056 prisoners.

Pelican Bay is entirely automated and designed so that inmates have virtually no face-to-face contact with the guards or other inmates. For 22½ hours a day, inmates are confined to their windowless cells that were built of solid blocks of concrete and stainless steel. Now the inmates would not have access to materials they could fashion into weapons. They do not work in prison industries; they do not have access to recreation; they do not mingle with other inmates. They are not even allowed to smoke because matches are considered a security risk. Inmates eat all meals in their cells and leave only for brief showers and ninety minutes of daily exercise. They shower alone, and they exercise alone in miniature yards of barren patches of cement enclosed by twenty-foot-high cement walls covered with metal screens. The doors to their cells are opened and closed electronically by a guard in a control booth.

There are virtually no bars in the facility; the cell doors are made of perforated sheets of stainless steel with slots for food trays. Nor are the guards walking the tiers with keys on their belts. Instead, the guards are locked away in glass-enclosed control booths, and they communicate with prisoners through a speaker system. The segregated housing unit has its own infirmary, its own law library (where prisoners are kept in secure rooms and slipped law books through slots), and its own room for parole hearings. Inmates can spend years without stepping outside the unit.

California's then-Governor George Deukmejian, dedicating the new prison on June 14, 1990, boasted that "California now possesses a state-of-the-art prison that will serve as a model for the rest of the nation.... Pelican Bay symbolizes our philosophy that the best way to reduce crime is to put convicted criminals behind bars." This prison is the most completely isolated prison since the early penitentiaries in Pennsylvania. Since the majority of the inmates housed at Pelican Bay are from the Los Angeles area, which is nine hundred miles away with no available air transportation, the prospect for regular visits from inmates' families is extremely remote.[14]

The description of the California SHUs is not unique. Here is a description of New York's new supermax, as reported in the *New York Times*:

> The New York prison, Southport Correctional Facility, has the same mission: to take the worst prisoners. They will include those who have dealt drugs behind bars, attacked guards, even murdered inmates. At Southport, they are being kept isolated, shackled at the waist and wrists when allowed out of their 6 by 10 foot cells and made to spend their daily recreation hour in newly built cages.[15]

Illinois constructed a supermax prison in the southern part of Illinois, far away from Chicago where about 60 percent of the inmates come from. Known as the Tamms supermax, it was opened 1995 A description of Illinois' supermax prison in a remote area of Illinois was reported by the *Chicago Tribune* in 2009:

> Situated amid rolling hills and farms in the southern tip of Illinois, the state's only "super-max" prison was built during the get-tough-on-crime wave that swept the nation in the 1990s. It was designed to house the state's most dangerous inmates.
>
> Conditions are harsh—and meant to be. For at least 23 hours a day, prisoners sit in solitary confinement in 7-by-12-foot cells. There is no mess hall—meals are shoved through a chuckhole in cell doors. Contact with the outside world is sharply restricted. For a rare visit from relatives or friends, inmates are strip-searched, chained to a concrete stool and separated from visitors by a thick glass wall. There are no jobs and limited educational opportunities.[16]

In describing the conditions at the eight-hundred-bed Ohio State Penitentiary (OSP) that was constructed as a state-of-the-art supermax prison, the U.S. Supreme Court made the following observations:

> Conditions at OSP are more restrictive than any other form of incarceration in Ohio, including conditions on its death row or in its administrative control units. The latter are themselves a highly restrictive form of solitary confinement. In OSP almost every aspect of an inmate's life is controlled and monitored. Inmates must remain in their cells, which measure 7 by 14 feet, for 23 hours per day. A light remains on in the cell at all times, though it is sometimes dimmed, and an inmate who attempts to shield the light to sleep is subject to further discipline. During the one hour per day that an inmate may leave his cell, access is limited to one of two indoor recreation cells. Incarceration at OSP is synonymous with extreme isolation. In contrast to any other Ohio prison, including any segregation unit, OSP cells have solid metal doors with metal strips along their sides and bottoms which prevent conversation or communication with other inmates. All meals are taken alone in the inmate's cell instead of in a common eating area. Opportunities for visitation are rare and in all events are conducted through glass walls. It is fair to say OSP inmates are deprived of almost any environmental or sensory stimuli and of almost all human contact.[17]

THE CONSEQUENCES OF LOCKUP

It is far from clear whether the expanded use of lockup has made prisons easier to manage. However, lockup certainly has a very negative effect on the prisoners who experience long periods of isolation in the various lockup units.

The Self-Fulfilling Prophecy

When people are believed to have certain characteristics, whether they actually have them or not, they are likely to develop those characteristics or have them magnified because of the treatment. This phenomenon frequently occurs when people are classified as recalcitrant and placed in lockup units. Many inmates, who have been minor "troublemakers," or who are mistakenly believed to be intensely or intimately involved in prohibited activities (such as revolutionary or gang activities), have been placed in lockup units and then have actually fulfilled the prophecy—that is, they have become serious troublemakers, committed revolutionaries, or gang members.

Several processes accomplish this transformation. In the first place, many people are filled with considerable frustration, anger, and a sense of injustice when they believe they have been unfairly placed in lockup. As mentioned earlier, the process of classifying inmates to lockup is often based on hearsay information of dubious reliability. Administrators have a great need to cultivate and rely on information supplied by informers, and they have regularly accepted anonymous information ("notes dropped") and have often coerced many inmates into supplying information on other prisoners. For example, administrators usually require a prisoner who is seeking protection or is trying to drop out of a gang to name persons who were threatening him or were involved in prohibited activities, such as gang activities.

They have also offered significant incentives to informers—transfers, letters to the parole board, or placement in protective custody. Although some of the information supplied by informers has been reliable, much has not been reliable. What occurred simultaneously with new forms of disruption, that prison administrations have been trying to control through the use of informants, was the loss of cohesion among prisoners and a weakening of the convict code, which dictated, above all, not to snitch. A new ethic has emerged, and it guides many prisoners; it is based on the general principle of everyone for himself or herself, or "dog eat dog." Informing for personal gain is consistent with this new code and has become much more commonplace. Even falsely accusing fellow inmates for personal advantage is a practice approved of by many prisoners. For example, a prisoner who was transferred from Soledad to San Quentin's segregated housing unit claimed to have been the subject of false accusations by an informer:

> I had this good gig, disc-jockey on the prison radio, and this black dude wanted my job. So he told them that I was active in the AB [Aryan Brotherhood]. I wasn't. I got a lot of friends who are AB. But I've never been AB. I played a lot of Western music, and a lot of people didn't like that and didn't like me. The rat who snitched me out of the job didn't like my music. But really he wanted to replace me. So he told the man I was an active AB.[18]

In making their decision to segregate, committees also regularly accept staff observations of questionable validity. The following is an example of statements taken from memos in files of persons assigned to lockup because of gang affiliations:

> I observed inmate A talking to inmates B, C, and D on many occasions. They seem to have been involved in gang-type activities together.[19]

The highly discretionary and arbitrary nature of the gang designation is revealed in the following California correctional officer's description of the process:

> There's three, four, five different ways that they can be designated as a gang member. They're either northern or southern Mexicans just by birth. If they're from south of Bakersfield, they're going to be southern unit. If they're from north of Bakersfield, they're going to be Nostra [Nuestra] Familia. And that's just something that doesn't change. Now after that, you get associations. If, for example, we're talking about Nostra Familia, and that's the northern gang, and there's an inmate you know associates, has been observed by staff who's seen writings in his letters, if you can use two of the five or six different methods of validation, then you can call him an associate. Letter writing, another inmate telling you, admission of the inmate himself, staff observation, there's several ways to observe and two of the five or six different ways, I believe, will validate him as an associate. Then to be a validated member, then I think it's four out of five or six, you have to be observed by staff, have another inmate tell you, though incriminating himself, he can tell you. Now, you may never ever take any of these vows or do any of their footwork or anything, but just because you hang with people from where you come, you associate with them. Once you've been validated as an associate, or validated as a member, then they can give you an indeterminate SHU term.[20]

Consequently, many inmates who have had minor behavioral problems in prison or have had a weak or no affiliation with some of the organizations suspected of engaging in extremely rapacious, violent, and disruptive behavior have been placed in lockup units.

A prisoner in Illinois recently explained that he has been identified as an escape risk that is keeping him in the state's supermax facility.

Q. Okay. I also see that you are wearing green stripes on your shirts. Can you tell us what that is?

A. Level E status. That means high escape risk.

Q. And how did you come to be classified as level E?

A. That happened at Tamms in 2002.

Q. What happened?

A. Well, they had placed me at Tamms and, you know, the monotony was getting to me, things like that. By being stuck in that cell and nobody to talk to and just minimum contact with other inmates or staff or whatever. And in order to move around and be able to talk to other people, things like that,

I wrote a letter to the major saying that if he doesn't move me out of the cell by 3:00 I will be halfway to Chicago. And things like that.

Q. And it was after that that they classified you as a high escape risk?

A. Yeah, they made me level E.

Q. Why is being classified as a high escape risk something that you wanted to happen?

A. Well, because I didn't actually—I just wanted to move around because I was stuck in that one cell. I wanted to move around from pod to pod, from wing to wing so I could be able to, you know, talk to other people, you know. I wanted to break up the monotonous routine.

Q. It is now seven years later and you are still—

A. Level E.

Q. Have they told you what you need to do to get out of level E?

A. No, they never told me.

Once in the lockup units, prisoners experience the ordinary deprivations inherent in lockup status, and they frequently witness or are subjected to the additional abuse that results from lockup guards; they express their extreme racism and general hostility toward lockup prisoners. This harassment further enrages many prisoners:

> One day when I got back from the visiting room, inmate M told me that the police had attacked W, a black inmate, while being handcuffed and taken to isolation. We protested according to their ways, and we threw some liquid on officer D, since he was the cause of W getting attacked. They came back and threw tear gas into our cells until we almost died—seriously—I had to wave a towel since I was choking from the gas. They told me that they wouldn't open the door until I got undressed, backed up to the door and stuck my arms out. I did just that. They handcuffed me and dragged me to the other side naked.[21]

In addition, the policy in many state prisons (such as Illinois, Texas, and California) throughout the 1970s and early 1980s was to locate suspected gang members in sections designated for a particular gang. This practice often forces prisoners, with weak or no affiliation, to become closer to the gang for two reasons. First, placing inmates in the unit with a particular gang results in their being viewed as a definite member of that gang, and it subjects them to the threats and attacks of other rival gangs. Second, if they are accepted by the other gang members, the dynamics of being held in close, exclusive interaction with these others strengthens the bonds between them. Consequently, weak or no gang affiliation is often converted to full membership by the lockup decision.

"Monsters"—"They Treat Me Like a Dog, I'll Be a Dog"   Many inmates held for long periods in lockup, during which they have been subjected to extreme racial prejudice, harassment by the guards, and threats and attacks from other prisoners, are converted into extremely violent, relatively fearless individuals who profess and conduct themselves as if they do not care whether they live or die. They frequently attack the staff as well as other prisoners. Examples of this extreme form of recalcitrance abound. George Jackson, held many years in lockup, writes:

> This monster—the monster they've engendered in me—will return to torment its maker, from the grave, the pit, the profoundest pit. Hurl me into the next existence, the descent into hell won't turn me. I'll crawl back to dog his trail forever. They won't defeat my revenge, never, never. I'm part of a righteous people who anger slowly, but rage undammed. We'll gather at this door in such a number that the rumbling of our feet will make the earth tremble. I'm going to charge them for this 28 years without gratification. I'm going to charge them like a maddened, wounded, rogue male elephant—ears flared, trunk raised, trumpet blaring. I'll do my dance on his chest, and the only thing he'll ever see in my eyes is a dagger to pierce his cruel heart. This is one nigger who is positively displeased. I'll never forgive, I'll never forget, and if I'm guilty of anything at all it's of not leaning on them enough. War without terms.[22]

Jackson, after he had succeeded in overpowering guards who had escorted him back to lockup in San Quentin and in releasing other prisoners in the unit, was shot and killed while running toward San Quentin's front gate. Some of the inmates Jackson had released proceeded to murder two prisoners and two guards in the lockup unit.

The two prisoners both murdered a guard while being escorted by four guards at Marion in 1983; they were fellow AB members who had been held in lockup for many years and who had vowed they would both kill a guard on that day. They murdered the guards even though they understood that they would suffer severe, immediate, and long-term consequences. They were beyond caring about consequences, or even their own lives.

In New York, Willie Bosket, who has served most of his life in prison and has been held in lockup for years, told the court that had just sentenced him to an additional twenty-five years to life for stabbing a prison guard:

> The sentence this court can impose on me means nothing. I laugh at you, I laugh at this court, I laugh at Mr. Prosecutor, I laugh at this entire damn system. I'll haunt this damn system. I am what the system created but never expected.[23]

Psychological Impairment

Since the introduction of the first "penitentiaries," in which prisoners were placed in complete solitary confinement, observers have concluded that isolation from others and am extreme reduction of activities produce considerable psychological damage. Charles Dickens, who visited Eastern Penitentiary, the first "solitary" prison, wrote:

> I am persuaded that those who devised this system [solitary confinement] ... do not know what it is that they are doing.... I hold that this slow and daily

tampering with the mysteries of the brain, to be immeasurably worse than any torture of the body.

My firm conviction is that, independent of the mental anguish it occasions—an anguish so acute and so tremendous, that all imagination of it must fall far short of the reality—it wears the mind into a morbid state, which renders it unfit for the rough contact and busy action of the world. It is my fixed opinion that those who have undergone this punishment, must pass into society again morally unhealthy and diseased.[24]

Regrettably, only a few systematic studies of the effects of confinement in lockup situations have been conducted. In one, Richard McCleery found that prisoners held in lockup settings for long periods were very prone to developing paranoid delusion belief systems.[25] Terry A. Kupers, a psychiatrist, with long experience with prisons who was assigned to give expert testimony in a suit involving California lockup units, wrote to the court:

Certainly, patients I see in the community who have spent any length of time in Security Housing, Management Control or Adjustment Center units at San Quentin have continued to display irrational fears of violence against themselves, and have demonstrated little ability to control their own rage. I know from many psychotherapies I have conducted and histories I have taken, that even when a patient entered prison angry, the largest part of the fear and rage was bred by the prison experience itself.

Some of these men [prisoners held in lockup for long periods] suffer mental "breakdowns," be they schizophrenic, depressive, hysterical or other. A much larger number suffer less visible but very deep psychological scars. They do not "break down," but they remain anxious, angry, depressed, insecure or confused, and then likely cover over these feelings with superficial bravado. They might later commit suicide, or merely fail to adjust when released, and become another statistic of recidivism.[26]

Kupers summarized the psychiatric literature on the effects of lockup in the following statement to the court:

There is general agreement today in the scientific community that the stress of life in segregation is the larger cause of high incidence rates of mental disorders amongst prisoners.[27]

A Pelican Bay SHU prisoner puts it well:

If you have not been informed of this new SHU program here in Pelican Bay, well, I think hell is a better place than this as it is built to break people. Since I have been here [one month] a man has gone literally nutty in the mind. What can you expect when you're isolated from all human contact? You sleep, eat, go to a yard by yourself, go to classification just to be told that you'll stay in the hole until you parole, die, or debrief, rat![28]

The Northern California Federal District Court states:

Based on studies undertaken in this case, and the entirety of the record bearing on this claim, the court finds that many, if not most, inmates in the SHU experience some degree of psychological trauma in reaction to their extreme social isolation and the severely restricted environmental stimulation in the SHU.[29]

More recently, inmates at the Tamms supermax stated the challenge of remaining sane.

For longtime inmates at Tamms, the biggest challenge is to stay busy and avoid "bugging out"—losing touch with reality. Tyrone Dorn, who was transferred to Tamms after prison assaults, passes the time reading the Quran and playing chess with an inmate housed upstairs in the same wing. They shout out moves to each other. "This place takes a toll on your entire body from a mental and physical standpoint," he said.

Chicago Tribune, 2009 p. 2

Isolation from communicating with other people. Communicating with other people just to go on the yard with other people, you know. To have that connection with someone, you know. You can talk to someone behind a door and you are isolated 23 hours a day. But it is a totally different situation if you are allowed to be with other inmates around and communicate, you know. And that type of way it's totally different. You got to have—you got to be in that situation to understand that. And it takes a toll. And it takes a big toll. I don't feel the same.

Interview with Prisoner Johnny Almodovar, Tamms, Illinois Department of Corrections, July 20, 2010.

Q. How about your mental state? Has that changed at all since you were in Tamms?

A. Well, I'm stressed out most of the time. A lot of anxiety. If I even think that I'm getting a call pass my stomach starts to hurting, I have murmurs—palpations [sic], I mean. The mornings of yard, stressed out. I'm not good around people anymore. I don't want to be around people.

Q. And were you that way before you went to Tamms?

A. No.

Interview with Prisoner Joe Sorrentino, Illinois Department of Corrections, July 20, 2010.[30]

Social Impairment

Prisoners confront extreme difficulties in adjusting to outside life and achieving basic viability; most of their problems stem from having been a prisoner. One of the reasons for this is that they have become profoundly habituated to the prison routine, which is quite different from outside patterns, and have been imbued with various forms and layers of the prisoner perspective. Prisoners who have been held in lockup encounter greater difficulties because the routine in lockup is rigid and "abnormal." In addition, many or most lockup prisoners have been influenced by the more extreme and deviant viewpoints (for instance, that of the "outlaw") that prevail in lockup and suffer extreme anxiety and paranoia about living in a world of conspiracies, threats, and actual violence.

Most persons held in lockup settings are eventually released to the outside, often directly from lockup. An SHU prisoner makes this point well:

> OK. I've been in jail now eight years. Let's say I was going home tomorrow, do you mean to tell me I sit here for eight years confined in a cell resentful of things, chained every minute of my time inside my cell. And they say I am just too dangerous for anything but tomorrow they will parole me to the streets. Is there logic there? There is no logic there. The guy is paroled from these units, straight from the cells, straight to the situation, straight to the streets. How in the hell are they suppose to function out there? Is it possible? It is not anywhere possible. There is no decompression time, there is no reorientation time or nothing. When I am paroled I will be paroled to the streets, the outside to where you're at, you know what I mean. But in the meantime every time I see you, I will be setting like this.[31]

We should be concerned by the fact that the prison systems are spewing out such damaged human material, most of whom will disappear into our social trash heap, politely labeled the "homeless" or the underclass, or, worse, will violently lash out, perhaps murdering or raping someone and then be taken back to the dungeon.

THE DECLINING USE OF SUPER MAXES

It now appears that the supermaxes are beginning to wane. This has occurred for two reasons. First, some states overestimated the need for a supermax facility. Once built, these facilities have never been filled to capacity. In 2006, Wisconsin Department of Corrections officials announced that over the past sixteen years, the state's Supermax facility in Boscobel—built at a cost of $47.5 million (in 1990 dollars) and with a capacity of 500 inmates—has always stood at 100 cells less than its capacity. It will now be housing maximum security prisoners—serious offenders, but a step down from the worst of the worst.[32]

Similarly, the Maryland Correctional Adjustment Center, which was the state's supermax located in Baltimore, was opened in 1989 at a cost of $21 million (in 1989 dollars) with room for 288 inmates. Like Wisconsin, the structure has never been at capacity. Not only does it hold the state's most dangerous prisoners, it also houses 100 or so inmates who are working their way through the federal courts; it also serves as the home for Maryland's ten death row convicts. By 2010, the state had decided to sell the facility to the BOP.

In Illinois, the Tamms Supermax was built with a capacity of over 500 inmates, has never been more than half full. Operating only at 50 percent capacity, the average cost per inmate at Tamms is three times the average cost for a general population inmate.

But the second reason that supermax facilities are in decline has been the amount of litigation that has been directed at such prisons. At Tamms, a lawsuit was filed in 2006 that challenged the state on the conditions of confinement and lack of due process. In a 2010 decision, the federal court imposed restrictions on who can be admitted there and for what reasons. These restrictions plus an agreement by the Illinois Department of Corrections has slowed the number of admissions to Tamms and has expedited the releases.[33]

Similarly, the Ohio supermax (Ohio State Penitentiary or OSP) saw its population drop from 800 to less than 150 after litigation was filed with the federal court on the criteria for admitting someone to OSP. The court also ruled that similar criteria must be established governing how long someone could be retained in the supermax.[34] Once the court ruled and objective criteria were established, the population began to decline. To fill the void it has added death row and other inmate populations to the Ohio State Penitentiary.

A GLIMMER OF HOPE—HOW AND WHY MISSISSIPPI CLOSED ITS SUPERMAX[35]

Like Ohio and Illinois, Mississippi was sued in 2003 by the ACLU and by the law firm of Holland and Knight to challenge the plight of prisoners in Unit 32 at Mississippi State Penitentiary, Parchman (*Russell v. Epps*, 2003; *Presley v. Epps*, 2007). Unit 32, a one-thousand-cell super-maximum security facility, contained the state's death row plus a large number of cells for Administrative Segregation or long-term isolated confinement. The prisoners described a harsh environment: deep isolation, unrelieved idleness and monotony, little access to exercise, stench, and filth. The toilet in every cell had a "ping-pong" mechanism: whenever it was flushed, it pushed the waste back up into the bowl in the adjoining cell. Infestations of mosquitoes, flies, and other stinging insects were so bad, the prisoners wrote, that they had to keep their windows closed and their bodies completely covered even in the hottest weather—and the temperatures in the cells during the long Mississippi Delta summers were extreme. Leaks in the roof and water from flooded toilets filled their cells ankle-deep in foul water. They were moved into cells smeared from floor to ceiling with excrement by previous psychotic tenants. The light was so dim that many couldn't see to read or write. They complained that they didn't have access to necessary medical, dental, and mental health care.

Both guards and prisoners were under constant intense stress. Psychotic inmates started fires, flooded the tiers, and smeared feces; their screams, sobs, and ranting made it virtually impossible for the other prisoners to sleep or even to concentrate, day or night. Security officers, short-handed and exposed every day to conditions almost as punishing for them as for the inmates, responded with force to the chaos caused by mentally ill inmates. Take-down teams extracted prisoners from their cells and subdued them with pepper spray and other chemical agents, adding to the toxic environment caused by fire and flooding. An environmental expert later found heat index readings in excess of 120° F. The medical expert found that it was inevitable the excessive heat would result in illness, permanent disabilities, and premature deaths. The psychiatric expert found that the combined conditions in Unit 32 were likely to cause mental breakdowns in healthy inmates and profound psychosis in those with preexisting psychiatric problems.

In August, 2005, Federal Judge Jerry Davis who had been overseeing the cases for many years summoned the parties to his courtroom to urge the parties to sit down together to resolve the Unit 32 case without further discovery or trial. A follow-up study found that 80 percent of the 1,000 men at Unit 32 did not belong in administrative segregation and should be released from lockdown into the general prison population. A clearly defined incentive program was then developed that permitted prisoners to earn their return to the general population as they met behavior-based criteria. A dining hall was being constructed so that for the first time prisoners would be able to eat meals together. For the first time, prisoners were being allowed to play sports and to recreate together. Over a six-month period the number of inmates assigned to administrative segregation dropped from over 900 to less than 150.

During this time the number of violent incidents and the number of incidents requiring "use of force" (actions by security staff where force is employed, for example, spraying a prisoner with immobilizing gas or "taking down" a recalcitrant prisoner) plummeted. Monthly statistics showed a drop of almost 70 percent in serious incidents, both prisoner-on-staff and prisoner-on-prisoner incidents (see Figure 6-1). Similarly, the number of "uses of force" has declined significantly since 2007 (see Figure 6-2).

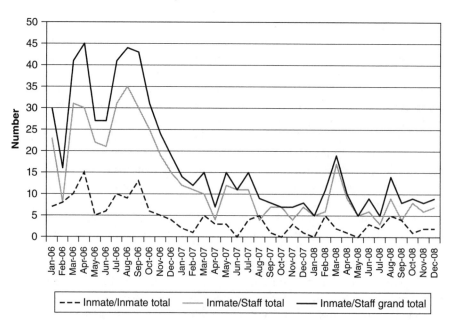

FIGURE 6-1 Serious Incidents at Unit 32 2006–2008

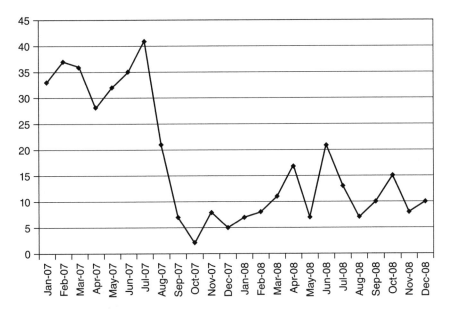

FIGURE 6-2 Use of Force at Unit 32 2007–2008

These reductions in serious incidents at Unit 32 as well as the number of uses of force were no doubt attributable, in part, to changes in classification and in the changed management of prisoners with serious mental illness. But it is also true that the Unit 32 population has declined dramatically from about nine hundred to below one hundred. It may be that the rate of incidents has either remained the same or even increased. The DOC did not have detailed population counts for Unit 32 by month so those rates cannot be computed. But one should note that those prisoners who remained in Unit 32 had serious misconduct records— more so than those who have been released.

In reviewing changes at one facility, it is important to also take into account changes that are occurring at other state facilities that may be counterproductive. In some states, compliance with a court's consent decree to downsize a super-maximum security unit or to exclude prisoners with serious mental illness from isolated confinement have resulted in the transfer of this population to isolated confinement at a different institution that is not under the court's jurisdiction. In the Mississippi DOC, recent statewide figures reflect that this "moving of the problem elsewhere" has not occurred. In fact, the Mississippi DOC has taken to heart the plan to revise classifications, establish effective mental health pro-gramming, and downsize isolated confinement in the entire state. As noted above, as of February 2009, the number of prisoners in administrative segregation at Unit 32 decreased from just over nine hundred to below one hundred (an additional ninety to one hundred prisoners are in segregation status on death row), and statewide, the number in administrative segregation (outside of death row) is 181. The population of MDOC is approximately twenty-one thousand, which means that about 1 percent of the entire prison system is housed in

Table 6-2 Pre- and Post-Step Down Unit (SDU) Graduate Disciplinary Rates

Time Period	Number of RVRs	Average RVR
Six Months Prior to Entering the SDU	203	4.7
While in the SDU	50	1.2
Six Months after Leaving the SDU	27	0.6

a long-term administrative segregation unit. Compared to most states, this is a very low rate.

One reflection of this outcome is the number of disciplinary infractions participants in the step-down program acquired prior to participating in the program, while traversing the phases of the program, and, subsequently, to being discharged or "graduated" from the program. A compilation reflects that forty-three prisoners with serious mental illness have completed the step-down unit program and have been discharged. A search of their disciplinary records reveals that in the six months prior to their admission to the program this group of forty-three prisoners received 253 rule violation reports (RVRs or "tickets") or an average of 4.7 RVRs per prisoner; while in the program (approximately six months), this group accounted for fifty RVRs or an average of 1.2 RVRs; and in the six months since they completed the program, they have accounted for 30 RVRs or an average of 0.6 per prisoner (see Table 6-2). Such a pre- and posttest analysis cannot "prove" that it was the step-down program that produced these results. But one would be hard put to explain how such a reduction would have occurred anyway.[36]

In October 2007, plaintiff's counsel Margaret Winter, who had been visiting Unit 32 for five years and walking across the vast empty field between the entrance and the cell blocks, paid another visit to the facility and, upon entering the courtyard of Unit 32, noted: "We came upon an amazing, almost unbelievable, scene: Dozens of prisoners laughing and shouting as they played basketball in the sunshine on yards that had been almost entirely empty prior to the litigation." On August 2, 2010 Judge Davis in a hearing to close the consent decree made the following comments:

> What you have been able to agree to, I'm just floored, candidly.... [I]t's a tremendous step forward in corrections that 80 percent of the people basically, now are able to go back into general population.... I want to commend both sides. You did exactly what I hoped you would do. I had my fingers crossed, and I was holding my breath because ... you did a lot better than I could have done.... I have spent an awful lot of my career dealing with prison cases ... The State of Mississippi should be real proud of (all parties to the changes), because we've made tremendous progress.[37]

One year later, Unit 32 was closed by the Mississippi Department of Corrections and the consent decree was dismissed without prejudice by the Federal Court.

NOTES

1. C. Riveland, *Supermax Prisons: Overview and General Considerations.* (Washington, DC: U.S. Department of Justice, National Institute for Corrections, 1999) P. Scharff-Smith, *The Effects of Solitary Confinement on Prison Inmates: A Brief History and Review of the Literature*, in M. Tonry (ed.), *Crime and Justice*, Vol. 34. (Chicago: University of Chicago Press, 2006), pp. 441–528.

2. Donald Clemmer, *The Prison Community* (New York: Holt, Rinehart, 1958).

3. When they first began this expansion, prison administrators usually presented the new policies as nonpunitive and planned new segregation units so they would not be as cruel as solitary confinement. In California, where segregation has been used more than in any other state, initial expansion of segregation units was justified with a therapeutic rationale. In 1956, California prison administrators requested and received funds from the state legislature to construct new housing units or convert existing units to sections called "adjustment centers," which were intended to hold prisoners who were not responding to their rehabilitative programs. According to the original plan, these prisoners would receive more intensive rehabilitative strategies, such as intensive counseling and therapy. The adjustment centers were built, but no special rehabilitative programs were introduced.

4. From a letter sent to the Prison Law Collective in San Francisco, California, and distributed by them in 1975 in an unpublished document titled "Descriptions of O Wing Soledad."

5. George Jackson, *Soledad Brother* (New York: Bantam Books, 1970), pp. 23, 164.

6. Ruling of Alfonso Zirpoli, federal district judge, Northern California District, in *Johnny L. Spain v. Raymond K. Procunier*, December 18, 1975, p. 5.

7. Interview by John Irwin, San Quentin prisoner, 1979.

8. See Min S. Yee, *The Melancholy History of Soledad Prison* (New York: Harper & Row, 1973), for a complete description of the events and the court decision.

9. Declaration for U.S. District Court for Northern California by Terry Kupers, M.D., *Wright v. Enomoto*, June 30, 1980, pp. 5, 7, 9.

10. Robert Slater, "Psychiatric Intervention in an Atmosphere of Terror," *American Journal of Forensic Psychiatry* 7, 1 (1986): 8, 9.

11. This description of Marion was taken from David A. Ward and Allen E. Breed, *The United States Penitentiary, Marion, Illinois: A Report to the Judiciary Committee, United States House of Representatives* (Washington, DC: U.S. Government Printing Office, October 1984).

12. Ibid., pp. 11–12.

13. Ibid., p. 32.

14. *Corrections Digest*, June 27, 1990, p. 9.

15. *New York Times*, February 20, 1991.

16. Chicago Tribune, 2009. "A Look Inside Illinois' Only Super-Max Prison," p. 1.

17. *Wilkinson v. Austin*, 545 U.S. 209 (2005).

18. Interview with John Irwin, San Quentin, March 1983.

19. From prisoners' files read in March 1983.

20. Robert Schultz, *"Life in SHU": An Ethnographic Study of Pelican Bay State Prison*, M.S. thesis, Humboldt State University, April 1991, p. 104.

21. From a letter written to the Soledad Defense Committee in 1971 and circulated in an unpublished document labeled "Descriptions of O Wing Ciliated," p. 3.

22. George Jackson, *Soledad Brother*, (New York: Bantam Books, 1970), pp. 164–165.

23. *New York Times*, (New York: Bantam Books, 1970), April 20, 1989.

24. Charles Dickens, *American Notes and Pictures from Italy* (London: Oxford University Press, 1957), pp. 99, 109.

25. Richard McCleery, "Authoritarianism and the Belief System of Incorrigibles," in Donald R. Cressy (ed.), *The Prison* (New York: Holt, Rinehart, 1961).

26. Declaration to the U.S. District Court for the Northern District of California,

Wright v. Enomoto, July 23, 1980, pp. 5, 15.

27. Declaration to the U.S. District Court for the Northern District of California, *Wright v. Enomoto*, July 23, 1980, p. 4. Kupers specifically cited the following articles in reaching his conclusions: W. Bromber et al., "The Relation of Psychosis, Mental Defect, and Personality Types to Crime," *Journal of Criminal Law and Criminology* 28 (1973): 70–89; S. B. Guze et al., "Criminality and Psychiatric Disorders," *Archives of General Psychiatry* 20 (1969): 583–591; J. Kloech, "Schizophrenia and Delinquency," in *The Mentally Abnormal Offender* (1968): 19–28; D. Wiersnian, "Crime and Schizophrenics," *Excerpta Criminologica* 6 (1966): 169–181.

28. Letter from Pelican Bay prisoner sent to Prisoners' Rights Union, Sacramento, California.

29. *Madrid v. Gomez*, 889 F. Supp. 1149 (N.D. Cal. 1995), p. 215.

30. *Robert Westefer, et al., Plaintiffs, v. Donald Snyder, et al., Defendants.* Civil Nos. 00-162-GPM, 00-708-GPM. United States District Court, S.D. Illinois. July 20, 2010.

31. Schultz, *"Life in SHU,"* p. 153.

32. http://www.forbes.com/2006/04/15/prison-supermax.-ross_cx_jr_06slate_0418super. html.

33. *Robert Westefer, et al., Plaintiffs, v. Donald Snyder, et al., Defendants.* Civil Nos. 00-162-GPM, 00-708-GPM.

34. *Wilkinson v. Austin*, 545 U.S. 209 (2005).

35. Much of this section is drawn directly from an article by Terry A Kupers, Theresa Dronet, Margaret Winter, James Austin, Lawrence Kelly, William Cartier, Timothy J Morris, Stephen F Hanlon, Emmitt L Sparkman, Parveen Kumar, Leonard C Vincent, Jim Norris, Kim Nagel and Jennifer Mcbride. (2009). *Beyond Supermax Administrative Segregation: Mississippi's Experience Rethinking Prison Classification and Creating Alternative Mental Health Programs*, Criminal Justice Behavior. 36(10):1037-1050

36. The most common other explanations for such a reduction would be regression to the mean, natural maturation or the participants and instrumentation or measurement.

37. *Presley V. Epps Consent Decree*, Fairness Hearing, August 2, 2010.

7

■

Private Prisons—Can
They Do It Better?

LEARNING OBJECTIVES

1. To understand the difference between public and private prison systems and their key attributes.
2. Review the key legal issues surrounding the use of private versus public prisons.
3. Review the major studies that have been completed on whether private prisons are cost-effective compared to public prisons.
4. To assess the future of the private prison system and the challenges it will face.

BACKGROUND

Arizona puts more of its inmates into privately run prisons every year, even though the prisons may not be as secure as state-run facilities and may not save taxpayers money. Lawmakers began using private prisons to ease overcrowding and have supported their use so aggressively that today, one in five Arizona inmates is housed in a private facility. A high-profile escape of three Arizona inmates last month from a Kingman-area private prison, which spurred a nationwide manhunt and is believed to have resulted in two murders, raises questions about the industry's growth and the degree of state oversight.

http://www.azcentral.com/news/articles/2010/08/22/20100822arizona-private-prisons.html#ixzz192PLJU2D

10 California Inmates Injured In AZ Private Prison Riot

Ten inmates were injured in a riot yesterday in a private prison in central Arizona, reports the Associated Press. Eloy police say the disturbance occurred during the lunch hour at the Red Rock Correctional Facility and involved an estimated 110 inmates. They say the riot was in an area of the prison that houses only California inmates. Staff used pepper spray and ended it within 10 minutes. The 1,596-bed facility now is in lockdown. Red Rock Correctional Center is owned by Corrections Corporation of America and houses male inmates for California, Hawaii, and the U.S. Marshals Service.

Associated Press/San Francisco Chronicle December 24, 2010.

The rise and associated costs of U.S. prison and jail systems has been a major catalyst for the relatively recent growth in private prisons. Compounding the problems created by the growing demand for prison space and funding is the lack of public confidence in the quality of correctional services provided by federal, state, and municipal governments. Programs designed to rehabilitate offenders have not demonstrated a reduction in crime or recidivism and have thus lost credibility with the public and policy makers. In short, there is an increasing belief that government is not equipped to meet the challenges of contemporary, institutional confinement.

In the 1980s, some saw private prisons and jails as part of the solution to meet the increasing pressure for prison bed space, at a time when taxpayers were reluctant to pay for correctional services and were not supportive of divestiture of resources from other areas of state responsibilities and services.[1] As a means of confronting escalating prison populations and costs, policy makers have considered turning to the private sector for assistance.

"Privatization" is commonly defined as a contract process that shifts public functions, responsibilities, and capital assets, in whole or in part, from the public to the private sector. Privatization in correctional services can assume a number of institutional characteristics. For instance, the most common form of privatization in corrections is the contracting-out (or out-sourcing) of specific services that entails a competition among private bidders to perform governmental activities. Over the past two decades, the practice of state and local correctional agencies contracting with private entities for medical, mental health, education, food services, maintenance, and administrative office security functions has risen sharply. Under these circumstances, the correctional agency remains the financier and continues to manage and maintain policy control over the type and quality of services provided.

A more radical approach occurs when government transfers ownership of assets, commercial enterprises, and management responsibilities to the private sector. This is called an "asset sale," leaving the government with a limited or nonexistent role in the financial support, management, and oversight of the sold asset.[2] This form of privatization is more radical and, until the 1980s, was not adopted by government in operating correctional facilities.

Table 7-1 Private Prison Market-Share of Prison Facilities 2000 and 2009

Year	Total	Federal	State	% Share
2000	87,369	15,524	71,845	7%
2009	129,482	33,162	96,320	8%

SOURCE: U.S. Department of Justice, Bureau of Justice Statistics, *Prisoners in 2000* and *Prisoners 2009*.

There is no doubt there has been a dramatic increase in the use of private correctional facilities, initially in the United States, and more recently in the United Kingdom, Australia, Scotland, and South Africa. We use the term correctional facilities, as many of the so-called private prisons are actually jails and detention centers that do not house state or federal prisoners.

In 1987, the total number of inmates in privately operated prisons and jails worldwide was approximately 3,100. By 2009, the number just in U.S. state prisons and the federal Bureau of Prisons (BOP) had increased to about 130,000 (see Table 7-1). Despite the rapid increases in the presence of private correctional facilities, they represent only a small share of the entire state and federal prison population. Based on the total state and federal prison population of approximately 1.4 million in the United States, the 130,000 private prison count reflects only 8 percent of the U.S. market. Furthermore, while the number in private prisons increased by over 40,000, there are some indications that growth in the use of privatization may be losing steam and has reached a plateau as the private prison market share in the national prison population has increased by only 1 percent since 2000.

There are a wide variety of private facilities (see Table 7-2). Most are traditional secure prisons with secure perimeter walls or fences and cell blocks. From an architectural perspective, they are no different from public prisons as they are designed and built by the same companies that build public prisons. There is a sizeable number of community-based low-security facilities; they are often operated by not-for-profit or religious organizations. These are generally small organizations that have

Table 7-2 Number of Public and Private State and Federal Correctional Facilities by Type of Facility

U.S. Prison Facilities	N	%
Total Prison Facilities	1,821	100%
Secure Prisons	1,292	71%
Community-based Halfway Houses	529	29%
Total Publicly Operated Prisons	1,406	77%
Secure Prisons	1,185	65%
Community-based Halfway Houses	221	12%
Privately Operated Prisons	415	23%
Secure Prisons	107	6%
Community-based Halfway Houses	308	17%

SOURCE: U.S. Department of Justice, Bureau of Justice Statistics. *Census Of State And Federal Adult Correctional Facilities, 2005.* Washington, DC.

long-standing relationships with local governments and are not involved in traditional prison operations. About 30 percent of these community-based facilities make up the entire private corrections market.

There is a dwindling number of corporations who operate these private prisons. In 1998 there were 14 private prison corporations. Today there are only three such organizations in the U.S.—the Correctional Corporation of America (CCA trading on the NYSE as CWX), the GEO Group (GEO) and Cornell Companies, Inc. (CRN). In 2010, GEO and Cornell finalized a merger valued at $730 million. CCA is the largest corporation, boasting of managing approximately 75,000 inmates including males, females, and juveniles at all security levels in more than sixty facilities in nineteen states and the District of Columbia.[3] There is also a dwindling number of smaller companies operating juvenile and adult systems. The number also includes some private not-for-profit organizations and faith-based organizations that operate very small halfway houses.

The vast majority of private prisons are located in the southern states with 58,102 of the total number of 130,000 inmates in private prisons followed by the western states (27,563). The states with the largest number of inmates are Texas (20,265), Arizona (9,355), and Florida (9,316). The states with the largest share of private prisons are New Mexico (46%), Montana (37%), Hawaii (35%), Vermont (30%), Alaska (26%) and Mississippi (25%). However, the BOP has the largest number of any state with 32,879 (Table 7–3).

Table 7-3 Number of State and Federal Prisoners in Private Prison by Region and Selected States

Region	Jurisdiction	December 2000	December 2008	December 2009	% of All Prisoners
U.S. Total		87,369	129,482	129,336	8%
	Federal	15,524	33,162	34,087	16%
	State	71,845	96,320	95,249	7%
Northeast		2,509	5,113	5,423	3%
	Vermont	0	726	668	30%
Midwest		7,836	5,448	4,895	2%
South		45,560	57,888	58,737	9%
	Florida	3,912	9,158	9,812	9%
	Mississippi	3,230	5,497	5,286	25%
	Texas	13,985	20,041	19,207	11%
West		15,940	27,871	26,194	8%
	Alaska	1,383	1,450	1,626	31%
	Arizona	1,430	8,369	8,971	22%
	Hawaii	1,187	2,108	1,648	28%
	Idaho	1,162	2,114	2,066	28%
	Montana	986	1,312	1,434	40%
	New Mexico	2,155	2,935	2,825	43%

SOURCE: U.S. Department of Justice, Bureau of Justice Statistics, *Prisoners in 2000*, *Prisoners 2008* and *Prisoners 2009*.

PRIVATIZATION OF CORRECTIONS: A HISTORICAL OVERVIEW[4]

Private enterprise in the United States has an extensive history of involvement in the provision of correctional services. According to Malcolm Feeley, the involvement of the private sector in corrections stems, in part, from an Anglo-American political culture that is somewhat skeptical of governmental authority yet promotes private initiative.[5] Feeley traces the private sector involvement back to the first colonists who arrived in Virginia in 1607. The colonists followed with a handful of convicted felons transported by private entrepreneurs to America as a condition of pardon to be sold into slavery and servitude.[6]

Merchants transported convicts in exchange for the privilege of selling them as indentured servants.[7] Transporting convicts to America (and later many more to Australia following the American Revolution) was an innovation that radically transformed the administration of criminal justice. This innovation expanded the sanctioning power of the state without the need to increase its administrative structure. In other words, the transportation policy multiplied the state's penal capacity at a low cost to the government.

During the eighteenth century, the modern prison emerged in America as a viable alternative to servitude or the death penalty. Also during this time, the use of privately operated facilities became popular. In the colonies, criminal justice procedures were copied from English customs that had a long history of private involvement in operating jails. Privately operated jails date back to medieval England.[8]

For a fixed fee, states allowed private contractors to supervise prisoners inside prison walls.[9] Although appointed by the government, a head jailer was considered an independent operator of a profit-making enterprise functioning as a government contractor. Jailers often provided employment for prisoners.[10] In privately operated facilities, inmates were often engaged as laborers and craftsmen in private sector activities. Early American jails may be characterized as exploitative. Clair Cripe describes the conditions as follows:

> There was seldom any separation of types of prisoners—women and children were often confined with hardened criminals. Many jails were very crowded; most were unsanitary. Payments were extracted for special services, such as better meals or other privileges. Some money was given to the jailer (often the sheriff) for basic services. But it was widely accepted that jailers could charge additional money for virtually any type of special benefit.[11]

By 1885, thirteen states had contracts with private enterprises to lease out prison labor.[12] One of the more interesting situations occurred in California. San Quentin prison was first constructed and operated under a private provider in the 1850s. Private entrepreneurs persuaded state officials that the facility could best be operated under a long-term lease arrangement with an entity having experience in law enforcement. Even back then the debate centered on costs; it was argued that the private sector would be less expensive and less corrupt than government. However, after a number of major scandals surrounding the mismanagement of the facility by the private provider, the state decided to turn the facility over to the control of state government. Eventually, government turned out to be as ineffective and corrupt as the private provider.

> As the year [1856] went on it became increasingly clear to more and more people that, regardless how much money it might save the taxpayers, a private contract was no way to run the state prison. The Bulletin was not alone when it demanded that, whatever it cost, a final end had to be put to the system of farming out the management of the state convicts.... After the final ejection of [Warden] McCauley, however, the prison fell into the hands of men who were primarily professional politicians rather than pirates. The distinction is a nice one, and the change was more a matter of style than of substance. The prison remained a rich piece of political spoils, but the looting was now carried on more in line with the ancient traditions of American state politics.[13]

Even back then, private contractors claimed they could both manage prisons and employ convicts in labor, arguing that the practice would be both rehabilitative and financially rewarding. Prison models of convict labor took various forms. At some prisons, companies outside the prison provided raw materials that were refined in prison workshops and later sold by private companies. At others, prisons leased out their inmates to private farms or other businesses if they could not produce saleable items within the prison. In a number of states, contractors paid the prison a fee or a percentage of profits for the right to employ convicts. For example, in the 1860s the Texas legislature directed state correctional administrators to contract out inmate labor to the private sector. Even when prisons were not operated entirely by private entrepreneurs, inmates were used as a cheap source of labor. Prisoners often worked on farms, for railroads, and in mines, in addition to other public work programs.[14]

For most of the correctional history of the United States, prison labor was expected to generate a profit for the institution. If generating a profit was not feasible, it was incumbent upon the prisoner to pay the costs of incarceration and become self-supporting. The "managers" of early detention facilities charged their inmates for food and clothing, while providing substandard service. The income generated by inmate labor, however, was not sufficient to cover the high costs of operating correctional systems, despite persistent and intense efforts to make the system pay for itself. Without independent oversight and monitoring, the convict labor system eventually succumbed to bribery and corruption.

Moreover, there was strong opposition to the convict lease system from organized labor, manufacturers, and farmers. This broad constituency opposed what was considered unfair competition and pressed for legislation to restrict the use of convict labor and convict-produced goods. Public opposition was also mobilized by reformers and religious groups who protested the scandalous conditions found at many of the privately run facilities and in labor lease systems. State legislatures began investigating alleged incidents of mismanagement and cruelty within privatized institutions, which resulted in modifications to the leasing system.[15]

An executive order signed by President Theodore Roosevelt in 1905 prohibited the use of convict labor on federal projects. In 1929 Congress passed the Hawes-Cooper Act permitting states to ban the importation of inmate products from other states.[16] Congress and state legislatures also passed laws during the Depression that further curtailed the use of inmates in private enterprises.

By the 1920s, the prevailing practice in American correctional agencies was to increase governmental involvement. The subsequent demise of the convict lease system eventually gave way to state-run institutions. Their operations and administrative functions were delegated to governmental agencies, authorized by statute, staffed by government employees, and funded solely by the government.[17]

Since the early twentieth century and until more recently, the custom in all American correctional agencies has been to provide virtually all correctional services as governmental functions in institutions constructed and maintained at the government's expense.[18] In some program areas, rehabilitative services (religious and educational) were provided by volunteer associations. Generally, private involvement in the provision of correctional services diminished.

During the past thirty years, private enterprise again began to play an influential and expanded role in the functioning of the criminal justice system. In an attempt to manage escalating costs associated with supporting the many functions required to effectively run penal institutions, a trend gradually developed in the twentieth century for the contracting-out of prison services to both profit-making and not-for-profit firms. While prisons continued to contract out the provision of medical, dental, and psychological services, more services—such as food preparation, vocational training, and inmate transportation—were added. By the mid-1970s, federal, state, and municipal governments were again willing to expand their association with the private sector, moving beyond the conventional contractual relationship that became common in the early twentieth century. According to Alexis Durham, the 1970s ushered in a new phase in the development of private corrections, beginning with juvenile correctional operations:

> In 1976 RCA Services, a private company, assumed control of the Weaversville Intensive Treatment Unit located in North Hampton, Pennsylvania. This facility was designed to handle male delinquents. Although the private sector had long been involved in providing a wide range of correctional services…this was the first modern institution for serious offenders to be completely operated in what has become an increasingly lengthy line of such institutions in the American correctional system.[19]

The Weaversville Intensive Treatment Unit for juvenile delinquents is widely regarded as the first high-security institution that was entirely privately owned and operated under contract to the state. The second such institution did not appear until 1982, when the state of Florida turned over the operation of the Okeechobee School for Boys to the Eckerd Foundation.[20] The trend toward privately operated juvenile correctional facilities has continued, with over 40,000 youth now housed in privately operated juvenile facilities. It is noteworthy that these operations have not received nearly the level of scrutiny and criticism as have their adult counterparts. This may be due to the fact that some, but not all, are not-for-profit operations.

The U.S. Immigration and Naturalization Service (INS) was among the first governmental agencies to take advantage of the emerging market of private prison operators. At the end of 1984, the INS had contracts with two private companies for the detention of illegal aliens; by the end of 1988, the number of private INS detention facilities had grown to seven, housing roughly 800 of the 2,700 aliens in INS custody.[21] Also, during this period, Corrections Corporations of America (CCA) was awarded a contract to manage the Hamilton County Jail in Chattanooga, Tennessee, near the location of CCA's national headquarters in Nashville Tennessee. This was followed by the first state-level contract award in 1985, when Kentucky contracted with the U.S. Corrections Corporation.

These developments initially provoked little controversy or even notice, the likely reason being that private sector involvement in correctional management was still limited in size and scope. The importance of these early contracts has been noted by Charles Thomas, an early advocate of private prisons:

> The importance of these contract awards to the subsequent development of correctional privatization would be difficult to overestimate and the fact that all remain still in force today with the same management firms is not inconsequential for those who would be willing to accept this fact as at least an oblique performance indicator. Each provided a real world opportunity to test the hypothesis that contracting could yield meaningful benefits to government. Each also provided a valuable model that subsequent units of government could examine and improve upon in such critical areas as procurement strategies, the formulation of sound contracts, and the creation of effective means of contract monitoring.[22]

Secure adult institutions, once considered the near exclusive and inextricable preserve of government, emerged as one of the central issues debated among correctional agencies. Finally, in the last few years, governments have sought to contract out capital expenditure costs and operational services, including prison design, construction, and management.[23]

Thus, the pressure of increased incarceration rates combined with rising correctional costs enabled privatization of penal facilities to reemerge as an acceptable political and correctional concept. This reemergence, however, has stirred considerable debate over the viability of privately operated prison facilities. The current enthusiasm for privatization is fueled by the prospect of more innovative, cost-effective prison management, including the anticipated private sector involvement in the financing of new prison construction. This enthusiasm is not shared by all. Much of the contention is reflected in the literature, especially with regard to the alleged advantages and disadvantages of private facility management.

THE DEBATE

There have been many claims by observers on the advantages and disadvantages of privatization. Dennis Cunningham has summarized the major reasons to either accept or reject the privatization concept (see Table 7-4). These

Table 7-4 Public Strategies for Private Prisons

Reasons to Privatize

1. Private operators can provide construction financing options that allow the governmental client to pay only for capacity as needed in lieu of encumbering long-term debt.

2. Private companies offer modern state-of-the-art correctional facility designs that are staff-efficient to operate, built based upon the value of engineering specifications.

3. Private operators typically design and construct a new correctional facility in one-half the time of a comparable governmental construction project.

4. Private vendors provide government clients with the convenience and accountability of one entity for all compliance issues.

5. Private corrections management companies are able to mobilize rapidly and to specialize in unique facility missions.

6. Private corrections management companies provide economic development opportunities by hiring locally and, to the extent possible, purchasing locally.

7. The government can reduce or share its liability exposure by contracting with private corrections companies.

8. The government can retain flexibility by limiting the contract duration and by specifying the facility mission.

9. Adding other service providers injects competition among the parties, both public and private organizations alike.

Reasons Not to Privatize

1. There are certain responsibilities that only the government should provide, such as public safety and environmental protection. Major constitutional issues revolve around the deprivation of liberty, discipline, and preserving the constitutional rights of inmates. Related issues: use of force; loss of time credit; segregation.

2. There are few companies available to choose from.

3. There may be private operator inexperience with key corrections issues.

4. The operator may become a monopoly via political ingratiation, favoritism, and so on.

5. The government may lose the capability to perform the function over time.

6. The profit motive will inhibit the proper performance of duties. Private prisons have financial incentives to cut corners.

7. The procurement process is slow, inefficient, and open to risks.

SOURCE: Dennis Cunningham, Oklahoma Department of Corrections, *Privatization Division, Public Strategies for Private Prisons*. Paper presented at the Private Prison Workshop at the Institute on Criminal Justice, University of Minnesota Law School, January 1999.

various reasons can be reduced to the overriding desire of many states and local governments to rapidly increase desperately needed prison bed capacity and to reduce prison operational costs. Others have raised the issue of whether private prisons enhance the quality of care for inmates (including enhanced protection from harm for inmates and staff) and reduce litigation. Thus far, there has been little need on the part of the private providers to argue that inmates incarcerated in privately operated prisons are more likely to be rehabilitated and less likely to recidivate, as the essential question has focused on costs.[24] Each of these claims that form the core of the debate on whether to privatize are discussed next.

Faster and Cheaper Bed Capacity

It is often cited that the major impetus behind the move toward privatization has been the dramatic increase in prison and jail populations and the associated need to construct new and less costly prison and jail bed capacity in a timely manner. Contracting with the private sector allows prospective prisons to be financed, sited, and constructed more quickly and cheaply than government prisons. This flexibility is especially advantageous when a new facility is under consideration.

Based on experience, it takes the government five to six years to build a facility, while some private companies claim they can do it in two to three years (or less). For example, the CCA built a 350-bed detention center in Houston for the Immigration and Naturalization Service (INS) in five-and-a-half months at a cost of $14,000 per bed. INS calculated the construction to take two-and-a-half years at a cost of $26,000 per bed.[25] In a comprehensive study of privatizing the District of Columbia's Department of Corrections, it was estimated that rebuilding several prison facilities would take the public sector five to six years while it would take the private sector only three to four years.[26]

Based on these and other reports, it seems clear that the private sector can add prison bed capacity faster and at less cost than most public entities. Cripe cited the numerous advantages advocates assert in support of private prison construction:

> Because private firms are not bound by governmental rules that tend to slow down prison construction, such as political pressures from unhappy neighbors, environmental hassles, and requirements of competed bidding and construction contracting, private firms have shown an ability to open new facilities more quickly. They claim they can also get the money to build new institutions more quickly from private investors or from lenders, while the government has to work more slowly, getting appropriations from the legislature or going through a bond issue process.[27]

On the other hand, Ira Robbins points out that privatization often allows prisons to be built without the approval of the public.[28] For example, the construction costs of a privately operated facility can be lumped together in the state's prison operating budget as opposed to requiring the state to seek voter approval on a construction bond, as is usually the case.

Reduced Operational Costs

Perhaps the most often cited claim made by the private sector is that it can save taxpayers more money by providing correctional services traditionally supplied by government at less cost. This can be achieved by reducing the costs of labor associated with operational costs. Labor costs are controlled by reducing one or all three of the following personnel cost factors: (1) number of staff, (2) wages, and (3) fringe benefits.

Prisons are extremely labor-intensive, with approximately 65 to 70 percent of the costs of operating a prison related to staff salaries, fringe benefits, and overtime. Controlling these costs is more difficult to achieve with unionized government workers. Private firms typically use nonunion labor, allowing for the lowest benefit packages. Typically, private firms claim that they can save 10 to 20 percent in prison operations largely due to efficiencies in labor costs.

This claim is borne out in the 2005 BJS correctional facility study showing that private facilities have higher rates of inmates per total staff and per correctional officers as compared to public agencies (Table 7-5). It is also noteworthy that the inmate-to-staff ratios are increasing, which is caused by states and the federal government trying to reduce operational costs by reducing the most expensive operational cost—staff.

Another, less powerful argument in favor of private contracting is that there is greater flexibility in the procurement process. Private contractors are not bound by the cumbersome and rigid government procurement system. Private vendors can purchase more quickly; maintain lower food, supplies, and equipment inventories; and negotiate better prices.[29]

It is by no means an uncontested fact that a private institution would be more cost-effective. It needs to be pointed out that the incentive to contain costs will be directly related to the type of contract structured:

> A public utilities or "pentagon" model reimbursement where a contractor receives costs plus a profit percentage would not necessarily provide an incentive to contain costs of service. On the other hand, a client charge may result in cost-overruns or even bankruptcy should the initial estimate prove wrong.[30]

One expense not normally included in the financial calculation of private firms is the cost to the government for monitoring contract performance. Constant

Table 7-5 Inmate to Staff Ratios in Federal, State, and Private Facilities 2000 and 2005

	Inmates per Staff		Inmates per Correctional Officer	
	2000	2005	2000	2005
Federal	3.4	4.9	9.0	10.3
State	3.0	3.3	4.6	4.9
Public	3.0	3.4	4.7	5.0
Private	3.8	4.2	6.4	6.9

SOURCE: Census of State and Federal Correctional Facilities, 2005, Table 5. Bureau of Justice Statistics, October 2008.

monitoring of all aspects of internal performance is essential to a good contractual relationship that may become expensive over time. If continual federal or state monitoring of private institutions is required for accountability purposes, the costs of monitoring will ultimately raise the price of privatized services. The potential costs of increased prison litigation are also rarely discussed by private prison advocates.

As a policy matter, opponents claim it is inappropriate to operate prisons based on a profit motive. In many instances, private prison operators are paid according to the number of inmates housed. Arguably, it is in the operator's financial interests to encourage lengthier sentences for inmates in order to keep bed spaces filled. If the private vendor enters into a contract based on a per-client charge, the profit margin and even the continued operation of the private facility is subsidized depending upon total population size. Firms driven by the profit motive could adversely influence prison population size by campaigning for longer sentences and stricter sentencing guidelines. Similarly, as private firms are in business to make a profit, high returns on their investments must be guaranteed.

Improved Quality of Service

BOISE, Idaho—The surveillance video from the overhead cameras shows Hanni Elabed being beaten by a fellow inmate in an Idaho prison, managing to bang on a prison guard station window, pleading for help. Behind the glass, correctional officers look on, but no one intervenes when Elabed is knocked unconscious. No one steps into the cellblock when the attacker sits down to rest, and no one stops him when he resumes the beating. Videos of the attack obtained by The Associated Press show officers watching the beating for several minutes. The footage is a key piece of evidence for critics who claim the privately run Idaho Correctional Center uses inmate-on-inmate violence to force prisoners to snitch on their cellmates or risk being moved to extremely violent units.

AP, November 30, 2010.

In addition to the proposed cost savings and associated efficient services, one must also remember that the nation's prison and jail systems have been facing widespread allegations regarding the quality of care being afforded staff and inmates. In the 1980s and up to the present, most of the state prison systems as well as the major urban jails have been under far-reaching consent decrees regarding medical, mental health, education, overcrowding, and protection from harm issues. There have also been major prison disturbances in New York, California, Illinois, and New Mexico, to name a few, that have added to the public perception that public prisons are not doing a good job in managing prisons.

However, one of the central concerns raised by critics of correctional privatization is that firms motivated by financial gain will make decisions that enhance profits at the expense of the rights and well-being of inmates.[31] History demonstrates that privately operated facilities have been plagued by problems associated with the quest for higher earnings. The profit motive produced such abominable conditions and exploitation that public agencies were forced to assume responsibility. The lack of contract supervision contributed to the squalid and inhumane conditions in privately run prisons. The current movement to reprivatize primary facility management assumes that modern entrepreneurs are somehow more benevolent and humanistic, so the exploitation of the past will not reoccur.[32] On the contrary, critics contend that privately managed facilities will bring new opportunities for corruption. Given poorly paid, undereducated, and inadequately trained staff, opponents question the professionalism and commitment that privatized staff will bring to the job.

Proponents, on the other hand, suggest that present-day judicial activism provides control over private prison operations. The threat of inmate lawsuits and court-mandated consent decrees act as a deterrent to abusive behavior. Further arguments suggest that these kinds of abuses defeat the long-term interests of private contractors and can be avoided with careful monitoring mechanisms. Moreover, competition between firms will hold down costs and provide superior service because contract renewals will depend on job performance. To date, the limited experience with privately managed prisons does not allow a thorough evaluation of public and private prisons in terms of overall quality of inmate services.

Legal Issues

Disagreements surrounding cost and efficiency may eventually be resolved with more complete data. Better contract monitoring and judicial oversight will curtail instances of exploitation and abuse of the inmate population. However, the legal ramifications of privatization pose challenging questions that are not easily rectified. Three complex issues stimulate heated debate on correctional privatization:

1. The propriety of private firms taking over state functions;
2. Inmate rights and due process considerations; and
3. Liability and accountability for state actions.

A fundamental issue is public responsibility for the well-being of society. It is often taken for granted that the apprehension and conviction of offenders is a public responsibility. Hence, the notion that convicted offenders should be the responsibility of private entrepreneurs motivated by profit seems contradictory. The central question becomes whether government has the authority to issue contracts for what is now widely regarded as a public function. Commenting on the issue, Durham states with some urgency that "if the transfer of responsibility to penal institutions is not carefully executed, the consequences may be disastrous. Beyond inconvenience and unanticipated costs, both public safety and inmate well-being may be at stake."[33]

At this time, it is clear that the courts have decided that private prisons can be assigned the same management responsibilities as those undertaken by state and local governments. This is not to say that governments can wholly delegate its functions and duties to a private provider. Indeed, based on a number of recent incidents in private facilities, the courts will hold governments responsible for actions taken by a private provider that violate an inmate's constitutional rights or put the prison staff, inmates, or surrounding community in harm's way.[34]

What has not yet been resolved is whether privatization will undermine or enhance prisoners' rights as compared to publicly operated systems.[35] The U.S. Constitution protects individuals against the violation of due process (Fifth and Fourteenth Amendments) as well as the related issue of cruel and unusual punishment (Eighth Amendment). The past few decades have witnessed a large volume of prison litigation concerning inmate rights and prison conditions that has resulted in most state correctional systems (or a facility within a state) operating under an imposed consent decree. The concern is whether private prisons operate in such a manner that the exposure to litigation against government is reduced.

There is a string of U.S. Supreme Court cases that have held that a person can only assert a denial of due process rights if that deprivation resulted from "state action."[36] The ultimate issue in determining whether an entity is subject to a suit for violation of an individual's rights is whether the alleged infringement is attributable to the state.

A person acts under the "color of state law" only when exercising power possessed by virtue of state law and made possible only because the wrongdoer is clothed with the authority of state law.[37] Federal civil rights law prohibits state officials or agencies from being named as defendants in their official capacities in civil suits if the plaintiffs seek monetary damages. The question remains whether the actions of private corrections facilities regulated by the state can be considered transformed into state actions.

Thus far, the courts have decided that people who provide services to inmates under contract are not immune from litigation for constitutional violations. What is yet to be settled is the propriety of private firms running entire correctional facilities and broad legal or constitutional questions.[38]

The issues raised have practical implications in the day-to-day operations of a private correctional facility. Before entering into a contractual agreement with a private firm for the operation of a prison or jail, it would be necessary to identify whether the private company can be authorized to exercise force (even deadly force) to prevent escapes, to imprison citizens against their will, and to impose penalties on those who violate the regulations and rules of the institution. In the event that private individuals are not allowed to enforce the rules and regulations of the institution, the likelihood of success of these corporations is obviously diminished. However, allowing a private prison to punish inmates who have violated institutional rules (which may differ from those of publicly operated facilities) without oversight by the state could be a denial of due process, especially if the punishment entails the loss of good time that could serve to lengthen an inmate's period of imprisonment.

The other area of concern has to do with actual prison conditions, such as access to medical care, mental health services, work, and vocational and educational services; crowding; and protection from harm. A series of questions must be considered before full privatization of correctional facilities becomes commonplace. For example, is the state liable for illegal actions of the contractor if conditions in the contracted penal facility are found to violate constitutional requirements is immune from not only the actions of the contractor but also for any negligence that results in the escape of prisoners or the financial mismanagement of the facility and would be responsible for "bailing out" a bankrupt contractor. With no clear Supreme Court precedent on whether private prisons will come under the state action doctrine, prisoners' rights may ultimately depend on the nature of the contractual agreement between the state and the private operator.

WHAT THE RESEARCH SHOWS

Despite the level of debate in the United States, there has been little research to answer the issues raised above. In this section we will review the most rigorous evaluations and analysis that have been published to date.

The only national study was undertaken by James Austin and Garry Coventry was funded by the U.S. Department of Justice's Bureau of Justice Assistance (BJA).[39] The BJA study was designed to make direct comparisons between the privately operated facilities that existed in 1997 and the nation's state prison facilities that existed in 1995. The 1995 data on public facilities came from a national survey of those facilities conducted by the U.S. Department of Justice's Bureau of Justice Statistics (BJS). Known as the BJS Survey of State and Federal Correctional Facilities, it provides a wide array of data on state and federal agencies. However, in 1997, the survey did not include the growing number of private facilities. To close that gap, the BJA study administered the same survey to all of the existing private facilities. Not all of the private facilities participated but information was gathered on forty-nine of the existing sixty-five private state facilities identified. What follows is a summary of major findings from that study.

1. A higher proportion (93%) of the private prisons consisted of medium and low custody inmates. This reflected at the time the inability of private companies to secure contracts to house higher security inmates.

2. The average salary for correctional officers ranged from $14,824 to $18,785. The starting salaries were not much lower ($12,958 to $16,640), suggesting that most of the private facility staff were new hires. By contrast, the average minimum starting salary in the public sector was $20,888.

3. Public correctional agencies in the South, where most of the private facilities were located, had an average starting salary of $18,127, which was much higher than that of the private facilities.

4. Basic management information systems (MIS) and inmate classification capabilities were lacking in the private facilities.

5. Inmate-on-inmate assaults per 1,000 were significantly higher at private prisons (35) than at public facilities (25).

6. When one controls for the facility security level, the rate of assaults at private prisons are magnified. As shown in Table 7-6 the misconduct analysis is repeated but it deletes surveys of public facilities that identified themselves as maximum- or higher-custody levels.

The differences in assault rates may be related to other factors, such as reporting standards or the fact that most correctional facilities experience management difficulties when they are newly opened. However, one must also entertain the notion that insufficient training and the lack of qualified staff in key positions may be a valid explanation for these differences. This would be consistent with the claims of critics of privatization who charge that private prisons are inadequately staffed by inexperienced and poorly trained correctional officers, in which case, coupled with a lack of programs and work assignments, higher rates of misconduct would predictably occur. These and other findings led Austin and Coventry to make the following predictions:

1. The number of privatized prisons is likely to increase, but not at the pace exhibited during the past decade.
2. The number of privatized prison companies is likely to decrease as competition and the costs of doing business increase, thus forcing a consolidation of firms within the industry.
3. It is unlikely that privatized prisons will develop a strong market in the high-security inmate population market due to a recent flurry of well-publicized disturbances. However, important inroads can be expected for the private sector within low-security medical, mental health, and geriatric inmate populations.[40]

In terms of evaluations of individual private prisons, there have been some that used varying levels of evaluation designs. Under ideal circumstances, the best test would be to randomly assign prisoners to two prisons that have the exact same design. One would be operated by a public sector agency and the other by a private prison company. In this manner the only factor that distinguished the two prisons would be the private versus public agencies. Simply stated, such a study has never been conducted.

There have been several quasi-experimental studies where comparisons were made between existing private and public agencies. Such studies have tried to

Table 7-6 Major Incidents in Public and Private Medium and Minimum Security Facilities

Types of Violations	Rate per 1,000 Inmates	
	Private 1997	Public 1995
Totals	48.0	29.6
Assaults on Inmates	33.5	20.2
Assaults on Staff	12.2	8.2

SOURCE: Bureau of Justice Statistics (BJS), Census of State and Federal Correctional Facilities, 1995 (1997).

control for various external factors like facility design and the attributes of the inmate population. The GAO reanalyzed data from what they considered to be the most rigorous studies attempting to apply adequate matching methods to make the comparisons meaningful. They concluded:

> Of the five studies reviewed, two (New Mexico and Tennessee) assessed the comparative quality of service between private and public institutions in great detail. Both studies used structured data-collection instruments to cover a variety of quality related topics, including safety and security, management, personnel, health care, discipline reports, escapes, and inmate programs and activities. The New Mexico Study reported equivocal findings, and the Tennessee study reported no difference between the private and public institution.[41]

More recently, the Federal Bureau of Prisons (BOP) was required to conduct a study of its first privatized prison known as the Taft facility. The study is noteworthy as there were two sets of researchers charged with conducting the evaluation. One set of researchers were from the BOP while the other research team was from the respected Abt Associates. Both teams were asked to determine if the Taft facility run by the private company was less expensive than three "control" facilities that were comparable to the Taft facility. What is most interesting is that on the issue of costs, the researchers reached very different conclusions on this topic even though they had the same data (see Table 7-7). The BOP researchers concluded that the Taft facility was as expensive as the three BOP facilities. The Abt study concluded just the opposite. The two basic reasons why the two researchers differed is that the BOP researchers took into account that the three BOP facilities were holding a higher number of prisoners and thus were benefiting from a higher scale of economy. The second reason is that overhead rates were not being applied to the BOP facilities but were assigned to the private prison.[42]

There were two significant studies conducted in Florida that dealt with the issue of whether private prisons were "more rehabilitative" than public facilities.[43] Here again we find some different results by two sets of researchers analyzing the

Table 7-7 Comparison Between BOP Public and BOP Private Prisons by Research Group

	1999		2000		2001		2002	
	Abt	BOP	Abt	BOP	Abt	BOP	Abt	BOP
Public								
Elkton	$39.72	$35.24	$39.77	$34.84	$44.75	$36.79	$46.38	$40.71
Forrest City	$39.46	$35.29	$39.84	$35.28	$41.65	$37.36	$43.61	$38.87
Yazoo City	$41.46	$36.84	$40.05	$34.92	$43.65	$37.29	$42.15	$38.87
Private								
Taft	$33.82	$34.42	$33.25	$33.21	$36.88	$37.04	$38.37	$38.62

SOURCE: Gaes, Gerald G., et al., Appendix 2: Comparing the Quality of Publicly and Privately Operated Prisons: A Review (1998).

prison system. Both studies found no difference in recidivism rates among adult and youthful males being released from private prisons as compared to public facilities. However, both studies found that women released from the private facilities had a *lower* recidivism rate. The Farabee and Knight study claimed it was a major finding, while the later Bales study using the same information found a weaker effect and only for a smaller portion of the females being studied. So the overall finding from both studies is that for the vast majority of Florida prisoners, the private prisons were not having an impact on recidivism. The fact that the women had a lower rate of recidivism may speak to the issue that some private prisons, like some public facilities, can provide effective services.

Finally, James Blumstein and Mark Cohen conducted a study where they compared the costs of prisons in states where private and public prisons existed with states where there were no private prisons.[44] The theory was that private prisons create a competitive economic climate that results in the costs of public prisons declining to remain competitive with the private prisons. The analysis is limited as it only looks for changes in the growth of corrections from 1999 to 2001. Further, although the authors attempt to control for external factors that may be unique to specific states, one must question whether that is actually possible. For example, the vast majority of states with private prisons are southern states where unions are either nonexistent or are not as strong in other parts of the country. It may be that these states, due to their traditional conservative fiscal philosophy, would have lower growth rates than other states. It may also be that other non-southern states are increasing their growth rates at a faster pace in order to meet court mandates or decisions to enhance the quality of medical, mental health, and other treatment services.

In the end, the researchers found that nineteen states that had no private prisons increased the costs of their correctional budgets by 19 percent whereas the other thirty states with some presence of private prisons grew by 11 percent. More significantly, states where over 20 percent of their prisoners were in private facilities grew by only 6 percent.

THE FUTURE OF PRIVATIZATION

Baldwin, Mich., (population 1,107), will soon have more prison beds than full-time residents. On the outskirts of town, one of the country's largest private prison companies recently spent $60 million to expand a former juvenile prison into a 1,755-bed facility meant to house illegal immigrants before deportation.... Baldwin residents were counting on the private prison to create jobs, but this past March, the federal government pulled back its funding on the bid. This left the GEO Group, Inc., with an empty fortress in the middle of rural Michigan, 85 miles north of Grand Rapids.

Newsweek, June 30, 2010. "How The Recession Hurts Private Prisons"

In general there is no consistent trend that private prisons can systematically out-perform public prisons. Some studies support and others do not. Although they tend to house a higher proportion of minimum-custody inmates in relatively new facilities, private facilities tend to have the same staffing patterns; provide the same levels of work, education, and counseling programs for inmates; and have the same rates of serious inmate misconduct as public facilities. This is not surprising since the administrators of private prisons generally come from the public sector. Thus, the same administrators are applying the same management methods and staffing configurations.

The few credible impact studies also show few differences and more similarities between the two methods of operation. What seems to have evolved in the United States is a model that essentially mimics the public model but achieves modest cost savings, at least initially, by making modest reductions in staffing patterns, fringe benefits, and other labor-related costs. But there is no evidence that private prisons will have a dramatic impact on how prisons operate. The promise of 20 percent savings in operational costs has simply not materialized. Even if it had, the fact that private prisons hold less than 10 percent of the total prison population means that private prisons can only have a limited impact on total prison budgets.

For example, assume that 10 percent of a state's prison system becomes privatized and that each private prison produces a 10 percent savings in operational costs. Even at this level, the overall impact on the state prison budget would be only 1 percent (10% of 10% is 1%). This is not a number that will revolutionize modern correctional practices.

But it now appears that achieving even a 10 percent market share is proving to be increasingly difficult for the following reasons. First, there has been a number of well-publicized stories of poor performance in Texas, Oregon, Colorado, Kentucky, Louisiana, and South Carolina. The problems, associated with the CCA-operated Northeast Ohio Corrections Center have dramatized how badly a privatized prison can be operated. In this facility, sixteen inmates were stabbed, two were murdered, and six escaped in less than a year of operations. Operational weaknesses were linked to inexperienced staff, inadequate training, and a willingness to accept inmates from the District of Columbia who should not have been transferred to the facility.[45] If nothing else, the private sector has shown that it is equally capable of mismanaging prisons as the public sector.

These recent problems suggest the "sales division" of the private sector may well be outstripping the "production division." It may be that private prisons will face increasing difficulties in expanding their market simply because they, like the public sector, are finding it more difficult to recruit competent staff. Further as noted in Chapter 10, the size of the nation's prison population has flattened out and is declining is several states. If one also recognizes that as of 2011, many states are facing sever budget deficits, the prospects of expanding the number of private prisons in the near future may have been dimmed.

Although promises of superiority in privatization as compared to the public sector have not been realized, the mere presence of private facilities has had a significant impact on traditional prison operations. The Blumstein and Cohen study noted above plus others have suggested that privatization has been successful in forcing the public sector to reexamine how it does its business. Certainly in those markets where the correctional officer salaries and fringe benefits have been excessive, privatization has fostered a reexamination of those costs that has often led to cost savings. In this sense, privatization has served as a catalyst for change by demonstrating other means for doing the business of corrections. But these cost saving innovations, as limited as they are, should not be the sole agenda nor the means for reducing the size or costs of incarceration.

It would be extremely interesting and productive for the private sector, in a partnership with the public sector, to become the vehicle for testing far more substantive changes in correctional policy in a number of areas—and not just in prisons and jails. For example, an extremely promising strategy would be for the private sector to test the long-term effects of state-of-the-art correctional programming in the areas of education, vocational training, and various forms of counseling—both in prison and after release—in reducing recidivism. The flexibility of the private sector would allow innovations in testing for the effects of reducing prison terms and other correctional policies on a limited basis. Finally, new management techniques, staff training, and facility designs could be tested by the private sector under controlled conditions. All such innovations would be directed at reducing the use and ineffectiveness of current correctional practices rather than producing a less expensive but just as ineffective system.

NOTES

1. Lawrence F. Travis, III, Edward J. Latessa, and Gennaro F. Vito, "Private Enterprise and Institutional Corrections: A Call for Caution," *Federal Probation* 49, 4 (1985): 11–16.

2. General Accounting Office, *Privatization: Lessons Learned by State and Local Governments* (Washington, DC: General Accounting Office, 1997; GAO/GGD-97-48).

3. http://www.cca.com/about/

4. Much of the data presented in this section was supported by a grant funded by the U.S. Department of Justice, Bureau of Justice Assistance, which is a component of the Office of Justice Programs (February 2001; Grant No. 97-DD-BX-0026). Points of view or opinions in this chapter are those of the authors and do not necessarily represent the official position or policies of the U.S. Department of Justice.

5. Malcolm M. Feeley, "The Privatization of Prisons in Historical Perspective," *Criminal Justice Research Bulletin* 6, 2 pp. 1–10.

6. During the North American phase of transportation, some 50,000 convicts were shipped across the Atlantic, where they were sold as agricultural laborers.

7. David Ammons, Richard Campbell, and Sandra Somoza, *The Option of Prison Privatization: A Guide for Community Deliberations* (Athens: University of Georgia, 1992).

8. R. B. Pugh, *Imprisonment in Medieval England* (Cambridge, UK: Cambridge University Press, 1968).

9. Philip A. Ethridge and James W. Marquart, "Private Prisons in Texas: The New Penology for Profit," *Justice Quarterly* 10, 1.

10. Robert D. McCrie, "Private Correction: The Delicate Balance," in Gary Bowman et al., *Privatizing Correctional Institutions* (New Brunswick, NJ: Transaction Publishers, 1993).

11. Clair A. Cripe, *Legal Aspects of Correctional Management* (Gaithersburg, MD: Aspen Publications, 1997), p. 378.

12. Robert D. McCrie, "Private Correction: The Delicate Balance," p. 24.

13. Kenneth Lamott, *Chronicles of San Quentin: The Biography of a Prison* (New York: David McKay Co., 1961), pp. 74, 78

14. Ethridge and Marquart identify other forms of private inmate labor such as the piece-rate system and the public account system. Under the piece-rate system, inmates worked inside prison walls under the supervision of state employees. In the public account system, prisoners worked under state supervision and produced goods for state institutions. However, the convict lease system was considered the most profitable, and the most brutal and corrupt, of all inmate labor systems.

15. McCrie, "Private Correction," refers to the case of the privatized Huntsville prison in Texas, which was the subject of a legislative investigation into prison conditions. The investigation resulted in modifications to the leasing system in which the state maintained control of the penitentiary and convicts but continued contracting arrangements with private interests beginning in 1883.

16. Ammons, *Option of Prison Privatization*, pp. 4–5.

17. Clair A. Cripe, Legal Aspects of Correctional Management, p. 380.

18. Health services was the exception. Smaller jails and prisons could not economically provide the full range of specialized care by competing for staff in the health-care market. These services were usually contracted out with local hospitals.

19. Alexis M. Durham, III, "The Future of Correctional Privatization: Lessons from the Past," in Gary Bowman et al., *Privatizing Correctional Institutions* (New Brunswick, NJ: Transaction Publishers, 1993), p. 33.

20. Charles Logan and Sharla Rausch, "Punishment for Profit: The Emergence of Private Enterprise Prisons," *Justice Quarterly* 2, 3 (1985): 303–318.

21. Douglas C. McDonald, "Public Imprisonment by Private Means: The Reemergence of Private Prisons and Jails in the United States, the United Kingdom, and Australia," *British Journal of Criminology* 34 (1994): 29–48.

22. Charles W. Thomas, Testimony Regarding Correctional Privatization, presented before The Little Hoover Commission of the State of California, August 21, 1997.

23. David Yarden, "Prisons, Profits, and the Private Sector Solution," *American Journal of Criminal Law* 21, 1 (Fall 1993): 325–334.

24. Charles W. Thomas, "Issues and Evidence from the U.S.," in Stephen T. Easton (ed.), Privatizing Correctional Services (British Columbia: Vancouver, 1998), pp. 15–61.

25. Yarden, "Prisons, Profits," p. 328.

26. James Austin, *District of Columbia Department of Corrections Long-Term Options Study* (Washington, DC: National Institute of Corrections, January 31, 1997).

27. Clair A. Cripe, *Legal Aspects of Correctional Management*, p. 384. Privately operated facilities for juveniles tend to be small and residential, with flexible programming catering to individual needs. See Robert D. McCrie, "Three Centuries of Criminal Justice Privatization in the United States," in Gary Bowman et al., *Privatizing the United States Justice System* (Jefferson, NC: McFarland & Co., 1992).

28. Ira P. Robbins, "The Case Against the Prison-Industrial Complex," *Public Interest Law Review* (Winter 1997): 23–44.

29. Ammons et al., The Option of Prison Privatization: A Guide for Community Deliberations, p. 10.

30. Travis, "Private Enterprise," p. 14.

31. Alexis M. Durham, III, *Crisis and Reform: Current Issues in American Punishment* (Boston: Little, Brown, 1994).

32. Donald B. Walker, "Privatization in Corrections," in Peter C. Kratcoski (ed.), Correctional Counseling and Treatment (Prospect Heights, IL: Waveland Press, 1994).

33. Durham III, "Future of Correctional Privatization," p. 43.

34. John L. Clark, *Inspection and Review of the Northeast Ohio Correctional Center* (Washington, DC: Office of the Corrections Trustee for the District of Columbia,

November 25, 1998); Eric Schosser, "The Prison-Industrial Complex," *The Atlantic Monthly* 283 (1998): 51–80.

35. Charles W. Thomas, "How Correctional Privatization Redefines the Legal Rights of Prisoners," *Privatization Review* 6, 1 (Winter 1991): 38–55.

36. Ira P. Robbins, "Privatization of Corrections: Defining the Issues," *Judicature* 69 (1987): 324–331, or *Federal Probation* 50 (1987): 24–30.

37. The leading case on this is *West v. Atkins,* 108 S. Ct. 2250 (1988). The case addresses the question of whether private persons under contract with the state can be sued under section 1983, or whether only public employees can be sued under this federal law. By deciding that such persons can be held liable and are acting under the "color of the law" when performing services, the Court expanded the number and categories of individuals who may be sued under section 1983. In 1997 the Supreme Court held that private prison guards employed by a private firm are not entitled to qualified immunity from suit by prisoners charging a section 1983 violation (*Richardson v. McKnight*).

38. Cripe, *Legal Aspects,* p. 394; Travis, "Private Enterprise."

39. J. Austin, and G. Coventry. (2001). *Emerging Issues on Privatized Prisons* (Washington, DC: Bureau of Justice Assistance, U.S. Department of Justice, 2001).

40. Austin, *Emerging Issues,* p. xi.

41. U.S. General Accounting Office. *Private and Public Prisons: Studies Comparing Operational Costs and/or Quality of Services* (Washington, DC: U.S. Government Printing Office, 1996), p. 6.

42. Gerald G. Gaes, Scott D. Camp, and William G. Saylor, "Appendix 2: Comparing the Quality of Publicly and Privately Operated Prisons: A Review," in D. McDonald, E. Fournier, M. Russell-Einhorn, and S. Crawford (eds.), *Private Prisons in the United States: An Assessment of Current Practice* (Boston: Abt Associates, 1998), pp. 1–38.

43. W. Bales, L. Bedard, and S. Quinn. (2003). *Recidivism: An Analysis of Public and Private State Prison Releases in Florida* (Tallahassee: Florida State University); D. Farabee and K. Knight. (2002). *A Comparison of Public and Private Prisons in Florida: During- and Post-Performance Measure Indicators* (Los Angeles, CA: Query Research).

44. J. Blumstein, and M. Cohen (2003). *The Interrelationship between Public and Private Prisons* (Nashville, KY: Vanderbilt University).

45. Clark, *Inspection and Review.*

8

■

Release, Recidivism, and Reentry

LEARNING OBJECTIVES

1. To understand the methods by which prisoners can be released from prison and how long they are imprisoned and under supervision for the crimes they have been convicted of.

2. To become familiar with the methods that measure recidivism, how such rates are changing over time, and how they vary by state.

3. To review the evidence on whether parole supervision is effective.

4. To learn how released prisoners adapt to life on the outside.

5. To review the evidence on whether reentry programs are or can be effective.

BACKGROUND

It's been over 150 years since John Augustus, the "father of probation," initiated what has today become the most common and prevalent form of correctional supervision. From 1841 to 1859, he convinced Boston judges to either release mostly drunkards to him by paying their bail or having them serve short probation sentences. His pioneering efforts were so inspiring that in 1878, Massachusetts passed the first legislation that allowed probation to become an official sanction for the court. Unlike today, these probation officers were unpaid volunteers. Some eighty years later, all states had some form of probation supervision with the probation officer being a professional, government employee. Shortly thereafter, Massachusetts was also the first state to implement parole supervision in 1846; by the 1950s all states had some form of parole supervision.

Over the past 159 years, parole has generally flourished with some bumps along the way. The most serious "bump" began in the 1970s when the indeterminate sentencing structure was questioned in terms of its fairness and effectiveness. While many but not a majority of states have abolished discretionary parole by a parole board, no states have completely abolished parole or post-prison release supervision. So the vast majority of the 600,000–700,000 prisoners released each year face some form of correctional supervision after completing their prison term.

THE GROWING NUMBER OF PRISON RELEASES

Eventually all prisoners leave prison, and the numbers have been escalating each year just as the number being admitted has been increasing. In 2009, about 680,000 state prisoners and another 50,000 federal prisoners were released after completing some portion of their sentence. Another 12.7 million will be released from the nation's jail system. Table 8-1 shows the two primary methods or forms· of release. "Conditional" releases are given to inmates who are released to some form of community supervision—usually parole. "Unconditional" releases are for people who are released with no supervision due to the expiration of their sentence. An increasing number of releases are not being paroled and are given minimal to no supervision; some states have abolished parole supervision or have become increasingly reluctant to parole inmates. The numbers of inmates released with no supervision or access to services will increase as the full effects of "truth in sentencing" and more restrictive parole-granting policies take hold. We will also examine what happens to people who are released from prison after having spent several years in confinement and the obstacles they face in trying to make it on the streets without reverting to criminal behavior. Interviews were originally

Table 8-1 Jail and Prison Releases—2009

Correctional System	Number	%
State Prison Releases—Total	**678,575**	**100%**
Conditional/Parole Releases	504,057	75%
Unconditional Releases	161,606	24%
Federal Prison Releases—Total	**50,720**	**100%**
Conditional/Parole Releases	1,479	3%
Unconditional Releases	49,208	97%
Jail Releases	**12.7 million**	**100%**

SOURCE: U.S. Department of Justice, Bureau of Justice Statistics, *Prisoners in 2009* (December, 2010). http://bjs. ojpusdoj.gov/index.cfm?ty=pbdetail&iid=2232.

conducted by the authors in 1999.[1] These are supplemented by a more recent study conducted on Maryland's parole system in 2009 by the Brennan Center for Justice.[2]

How Long Do They Stay in Prison and How Are They Released?

One of the objectives of this chapter is to estimate the total amount of supervision and incarceration convicts will experience before they are fully clear of their "legal obligations" to the state for the crime committed. For many years, the U.S. Department of Justice only reported the amount of time inmates spent in prison until they were granted their "first release," either by the parole board or by virtue of the expiration of their sentence. The most recent number represents people released in 2006 and shows the average length of stay (LOS) to be 28 months. The median number is much lower (15 months), which suggests that a large number of people sentenced to prison spend less than a year of incarceration for nonviolent crimes and probation violations.

However, this number greatly underestimates the total length of incarceration for many prisoners for several reasons. First, it excludes the amount of time an inmate will spend in jail before going to prison. This period of incarceration occurs when the defendant (at that time) is arrested and detained in the local (usually county) jail. Although many defendants arrested for minor crimes (ranging from drunk driving, failure to pay parking tickets, and petty theft) are quickly released within one to three days, those defendants who eventually are sentenced to prison will spend many months in jail awaiting the court's sentencing decision. According to the U.S. Department of Justice, the LOS in jail for inmates admitted to state prison is approximately five months. Thus, the total period of incarceration before being granted a "first" release averages 33 months (Table 8-2).

Table 8-2 Prison Releases and Time Served—Pretrial Jail, Prison, and Parole 2006 Prison Releases

Original Sentence	Average 60 mos	Median 36 mos
Incarceration		
Pretrial time in local jail awaiting sentence	5 mos	5 mos
Prison time until first release	28 mos	15 mos
Total incarceration time until first release	33 mos	20 mos
Parole Supervision		
Successful parole releases	27 mos	20 mos
Unsuccessful parole releases	21 mos	15 mos
Additional prison time for parole violators	27 mos	16 mos
Total Time Under Supervision	**60 mos**	**36 mos**

SOURCE: Bureau of Justice Statistics, National Corrections Reporting Program, 2006 (2010).

Second, this figure only refers to persons who are referred to as "first releases". This means that they are not parole violators who are being re-released again on their prison setence. Technically it means prisoners being released at their first parole hearing or a subsequent parole hearing date, or are being discharged after being denied parole or not being eligible for parole.[3] This category of releases excludes the large number of inmates who return to prison for parole violations and who spend many additional months in confinement before being rereleased to parole or being discharged after completing their entire sentence (that is, "maxing out"). Once released from prison, the inmate must deal with the rules and regulations of parole supervision for many more months. And, if an inmate fails to abide by these rules or is arrested for a new crime, he or she will be returned to prison for further incarceration. The latest national data show that about 40 percent of all prison releases return to prison after three years.

There are no national data on the amount of time parole violators remain in prison until they are rereleased. The practices vary substantially by the state. In California, most parolees spend about 3 to 5 months in custody before being rereleased.[4] In Louisiana, they can spend years as they "lose" all of the time they spent on parole supervision, starting over when they were paroled. For example, if a person gets a five-year prison sentence and is paroled at two years there are three years left to serve on parole. If the parolee violates the terms of supervision after serving two years on parole, he or she must start over with the two-year prison sentence to serve another three years in prison until the original five-year sentence is completed. In this example, the person will do a total of seven years on the five-year sentence (two in prison, two on parole, and another three in prison as a parole violator).

Based on the national average of 60 months, successful parolees will do 33 months in jail and prison and then another 27 months on parole. So-called unsuccessful parolees do the same 33 months in jail and prison and 21 months on parole. Their parole time is shorter since violations tend to occur sooner rather than later, but when they return, they are likely to do more time in prison. Using these figures, the total length of stay for released prisoners can range on average from 33 to 60 months—not 28 months as reported in government reports.

Third, the current cohort of prison releases does not accurately reflect the recent changes in sentencing laws that require greater numbers of inmates to serve extremely long periods of time in prison. It will take many years for the full effects of various sentencing laws, designed to greatly increase the length of stay, to show up in subsequent release cohorts in certain states. In summary, persons sentenced to prison can expect to spend on average 5 to 7 years either in jail, prison, or on parole.

Recidivism

During this period of supervision, many released inmates experience tremendous difficulties in adjusting to the outside world without being rearrested and returning to prison and jail. In general, most inmates are rearrested at least once after being released from prison but most (60%) do not return to prison. What is the source of these recidivism rates and what are the implications of these numbers?

There are three ways that recidivism is defined by most criminologists:

1. Percentage of people arrested for a new crime after being released from prison;

2. Percentage of people convicted of a new crime after being released from prison; and,

3. Percentage of people returned to prison after being released from prison.

In order to standardize these recidivism rates, a fixed period of time is set to record the rearrests, reconvictions, and returns to prison. The most universal time period is 3 years because most new arrests, convictions, and returns to prison occur within a three-year (36 month) period.

The U.S. Department of Justice has conducted two so-called national studies of recidivism. The first was conducted on 108,580 people released from eleven state prison systems in 1983. That study found that 63 percent were rearrested at least once for a felony or a serious misdemeanor within three years, another 47 percent were convicted of a new crime and 41 percent were returned to prison because of a new felony conviction or a parole violation. In 1994, BJS conducted another study that involved fifteen states and consisted of 272,111 people released from prison. That study showed basically the same results with a higher rate of arrests (69%) but the same number of people convicted of a new crime. The return-to-prison rate is a bit more complicated. This is because California, which is one of the fifteen states in both the 1983 and 1994 studies, had greatly increased its return-to-prison rate for reasons that will be discussed later in this chapter. Because California has so many more people being released from prison than the other fourteen states, it skews the results. If you include California in the data, the overall return-to-prison rate is 50 percent. If you exclude California, the rate goes down to 40 percent (see Table 8-3).

A more recent study on recidivism rates has been released by the Pew Charitable Trust Center.[5] That study was based on the three year follow-up recidivism rates as reported by the states for prisoners released in 1999 and 2004. That study found that the 1999 three year re-incarceration rate was 45 percent while the 2004 rate was 43 percent. If California is excluded, the overall re-incarceration rate is 40 percent.

Table 8-3 National Recidivism Rates for 1983 and 1994 Prison Releases

Recidivism Measure	1983 Prison Releases	1994 Prison Releases
Rearrested	63%	69%
Reconvicted	47%	47%
Reimprisoned	41%	40% to 52%*

40 percent deletes California data while 52 percent includes California

SOURCES: Patrick Langan and David Levin, *Recidivism of Prisoners Released in 1994* (Washington, DC: U.S. Department of Justice, Bureau of Justice Statistics, [June 2002]); Allen J. Beck and Bernard E. Shipley, *Recidivism of Prisoners Released in 1983*, BJS Special Report

So what do we make of these results? One conclusion is that a significant proportion of the people released from prison do not get rearrested, reconvicted, or return to prison. This is contrary to public perceptions that most people return to prison—they don't. Many are rearrested but a good proportion of those arrests (about one-third) don't result in a conviction. This is understandable since police tend to round up the usual suspects.

It also suggests that we are not seeing any progress in the recidivism rates, at least not between the BJS 1983 and the Pew 2004—a time when the imprisonment binge was in full throttle and prison systems were badly crowded. We would wonder why, under these circumstances, we would expect any reduction in recidivism rates.

Finally, in the two BJS reports, it was found that there was no relationship between how long a prisoner was imprisoned and recidivism rates (Table 8-4). This means that keeping someone in prison for longer or shorter periods of time has no impact on recidivism rates. One can then question the value of longer prison terms in deterring future criminal conduct by released prisoners.

Similar to our discussion of how incarceration rates vary dramatically between states and within states, so to do recidivism rates. It becomes a bit more complicated as each state computes its recidivism differently. But as shown in Figure 8-1, there are considerable differences among the states. Again, part of these differences have to do with the sentencing structure of the state. For example, Arizona and Florida have very low three-year return-to-prison rates because they are "truth in sentencing" states with little time spent on parole after release from prison. Thus, in these two states, very few people can return to prison as a technical parole violator.

The often-neglected study by the Rand Corporation, sponsored by the U.S. Department of Justice, compared the two-year rearrest rates of a group of felons sent to California prisons with a group who was matched on crime seriousness, past records, and other relevant characteristics but who were granted probation instead of prison. The results revealed that the persons

Table 8-4 Three-Year Follow-Up Rate of Rearrest of State Prisoners Released in 1994, By Time Served in Prison

Time Served	3 Year Rearrest Rates
6 months or less	66.0%
7 to 12 months	64.8%
13 to 18 months	64.2%
19 to 24 months	65.4%
25 to 30 months	68.3%
31 to 36 months	62.6%
37 to 60 months	63.2%
61 months or more	54.0%

SOURCE: U.S. Department of Justice, Office of Justice Programs, Bureau of Justice Statistics, *Prison Statistics*. Online. Available: http://www.ojp.usdoj.gov/bjs/prisons.htm. Accessed August 1, 2006.

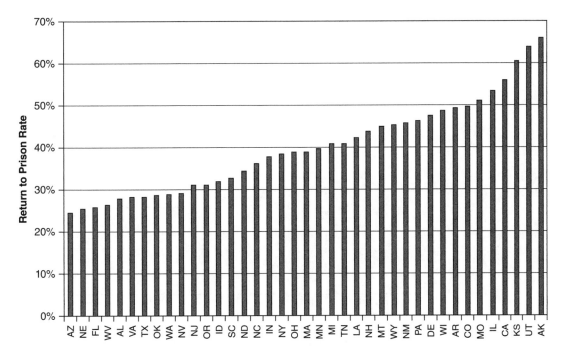

FIGURE 8-1 Differences in Three Year Recidivism Rates by State

sentenced to prison were rearrested, reconvicted, and resentenced to jail or prison at significantly higher rates than the persons who were sentenced to probation (Figure 8-2).[6]

Even though prison has apparently increased the likelihood that they will commit future crimes, ex-prisoners are still less likely to commit crime than they were before being sent to prison. In other words, their rate of rearrest declined compared to the rate that existed before they were sentenced to prison. Two studies of released felons in California and Illinois showed that the arrest rates of released prisoners was about half of the rates before imprisonment. The California study found that the number of arrests for prisoners released to the streets over two years dropped by over 50 percent compared to the number that occurred two years before the inmates were sentenced to prison and that the severity of the crimes also declined by 50 percent during the same two-year follow-up period.[7]

The Illinois study also found a 64 percent decline in the rate of arrests twelve months after release from prison as compared to the twelve months before imprisonment (0.8 arrests per year per released inmate versus 2.2 arrests per year before prison).[8] In addition, the study showed that significant proportions of those arrests were for minor property or drug use crimes that did not result in a conviction or resentencing to prison. Instead, high arrest rates often reflected traditional police practices of "rounding up the usual suspects." The National Council on Crime and Delinquency (NCCD) studies also demonstrated that

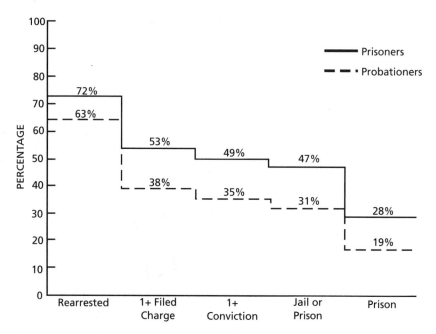

FIGURE 8-2 Recidivism Among Probationers and Matched Prisoners: Total Sample Combined

although prison releases were frequently rearrested, their overall impact on crime rates in the two states was about 2 percent or less.

The reductions in the arrest rates for released inmates are largely the result of maturation effects: as inmates get older, they burn out and are unable to maintain their previous criminal lifestyles. The highest crime rates are for males between the ages of 15 and 24, whereas the average age for released prisoners is over 30, well beyond their most productive crime-producing years. This point, in part, explains the limits of incarceration as a workable crime-reducing strategy. As noted in Chapter 2, the ranks of released prisoners are replaced each year by another cohort of lower-class prison-bound males nurtured in inner-city communities riddled with poverty, drug abuse, and violence.

THE CRIMINOGENIC EFFECTS
OF PAROLE SUPERVISION

Today, most inmates do not get off of parole without some further legal difficulties. Table 8-5 shows that only about half of parolees "successfully" complete parole. This measure is different from the prison recidivism rate since a sizeable share of the prison releases are not placed on parole. Another 34 percent are re-incarcerated mostly for a parole revocation rather than being re-incarcerated for receiving a new felony sentence. Another 9 percent absconded from supervision meaning they cannot be located.

Table 8-5 Terminations from Parole in 2009

Type of Exit	2009
Completion	51%
Incarcerated	34%
New Sentence	9%
Revocation	24%
Absconder	9%
Other	4%
Transferred to Another State	1%
Death	1%

Since 1980, the success rate of parole declined and has recently begun to increase, but it is no where near the rate that existed in 1985 (Figure 8-3). Since 1980, the number of parole violations has increased nationally from 28,817 to 242,007 in 2009, representing a nearly tenfold increase. This trend is attributable in large part to the dramatic changes in the nature of parole supervision and the imposition of increasingly more severe conditions of supervision on parolees. Instead of a system designed to help prisoners readjust to a rapidly changing and more competitive economic system, the current parole system has been designed to catch and punish inmates for petty and nuisance-type behaviors that do not, in themselves, draw a prison term.

Technical violations represent a wide array of noncriminal behaviors (see Table 8-6). For example, an inmate may have failed to appear for scheduled office visits with the parole agent, failed to attend counseling sessions, failed to notify the parole agent of a change of address, or failed to maintain "gainful"

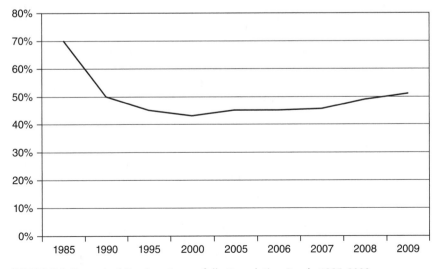

FIGURE 8-3 Percent of Parolees Successfully Completing Parole 1985–2009

Table 8-6 Selected Conditions of Parole in Effect in 51 Jurisdictions

Condition of Parole	Number of Jurisdictions	%
Obey all federal, state, and local laws	50	98.0
Report to the parole officer as directed and answer all reasonable inquiries of the parole officer	49	96.1
Refrain from possessing a firearm or other dangerous weapon unless granted permission	47	92.2
Remain within the jurisdiction of the court and notify the parole officer of any change in residence	46	90.2
Permit the parole officer to visit the parolee at home or elsewhere	42	82.4
Obey all rules and regulations of the parole supervision agency	40	78.4
Maintain gainful employment	40	78.4
Abstain from association with persons with criminal records	31	60.8
Pay all court-ordered fines, restitution, or other financial penalties	27	52.9
Meet family responsibilities and support dependents	24	47.1
Undergo medical or psychiatric treatment and/or enter and remain in a specified institution, if so ordered by the court	23	45.1
Pay supervision fees	19	37.3
Attend a prescribed secular course of study or vocational training	9	17.6
Perform community service	7	13.7

SOURCE: Edward E. Rhine, William R. Smith, and Donald W. Jackson, *Paroling Authorities: Recent History and Current Practice* (Laurel, MD: American Correctional Association, 1991).

employment. Technical violations can also include subsequent arrests without convictions or failure to pass drug tests—which suggests continued drug use—or may simply reflect unsubstantiated suspicions by parole authorities.

Unlike the criminal courts, parole revocation hearings do not require the same level of proof to trigger a return to prison. Although the *Morissey* decision by the U.S. Supreme Court grants parolees the right to a partial "due process" hearing, they still are not afforded such basic rights at these hearings as the right to counsel, the right to call witnesses, an impartial judge and jury, or most of the features of a full due process proceeding. More important, a parolee's parole status can be revoked if the board feels there is a preponderance of evidence that the parolee was not meeting parole obligations. This means that parolees who are arrested but not found guilty can have their parole status revoked, be returned to prison, and remain in prison until their original sentence expires.

Some parole board officials view these broad discretionary powers over parolees as a positive feature of parole, because it allows them to re-imprison prisoners with greater speed and certainty than if the charges had been brought before the criminal courts. For example, revoking parole status and re-incarcerating the prisoner is accomplished without involving the district attorney, a public defender, a law enforcement official, or a judge. Parole revocation hearings often are pro forma ceremonies lasting less than five minutes before a parole board officer, whose recommendation is forwarded to the full board for approval. Often there is no interview by the parole board member and the parolee.

OBSTACLES TO MAKING IT AFTER RELEASE

Why is it that so many prisoners have such a difficult time "making it on parole"? Given their social and economic situation, one might better ask, why do so many actually make it? Their transition to the outside world is replete with hurdles, pitfalls, and traps that make it extremely difficult for all and that defeat many. These obstacles range from finding a job and staying off drugs to dealing with the parole agent. But there are many organizational obstacles imposed by the parole system that serve to encourage failure.

Parole Supervision and Drug Testing Fees

Most states and counties require the parolee to pay for supervision. These costs vary but they generally cost $10 to $25 per month. In Kentucky, the fee is $25 a month plus a $1,000 initial placement fee. In Maryland, the fee is $40 a month, and in addition to the supervision fees there are drug testing costs that also cost about $25 a test. The most powerful tool for the new parole agent is the urinalysis test. The first thing a parolee is instructed to do on arrival at the parole officer's office is to urinate in a bottle and have a chemical test completed. Because most of these inmates have rather extensive histories of drug use, it is predictable that many will occasionally fail the drug test and subsequently have their paroles revoked. Generally, a parolee usually is required to pay $50 to $75 a month over the course of a three-to-five-year probation period. If one fails to pay the monthly fees, a revocation may occur or a surcharge may be added to the amount that has not been paid. In Maryland the surcharge is set at 17 percent of the unpaid balance.

Child Support

In addition to monthly supervision and drug testing fees, many parolees are faced with outstanding child support obligations. In general, these debts stack up during incarceration and must be paid once the person is released from prison. A 2005 University of Maryland study found that there were 17,214 child support cases in Maryland with incarcerated parents or previously incarcerated parents. The average arrears owed for each incarcerated parent was $15,933 and average arrears for parolees was $13,472.[9]

The Shock of "Reentry"

Most ex-inmates pass suddenly from a highly routinized, controlled, reduced, and slow-paced prison life into the complex, fast-moving, impersonal world of the "streets." Because they are assimilated into prison routines and culture, the transition usually disorganizes, disturbs, and depresses them—especially those inmates who have spent many years incarcerated. Think of the problems that highly skilled, well-educated white males would have in getting a job, buying a car, and finding a place to live after two years of imprisonment. For the uneducated and unemployable who must face a rapidly changing and increasingly competitive and unforgiving society, the odds are almost insurmountable.

> The cars, buses, people, buildings, roads, stores, lights, noises, and animals are things [they have not] experienced firsthand for quite some time. The most ordinary transactions of the civilian have dropped from [their] repertoire of automatic maneuvers. Getting on a streetcar, ordering something at a hot dog stand, entering a theater are strange. Talking to people whose accent, style of speech, gestures, and vocabulary are slightly different is difficult. The entire stimulus world—the sights, sounds, and smells—is strange.[10]

> My family passed while I was inside. I have no family out here. I got out in November 2007 after fifteen years....I've been here [Goodwill] three weeks. I do a little on my own. I don't want to go back in [the] street.[11]

Beyond overcoming the initial shock of "reentry," released prisoners must struggle to achieve some minimal level of economic viability. To do this in a conventional fashion, they must immediately locate some form of affordable housing, gather sufficient clothing and other basic accoutrements—tools, toiletries, and get a job. They have scant resources for accomplishing these meager goals. State prison systems usually provide a small amount of money ($200 or so), and a few provide transitional institutional supports, such as halfway houses or arrangements with social welfare agencies. In Nevada, inmates receive $21 to help them "transition" from prison to parole. These limited supports, however, are temporary and merely prolong the eventual problem of trying to make it without going back to prison.

Some prisoners have saved a little, even several hundred dollars, from money earned in prison "pay" jobs that usually pay considerably less than $7 per day. A minority have help from their families. However, most must make it on their own resources and capabilities, which are typically limited and damaged. As pointed out in Chapter 2, most prisoners enter prison poorly educated and vocationally unskilled, with limited work experience. And prison has done little to improve their preparation for the outside work world; in fact, it has often worsened it. As stated earlier, prisoners seldom receive any appropriate job training, and the habits they learn in prison are inconsistent with outside work routines.

Finding a Job

Despite research showing that providing employment or other forms of economic assistance significantly reduces the likelihood of recidivism, most prison systems are unable or unwilling to assist inmates.[12] Released inmates confront sizeable barriers to getting even the most demeaning forms of employment because they are stigmatized as ex-convicts. Most employers will not hire ex-convicts; and so, when applying for a job, the "ex" must either tell the employer that he has a record and is likely to be denied employment or the ex-convict will take the chance that the employer will not run a record check and that a parole agent will not inform the employer. Also, many jobs require bonding, special licenses, or union memberships, all of which are unavailable to most ex-convicts.

The ex-convict stands at the very end of society's growing line of job seekers. At the end of the 1960s, when the country had more employment opportunities for blue-collar workers than it does presently, there was some movement to reduce the employment barriers for ex-convicts when studies revealed an employment rate of around 50 percent (which seemed dismal at the time). At present, this rate is much lower. In the Maryland study, 75 percent of the parolee population was unemployed. The following two cases reveal the difficulties released prisoners have in trying to locate a job.

> I've been looking for work for two weeks. I'm living with friends 'cause my mother can't help me. I've been staying away from my old neighborhood and friends 'cause I don't want to get back into that life. I've been pretty nervous 'cause I don't know how to live like this. If I was going back to selling drugs, I wouldn't be nervous 'cause I would know what I was gonna do. But I made up my mind I wasn't gonna sell no drugs. I go to different places, fill out applications. I've been to San Leandro, Hayward, Oakland, Berkeley. I'm in the process of getting my California ID. I have to have that. Now every day I am going to different places and trying to get a job. I got a friend who got a job at the Oakland Airport. He says something might come up there. If I don't get a job through some agency or friends, I'm gonna do something I thought I would never do—work for McDonald's. [R.C., a twenty-two-year-old black man]

> I been meeting R.C. [above] and we been going up and down the streets applying everywhere. Wherever I tell him to meet me, he is there on time. I was supposed to get this light industrial job. They kept putting obstacles in front of me and I talked my way over them every time, till she brought up my being on parole and then she went sour on me. If they catch me lying on the application about being in prison or being on parole, they will violate me and give me four months. I was over to Hertz, applying for a job detailing cars. They pay $9 a hour. They told me they would give me a job if I had a driver's license. I gotta have $50 to get my license reissued, $35 for a ticket and $15 for the fee. The agent doesn't have a fund to loan me any. They used to have a fund, but the parolees didn't pay the money back. If I could get my license, I could work for Avis or Hertz. I had dry-cleaning training a long time ago, but this time I wasn't in long enough to go through the program. It takes several years. You have to have the paper to get a job. I could jump in and clean anything—silks, wools, remove any spot, use all the chemicals, but I don't got any paper. They won't let you start without the paper. And they don't have any programs where they are giving you the old training and certifying you. [K.B., a thirty-eight-year-old black man][13]

Trail 'Em, Nail 'Em, Jail 'Em

Being on parole means being under the supervision of parole agents who have peace officer status. Parole officers are equipped with extraordinary police powers: they can enforce a set of "conditions of parole," which are much more restrictive than penal statutes, and they are not restrained by constitutional protections against invasion of privacy and illegal search and seizure. Parole agents can enter a parolee's residence at any time of the day or night, search the parolee at the agent's discretion, place the parolee in jail any time they desire, and charge the parolee with violation of parole, either for new crimes or for violation of the conditions of parole.

> I go to the parole agent and tell him I want to get a job. "Uh, come back and see me next week." I mean, it's not really his fault because he's got 300 other guys. And he doesn't even know me. All he knows is my number is three seven such and such. All he knows—if he wants to keep his job, all he's got to do is have me come in once a week, piss in the bottle. As long as the bottle don't show no drugs in it, I can stay on the street another week. First time the piss is not good, all he gotta do is send me to jail, that's it. He put my file over there in "inactive," and that's it. He's still got his job, he goes on—you know, they don't have to get personally involved with you. 'Cause they can't. You got 300 guys—how you get involved with 300 guys?[14]

Commensurate with the toughening of sentencing laws and the demise of the rehabilitation model, parole supervision has been transformed ideologically from a social service to a law enforcement system. During the rehabilitative era (the 1950s and 1960s), most states sought to combine policing and rehabilitative services in their parole administration. Parole agents were viewed as paternalistic figures who mixed authority and help. The punitive swing in corrections and the fiscal crisis experienced by most states have transformed parole more and more into a policing operation. Instead of developing individualized plans to help the prisoners locate a job, find a residence, or locate a needed drug treatment service, the new parole system is bent on surveillance and detection. Parolees are routinely and randomly checked for illegal drug use, failure to locate or maintain a job, moving without permission, or any number of other petty and nuisance-type behaviors that do not conform to the rules of parole.

On detection of any of these acts or on the parolee's arrest for any crime, the parole officer holds the option of having the parolee arrested and placed in the local jail until the parole board can review the charges. In many states, parolees can wait weeks in the local jail until a representative from the parole board makes a determination on whether the behavior is sufficiently serious to warrant revocation and return to prison.

A parolee we interviewed ended up on general assistance He had been abusing drugs, but had finally gotten into a drug program; in spite of this, he lost a good job because of his agent's enforcement of the rules:

> I looked for a place to stay in San Francisco, so I moved in with a friend across the bay in Hayward. I got a job as a bank courier. I wasn't carrying any

money, and it was a good job. My agent told me to quit it and move back to the city. I hadn't been able to find a job in the city, so I told him, "Would you rather have me back on GA [general assistance welfare] and selling dope?" He said he couldn't tell me to do that. [D.H., a fifty-one-year-old white man]

Similar sentiments were voiced in the 2009 Maryland study:

I'm on parole to 2011. They give you the whole fee, $2000. People who are on the street will just try to find a way to pay....I went back to boosting (stealing) before because they threatened to lock me up. I was thinking "I just did time in prison, does that count for anything."....It's a little discouraging to get out and owe $2000 right away. [Diller et al., (2009), p. 19]

I had three cases. I couldn't pay the money. The agent started calling me to say come and see them. They would call during the job time. I told them I couldn't right now, I'm working and they would say, "It's your responsibility. Keep the job and go to jail or come and see me." My appointments were between 9am and 1pm. I didn't go. I had to work. They did come and lock me up. [Diller et al., (2009), p. 18]

It's stressful. You come home with three felonies and are faced with a large fee. You have a felony and you're trying to find a job with felonies. I owed $3200—got it down to $2000 and haven't paid a penny since. My other bills are lacking. I'm faced with violation of parole. I don't want to go back. [Diller et al., (2009), p. 18]

Intensive Supervision Programs

Intensive supervision programs (ISPs) also place additional obstacles in the path of parolees and result in more parole failures. Hailed by criminologists as the new wave of "intermediate sanctions," these programs were first created by the courts to divert offenders who otherwise would have been imprisoned had the program not existed. However, they have also been used by parole agencies to escalate levels of supervision for offenders paroled from prison. The ISPs, the "back end" of the correctional system, are intended to encourage parole boards to release offenders who pose a somewhat higher risk to public safety and who would not have been released had the ISPs not existed. By releasing these marginal cases on ISP, the inmate's expected length of stay in prison can be shortened, thus reducing the prison population. For both probationers and parolees, specialized treatment programs were also to be part of the ISP regimen, although this rarely has been the case. The overall expectation was that these programs would also reduce these offenders' recidivism rates and therefore be more cost-effective as compared to traditional forms of incarceration.

Evaluations of these programs have shown just the opposite results. A number of experimental studies by the Rand Corporation have found that persons placed in these programs violate parole for technical reasons at a far greater rate than those receiving regular supervision, even though their rearrest rates are essentially equal.[15] These programs also tend to be far more expensive than regular supervision and have had little if any impact on prison crowding. Because of the highly restrictive nature of the programs' eligibility criteria, these programs are quite small in size (50 to 150 offenders diverted or released on parole each year) and often cease to exist. The higher technical violation failure rates for ISP cases are simply the result of programs that provide more supervision but not many more services. Consequently, parole and probation officers are able to detect more petty behavior than before. But more important, the parole officer is able to use this information against the inmate to justify revocation and recommitment to prison.

Electronic Monitoring

Many ISP programs are also adding electronic monitoring technology to their capabilities. In such a situation, the inmate cannot, without calling his or her parole officer, leave his or her residence to do such normal things as purchasing groceries, picking up the mail, and running any number of regular errands associated with modern life.

As with the ISP evaluations, rigorous studies of electronic monitoring programs have found neither negative nor positive results relating to rearrest.[16] Offenders admitted to such programs respond the same as or worse than offenders placed under normal supervision. In fact, a study of the Oklahoma electronic monitoring program found that released inmates placed on electronic monitoring did worse, as a greater proportion were returned to prison for not abiding by the strict house arrest rules imposed by the electronic monitoring program.

THOSE WHO MAKE IT

Most prisoners we interviewed in our three-state study aspired to a relatively modest, stable, conventional life after prison. "I want a nice job, paying pretty good. Something to keep me busy instead of running the streets." "When I get out I want to have my kids with me, have a good job so I can support them." "I'm going to try to get into electronics. I want a job I won't get laid off on."[17] However, their chances of achieving these modest goals are slim. As already suggested, released prisoners are socially and economically damaged goods. Parolees are certainly no better equipped to make it in society after imprisonment than when they were admitted. They remain largely uneducated, unskilled, and without the necessary family support system to help them make a law-abiding transition from prison to the community.[18]

Despite these obstacles, most released prisoners eventually quit or scale down their criminal activities to a level that avoids arrest or at least arrest for serious crimes. Because so many continue to have extreme difficulty finding and holding jobs, how, then, do they get by? What kind of life do they live?

Doing Good

A few released prisoners "do all right," that is, achieve more or less permanent viability in a relatively conventional manner. They usually do so only because of the random chance of securing a good job and a niche in some conventional social world by virtue of their own individual efforts to "straighten up," often with the help of their family, friends, or prisoner assistance organizations. But even members of this group are likely to face periodic obstacles in being accepted as full citizens. In applying for a job from which they are not excluded by virtue of their prior criminal record, they must publicly admit their ex-convict status. When crimes are committed in their neighborhoods, they are often arrested simply because they are known to the police. Their friendships and memories are forever tied to their past prison experiences. They will always be treated by others with suspicion, fear, and distrust.

A very few released prisoners—usually persons with better preparation when they leave prison; significant support from friends, family, or some program; and some luck—realize some of their higher aspirations. A twenty-nine-year-old white male who had had a drug and alcohol problem since he was fifteen and served two years for vehicular manslaughter was about to graduate from San Francisco State with a 3.7 grade point average and was applying for graduate school when we interviewed him. His progress demonstrates the difficulty experienced by persons who do make it.

I had about $1,200 when I got out that I had saved when I was out on OR [release on own recognizance program]. I knew from my crime and record I was gonna get time, so I worked and saved my money. I first got a hotel room in downtown Burlingame, the only flea bag hotel there, and went to an AA meeting that night. The next day I went to see my parole officer, and he started right off reading all my arrests, saying you did this and that. But I finally struck a deal with him that if I didn't drink or drive a car without a license he would keep off my back. But if I did, he would violate me and charge me with everything he could. He lived up to the bargain for a year and then I got another parole agent.

By then I was already in San Francisco State. I had signed up with the Rebound Project [a program that helps ex-prisoners enter San Francisco State University] while I was in CMC [a state prison near San Luis Obispo]. I had a small apartment in San Carlos for $400 a month. I was busing it to school three days a week. Two hours there and two hours back. I got a job at Walgreen's. I was selling liquor at night to guys who were just like me. But I was attending AA and had made up my mind that I was gonna change my life. And I never took a drink. Then I worked for a while selling cars. Then selling TVs at Mathews in Daly City. I bought an old beat-up Buick that had a pretty good motor and I got two years out of it. About 25,000 miles.

The next parole agent was a real tough guy. First thing he told me was, "It's obvious you've been pulling some scam for a year." So he put me back on maximum custody. The other agent, even though he put on the tough-guy act, he left me alone. This guy had me coming in once a week, had me pissing in the bottle, and he would show up at my house at six in the morning trying to catch me at something. But I had decided that if they were going to send me back, they were gonna have to fabricate something. I wasn't doing nothing. I didn't even have kitchen knives in my house. I made the decision, also, that I was gonna stay out of their face. I learned that in prison. If you stayed out of people's faces and stayed away from places where shit started, you wouldn't have any trouble. I never went in the day room or to the iron pile [the weight workout area]. That's where guys got stuck. So I did the same on the outside. I had to learn to keep out of people's faces outside, too. One time some guy in the library got in my face and I got back in his. I didn't have the little stamp on my ID card that you had to have to check out reference books and he wouldn't give me a book. They hadn't sent me the stamp yet. So we got into it. But I try now to keep out of everyone's face. Sometimes some of these PC [politically correct] students get on my nerves. The little assholes don't know shit, and they're telling me what's politically correct. But I still stay out of their faces.

Then I got another agent. They didn't tell me and I went to the office and the old agent said he had sent me a letter telling me that I had been transferred to a new agent. He didn't send me no letter. It's lucky I had gone to see the old agent when I did, because I was supposed to report to the new agent the next day and I wouldn't have known it and they could have violated me. This guy was an asshole too, but then I got another agent and he was like the first one. By that time I had finished two years of college and had no arrests. So he left me alone. Now, I am gonna graduate with a 3.7. But I had a lot of luck, too. A lot of times I got behind in my rent, but I had good landlords. Really nice guys and they let me slide. They could have kicked me out and where would I have been? The parole agency wasn't gonna help me. They're too busy trying to bust guys. [1999 California interviews]

Dependency

Many ex-prisoners refrain from further law violations but remain completely dependent on their families or social welfare. This is true for the following four parolees.

I got out on Friday a year ago, and I got high right away. When I went to the parole agent on Monday, he asked me if I had been using and I told him I had. He said he liked my honesty, but he sent me right then to a ninety-day detox at San Quentin. I didn't use no more. I been staying at home with my mother. She is just happy I'm clean. I haven't been able to find no job, but she thinks that's alright, just so I'm clean. You see, I got a younger brother and sister and an older sister, all on crack. I help them a little and protect the house. My mother is just glad I do that. She is proud of me. Shows me to her friends, says, "See how good he looks?" I go to meetings and just stay home. I got a lady and a seven-year-old daughter, too, who I see a lot. I'm on GA and get $340 a month. I couldn't live on that. It's lucky I got my mother. I got phlebitis in my leg and have to take medicine. It hurts

when I stand or walk too much. But I'm still gonna take a job if I get one.
I want the extra spending money. But I'm not going back on drugs. If I did,
I'd just be back into buying some drugs, flipping them or burglarizing houses
and factories like before. [K.W., a thirty-year-old black man]

I get $620 a month through SSI [supplemental security income]. I got a room
on Sixth Street [skid-row area] through Tenderloin Housing. It costs me $260
a month. I eat breakfasts at one of the restaurants around the hotel. For $2.50
I get eggs, bacon, and potatoes. Sometimes I eat at Glide for lunch, sometimes
dinner, too. Once in a while I treat myself to steak dinner. I don't use drugs or
alcohol. I mostly stay to myself, watch TV in the room. It's safer that way.
Sometimes, I walk to Golden Gate Park. And I go to a movie once in a while.
I can't read very much because I'm too nervous. I have a hyperactive thyroid.
They found out I had it in prison. I kept losing weight. I went from around
190 to 130. The doctors there didn't know what it was and wouldn't give
me any time. So I swallowed glass and told them I had. They sent me to the
General Hospital and when I got there, I told them why I had done it. So
they gave me all kinds of tests and found out I had the hyperactive thyroid.
So I'm waiting to get some drugs for it. I've been on the list for seven months.
I have an appointment in May. I'm not going back to prison. I can't live there.
I don't know how they can treat a person like that. Least they could do is have
some kind of program. There is no rehabilitation. They just shove you out the
door with no support. It's scary as hell. What I want is a job. Any job. I don't
give a fuck what it is. I'll clean shitters, or whatever. At least it is something to
fill my time and make me feel better about myself, something constructive.
[L.E., a forty-eight-year-old white man]

I used drugs, speed, the first day. It scared the hell out of me. I've been clean
ever since, since July, nine months. It's the first time I've been clean when
I was out since I first went to the joint in the '60s. I feel kinda weird. I'm
gonna stay clean and get off this parole. It's hard to do, but I'm not going
back. I tried to get work, but there is this thing, you have to say you were in
prison. If you don't, it's a violation. Who's gonna hire a fifty-one-year-old
that's been in prison most of his life? I'm getting GA. My room's $270. That
leaves me 70 bucks. Not much. I'm trying to get SSI and drugs after having
been in the system all these years. They tell me that you go once and they
deny you. You go again and they deny you. Then the third time they give it
to you. I eat in restaurants once in a while. But usually I buy food at the food
bank. A friend of mine has a hot plate. Sometimes I eat at Glide or that gay
church on Gough. I go there on Christmas, New Year, and Easter. I go up
to the firehouse on Third Street where they collect toys for kids. They give
hot soup in the afternoon. My sister sent me some clothes and every month
I buy something, like these jeans. Most of the time I stay alone. I stay away
from the TL [Tenderloin district, where there is a lot of drug dealing, prostitution, and crime]. I watch TV a lot. I go to the library and walk around a
lot. I like to go to Golden Gate Park and the wharf. Last month I went back
to Arkansas and visited my sister. The parole agent let me go. When I got
back, he said he won a bet on me. The supervisor said I would never come

back. I go to the shelters sometimes to talk to people. I try to tell the youngsters how it is. Maybe I can help them a little, so they can stay away from the shit I got into. [D.R., a fifty-one-year-old Chicano]

I have a drug-related offense. I'm on parole until March 2009. Right now I'm in a residential treatment program, and you can't work while you are in there. I get a letter saying I have to pay these costs. They keep shooting letters at you. It makes you depressed and it can mess around and make you use. But I've learned that's not the way. I can't get bus fare to see my parole officer. The bus costs $3.50 twice a month and then I have urinalysis every week. Some people have it twice a week or even three times. You need bus fare for each of those times and the urinalysis fee. If you get in a job program they want you to train, you're not getting paid, so you have to manage to live without getting paid. Even your family doesn't want to take care of a grown man. It can drive some one into the street just to make ends meet. Then you get violated Maryland parolee. [Diller et al., (2009), p 17–18.]

Drift

Other parolees, even though their intentions before release and at the time we interviewed them were to avoid going back to prison, cross back and forth— outside and inside the law and the parole rules. For a while they hold menial jobs or live with their families, in halfway houses, or on welfare. Then they slip, start using drugs, lose their job, and begin selling drugs or stealing. Usually they are arrested or "violated" by their agent and sent back, often for short periods, perhaps a thirty-day detox, which in California can be done with no formal proceedings. Then they begin again to attempt to live within the law and parole rules. Two parolees we interviewed had been drifting for more than a year.

When I got out I moved in with my cousin in the Haight [the Haight-Ashbury district]. I wanted to stay away from the crime element, the prey-type environment. I met this guy at a club who said he thought I would be a good bouncer because I was big, so I worked at this place at Turk and Eddy [in the Tenderloin district] for ten months. I lost that job because I was staying up so late and I started using some drugs. So then I started selling a little dope. I'd take $100 and buy some crack and make $300. But I was using and the agent sent me back to San Quentin for a ninety-day violation. Then I got out and started scuffling to get by. I was cleaning the streets. A friend had a pickup and we'd go around and pick up anything. An old stove or refrigerator, sitting on the sidewalk. We picked up this old dirty Persian rug and we cleaned it up and sold it to some hippie. We were living from day to day. Then I got to using crack again and was busted in a car with a white guy, scoring. I got sent back for six months that time. Now I'm out, no job, and I don't want to go back; I'm not going back. My aspiration is to be a public relations man, but I haven't had any luck in finding anything like that. [A.R., a thirty-year-old black man]

I stopped in Oakland on the way home and went to MacArthur and Telegraph, saw a couple of friends, and got high. I got a room in a little hotel there. After a few days I went to see my agent in San Francisco and told him I was high and needed some help. He put me in a detox program for 72 hours and then put me in Milestone. It's a halfway house for parolees. I stayed there for four months. I had a job in temporary service and had a bank account, $300. On a Friday I wanted to get high. I went back to Milestone, got my clothes, and went to the Tenderloin. I got busted on Turk Street. I had just bought some crack, had it in my mouth. I got sent back. When I got out, I went back to Milestone and I couldn't get no job, so I was hustling. I'm not gonna walk around begging, dirty, homeless when everyone else in America is eating. I was doing the smallest crimes so I'd do less time. I passed a few $2 bills for a twenty. Whenever I got a twenty, I'd tear a couple of corners off and then I would get some $2 bills from the bank. Most people never see a $2 bill. So you glue the twenty on it and you just hand it to somebody and keep talking to them while they get your change. If they give you change for a twenty, well, they gave it to you, you didn't tell them it was a twenty. But I tried to pass one in this little store and this Chinese lady followed me out on to the street and started yelling. I got busted again. Now I been out since last month. I'm living in the FAD [Freedom Against Drugs] program out on 48th Avenue. I'm getting GA. I get $172 every two weeks. They help you get on welfare. I'm going to go to the Northern California Service League to see Nancy Lopez. She tries to get ex's a job. I'm gonna get a job, save me some money, become a functioning citizen of society. [R.R., a thirty-year-old black man, 1999 California interviews].

Dereliction

Most of those who do not find a rare niche in some conventional or marginal realm steadily gravitate to the world of homeless street people who live from day to day, drinking, hanging out, and surviving (but not for too many years) by making the rounds of soup kitchens and homeless shelters. A study of homelessness by Martha Burt found that 80 percent of the homeless population has been in jail, prison, or a mental hospital.[19] A more recent report by the Urban Institute found that 30-50 percent of all parolees in San Francisco and Los Angeles were homeless.[20] We believe that a follow-up study (which has not been done) of prisoners after release would reveal that more than 25 percent eventually end up on the streets, where they live out a short life of dereliction, alcoholism, and drug abuse. A forty-three-year-old black man we interviewed appeared to have become a derelict.

I been violated three times. Twice for absconding, once for a dirty drug test. I've been to the county jail four times. I was in a substance abuse program for a little while. One time I had a little job for a while as a janitor in a machine shop. They fired me. Said I had a drinking problem. Now I'm living on the street. I just got out of an alcohol program. I stay at the shelters when I can. You sign up and they have a lottery. I'm getting welfare and am waiting for a room through the Tenderloin Housing. As soon as I get a room, I can clean up and keep my clothes clean and get a little job. Been staying away from Safeway, stealing booze. I'm determined to stay out this time. I've been to the shelter on 5th and Bryant, a multiple service center for the homeless. They're gonna develop a job around my skills, fix my résumé.

Generally speaking, this is a very grave situation. Some ex-prisoners—with luck, resolve, and some help—do all right. But most of those who eventually stay out of prison do not live successful or gratifying lives by their or conventional society's standards. They remain dependent on others or the state; drift back and forth from petty crime to subsistence, menial, dependent living, or they gravitate to the new permanent urban underclass—the "homeless." Many die relatively young: "I started getting real nervous. Most of the guys I ran with were dead from AIDS, shot, drugs, or whatever."[21]

Imprisonment is not the total cause of this depressing outcome, but its contribution is considerable. Any imprisonment reduces the opportunities of felons, most of whom had relatively few opportunities to begin with. Doing time in the new generation of warehouse prisons, in which routinization and isolation have increased and rehabilitative efforts have all but completely disappeared, only makes matters worse.

Will Prison Reentry Save Us?

Reentry has become the new buzzword in correctional reform. The term became popularized during the latter part of the Clinton administration when then-Attorney General Janet Reno suddenly discovered that there were hundreds of thousands of people being released from prison each year and that many of them fail to make it. With great fanfare, she announced a major federal effort, that was oddly only directed at the states and not the federal government, to launch a reentry movement.

> We have initiated programs for re-entry offenders, since some 500,000 to 600,000 offenders will come out of prison each year for the next three or four years. We want to have positive alternatives when they come back to the community.
>
> Janet Reno, 1999

After three decades of passing laws and implementing policies designed to increase the number of people incarcerated, providing hundreds of millions of federal dollars to the states if they pass truth-in-sentencing laws, adding 100,000 cops on the streets, hardening the conditions of confinement, and imposing more conditions on parolees, there was a new concern that having over 600,000 people released under such conditions might be a problem. Ironically, concerns were voiced about the lack of programming both in and outside prison.

For those who have been toiling in the vineyards of prison and prison reform advocates, the newfound interest in prison release has been met with a fair degree of skepticism and suspicion. For them, reentry is simply another word for parole supervision that many have tried to discredit and dismantle. The basis for eliminating parole as we know it is grounded in data that shows that the imposition of parole supervision on released prisoners either has no impact or a negative impact.

First, prisoners are far less likely to be returned to prison if they are not placed on parole. This is because they cannot be returned for a parole revocation. We have already noted that states that have low periods of parole supervision have lower return-to-prison recidivism rates. Table 8-7 shows that for three states, prison discharges have substantially lower return-to-prison rates. These lower rates for the discharges explain why many prisoners in a number of states choose to "max out" rather than be paroled, even if it means spending many more months in prison.

> Are you kidding? Why should I go on parole and have to see a parole agent who doesn't really care about me, be drug tested, and have them bust down my door for some bullshit reasons. I'd rather lay up and get it over and be totally free when I get out.[22]

A more sophisticated analysis was done by the Urban Institute based on the BJS 1994 recidivism file. That analysis used the recidivism measure of rearrest after three years versus the return-to-prison rate. The objective was to see if persons placed on parole fared better than prisoners released to other forms of supervision or no supervision at all. Table 8-8 shows the results of the study. The first row of the table shows that people released by parole boards in indeterminate sentencing states had a lower rearrest rate. But when one controls for the attributes of the releases (the "adjusted" row), the differences largely disappear. So at a minimum, parole supervision, as it existed in the 1990s, was not effective in reducing recidivism.

We have already shown that the success rate for parolees has remained well below what it was in the early 1980s. Yet some have no doubt that great progress has been made.

> Yet it is fair to say—even after discounting for the unavoidable bias inherent in my observation—that the interest in "prisoner reentry" has been nothing short of remarkable. At the national level, both the Clinton and Bush administrations have promoted major initiatives to spur new approaches to prisoner reentry. The Second Chance Act, developed at the request of President George W. Bush following his eloquent call for new thinking about the reentry challenge in his 2004 State of the Union Address, stands poised for enactment by Congress later this year. Every state in the nation has convened, at the gubernatorial level, a task force of cabinet-level officials—typically including

Table 8-7 Return-to-Prison Rates by Methods of Release

Release Type	Kentucky	Texas	Pennsylvania
Parole Supervision	53%	26%	50%
Discharges	18%	11%	19%
Total	35%	25%	42%

SOURCE: James Austin and Patricia Hardyman, *Exploring the Needs and Risks of the Returning Prisoner Population* (Washington, DC: Urban Institute, April 2002).

Table 8-8 Three-Year Rearrest Rates for Prisoners Released in 1994

Rearrest Rate	Unconditional Releases	Mandatory Releases	Discretionary Paroles
Unadjusted	62%	61%	54%
Adjusted	61%	61%	57%

SOURCE: Urban Institute, *Does Parole Supervision Work? Research Findings and Policy Opportunities.* (Washington, DC: Urban Institute, 2008).

secretaries of health, child welfare, workforce development, veterans' affairs, public safety, corrections, and education—charged with developing new policies to improve the outcomes for individuals leaving prison. Dozens of mayors and county executives have assigned staff to serve as reentry coordinators, or liaisons, to coordinate city services better to address the profound harms experienced by communities struggling with high rates of incarceration and reentry.

Jeremy Travis, Former NIJ Director during Clinton Administration. http://www.jjay.cuny.edu/extra/president_articles/ReflectionsOntheReentry Movement.pdf.

But what is the evidence to date? The only national evaluation completed to date suggests not much success. Pamela Lattimore and Christy Vishermore issued their findings on what is called the Serious Violent Offender Reentry Initiative (SVORI), the initial wave of federally funded reentry programs. Here are their findings:

For the adults, the significant—albeit less-than-universal—increase in service receipt associated with participation in SVORI programs was associated with moderately better outcomes with respect to housing, employment, substance use, and self-reported criminal behavior, although these improvements were not associated with reductions in official measures of reincarceration.

Although adult SVORI programs were successful in increasing the types and amounts of needs-related services provided before and after release from prison, the proportion of individuals who reported receiving services was smaller than the proportion that reported need and, generally, was smaller than the proportion that the SVORI program directors expected to have received services. This finding is consistent with the fact that SVORI programs were still developing and implementing their programs and serves as a reminder that starting complex programs may require sustained effort over several years to achieve full implementation. Service delivery declined after release; therefore, overall, the programs were unable to sustain support of individuals during the critical, high-risk period immediately after release. This decline may be due to the programs' difficulty identifying and coordinating services for individuals released across wide geographic areas and, again, suggests the need for sustained effort to achieve full implementation.[23]

One other study should be noted as well. Project Greenlight is a re-entry program operated by the New York Department of Corrections (NYDOC).

The prestigious Vera Institute helped the NYDOC design and implement the program. A rigorous experimental study found that prisoners released to the program had higher or the same recidivism rates than those in two control groups.[24] One control group received no services and the other received alternative pre-release services. The control group that received no services had the same re-arrest rate as the Project Greenlight participants while the prisoners in the alternative program had lower re-arrest rates. The author of the study, James Wilson, attributes the negative results to poor program design and implementation. He makes the following conclusion:

> If we continue to place offenders in programs that are positively perceived but that remain untested, we might continue to produce outcomes similar to Project Greenlight. Without effective evaluations of our programs, we run the risk of programming offenders nearly to death—and it still will not make one whit of difference.[25]

One might say that reentry as attempted by public agencies is difficult to work for several reasons. First, federally funded programs are limited in terms of how long they last (usually no more than three years) and their ability to be properly implemented. Second, prisons are not designed, funded, nor staffed to provide treatment services. Rather, they are designed to punish people—for which they do a very good job For these reasons the better option is to divert as many people who pose little or no risk to the public and/or reduce the period of imprisonment. We have already shown that reducing the length of stay and eliminating parole supervision for most people either reduces recidivism rates or has no impact. And the diverting of similarly situated offenders to probation versus sending them to prison reduces their recidivism rates. These are better and more direct methods than launching questionable or ineffective prison-based reentry programs.

NOTES

1. The California sample was not randomly determined. We had requested permission from the California Department of Corrections (CDC) to conduct a far more systematic study that would have entailed a more rigorous design. However, the request to have access to lists of parolees was refused by the then Director of the CDC. We were flooded with respondents and had to refuse to take any more after four days of interviewing. It should be noted that more than 112,000 parolees are on supervision in California as of 1999.

2. Rebekah Diller, Judith Greene, and Michelle Jacob, *Maryland's Parole Supervision Fee: A Barrier to Reentry.* (New York: Brennan Center for Justice, New York University School of Law, 2009).

3. The rate at which parole boards grant parole at the first release varies dramatically by the type of crime the inmate was sentenced to prison for and from state to state. Parole boards in general, however, do not release the majority of inmates eligible for parole at the inmate's first hearing.

4. California Expert Panel Report, 2007.

5. Pew Center on the States, State of Recidivism: The Revolving Door of

America's Prisons (Washington, DC: The Pew Charitable Trusts, April 2011).

6. Joan Petersilia, Susan Turner, and Joyce Peterson, *Prison Versus Probation in California: The Implications for Crime and Offender Recidivism* (Santa Monica, CA: Rand).

7. James Austin, *Parole Outcome in California: The Consequences of Determinate Sentencing, Punishment, and Incapacitation on Parole Performance* (San Francisco: National Council on Crime and Delinquency, 1989).

8. James Austin, *The Effectiveness of Reduced Prison Terms on Public Safety and Costs: Evaluation of the Illinois Supplemental Meritorious Good-Time Program* (San Francisco: National Council on Crime and Delinquency, 1993).

9. Pamela C. Ovwigho, Catherine E. Born, and Correne Saunders, *Intersection of Incarceration and Child Support: A Snapshot of Maryland's Caseload* (University of Maryland School of Social Work, July 2005).

10. John Irwin, *The Felon* (Upper Saddle River, NJ: Prentice-Hall, 1970), pp. 113–114.

11. Rebekah Diller, Judith Greene, and Michelle Jacob, *Maryland's Parole Supervision Fee: A Barrier to Reentry* (New York: Brennan Center for Justice, New York University School of Law, 2009).

12. Richard Berk and David Rauma, "Remuneration and Recidivism: The Long-Term Impact of Unemployment Compensation on Ex-Offenders," *Journal of Quantitative Criminology* 3, 1(1987): 3–27.

13. Interviews with authors.

14. From interviews conducted by staff at the Center on Juvenile and Criminal Justice, San Francisco, California, reported in its *Parole Violators in California: A Waste of Money, A Waste of Time* (September 1991), p. 8.

15. Joan Petersilia and Susan Turner, "An Evaluation of Intensive Probation in California," *Journal of Criminal Law and Criminology* 82, 3(Fall 1991): 610–658.

16. James Austin and Patricia Hardyman, *The Use of Early Parole with Electronic Monitoring to Control Prison Crowding* (San Francisco: National Council on Crime and Delinquency, 1992); Terry L. Baumer and Robert L. Mendelsohn, *Final Report: The Electronic Monitoring of Non-Violent Convicted Felons: An Experiment in Home Detention* (Indianapolis, IN: School of Public and Environmental Affairs, Indiana University, January 1990).

17. Excerpts from interviews of prisoners included in Chapter 2.

18. According to the U.S. Department of Justice, over 50 percent of all prison releases to parole had less than a high school education, with a median education level at the eleventh grade. The eleventh-grade level is the same for prison admissions, which indicates the absence of any improvement in education level while imprisoned. Bureau of Justice Statistics, Washington, DC. Data collected in the 2008. National Corrections Reporting Program. Draft table delivered uponspecial request on May 2, 2011.

19. Martha Burt, *Over the Edge* (New York: Urban Institute and Russell Sage Foundation, 1992).

20. Jeremy Travis, Amy L. Solomon, and Michelle Waul, *From Prison to Home: The Dimensions and Consequences of Prisoner Reentry* (Washington, DC: The Urban Institute, 2001), p.36.

21. Interview, 51-year-old parolee, San Francisco, April 1993.

22. Interview with Kentucky ex-prisoner, 2010.

23. Pamela Lattimore and Christy Visher (December 2009). *The Multi-Site Evaluation of SVORI: Summary and Synthesis*. Washington, DC: U.S. Department of Justice, National Institute of Justice.

24. J. A. Wilson and R. C. Davis (2006), Good Intentions Meet Hard Realities: An Evaluation Of The Project Greenlight Reentry Program. Criminology & Public Policy, 5: 303–338.

25. J. A. Wilson (2007). Habilation or Harm: Project Greenlight and the Potential Consequences of Correctional Programming. NIJ Journal, 257:7.

9

■

Special Topics

LEARNING OBJECTIVES

1. To become familiar with some of the most highly publicized and controversial topics that are impacting correctional and prison reform policies.
2. To understand the use of confidential informants and how they are impacting the size of the federal prison system and the number of people being sentenced for drug crimes.
3. To review the question of whether today's prison system can serve as a breeding ground for homegrown terrorists.
4. To become familiar with the three strike movement and understand its impact on prison population growth.
5. To learn more about those prisoners who are convicted of the most serious crimes (murder and sex crimes) and whether they pose a danger to public safety.

INTRODUCTION

This chapter reviews five contemporary and controversial issues in criminal justice that have been popularized by the media and public officials—the use of confidential informants in the "war on drugs," prisons as breeding grounds for terrorists, the "three strikes and you're out" movement, the growing number of people sentenced as lifers, and sex offenders. While each topic is not discussed in great detail, information is provided to offer an overview of these topics and their relationship to the use of imprisonment.

CONFIDENTIAL INFORMANTS
AND THE WAR ON DRUGS

The Bureau of Prisons (BOP) is the federal prison system and is largest and fastest growing prison system in the United States and probably the world. As shown in Figure 9-1, the BOP system has grown from 21,000 in 1970 to 210,000 by 2010. There are two major reasons for this massive increase—the U.S. sentencing guidelines that require people to serve 85 percent of their imposed sentence and the war on drugs. With regard to the war on drugs, the federal government has provided funding for a large number of federal drug task forces, providing money to local law enforcement agencies to investigate, arrest, and prosecute people believed to be trafficking in drugs. A key component of this initiative is the widespread use of confidential informants (CIs).

The History of CIs

CIs always been used by police and prosecutors to secure information about criminal activities that are only known by those who are participating in such activities. In most portrayals of police work in the mass media, there are usually characters that demonstrate the informant being paid or receiving preferential treatment for insider information about a larger criminal enterprise. In some cases, the informant is a police officer operating undercover to either infiltrate a criminal enterprise or to expose corruption within the police force itself.

Perhaps the most well-known informants have exposed corruption and criminal activity in governments are Frank Serpico, who exposed corruption in the

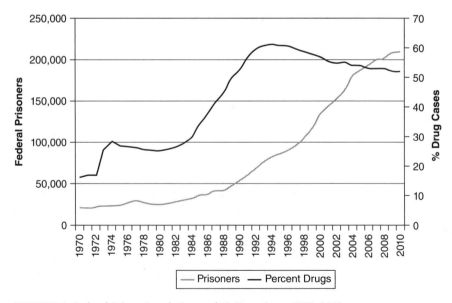

FIGURE 9-1 Federal Prison Population and % Drug Cases 1970–2010

New York Police Department; Daniel Elsberg, who released the Pentagon Papers; and Deputy Director of the FBI, Mark Felt, aka "Deep Throat," who provided confidential information on the Watergate break-in to the *Washington Post* that led to the resignation of President Nixon. There are many other examples, both historic and less well known where informants have exposed criminal activity or prevented serious crimes from occurring.

The increased use of CIs has received greater scrutiny, partly due to the number of cases that were extensively covered by the media. As will be shown, in some of these high-profile cases, innocent Americans have been wrongfully convicted of drug crimes and, in some situations, even killed by police because of false information provided by CIs who have either been paid for the faulty information or have received lenient treatment from the courts.

Such high-profile cases led to the controversial "stop snitching" campaign popularized by rap singers and community activists. Rappers and hip hop artists, such as Mac Dre, Lil' Kim, Camron, and Ice T, have warned about the dangers of snitching. This is not because they endorse crime, but because they see snitching as actually contributing to crime, especially violent crime and the wrongful convictions of persons targeted by CIs.[1]

There are different levels of CIs. In the simplest terms, a confidential informant is someone who provides information to police or the prosecutors on the alleged criminal activities of another person or group of people. As defined by the U.S. Department of Justice, a confidential informant (or CI) is defined as follows:

> any individual who provides useful and credible information to a Justice Law Enforcement Agent (JLEA) regarding felonious criminal activities and from whom the JLEA expects or intends to obtain additional useful and credible information regarding such activities in the future.[2]

A criminal informant is a person who has been arrested on criminal charges but who has not been charged or convicted in exchange for his or her willingness to secure additional information about the criminal conduct of other people while posing as a criminal to his or her unsuspecting associates. Such "information" may take the form of a simple "tip" that identifies people who are alleged drug dealers or may be involved in what is known as a "controlled buy." This is a situation where the CI is used to purchase drugs from a dealer under the observation of the police. But in order to do this and to demonstrate that one is not working for law enforcement, the CI continues to be involved in or a witness to the criminal activities of others.

Career and High-Level Informants

The forms of compensation can be attractive, especially to people who themselves are drug abusers and have little opportunity or ability to maintain a legitimate lifestyle. This helps explain why some make a career as an informant. Career CIs, who are relatively rare, can make a steady and reliable income by buying and selling drugs. But the use of so-called "career informants" can foster many significant violations of policies governing the use of CIs.

The Department of Justice (DOJ) has a special category for such CIs—high level confidential informant. The U.S. Department of Justice defines these people as "senior" CIs who are associated with international criminal enterprises or who are of "high significance" to the DOJ. These high-end CIs are able to command higher wages and longer periods of work as CIs.

The Use of Juveniles as Informants

While many law enforcement agencies do not use juvenile CIs in adult drug cases, there is increasing evidence that this practice is being used more frequently. The most widespread practice is to offer students cash for information. For example, in Rome, Georgia, high school students are being paid $10 for a tip on theft, $25 to $50 for a drug tip, and up to $100 for information on weapons. San Diego operates a similar program where youth can earn as much as $1,000 for a tip. In a recent documentary, the BBC reported that such informant operations exist in over two thousand U.S. public schools.[3]

The other use of juveniles is as paid CIs infiltrate drug rings that may be operating in the schools or in the community. While juveniles are not used as much as adults, the practice has become so widespread that professional organizations like the International Association of Police Chiefs (IACP) has established formal guidelines and standards for police agencies to follow when using children as CIs.

Numbers of CIs

Federal law enforcement agencies, as well as local and state law enforcement agencies, will not disclose the precise number of CIs they are using at any time nor the total number that are in their data rosters. Their own guidelines require them to maintain a listing of all current and terminated confidents. Their reason for not disclosing such information is that the numbers could somehow compromise the agency's efforts to infiltrate organized crime operations or the identity of their CIs.

Although precise numbers do not exist, a sizeable portion of these arrests are based on information provided by CIs. The FBI, which makes only a small percentage of the national drug arrests, has reported to have approximately 15,000 CIs on its payroll based on its Fiscal Year (FY) 2008 budget request to Congress. The Drug Eforcement Agency (DEA) is estimated to have another 4,000 CIs on its payroll.[4] But this is only the tip of the iceberg since the majority of police arrests, and thus the use of CIs, is largely a local police function.

Examples of Miscarriages of Justice through CIs

As the use of CIs in the "War on Drugs" has escalated, so has the number of cases where information has led to the wrongful arrest, conviction, and lengthy prison terms of innocent people. In some instances, innocent people have been assaulted and even murdered by police or by the CIs. A simple Internet search will produce hundreds of cases where such abuses have occurred. What follows are some recent examples of the most egregious abuses.

Kathryn Johnston   Ms. Johnston was a ninety-two-year-old grandmother from Atlanta, Georgia, who was fatally shot in the chest by Atlanta police SWAT agents. In this case, her house was wrongfully targeted as a source of illegal drug dealings. The officers fabricated an imaginary informant and then lied to the court about the sale of drugs from her house in order to get a warrant. After the murder occurred, they tried to get another informant, who was also working for the DEA, to lie that he had purchased drugs at Kathryn Johnson's home.[5]

The City of Tulia, Texas   In Tulia, Texas, the misinformation of a single white informant resulted in over a dozen black members of the community being falsely accused of selling drugs; this led to their conviction and sentencing of long prison terms. After an independent investigation showed that the informant's testimony was totally fabricated, the prison sentences were overturned and the innocent community residents were released from prison.[6]

"Whitey" Bulger   This case involved former Boston FBI agent John Connally. The recent Oscar award-winning film *The Departed* was based on Mr. Connally who was recently convicted of racketeering and obstruction of justice stemming from his mishandling of two Mafia CIs, Stephen "The Rifleman" Flemmi and James "Whitey" Bulger. Both Flemmi and Bulger were actively involved in organized crime activities, including illegal drug sales and acts of violence that were known to the FBI, while also serving as FBI CIs. In some instances, the FBI tipped off Bulger and Flemmi on pending law enforcement raids on their criminal organizations, and they even identified other CIs who were being used by other police agencies to break up their organized criminal activities.[7]

Cory Maye   In December of 2001, police in Prentiss, Mississippi, who were working as part of a multi-county narcotic task force, secured warrants to search both units of a duplex where it was believed that large amounts of marijuana were located. The basis for the raid was a tip from an informant. Upon entering, the police found only a small amount of marijuana. This suspect was never arrested of any charge. The police then went to the next unit where Cory Maye and his young daughter were sleeping. It's unclear whether the police identified themselves prior to breaking into the unit, but when they entered his bedroom, Maye, thinking they were burglars, fired his pistol and killed one of the officers. Maye, who had no prior arrest record, was subsequently sentenced to death for the murder. His death penalty was subsequently over-turned, but he remains in prison serving a life sentence.[8]

Jerrell Bray   Mr. Bray is a paid informant whose tips to police in Mansfield, Ohio, and elsewhere, led to the wrongful conviction and imprisonment of at least twenty-three people, some of whom spent years in prison before having their cases overturned. Under the guidance of a seventeen-year veteran, DEA agent Lee Lucas, accusations were made of people who later were found not to be in Mansfield at the time of the alleged drug purchases or did not fit the physical description of the drug dealer. In many cases, it appears that Mr. Bray simply concocted the stories for the sole purpose of being paid for information, regardless of its accuracy. According to published accounts, Bray was paid tens of thousands of dollars a year, was able to continue to use drugs as an informant, and stole thousands of dollars in "buy money" (money given to CIs by police to purchase illegal drugs) provided by the DEA.[9]

What Are the Forms of Compensation?

What is not spelled out, but is implied, is that the confidential informant is involved or has knowledge of criminal activity of others and that, in exchange for such information, he or she will receive compensation for the credible and useful information. As listed below, these forms of compensation are used to lure people into becoming CIs for extended periods of time. However, it can also encourage CIs to provide misleading and false information unless the prosecutor and police take steps to ensure the information is valid.

Lenient Sentences   The "lenient sentence" compensation occurs in the federal courts via what is known as a 5K1.1 letter. If the federal prosecutor decides that the defendant has provided "substantial assistance" in a particular case, a letter pursuant to 5K1.1 of the federal sentencing guidelines is submitted by the prosecutor, which allows the judge to give a sentence that is outside the guidelines. However, prior to issuance of this letter, the defendant may be required to disclose not only the current involvement in criminal activities, but also all other criminal activities. This letter allows the federal court to sentence the criminal to a term that is much shorter than the ones his co-defendants will receive or less proportional to the crimes the informant admits he or she has committed in the past.

Cash   The usual and customary practice for payments to CIs is sums of money. The amount of money paid to CIs can vary dramatically from a few hundred dollars for one tip to several hundred thousand dollars for another. For those who have been CIs for several years, there have been documented reports of them receiving millions of dollars over their careers as an informant.

For example, a well-documented investigation by the *Pittsburg Press* cited the case of Anthony Tait, a member of Hell's Angels and a drug user who was an informant for the FBI for several years in the 1980s. From 1985 to 1988, Tait received approximately $1 million from several FBI offices, the state of California, and the federal forfeiture fund.[10] The federal government sets aside tens of millions of dollars a year to support the cash payments of drug CIs either under their direct supervision or the supervision of local police agencies as part of the drug task forces.

The U.S. DOJ has published guidelines on the terms of financial payments to CIs. So-called "one time payments," generally range from $2,500 to $25,000 but can exceed these amounts with the approval of a senior field manager. Annual payments are allowable up to $100,000 and increased in amounts of

$50,000. Total payments made over a one-year period can reach $200,000 without a review by the LJEA senior field manager. These payments can be increased in amounts up to $100,000 at any given time.[11]

The DEA's internal guidelines show similar amounts of compensation, although it notes that CIs can be paid up to $250,000 if the informant's assistance leads to a successful seizure of assets. Particularly attractive is the option of rewarding CIs with up to ¼ of the determined value of the seized assets, but not more than $250,000 per case.[12]

A New Life   An often-overlooked vehicle for compensation to CIs or witnesses is placement in the Federal Witness Protection program. In the witness protection program, CIs are provided compensation ranging from housing to jobs. In the United States, the Witness Protection Program, also known as the Witness Security Program, or WitSec, was established by the Organized Crime Control Act of 1970, which, in turn, set out the manner in which the U.S. attorney general may provide for the relocation and protection of a witness or potential witness of the federal government, or for a state government in an official proceeding concerning organized crime or other serious offenses including major narcotics trafficking cases.

Sex and Drugs   Another form of compensation is illegal drugs to be used by the informant in ways not so easily identifiable, in particular the sale of drugs to other drug users. Such compensation is not allowable under the attorney general guidelines, but it often happens if sufficient controls are not imposed by the law enforcement agent or agency supervising the confidential informant or witness.

In a recent decision by the Texas Court of Criminal Appeals, the court ruled that an officer who had given a portion of the drugs he had seized from in an effort to make her an informant was not illegal. In this case, a police officer caught a potential informant with drugs, but before booking the evidence in her case, returned some of the drugs to her so she could get high. The officer's defense to the tampering-with-evidence charge? "I was trying to create a snitch."[13]

A more recent example of illegal drugs being used to pay CIs was reported by the *New York Times* on January 27, 2008. The *Times* reported that four Brooklyn narcotics officers were arrested after an investigation found that they had been paying their CIs with drugs seized from dealers identified by the CIs. The officers made no profit and were actually praised by their supervisor since "trading drugs for information in the pursuit of arrests could be described as a noble cause of corruption." The Brooklyn district attorney announced he will seek the dismissal of about 159 drug cases because of the police corruption, with hundreds more under review. Six additional officers were suspended and several others were placed on modified or desk duty, barred from doing enforcement work.

Having sexual relations with CIs has also been documented. A recent news article in the *Asbury Park Press* described a police officer's illicit relationship with an informant. In this case, a New Jersey police officer was accused of regularly having sex with a married informant and, at least once, brutally raping her, which resulted in her carrying his child. The informant has now accused the police department of permitting and encouraging police officers to sexually harass and have sex with female CIs and other women they encounter while on duty. The mayor proclaimed "no wrongdoing," and the police officer who fathered the informant's child is back on patrol.

Consequences of the Misuse of Confidential Informants in the "War on Drugs"

All of the above data and information suggests that the use of CIs often has unintended and negative consequences on the "War on Drugs." In some ways, the widespread use of CIs may serve to increase, rather than decrease, drug abuse and the violent criminal activity surrounding it. Listed below are the major negative consequences that result from the misuse of CIs.

1. Wrongful Convictions and Prison Sentences   Until CIs are properly screened and monitored, innocent people will be arrested, falsely convicted, and wrongfully sentenced to prisons. This happens when CIs, who themselves are drug abusers and criminals, become the sole basis for the issuing of search warrants. Until there is some certainty that CIs are being properly screened, managed, and monitored by law enforcement agencies, it is inevitable that an intolerably high number of people will be wrongly arrested, convicted, and imprisoned.

2. Disparate Impact in Black and Hispanic Communities   The disparities between who is using drugs and who is being arrested, convicted, and imprisoned for drug crimes implies that the use of CIs in the "War on Drugs" is having a more negative impact in Black and Hispanic communities than it is having in White communities. Not only are there many examples of Blacks and Hispanics being disproportionately arrested and convicted for such behavior, but the deployment of CIs who engage in criminal and violent behavior, with the knowledge of the police, only serves to increase the level of random violence occurring in these communities.

3. Ineffective and Inefficient Use of Criminal Justice Resources   When the system is more interested in drug arrests and convictions than reducing serious and violent crime, our criminal justice system loses its integrity and effectiveness. CIs and those associated with them understand that the criminal justice system actually tolerates and often encourages serious criminal activity in the pursuit of catching the so-called "big fish." Often the "big fish" are also CIs who are able to escape prosecution and conviction by trading people and information. The question becomes whether such a system is designed to arrest and prosecute the most dangerous and serious criminals or simply to secure the highest number of arrests and convictions while having no effect on public safety.

4. Undermining Our Core Democratic Values   A free and democratic society is based on a minimal level of government intrusion in our private lives. There are many current and historical examples where societies have trampled on individual rights by creating government forces, both military and police, that allow citizens to be arrested and imprisoned based on information that is hidden from the public. The increasing reliance on CIs to justify the entering of peoples homes or arresting them on the street without disclosing the basis for such governmental actions is one step toward a totalitarian society. The informant system has radically increased the ability of government to keep its functions secret. For example, the *WhosaRat* web site caused an official federal government memo that encouraged all courts to change their practices and seal many more documents, thus shielding a vast amount of fundamental police practices. The FBI stated before Congress on July 19, 2007, that it need not publicly disclose its own internal policies on the use of CIs. Local and state agencies refuse to willingly release any information on the number of CIs use, the amount of money being paid to CIs, and how many criminal arrests and convictions are based on such cases. The primary source of the atrocities associated with CIs comes largely from the media that has limited concrete information and is based predominantly on the CIs.

5. Funding Criminal Activities and Drug Use   The use of CIs means that the government is in the business of supporting individuals who, with the knowledge of the government, are actively involved in the commission of serious crimes and the use of illegal drugs. To be effective, an informant must be knowledgeable about current criminal activities and demonstrate to others that he or she is a criminal. One way this is done is by committing crimes in their presence. Similarly, since "potential" CIs are often drug users who have been recruited by police after their initial arrest, there is an incentive for them to continue their drug use without the fear of arrest by becoming an informant. Rather than steering people to treatment, the police will encourage the informant to stay active in his circle of fellow drug users.

6. Criminals Doing Police Work   By increasingly relying on CIs to uncover drug crimes, we are establishing a dangerous practice where drug users and dealers, with suspect backgrounds and intentions, are doing traditional police undercover work. This work used to be the domain of trained and professional law enforcement officers. The work of the informant is largely unregulated in terms of deciding who should be targeted and on what merit they should be targeted. The informant's motives are, at best, suspect. One of the major reasons for using CIs in lieu of undercover officers in such large numbers is to keep officers out of harms way. Or, as one of our CI sources stated, "I'd rather those scum bags take a bullet rather than one of my officers."

TERRORISM AND PRISONS[14]

As the war on terror continues without an end in sight, we continue to look for other groups or populations that might be able to pull off another 911 attack. This pursuit of terrorists leads us back to the American prison system. Research centers are being created and criminologists are publishing papers that examine the dangers that may exist with prisons serving as incubators of terrorists. As one criminologist ominously warned:

> Since the terrorist attack of September 11, 2001, much attention has been paid to the global spread of radical Islam, leading researchers to examine the influence of extremist websites, jihadist chat rooms, and incendiary fatwa issued by Muslim clerics…. Since 9/11, such networks have been discovered in mosques, bookstores, barbershops, military barracks, sports clubs, community centers, and, perhaps most disconcerting, prisons.[15]

Before addressing this subject in more detail, we'll call your attention to two movies. There was "Die Hard" in which Bruce Willis as detective John McClane single-handedly defeated a band of terrorists. But these were not the ordinary terrorists like the ones we fear so much and are fighting today. This group was led by a highly educated and stylish dressed German (Hans Gruber) who is plotting to steal $640 million in bonds stored in a vault. His associates are fluent in English and German and are skilled in weapons, explosives, and martial arts. One is a computer software expert who can penetrate any sophisticated telecommunication or alarm detection system. Even though they are all killed by Willis, one has to admit they were an impressive, formidable force.

The other film is less known but is also relevant to the information in this chapter. Titled "No Such Thing," the subject of this film is a Monster who is disgusted with the modern world's bent on instant gratification and materialism. The Monster lashes out at anyone who crosses his path because that is what we expect him to do. Efforts are made to kill him but the movie's twist is that no one is sure whether he exists or is just a figment of our imagination. At the end of the film, he is killed—or at least we think so. But how do you kill something that doesn't exist?

Both movies express two major themes that dominate our thinking on terrorism. First, we assume terrorists are sophisticated, extremely dangerous, and unless they are killed or incarcerated, they will inflict mass destruction. The second theme is that they exist in such large numbers that we must allocate huge amounts of our military and criminal justice resources to identify, kill, or contain these "Monsters"—assuming they exist.

By definition, terrorism is a political term. Students of criminology learn early on that in order for an act to be defined as criminal, we (usually the state) must apply the label to the act. The sheer act of killing someone does not constitute it being a crime. Depending on who does it and under what circumstances, the very act may be viewed as heroic or a brutal murder. This relative definition of hero versus terrorist also applies to the murder of large numbers of people. Such acts are usually carried out by people who are resisting the control of a foreign and more powerful state.

Just how likely is it that terrorists can be produced from our nation's 1.7 million inmates in the prison population? One would think that with all of the pressing issues that surround America's growing prison population, this topic would be among the lowest, if not the lowest, priority for criminologists to study and debate. But the politics of fear that have been successfully linked to September 11, 2001, seem to trump any rational assessment of the potential danger the U.S. population now faces from terrorism within the nation's prison system.

More significantly, at the time of this writing, this concern has been amplified by recent political events. President Obama promised to close the notorious Guantanamo Bay prison when he was on the campaign trail. According to our government, in 2010, the prison housed about 170 of the world's most feared terrorists. Now there are concerns that it would be dangerous to transfer them to the federal maximum security prisons on American soil.[16] FBI Director Robert Mueller argued that such a move would allow the bulging U.S. prison population to be radicalized by these 170 terrorists who would be contained in supermax single cells.

> The concerns we have about individuals who may support terrorism being in the United States run from concerns about providing financing, radicalizing others as well as the potential for individuals undertaking attacks in the United States. All of those are relevant concerns.[17]

As is common practice with our government, the FBI chief would not list any specific individuals reflect these concerns. And never mind the uncomfortable fact that this has not yet happened, even with the presence of over three hundred such terrorists already in the custody of the Federal Bureau of Prisons. But to further fuel our fears, the Department of Defense recently reported that 5 percent of the nearly six hundred people released from "Gitmo" have become involved once again in terroristic activities or "are suspected of being involved." Compared to U.S. prisoners, this is a very good recidivism rate. On a more serious note, we (criminologists and the public) cannot verify these facts, but they provide a useful image of fear to convince the public that without "Gitmo" terrorism would be breaking out all over the U.S.

Two of our leading academic institutions (George Washington University (GWU) and the University of Virginia) have published a detailed report ominously titled "Out of the Shadows: Getting Ahead of Prisoner Radicalism" that raises the same fears. GWU's Homeland Security Policy Institute and Virginia's Critical Incident Analysis Group believe that our U.S. prison population could easily become a breeding ground for future terrorists unless we take action now.[18] And the basis for this conclusion is five cases of which only three are examples of American-born prisoners who were radicalized by Islamic teachings while they were incarcerated in U.S. prisons. Like Director Mueller, the authors of the report say there are many more, but, as always, these cases cannot be shared with the public due to "the sensitive nature of ongoing investigations."[19] But despite the small sample, they confidently recommend the following steps be taken to preempt a terrorist attack by U.S. prisoners:

> Congress should establish a Commission to investigate this issue in depth. An objective risk assessment is urgently needed in order to better understand the nature of the threat and to formulate and calibrate proactive prevention and

response efforts accordingly. Enhanced information would enable officials to address this issue now, rather than forcing them to manage a crisis later.[20]

How Dangerous Are They?

One of the three examples cited by Cilluffo and his associates is the Kevin James case. A closer analysis of Mr. James illustrates quite effectively how he and his band of four other converts would be incapable of being effective terrorists. Kevin James was doing a lengthy prison term in California and became a converted Muslim. He and a fellow convert then formed a group called the JIS that in theory was dedicated to terrorist acts against U.S. military bases, synagogues, and Israeli government facilities. While incarcerated, James wrote a document called the "Blueprint 2005" that set forth the following somewhat comical goals for members of the JIS:

1. Learn Arabic

2. Acquire a steady job that does not interfere with learning Arabic

3. Acquire two weapons (pistols) with silencers

4. Appoint a member (from the five) to find contacts for explosives or to learn bomb making. We will need bombs that can be activated from a distance

5. And—in order to fulfill these task [sic] you must become legitimate. Acquire identification, drivers license, work/school, keep regular contact with your parole agent, attempt to remove your tattoos and monitor your looks. Your dress code must not bring attention … casual dress so as not to arouse "extremist suspicion." We have work to do.[21]

After James's fellow terrorists were paroled from prison, he and two others were rearrested by law enforcement after committing a series of petty gas station robberies. Apparently they had strayed from the Blueprint and returned to what they knew best—common holdups of gas stations.

The second example is Jeff Fort. One of the authors of this book met many of Mr. Fort's associates who were incarcerated at Stateville and Joliet prisons. At that time, Fort was the leader of a Chicago street gang called the Blackstone P. Stone Rangers. They were just "gangbangers" who knew how to steal, intimidate, assault, and murder rival gang members. Fort was not educated and had no skills that would make him a threat to anyone beyond those in neighborhoods on the south side of Chicago, which the Rangers controlled.

Over the years, Fort has transformed the Rangers into a group called El Ruken. He has been incarcerated in the BOP's supermax prison in Colorado; he was convicted after being taped on prison telephones, plotting to receive $2.5million from Libya to commit unspecified acts of terrorism. Fort and his band of would-be terrorists never got the money, and if they had, one suspects he would have spent it on activities he was more skilled a—drug dealing and assaulting/killing rival drug dealers. While James and Fort were threats to public safety, they were never capable of inflicting the kind of damage and mass destruction suggested by our domestic terrorism experts. Put differently, they were no Hans Gruber.

The Disproportionate Costs and Benefits
of the War On Terror

We would be remiss not to remind our readers of the cost-benefits of the war on terror. The United States is spending approximately $215 billion a year for the criminal justice system, of which almost $70 billion is spent on corrections.[22] Conversely, the total economic loss to victims of "street crime" in 2003, as reported by the U.S. Department of Justice, was an estimated $15.4 billion.[23]

Similar to the disproportionate costs of the wars on crime and drugs, the costs of the war on terror can only be seen as excessive. Approximately 3,000 people were killed in the 9/11 Twin Towers and Pentagon attacks. The estimated economic losses associated with 9/11 have been estimated at $27.2 billion. Included in this estimate is the destruction of private and public assets ($16.2 billion) and another $11 billion in rescue, cleanup, and related costs.[24]

In reaction to this attack, the United States launched two wars that as of 2011 have cost $1.3 trillion in military and associated support services. As of 2011, over 5,500 American troops have been killed and another 36,000 seriously wounded. An estimated 900,000 civilians have been killed and over 2.5 million Iraq citizens have been displaced. At what point do these mounting losses no longer the costs of 911?

The "No Such Thing" Hypothesis

Another issue that needs to be seriously discussed is why there have not been any further massive terror attacks on the United States since 2001. It defies common sense that the absence of any post-9/11 attacks is solely due to the greater use of military and law enforcement assets. The relative ease by which a few dedicated suicide bombers could enter our country and simultaneously detonate explosives in some of our major railroad stations or shopping malls is done almost on a daily basis in Iraq and elsewhere, strongly suggesting that such cells either do not exist or are extremely rare. Perhaps we should be devoting more of our criminological resources on the "no such thing" hypothesis rather than looking for incompetent "wanna-be" terrorists within our prison system.

THREE STRIKES

The past decade has witnessed many efforts by policy makers to increase the use of imprisonment. One of the most popular reforms has been "three strikes and you're out." It began in 1993 when an initiative was placed on the ballot in the state of Washington to require a term of life imprisonment without the possibility of parole for persons convicted for a third time of certain specified violent or serious felonies. This action was fueled by the tragic death of Diane Ballasiotes who was murdered by a convicted rapist who had been released from prison. Shortly after this release, twelve-year-old Polly Klass was kidnapped, raped, and murdered by a California-released inmate who had an extensive prior record of violence. The rallying cry of "three strikes and you're out" caught on, not only with Washington and California voters, who passed their ballot measures by wide margins, but with legislatures and the public throughout the country. As described later in this chapter, these horrific crimes led to the passage of mandatory imprisonment, sex registration, and civil commitment laws for sex offenders. By 1997, twenty-four other states and the federal government enacted laws using the "three strikes and you're out" phrase. In 1994, President Clinton received a standing ovation in his State of the Union speech when he endorsed three strikes as a federal sentencing policy.[25]

The three strikes movement is the most recent anticrime policy to sweep the United States. Such reforms include the Scared Straight Shock Incarceration programs in the 1970s, boot camps, mandatory minimum sentencing for certain crimes (for example, "use a gun, go to prison"), and truth in sentencing.[26] These often short-lived campaigns have widespread appeal to a disenchanted public, who, through the media, have perceived the criminal justice system as overly lenient and incapable of protecting them from violent offenders. Highly publicized cases, where the courts or correctional officials have allowed violent and habitual offenders to be released from prison only to commit yet another violent crime, have fueled the public's appetite for harsher sentencing policies to correct a criminal justice system run amok.

The theoretical justification for such policies in general, and for the "three strikes and you're out" policy in particular, is grounded in the punitive ideologies of deterrence, incapacitation, and/or just deserts. General deterrence is achieved by delivering swift, certain, and severe punishment (life imprisonment without parole) to habitual offenders in order to suppress the criminal tendencies of potential habitual criminals.[27] Knowing that the next conviction will result in life imprisonment, the offender would weigh the consequences of committing another offense or living a crime-free life to avoid such punishment. In order for this sequence of events to occur, however, two critical but highly questionable conditions must exist: (1) offenders must be well informed of the new sentencing policies; and (2) they must believe there is a high probability of arrest and conviction should their criminal activities persist.

Malcolm Klein has argued that three-strike-type legislation is unlikely to significantly enhance deterrence effects with respect to gangs, as the laws do little to "increase the likelihood of detection, apprehension and court conviction, which precede punishment."[28] Nor is it likely that would-be three strikers keep fully abreast of the complex and foreign legislative activities conducted by politicians in remote state capitals. For these and other reasons, the justification of three strikes legislation as an effective crime-control strategy remains problematic.

Incapacitation effects may be realized by accurately targeting habitual or career offenders who are unamenable to deterrence and rehabilitation and must be permanently separated from society. This perspective was popularized by Rand's research on habitual offenders in the 1970s and 1980s. Peter Greenwood and Joan Petersilia were early advocates of sentencing reforms that would isolate and incapacitate habitual offenders. This perspective assumed that (1) the courts could readily identify the so-called "career offender," and (2) the offender's career would continue unabated over time.[29]

Both assumptions have been widely criticized. First, previous studies have documented that the courts and social scientists have not been able to accurately identify the so-called high rate or career offender without also punishing an equal or higher number of "false positives." In fact, Greenwood's own, but less publicized, research discredits his claim that career offenders can be identified or that they even exist. Second, reforms such as "three strikes" run counter to research suggesting that criminals' careers are strongly impacted by age. As noted by the national panel on criminal careers:

> From the perspective of incapacitation, prison capacity is used inefficiently if offenders are imprisoned beyond the time their criminal activity would have terminated if they were free on the street. Therefore, it is reasonable to ask whether "habitual-offender" laws, which mandate very long sentences, may result in incarceration of offenders well after they ceased to be serious risks.[30]

The incapacitation effects of a three strikes law on crime rates must be viewed as long-term if the goal is simply to extend incarceration. Assuming a portion of the targeted offenders is already being incarcerated, the added benefits are not realized until the offenders' "normal" release dates have been extended. For example, if prisoner sentenced as a three striker already serves ten years, the crime reduction effects will not occur for ten years after the bill's passage.

The last possible justification for this policy is consistent with wide public and political appeal—punishment or just deserts. As Shichor and Sechrest noted, three strikes and you're out, in its purest form, is "vengeance as public policy."[31] This ideology requires no empirical validation or justification. As Greenwood and his Rand colleagues (the same scholars who had advocated selective incapacitation as a viable sentencing policy) note in their analysis of the California three strikes law:

> It is the "right thing to do." Aside from the savings and other effects, justice demands that those who repeatedly cause injury and loss to others have their freedom revoked.[32]

About half of the states and Congress have adopted some form of three strikes legislation. Although there are variations among the states in how they decided the rules of the three strikes game, there are some common themes.

First, in terms of what constitutes a strike, the vast majority of states include on their list of "strikeable" offenses violent felonies, such as murder, rape, robbery, arson, and assaults, and some states also include nonviolent charges. Some states have included other charges, such as:

- the sale of drugs in Indiana
- any drug offense punishable by imprisonment for more than five years in Louisiana

- the sale of drugs to minors, burglary, and weapons possession in California
- escape in Florida
- treason in Washington and
- embezzlement and bribery in South Carolina.

There are also variations in the number of strikes needed to be out, with two strikes bringing about some sentence enhancement in eight states. California's law is unique in that it allows for any felony conviction for any felony crime to be counted if the offender has a prior initial conviction for its list of strikeable crimes.[33]

The laws also differ regarding the length of imprisonment that is imposed when the offender "strikes out," although most are designed to incapacitate the offender for extremely long periods of time. For example, mandatory life sentences with no possibility of parole are imposed when offenders are "out" in Georgia, Indiana, Louisiana, Montana, New Jersey, North Carolina, South Carolina, Tennessee, Virginia, Washington, and Wisconsin. In three states, parole is possible after an offender is "out," but only after a significant period of incarceration. In New Mexico, these offenders are not eligible for parole until after serving thirty years, while those in Colorado must serve forty years before parole can be considered. In California, a minimum of twenty-five years must be served before parole eligibility.

Despite the passage of these laws, it has become clear that, with the noted exception of California, they are largely symbolic and are having no major impact except for the very small number of persons who are sentenced as third striker. This is because all of the states had habitual sentencing laws for repeat violent offenders *prior* to the enactment of three strikes laws. In other words, the new laws simply target a population already covered by existing laws.

In summary, from a national perspective, the "three strikes and you're out" movement was largely symbolic. It was not designed to have a significant impact on the criminal justice system. The laws were crafted so that in order to be "struck out," an offender would have to be convicted two, and often three, times for very serious but rarely committed crimes. Most states knew that very few offenders have more than two prior convictions for these types of crimes. More significantly, all of the states had existing provisions that allowed the courts to sentence these types of offenders for very lengthy prison terms. From this perspective, the three strikes movement is much ado about nothing and is having virtually no impact on current sentencing practices.[34]

The only noted exception to the national trend is happening in California. Today, there are about 45,000 people sentenced as either a second or third striker in California's severely crowded prison system. For both groups, the majority were not convicted of a violent crime. While the third strikers represent the smaller proportion, they must serve twenty-five years to life before they can be *considered* for release (Table 9-1).

Finally, we offer the case studies presented in Table 9-2 to further illustrate the types of crimes the strikers are committing. These five cases are drawn from

Table 9-1 California's Second and Third Strike Prison Population by Offense 2010

Offense	Second Strike	Third Strike
Violent	40%	49%
Property	26%	27%
Drugs	23%	15%
Other	10%	8%
Total Prisoners	37,027	8,837
Percent of Total California Prison Population	22%	5%

SOURCE: California Department of Corrections and Rehabilitation (CDCR), 2010.

Table 9-2 Selected Descriptions of Current Offenses by Three Strikers

Case Descriptions

Case 1. Person Offense: Carjacking

While attempting to steal a parked truck, the offender reportedly held the owner at bay with a buck knife. He fled on a freeway and was apprehended. No physical injuries or vehicle damage was reported. The offender was sentenced to 27 years to life with a minimum term of 22.95 years. The offender was employed at the time of arrest, earning between $300 and $500 per week net.

Case 2. Property Offense: Possession of Cellular Telephone to Defraud Telephone Company

The offender was in possession of a cellular phone that when used would be associated with a different number and individual. Telephone calls billed to the victim represent the harm imposed in this case. The offender will serve at least 25.6 months. The offender was employed, earning $873 each week.

Case 3. Property Offense: Petty Theft

The offender received a sentence of 27 years to life for attempting to sell stolen batteries to a retail merchant. The loss to the victim (cost of batteries) is $90. The offender was collecting disability pay at the time of arrest.

Case 4. Drug Offense: Sale of Marijuana

The offender sold a $5 bag of marijuana to an undercover police officer. The offense did not involve harm to person or to property. The offender will be incarcerated for at least 5 years.

Case 5. Other Offense: Reckless Driving, Evading the Police

The offender reportedly rolled his vehicle through a stop sign, panicked when police responded, and led police on a one-hour chase. He "decided to ride it out ... [to] smoke [his] cigarettes and run out of gas." Police apprehended the offender after blowing out the tires on his vehicle. No victim was involved in this case. The offender received a sentence of 25 years to life; he must serve 20 years. He was employed, earning $1,000 per week net.

interviews with inmates, and, in our estimation, here again, the pattern is the same. Inmates sentenced under this law for property crimes had committed relatively minor crimes where little if any harm was inflicted upon the victim. Furthermore, these cases were drawn from the three striker population, which is expected to reflect the more serious offender. Both the qualitative and quantitative data show that most inmates receiving the second and third strike sentences do not fit the profile of a violent and habitual offender for whom lengthy imprisonment is required.

Although the call for three strike legislation had its origins in the commission of horrible violent and sex crimes against children, the implementation of such laws has greatly expanded its original target population. Today, very few of the persons sentenced under three strikes law have anything in common with the offenders who murdered Diane Ballasiotes and Polly Klass.

THE GROWING NUMBER OF LIFERS

As with the other components of the U.S. correctional system, the number of lifers has been growing at a very fast pace. By 2009, there were an estimated 140,160 individuals (or 10%) of the entire prison population serving life terms in state and federal prisons, including 6,607 people who had been sentenced as juveniles (Table 9-3). Another 41,095 are known as LWOPs or life without parole. This sentence means the person must die in prison.[35] Louisiana has the highest percentage of LWOPs (11%) and that population continues to grow. Juvenile life without parole (JLWOP) sentences, which only exist in the United States, has resulted in at least 1,755 people are serving sentences for crimes committed when they were legally classified as juveniles. The vast majority of the JLWOP are people of color (77%). In 17 states, more than 60 percent

Table 9-3 Lifers and Lifers Without the Possibility of Parole in the U.S. by State, 2008

State	Life Sentence		LWOP	
	Number	**% of Prison Pop**	**Number**	**% of Prison Pop**
Alabama	5,087	17%	1,413	5%
Alaska	229	7%	NA	NA
Arizona	1,433	4%	208	1%
Arkansas	1,376	10%	541	4%
California	34,164	20%	3,679	2%
Colorado	2,136	9%	464	2%
Connecticut	430	2%	334	2%
Delaware	526	14%	318	8%
Florida	10,784	11%	6,424	7%
Georgia	7,193	13%	486	1%
Hawaii	412	12%	47	1%
Idaho	523	8%	102	2%
Illinois*	103	Unknown	103	Unknown
Indiana	250	1%	96	0%
Iowa	616	7%	616	7%

Table 9-3 Lifers and Lifers Without the Possibility of Parole
in the U.S. by State, 2008 (continued)

State	Life Sentence		LWOP	
	Number	% of Prison Pop	Number	% of Prison Pop
Kansas	806	9%	2	0%
Kentucky	1,073	8%	66	1%
Louisiana	4,161	11%	4,161	11%
Maine	58	3%	54	2%
Maryland	2,311	10%	321	1%
Massachusetts	1,760	17%	902	9%
Michigan	5,010	10%	3,384	7%
Minnesota	496	5%	48	1%
Mississippi	1,914	9%	1,230	5%
Missouri	2,582	9%	938	3%
Montana	171	5%	51	2%
Nebraska	515	12%	213	5%
Nevada	2,217	16%	450	3%
New Hampshire	177	6%	63	2%
New Jersey	1,257	5%	46	0%
New Mexico	391	6%	0	0%
New York	11,147	18%	190	0%
North Carolina	2,390	6%	1,215	3%
North Dakota	40	3%	11	1%
Ohio	5,202	10%	216	0%
Oklahoma	2,135	9%	623	3%
Oregon	719	5%	143	1%
Pennsylvania	4,349	9%	4,343	9%
Rhode Island	182	5%	32	1%
South Carolina	2,056	8%	777	3%
South Dakota	169	5%	169	5%
Tennessee	2,020	11%	260	1%
Texas	8,558	6%	71	0%
Utah	Unknown	Unknown	Unknown	Unknown
Vermont	89	4%	13	1%
Virginia	2,145	6%	774	2%
Washington	1,967	13%	542	3%
West Virginia	612	10%	251	4%
Wisconsin	1,072	5%	171	1%
Wyoming	197	10%	20	1%
FEDERAL	5,400	3%	4,514	2%
TOTALS	140,610	10%	41,095	3%

NOTE: Illinois did not provide usable data on life sentences or LWOP sentences in 2008. Estimate based on 2003 data.

of the JLWOP are black. In Alabama, 75 of the 89 persons serving JLWOP (84%) are black, as are 15 of the 19 (79%) in Maryland and 11 of the 14 (79%) in South Carolina.

In May 2010, the U.S. Supreme Court decided that JLWOP cannot be applied in cases where a homicide did not occur. In its opinion on *Graham v. Florida,* the Court reasoned that juveniles are fundamentally different from adults and have a unique ability to reform their lives. The Court ruled that young people must be given some "meaningful opportunity to obtain release based on demonstrated maturity and rehabilitation." Without the possibility of a death penalty for juveniles, life without parole is the toughest sentence available and is reserved for the most serious offenses, those involving homicide. In the majority opinion, Justice Kennedy wrote:

> The Court has recognized that defendants who do not kill, intend to kill, or foresee that life will be taken are categorically less deserving of the most serious forms of punishment than are murderers.[36]

Prior to this ruling, ten states and the federal government held a total of 129 juveniles serving life sentences without parole for crimes that did not include a homicide. These people can receive a new sentence but it is unclear or certain that parole will be granted on the new sentence.[37]

How Dangerous Are They?

Even though it is possible to receive a life sentence for crimes other than murder, the majority of lifers have been convicted of murder. There are numerous levels of murder but the three basic categories are first degree (premeditated), second degree (non-premeditated) and manslaughter (voluntary and nonvoluntary without malice or intent). Although murderers represent about 14 percent of the state prison population, they represent only 2 to 3 percent of prison releases (Table 9-4). The reason for the differences between these percentages has to do with the length of stay. Murderers who are released spend an average of 144 months (12 years) incarcerated in the state prison compared to 28-month average for all released prisoners. But the 144-month figure does not take into account the large number of LWOP and other current parole practices who have yet to show

Table 9-4 Key Attributes of U.S. Incarcerated Murderers and Other Prisoners

Attribute	Murderers	Other Prisoners
% of Prisoners	14%	86%
% of Prison Admissions and Releases	1%	99%
Time Served	144 mos	28 mos
Rearrested after 3 years	41%	68%
Reconvicted after 3 years	21%	47%
Returned to Prison after 3 years	31%	52%
Rearrested for a Murder Charge	1%	1%

up in the BJS release data files. In other words if a parole board has reduced the number of paroles for murders, they will serve a longer period of imprisonment but will not be counted in the prison release data until they start to be released.

For those who are released, they have among the lowest rearrest rates. The BJS data shows that compared to all prison releases, murderers have substantially lower rearrest, reconviction, and return-to-prison rates. Their probability of being rearrested for murder (about one-third of the charges are dropped or dismissed by the courts) is 1 percent So, from a public safety point of view, murderers (and other people convicted of violent crimes) are much lower risks to recidivate than people convicted of property or drug crimes. In terms of committing a murder upon release, we are far more likely to be murdered by a so-called "nonviolent" offender than someone released for murder. This is because there are far more people being released each year even though they all have a low rearrest rate for murder. Lifers, after they have become eligible for release, have even a lower recidivism rate by virtue of their advanced age. In California, over half of the current lifer population is assessed as a low risk to re-offend largely due to their advanced age plus the lack of a recent criminal career.

But despite these statistics, if they are eventually released, a murder will occur—the so-called "third rail" of politics meaning that no public official can survive polically if such an crime is committed by a lifer.

The Massachusetts Parole Board is under scrutiny after a local police officer was killed by a career criminal who was released despite serving a term of three concurrent life sentences. Dominic Cinelli was serving time for shooting a security guard during an armed robbery to feed his heroin addiction when he told the board in November 2008 that he was a changed man, the Boston Globe reported. Four months later the board unanimously voted to free Cinelli, but police say the 57-year-old returned to his ugly ways Sunday, fatally shooting Woburn police officer John Maguire, 60, while robbing a Kohl's department store. Cinelli also died in the shootout.

http://www.foxnews.com/us/2010/12/29/mass-cop-killed-career-criminal-parole-despite-life-sentences/#ixzz1BIphxGpK

Correctional officials have long understood the low-risk nature of lifers. They tend to have the most coveted work assignments as they represent a stable and productive workforce. In the 1970s, lifers were generally assigned to the warden's house to care for not only the warden but his wife and children. At Stateville in the 1970s, lifers prepared the food, did the laundry, cut the grass, and washed the warden's official and private cars.

Today, some states have curtailed this practice but in the southern states, it prevails. For example, in Louisiana, the governor's mansion is staffed by lifers who prepare the food and serve it to the governor and his or her guests. In Mississippi, during a study we conducted in 2009, we stayed at the commissioner's house at Parchment where two lifers served as our butlers. One had murdered a police officer and another had killed an acquaintance more than twenty years ago. They lived in a housing unit (with no fence) that was no more than fifty yards from the main highway. Their relationships with prison staff were so normal that one would think they were paid employees, except they had a uniform that said "MDOC Inmate."

Lifers also help create self-help programs for other inmates. Here is a listing of some of the programs run by lifers and other prisoners at California's San Quentin prison:

S.Q.U.I.R.E.S. (San Quentin Utilization of Inmate Resources, Experience, and Studies)

Started in 1964, SQUIRES brings California juvenile wards and probationers to San Quentin for "intervention," which is undertaken by San Quentin prisoners.

REAL Choices

Two prisoners and a San Quentin guard started this youth intervention program in 2001. Young people from around the Bay Area come to San Quentin for counseling from lifers, who, employing their experience and their transformation, try to guide the youth to more responsible and productive lives.

VORG (Victims and Offenders Rape Counseling)

Initiated by the Bay Area's Women Against Rape organization, VORG brings rape victims together with prisoners for reconciliation efforts.

IMPACT (Incarcerated Men Putting Away Childish Things)

This program was created by a group of prisoners in cooperation with the Protestant chaplain. The stated purpose is to "re-form the character of men seeking to bring their lives to full and responsible maturity."

Brothers Keepers

A peer support group that provides crisis intervention and suicide prevention services to San Quentin's population. It was started by two prisoners after one of their friends committed suicide.

Their Crimes

For his last book, John Irwin spent several years interviewing seventeen long-term lifers at San Quentin.[38] Based on the interviews, he classified the crimes that the lifers had committed. All of them were sentences for murder, but circumstances surrounding the murders varied dramatically.

In a review of the records of prisoners sentenced for homicide, Irwin distinquished three categories of typical homicides: (1) homicides resulting from deviant-group activities, such as "gangbanging" and drug trafficking, (2) homicides resulting from robberies or burglaries gone awry, and (3) homicides related to high pressure, emotional contexts, sequences, or relationships, such as in an ongoing spousal conflict. This breakdown corresponds to national data on homicides, which reveals that, in 2005, of the homicides in which the circumstances were known, 20 percent were related to drug crimes or gang activities; 23 percent to burglaries or robberies; and 36 percent to arguments among friends and family or love triangles.

Homicides are *very* serious crimes and are violent and tragic events that take the lives of individuals and deeply harm family members and friends of victims. Most, however, are not committed by monsters or fundamentally evil people. Instead, they are performed by relatively ordinary people who have either been caught up in special, often deviant, and criminal group dynamics or in unusual, perhaps ongoing, contexts, such as a hostile and stressful, even threatening, relationship with another person. They fall within the realm of understandable human behavior. What follows are examples of each type of homicide.

Gangbanging – Albert   We get to 24th and Mission, the bus stop. Wait for the bus. My old partners offered me a ride back to Daly City. Got back in the car. Maria was with me. We forget the bus, I accept the ride so my friends don't think I was a wimp. I did avoid them. I avoided them for a few months. So that day when they offered me a ride, I kept saying no, no, no. Finally I said ok, and I got in the car. Maria said no, wait for the bus. I said, get in the car, we'll get it over with and go home. Usually we go up Mission Street and get on the freeway and get off in Daly City. This day this guy decides to drive all the way up Mission Street. We get there, Colma, Daly City. I forgot the time, but I would say it was about 4:30 or 5:30. Late afternoon, fog time. It gets foggy there in Colma. One thing led to another. A red light. Another group of youngsters called "the Fog Town Gang" in Colma. They were standing on the corner in front of a 7-11. Like, you know, it was typical, so-called gang lifestyle, you mad dog each other. You look at each other. Then the little hand signals. Then you asked them, "Where you from?" Then the other gang will say, "We're from here." "We're from San Francisco, Mission District," yelling back at them. More hand signals, a few F-you's are thrown in there. Before you know it, the car does a U-turn, drives up into the parking lot and everyone starts running, dispersing. They see a car pull up, doors opening, couple of guys get out. Everyone runs away, except the victim of this crime. He's smoking a joint. He didn't think we were going to get out of the car or that it was going to go this far. Me too, I didn't think so either. He flipped the joint and started running. As he ran, he tripped. So it made it easier for us to catch up. We caught him and the ultimate sadly happened. No guns, just bats.

I go back to that day. I think to myself, if I only hadn't gotten into the car, if I hadn't accepted a ride to the hospital, if I hadn't been drinking or smoking weed that day. I think of them things. (Albert has served twenty-seven years for second degree murder and has no parole date.)

Robbery Gone Awry – Bobby   And so one night, I left the house and I went to do a burglary. And I found a gun at one of the incidents, at one of the places I burglarized and I took it with me and I went to another place to burglarize somewhere else and there was somebody home and we got into it and I shot and killed this person. Soon as I left from his house where I shot the guy at, I walked right into a policeman who was on foot patrol and he was on foot patrol because of the burglaries that were going on in the neighborhood. And so he happened to be on foot patrol because I'm the one that, you know, stirred up the community and so I walk right into him and he asks a bunch of questions and I end up getting arrested 'cause he found the gun on me 'cause I didn't throw it or anything like that. (Bobby has served twenty-three years and has no parole date.)

Relationships – Dannenberg   By May 1985, Dannenberg and his wife, victim Linda Dannenberg, had been undergoing severe domestic difficulties for a number of years. They had been engaged in marriage counseling and the victim had also sought individual psychiatric assistance. Apparently the victim was planning a dissolution of the marriage and a physical separation although there is no evidence that Dannenberg knew that. The marriage had been marred by verbal discord and at least one physical altercation (involving the victim and the minor child of [Dannenberg]) in the past.

On the morning of May 5, 1985, Dannenberg awakened the parties' five-year-old son. He noticed that the child had wet his bed, so he went into the bathroom to draw a bath for the boy. The tub drain was clogged, and the toilet was running. [Dannenberg] obtained tools (a pipe wrench and a screwdriver) from a nearby pantry and in the process chastised the victim for failing to clean the tub properly (apparently he blamed her for the clogged condition of the drain).

The victim followed Dannenberg into the bathroom. Dannenberg states that the victim picked up the screwdriver and came toward him, jabbing the screwdriver at him. Dannenberg had defensive wounds on his body. The victim attacked [Dannenberg], clawing and scratching his left arm with her fingernails and cutting his arm with the screwdriver. She told Dannenberg that she wanted him dead. Dannenberg picked up the pipe wrench and hit the victim once on the side of the head. The victim kept coming at Dannenberg who hit her a couple more times on the head.

The victim fell down, but kept kicking Dannenberg, who claims that he lost consciousness and that when he came to he found the victim lying motionless on the side of the bathtub, with her head partially under the water of the half-filled tub. Dannenberg called 911 and reported the incident. The autopsy revealed that the victim had been hit numerous occasions on the head but that the cause of her death was drowning. Dannenberg was convicted of second degree murder and served twenty-two years before being released in 2009.

Awakening, Programming, and Atonement

All of Irwin's lifers had spent over twenty years incarcerated for their crimes. Based on those interviews, he saw an emerging social process that follows a three-staged event. The awakening constitutes an understanding of their behavior, associations, and decisions that led to their life sentence. In particular, this occurs when lifers fully appreciate that there has been something fundamentally wrong with their former behavior. They realize that *their* actions have brought them to this disastrous end. They come to sincerely regret that they have taken the life of another human being. They further realize that there may be something fundamentally deranged in their personality or character. And they conclude that they better do something about it or they are not going to get out of prison, or they will not be able to avoid another disaster if released. They take inventory and ask themselves, who are they and what should they do to reform themselves?

One of the lifers expressed his awakening moment as follows:

And they put us in the hole and I'm in the hole with my brother. And I wake up one morning with him yelling at me. He says, "When you gonna quit this, man. You know the games over, man." He says, "You know I love you. You're a sharp man. You know what time it is about this penitentiary life. You know these fools are gonna rat, but you don't what to live by that old school morality. That went out in the 70s, by the 80s it was gone, man. You got more game than I do. But you're stupid. Would you do me a favor and quit this shit. Quit trying to run the child molesters off the yard, or beat them up or whatever you're doing.

What follows is a long-term effort to become involved in positive activities within the prison, not to gain release (while some may do so) but simply to start doing positive things that help justify living and that demonstrate to themselves and others that they are capable of good deeds. This includes dropping the self— as best one can do within a high-security prison.

I did everything I said. I made another promise: I'm gonna make myself, I'm gonna improve in every area in my life, in physical, mental, spiritual, and that's what I did. I got two trades. I finished one trade right before I left Tehachapi in '89. Did another one in Wasco, years later. I mean, that's pretty much my whole thing is on that and that's what I try to do now. I try to reach out. I try to teach other dudes the same thing, man. And all you got to do is be in control of you. You cannot be responsible about what some other fool gonna do, man. If you do, you're gonna drive yourself crazy, like I practically would of did to myself. All you got to do is control yourself, your own actions, be responsible for yourself. (Jerry)

One thing I came to realize is that we all are human. We are all God's creations. There is value in life. I began seeing the value in life—people. You start looking at yourself. Would you want someone to hurt your family? Would you want somebody to rob your family? I remember one time my mom got robbed. She never told me about it when I was on the streets. She told me after I got locked up. Someone had robbed her right there at gunpoint. I got so angry. How could someone do that to my mom. So I thought about that. And that's the way people feel. I started feeling how people feel. Soon I was realizing that this was not right. (Noel)

Irwin ends the study with the hope that lifers may still have a chance to be returned to society. Not because they deserve to be returned but because they have atoned for their crimes and have undergone a fundamental transformation. They simply are not the same people they were when they committed their crimes.

A dramatic change in the legal situation of California lifers is occurring. The federal courts have been vacating the denials of parole based on the lifers' crimes or their pre-conviction behaviors as "some evidence" that their release represents an unreasonable risk to public safety. In recent years, California courts have been ruling on cases where the prisoner has served more than their minimum sentences; the courts say that the crime alone is not a sufficient factor in establishing whether the individual is a danger to public safety.[39]

Most recently, in the case of *in re Sandra Davis Lawrence*, the court of appeals of the state of California, Second District, vacated the governor's reversal of the Board of Prison Terms' (BPT – the California Parole Board) fourth recommendation that Lawrence be released on parole. The governor had used Lawrence's crime as his main reason for reversing the parole board's decision. The court disagreed with the governor's characterization of her crime and her lack of remorse and decided that "Lawrence's commitment offense, now over thirty years in the past and after nearly a quarter century of incarceration, does not provide 'some evidence' that her present release would represent an 'unreasonable risk' of danger to the community."[40]

The other major case occurred in 2008, when the U.S. Court of Appeals for the Ninth Circuit in *Ronald Hayward v. John Marshal* vacated the governor's reversal of the decision of the BPT in granting Hayward a parole *and* the Los Angeles court's decision to uphold the governor's reversal. They stated:

> Hayward was initially sentenced to a term of fifteen years to life in prison. Hayward has been in prison for twenty-seven years. In *Irons,* we noted that in all the cases in which we have held that a parole board's decision to deem a prisoner unsuitable for parole solely on the basis of his commitment offense comports with due process, the decision was made before the inmate had served the minimum number of years required by his sentence. Specifically, in *Biggs, Sass,* and here, [in *Irons*] the petitioner had not served the minimum number of years to which they had been sentenced at the time of the challenged parole denial by the board. Therefore, we concluded that "all we held in those cases and all we hold today is that, given the particular circumstances of the offenses in these cases, due process was not violated when these prisoners were deemed unsuitable for parole prior to the expiration of their minimum terms." Here, by contrast, Hayward has served more than his minimum fifteen-year term of imprisonment. We hold that the governor's reversal of parole in this case was not supported by any evidence that Hayward's release would threaten public safety and that the governor's reversal of his parole thus violated his due process rights.[41]

It appears that the dam that has held back the release of thousands of lifers, who have served many years over the time, is finally cracking. Since Hayward, many lifers have had their habeas corpus petitions accepted by the federal courts. In the months to come, many more lifers may leave California prisons and enter free society.

SEX OFFENDERS

There probably is no class of people who are more universally despised by the public and the media than today's sex offender. It is not uncommon for sex offenders to receive more serious and longer prison terms than people who commit murder. Take the most recent case of Claude Foulk, who at age sixty-three, was sentenced to 248 years in California's prisons for sexually molesting his adopted son since age 9 for over ten years. Foulk, prior to his conviction, was the executive director of the Napa State Mental Hospital. His sentence ensures he will die in prison.[42]

The term sex offender actually includes a wide array of behavior and offenders. It can include statutory rape where consensual sex occurs between a person under the age of eighteen and an adult. There have been several well-publicized situations where female teachers have been sentenced to prison for having consensual sex with their teenage male students (see the following page). Other high-profile convicted sex offenders include celebrated film director Roman Polanski and former NFL player Lawrence Taylor. But it also includes horrific crimes of rape and murder of innocent children by habitual child molesters. Thus, lumping all sex offenders into one category fails to recognize the diversity of their crimes, victims, personal attributes, and their risk to the community.

To begin, the commission of a sex crime is one of the rarest forms of criminal activity and is declining. As shown in Figure 9-2, the rape and sexual

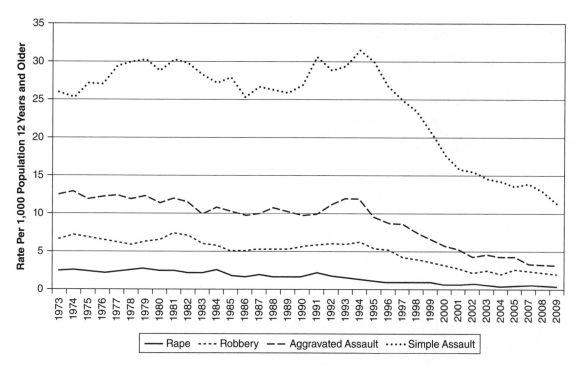

FIGURE 9-2 Rates of Violent Crime Per 1,000 Population Age 12 and Above 1973–2009

SOURCE: Bureau of Justice Statistics, Criminal Victimization, 2009.

Table 9-5 Victimization, UCR Reported Crimes, and UCR Arrests 2009

Source	Total		Rape/Sex Assault	
	Number	**Rates**	**Number**	**Rates**
NCVS Survey	20,057,180	6,533	125,910	50
UCR Reported	10,738,099	3,466	88,097	29
UCR Arrests	13,687,241	4,478	98,733	7

SOURCES: Bureau of Justice Statistics Victimization 2009 and Uniform Crime Reports 2009.

assault rate as reported by the U.S. Department of Justice's National Crime Victimization Survey (NCVS) survey shows that the chance of being raped or sexually assaulted is well below any other type of violent crime with the exception of murder. Table 9-5 shows the number of NCVS reported crime and arrests for 2009. Here one can see that the chances of being victimized are well below all crimes. The highest victimization rate is 50 per 100,000 per year whereas the total rate is over ten times that number.

The number of people currently incarcerated for various forms of sex crimes is about 152,400 (Table 9-6). The two primary sex crime categories are rape and other sexual crimes. The latter offense includes the more publically distained crime of child molestation. These people now represent about 11 percent of the entire state prison population with the two sex crime categories evenly split. In terms of demographics, sex offenders are overwhelming male

Table 9-6 State Prison Sex Crime Populations by Sex, Race, and Ethnicity, 2009

	Male		Female		Total	
Population	**N**	**%**	**N**	**%**	**N**	**%**
Total	1,259,400	93%	94,300	7%	1,353,700	100%
Rapes	69,700	99%	500	1%	70,200	5%
Other Sexual Assaults	81,100	99%	1,100	1%	82,200	6%
Total Sex Crimes	150,800	99%	1,600	1%	152,400	11%

	White		Black		Hispanic	
Population	**N**	**%**	**N**	**%**	**N**	**%**
Total	473,500	35%	517,500	38%	262,000	19%
Rapes	32,900	47%	23,500	33%	8,800	13%
Other Sexual Assaults	45,900	56%	16,200	20%	16,800	20%
Total Sex Crimes	78,800	52%	39,700	26%	25,600	17%

SOURCE: Bureau of Justice Statistics, *Prisoners in 2009.*

Table 9-7 Recidivism Rates for All Prisoners and Sex Offenders

3 Year Recidivism Rates	All Prisoners	Rape	Sexual Assault
Rearrest Rates	67%	46%	47%
Reconviction	47%	27%	22%
Rearrested for rape	1%	3%	NA

SOURCE: Bureau of Justice Statistics, *Recidivism of Prisoners Released in 1994.*

(99%) and white (52%) whereas Blacks and Hispanics represent 26 percent and 17 percent, respectively, of the sex offender population.

In terms of subsequent risk to public safety, sex offenders universally have *lower* recidivism rates compared to the overall recidivism rates for other prisoners. Table 9-7 shows prisoner recidivism rates published by the Bureau of Justice Statistics. Here, one can see that three-year recidivism rates for persons convicted of rape and sexual assaults are much lower (about one-third) than for all prisoners versus the overall prison recidivism rates. Furthermore, only 3 percent of released rapists are rearrested for another rape.

The national numbers can be used to estimate how much released rapists contribute to overall rapes as measured by arrests each year. Sex offenders represent about 5 percent of the 675,000 releases each year. The number of rapists released each year is even smaller at 1.5 percent. Assuming that 3 percent of these released rapists are rearrested for rape, that translates into about 254 prisoner-generated rape arrests for that release cohort over a three-year period. This number constitutes 1 percent of the total rape arrests that occur each year (Table 9-8).

This estimate of arrests attributable to released rapists excludes the number of rape arrests that were generated by earlier prison release cohorts, but since most arrests occur in the first year of release from prison, it is doubtful the number is much higher. And while this is a small percent of total rape arrests, it is a large number in terms of all the media stories that fuel the public's fear of rapists and sex offenders.

Table 9-8 Estimated Arrests Attributed to Released Prisoners

Prison Releases	678,575
# of Rapists Released Each Year @ 1.5%	10.179
# of Rapists Rearrested for Rape for the Next 3 Years	254
Total Rape Arrests	21,407
% of Released Rapists Rearrested for Rape, Based on the Total Number of Rape Arrests	1%

SOURCES: Bureau of Justice Statistics, *Recidivism of Prisoners Released in 1994* and FBI, UCR, 2009.

Selected Case Studies of Women Having Sex with Underage Students and Sentenced to Prison

Mary Kay Letourneau was a married elementary school teacher at Shorewood Elementary School in Burien, Washington, when she began a relationship with a sixth grade student she had previously taught in second grade. She was convicted of rape of a minor, for which she received probation. However, Letourneau refused to avoid contact with the victim, who was still a minor at the time, and she actually conceived the couple's first child while in violation of her probation; Letourneau was sent to prison for seven-and-a-half years. Today, the student, Vili Fualaau, and Letourneau are now married and raising the couple's two children.

Kelsey Peterson was employed as a teacher at Lexington Middle School before engaging in an affair with a sixth grade male student and fleeing with the child to Mexico in October of 2007. According to police, Peterson engaged in a sexual relationship with Fernando Rodriguez beginning in June of 2006 when the boy was twelve years old. When confronted, the pair fled to Mexico. Due to this decision, Peterson was sentenced to six years in federal prison for one count of crossing state lines to have sex with a person under the age of eighteen. This was part of a plea agreement that spared her facing federal kidnapping charges. Additionally, Peterson pled guilty to two counts of state charges for felony sexual assault on a minor.

Lisa Robyn Marinelli was a forty-year-old teacher at Mitchell High School in New Port Richey, Florida, where she was arrested and charged with unlawful sex with a minor. The charges stem from an incident when the boy's father saw his son exit the woman's vehicle and zip his pants up. Initially, the sixteen-year-old male in question was dating Marinelli's fifteen-year-old daughter. Following some legal moves, Marinelli eventually pled guilty to unlawful sex with a minor in April of 2009 and was sentenced to one year under house arrest and registration as a lifelong sex offender.

Vicky Lynn Lewallen was a forty-five-year-old biology teacher at Norman North High School in Norman, Oklahoma, as well as the school's basketball coach, when she was arrested for having sexual relations with a sixteen-year-old female student. According to police, the victim in the crime stated the acts were consensual and that she expressed no regret over the situation. She also stated that she had previously engaged in sexual relations with another educator at the school. Authorities eventually allowed Lewallen to plead guilty to two counts of oral sodomy, which, upon sentencing in March of 2009, led to a two-year prison sentence with an additional eight years of the sentence being suspended.

A more recent study of people arrested for sex crimes in Illinois in 1990 reached similar conclusions. In this study, the authors looked at all people who were arrested in 1990 and followed them for five years. That study found that 6.5 percent of the people arrested for a sex crime arrested again for the same crime within five years. Only homicides, kidnapping, and stalking had lower rearrest rates (5.7%, 2.8% and 5% respectively).[43]

Despite the lower risk associated with released prisoners to the overall rape and other sex offense crimes picture, people sentenced to prisons for such crimes have increased at a faster pace than almost any other crime group (Table 9-9).

Table 9-9 Prison Populations by Crime Category 1994–2009

Crime Category	1994	2009	% Change
All Prisoners	914,192	1,331,100	46%
Violence	433,218	693,400	60%
Rape	34,109	65,800	93%
Sexual Assault	54,824	93,600	71%
Property	211,668	258,200	22%
Drugs	203,935	264,300	30%
Other	65,371	114,600	75%

SOURCE: Bureau of Justice Statistics, *Prisoners* reports.

It is also noteworthy that sex offenders and rapists within the prison system have varying social statuses. The child molester or any prisoner who commits a crime against a child may often experience difficulties with other prisoners who often distain that type of crime. If the threats of violence become too great, these prisoners will seek refuge in protective custody units. But this is not necessarily the case. Many sex offenders are able to remain in the general population and programs like other prisoners. More significant is that sex offenders pose little threat within the prison setting to other staff and inmates. Most will quickly qualify for minimum custody because of their good conduct and lack of an extensive prior record. However, they are often unable to be placed in minimum custody prisons due to the fear that if one of them were to escape, the public would be outraged and the current administrator of the prison system would likely lose his or her job. For this reason sex offenders are generally over-classified within the prison system and housed in a more restrictive prison than warranted.

Megan's Law

On the other hand, there are incidents, while rare, where horrific violence is committed against children by sex offenders. These are the cases that strike fear in the public and have led to many sentencing reforms. The most infamous crime occurred in July of 1994, when Jesse Timmendequas, a sex offender, was released from a New Jersey prison after serving his ten-year maximum sentence. He could have been sentenced to thirty years under existing sentencing laws, but due to plea bargaining he received a lesser sentence (Ironically, the murderer of Polly Klass could have been sentenced to a life term as a "habitual" sentence but he received a sixteen-year sentence for kidnapping) Timmendequas subsequently raped and murdered seven-year-old Megan Kanka. Timmendequas was eventually sentenced to death but he had his death sentence commuted to life in prison without the possibility of parole when the New Jersey legislature abolished the state's death penalty in 2007.

The nature of this crime by a known sex offender resulted in all fifty states and the federal government adopting laws that require sex offenders to register with local law enforcement agencies, once they are convicted, to keep track of their whereabouts. In particular, sex offenders must notify police, parole, and probation agencies of their residence and employment. The sex offender registries are made public so that citizens can find out where they are residing and working. Some states require the registry requirements to be enforced for the person's entire life.

Many states have imposed restrictions on where sex offenders can or cannot live, and they do not allow them to reside in places near schools, day care centers, and even public parks. Furthermore, many local cities and municipalities have passed their own laws that prohibit sex offenders from living in their towns.

Civil Commitments of Sex Offenders

The other major development on the restriction of sex offenders is the passage of laws that allow a state to keep a prisoner incarcerated for an indeterminate period of time after they have completed their prison sentence. According to one study, seventeen states have adopted these "sexually violent predator" laws.[44] Typically, as a sex offender nears their prison release date, they can be evaluated regarding their suitability for release. Based on that review, the state can deny release and refer the person to a treatment facility that is usually part of the state's prison system. Until the person is judged suitable for release, he or she will remain incarcerated.

The Impact of the Sex Offender Restrictions

To date, there have been only two evaluations of the Megan's Law policies. The first was done in Washington state and the last one was conducted in New Jersey where Megan's Law was first introduced. Both have found that the passage of these laws has had no impact on the number of arrests for sexual crimes against children nor have they reduced recidivism rates.[45] These two evaluations examined trends in reported crimes and arrests both before and after the implementation of the laws. Both studies found no difference in the pre- and post-implementation trends for sex crimes and other violent crimes. They also found no differences between offenders under the notification restrictions and those who were not. Here again, there were no differences between the two groups. But they have had a dramatic impact on the sex offender prison population and its associated costs.

Several related studies offer clues regarding why the restrictions have had no effects on sex offenders re-offending. Tewksbury and Zevitz and Farkas both found that sex offenders often experience stress and depression that is associated with the registration requirements due to the stigmatization of the exclusion from geographic areas and residences, the threats and harassment, the loss of employment, and the humiliation of their family.[46] Such degrading experiences and the efforts to avoid being identified as a sex offender may result in not attending treatment or turning to drugs and alcohol and thus increasing recidivism rates. In this manner, restrictions and longer periods of supervision for sex offenders may be counterproductive.

NOTES

1. An example of one of the songs is the late Mac Dre's "Punk Police," where he points to activities of a Drug Enforcement Administration (DEA) agent he believes to be corrupt; Mac Dre, "Punk Police," The Best Of Mac Dre II [Explicit], 2004; Thizz Nation, CBS, "60 Minutes"; "Anderson Cooper Reports on "Stop Snitchin"; Rapper Cam'ron: Snitching Hurts His Business, "Code Of Ethics," April 22, 2007.

2. These guidelines are described in detail in U.S. Department of Justice. September 2005. *The Federal Bureau of Investigation's Compliance with the Attorney General's Investigative Guidelines.* Washington, DC: Office of Inspector General., US Department of Justice. Specifically see CI Guidelines § I.B.6 at B-8.

3. Blenford, Adam, April 28, 2005. *U.S. Schools Pay Classroom Informants.* BBC News.

4. Alan Feurer and Al Baker, January 27, 2008, "Officer's Arrests Put Spotlight on Police Use of Informants," *New York Times*, New York Region Section.

5. *Kathryn Johnston* (c. 1914–November 21, 2006): Article detailing her murder and surrounding circumstances with source links, available at: http://en.wikipedia.org/wiki/Kathryn_Johnston.

6. *Tulia, Texas:* Article detailing 1999 drug arrests with source links, available at: http://en.wikipedia.org/wiki/Tulia Texas.

7. Article detailing history of case with source links, available at: http://en.wikipedia.org/wiki/James_J._Bulger.

8. *Cory Maye* (c. September 9, 1980–): Article detailing his conviction of murder in 2001of a Mississippi police officer with source links, available at: http://en.wikipedia.org/wiki/Cory_Maye.

9. Mike Tobin; Amanda Garrett, and John Caniglia, July 30, 2007, *"DEA snitch Jerrell Bray says he decided to come clean, But when Jerrell Bray finally 'came clean,' who would believe him?" Plain Dealer*, available at: http://truthinjustice.org/lee-lucas2.htm.

10. Andrew Schneider and Mary Pat Flaherty (1991), "Part Four: Crime Pays Big For Informants in Forfeiture Drug Cases," *Presumed Guilty: The Law's Victims in the "War on Drugs,"* Pittsburg, PA: Pittsburg Press.

11. These payment limits are spelled out in the January 8, 2001, *Department of Justice Guidelines Regarding the Use of Confidential Informants*, Appendix D, p. 142.

12. A related form of compensation can occur if a DEA informant is killed or injured as a result of their cooperation with the DEA. In such instances, the informant is eligible for benefits under the Federal Employees Compensation Act, the same benefits federal employees can receive.

13. *Clinton Shane Stewart v. The State of Texas* 04-06-00488-CR. Texas Fourth Court of Appeals.

14. Much of this section is taken directly from an earlier article by James Austin (2009), "Prisons and fear of terrorism." *Criminology & Public Policy*, 8: 641–646.

15. Mark S. Hamm. "Prisoner Radicalization and Sacred Terrorism: A Life Course Perspective," in R. Rosenfeld, K. Quiner, and C. Garcia (eds.), *Contemporary Issues in Criminological Theory and Research: The Role of Social Institutions.* (Belmont, CA: Wadsworth, 2010), p. 174.

16. The 2009 budget request from the Department of Justice says that it would cost anywhere from $50 million to $80 million as requested to effect such a transfer (that's $207,000 to $330,000 per transferred prisoner). Those familiar with the business of transferring prisoners know that the costs are more likely to be zero. The U.S. already has a considerable infrastructure designed to move known and suspected terrorists from one place to another for detention and torture. In fact, a recent editorial by Harvard law professor Jack Goldsmith points out that there is an even larger but unspecified number of detainees at the Bagram U.S. Air Force Base in Afghanistan. Further, the U.S. continues to transfer suspects to

other countries as part of its rendition program for purposes of using interrogation methods that are not legal in the U.S. "The Detainee Shell Game," *Washington Post*, May 31, 2009, pA17.

17. http://www.msnbc.msn.com/id/30846430/#.

18. Frank Cilluffo, Gregory Saathoff, and others. 2006. "Out of the Shadows: Getting Ahead of Prisoner Radicalization," report by George Washington University, Homeland Security Policy Institute, and University of Virginia Critical Incident Analysis Group http://www.gwu.edu/~dhs/reports/rad/Out%20of%20the%20shadows.pdf.

19. Cilluffo et al., 2006: iii.

20. Cilluffo et al., 2006: v.

21. http://nefafoundation.org/miscellaneous/FeaturedDocs/U.S._v_James_PleaAgreement.pdf.

22. http://www.ojp.usdoj.gov/bjs/glance/tables/exptyptab.htm.

23. U.S. Department of Justice, Bureau of Justice Statistics, *Criminal Victimization, 2002* (Washington, DC, August 2003), NCJ 199994.

24. One should be reminded that these are not necessarily losses as many companies and individuals profited from the disaster by being awarded large government cleanup and construction contracts and replacing lost jobs that occurred only in Manhattan.

25. Ted Gest, "Reaching for a New Fix to an Old Problem," *U.S. News & World Report* (February 7, 1994), p. 9.

26. Ray Surette, "News from Nowhere, Policy to Follow: Media and the Social Construction of 'Three Strikes and You're Out,'" in David Shichor and Dale K. Sechrest (eds.), *Three Strikes and You're Out: Vengeance as Public Policy* (Thousand Oaks, CA: Sage Publications, 1996).

27. For a summary of this literature, see J. P. Gibbs, *Crime, Punishment, and Deterrence* (New York: Elsevier, 1975); and F. E. Zimring and G. J. Hawkins, *Deterrence: The Legal Threat in Crime Control* (Chicago: University of Chicago Press, 1973).

28. M. Klein, "Street Gangs and Deterrence Legislation," in David Shichor and Dale K. Sechrest (eds.), *Three Strikes and You're Out: Vengeance as Public Policy* (Thousand Oaks, CA: Sage Publications, 1996).

29. J. Petersilia, P. W. Greenwood, and M. Lavin, *Criminal Careers of Habitual Felons* (Washington, DC: National Institute of Law Enforcement and Criminal Justice, 1978); and P. W. Greenwood and A. Abrahamse, *Selective Incapacitation* (Santa Monica, CA: Rand Corporation), Report prepared for the National Institute of Justice, 1982.

30. Blumstein, J. Cohen, J. A. Roth, and C. Visher (eds.), *Criminal Careers and "Career Criminals"* (Washington, DC: National Academy Press, 1986), p. 15.

31. Shichor and Sechrest (eds.), *Three Strikes*.

32. P. W. Greenwood et al., "Estimating Benefits and Costs of Calculating New Mandatory-Sentencing Law," in D. Shichor and D. K. Sechrest (eds.), *Three Strikes and You're Out: Vengeance as Public Policy* (Thousand Oaks, CA: Sage, 1996).

33. John Clark, James Austin, and D. Alan Henry, "Three Strikes and You're Out: A Review of State Legislation," in *Research in Brief* (U.S. Department of Justice, National Institute of Justice, September 1997).

34. For example, in Washington, the state that started the three strikes movement, only 115 offenders were admitted to the Washington state prison system on their third strike for the first five years. The Federal Bureau of Prisons reported that no inmates had been sentenced under the three strikes law as of 1998. In Georgia, a two strikes state, Fulton County (Atlanta) has reported that less than ten cases are being prosecuted under the new law per year.

35. Ashley Nellis, "Throwing Away the Key: The Expansion of Life Without Parole Sentences," United States. *Federal Sentencing Reporter*, 23, 1, 2010: 27–32.

36. *Graham v. Florida*, (N0. 08-7412), 982 So., 2nd 43, Reversed and Remanded, 560 U.S. (2010) Opinion of the Court, p. 18

37. The Sentencing Project, *Juvenile Life Without Parole* Fact Sheet (May 2010), http://www.sentencingproject.org/detail/publication.cfm?publication_id=305&id=156.

38. John Irwin, *Lifers: Seeking Redemption in Prison*. New York: Routledge, 2009.

39. See *In re Smith* (2003), 109 Cal.App. 4th, *in re Scott* (2004), 109 Cal.App. 4th, and *in re Lee* (2005), Cal.App. 4th.

40. See *in re: Sandra Davis Lawrence* on habeas corpus. California Supreme Court, No. S154018. August 21, 2008

41. *Ronald Hayward v. John Marshal* (9th Cir. 2008) 512 F.3d 536., pp. 29–30.

42. http://www.ktla.com/news/landing/ktla-hospital-director-molest-guilty, 0,5410163.story

43. Lisa Sample and Timothy M. Bray, 2003. "Are Sex Offenders Dangerous?" *Criminology & Public Policy*. 3,1: 59–82.

44. Marcus Nieto and David Jung, *The Impact of Residency on Sex Offenders and Correctional Management Practices: A Literature Review* (Sacramento: California Research Bureau, August 2006).

45. Kristen Zgoba, Phillip Witt, Melissa Delessandro, and Bonita Veysey, *Megan's Law: Assessing the Practical and Monetary Efficacy*. December 2008; D. D. Schramm and C. D. Malloy, *Community Notification: A Study of Offender Characteristics and Recidivism* (Seattle: Washington State Institute for Public Policy, 1995).

46. Richard Tewksbury, "Collateral Consequences of Sex Offender Registration." *Journal of Contemporary Criminal Justice*, 21, 1, 2005: 67–81; R. G. Zevitz and M. A. Farkas, *Sex Offender Community Notification: Assessing the Impact in Wisconsin* (U.S. Department of Justice, National Institute of Justice, 2000), Research in Brief (NCJ 17992).

10

■

Unlocking America

LEARNING OBJECTIVES

1. Understand the various costs associated with incarceration as compared to the costs of crime and how they are computed.

2. Become familiar with the various arguments and evidence on whether higher incarceration rates or other factors have lowered crime rates.

3. Develop an understanding of which sentencing reforms would be required to reduce the U.S. correctional system.

4. Develop analytic skills to assess the relative effects of various reforms that will significantly reduce prison populations.

> "Everything is on the table. ... But corrections reform is critical. It's one of the big cost sinks that we have. We've got some states that are releasing people because they can't control their costs. We have to think intelligently about how we're going to do this... locking up offenders who have committed relatively minor crimes in costly state prisons doesn't make sense to me."

Governor John Kasich, December 3, 2010

> "We know from long experience that if [former prisoners] can't find work, or a home, or help, they are much more likely to commit more crimes and return to prison. ... America is the land of the second chance, and when the gates of the prison open, the path ahead should lead to a better life."

President George W. Bush, State of the Union Address, 2004

"In this whole thing, nobody is being soft on crime. ... The system has a very strong tendency to change them [offenders] for the worse. Everybody knows that, I think. Our current system is fundamentally immoral."

Chris Cannon, U.S. Representative, Utah

Viewed through the skeptical eye I train on all other government programs, I have concluded that mandatory minimum sentencing policies are not worth the high cost to America's taxpayers."

Grover Norquist, Americans for Tax Reform

INTRODUCTION

While the past three decades have seen a concerted effort to dramatically increase the use of imprisonment, today the country seems poised to reverse that trend. Even among conservatives, there is a growing chorus to begin dismantling our prison system. The science of criminology, as we have shown in the previous chapters supports this reform. Our study of the American prison system revealed that most (about 80%) of the unprecedented numbers of people sent to prison are guilty of petty property and drug crimes or violations of their conditions of probation or parole. Their crimes or violations lack any of the elements that the public believes are serious or that they associate with dangerous criminals. Even people who commit frequent felonies and who define themselves as "outlaws," "dope fiends," crack dealers, or "gangbangers" commit mostly petty felonies. These "high-rate" and "superpredator" offenders, as they have been mislabeled by policy makers and criminologists, are, for the most part, uneducated, unskilled (at crime as well as conventional pursuits), and highly disorganized persons who have no access to any form of rewarding, meaningful conventional life.[1] They usually turn to dangerous, mostly unrewarding, petty criminal pursuits as one of the few options they have to earn money, win some respect, and avoid monotonous lives on the streets. Frequently, they spend most of their young lives in and out of trouble and behind bars. With time, they either "grow out" of these behavioral patterns or they transition to an even more desperate existence that often leads to alcoholism, drug addiction, chronic unemployment, homelessness, mental illness, bad health, and an early death.

What may be more surprising is that a majority of all persons sent to prison, even the high-rate offenders, aspire to a relatively modest conventional life and hope to prepare for that while serving their prison sentences. This point should be considered particularly important because very little in the way of equipping prisoners for a conventional life on the outside is occurring in our prisons. In preceding decades, particularly the 1950s and 1960s, a much greater effort was made to "rehabilitate" prisoners. Whatever the outcome of these efforts (and this is a matter of some dispute), rehabilitation has been all but abandoned. Prisons have been redefined as places of punishment. In addition, rapid expansion has crowded prisoners into physically inadequate institutions and has siphoned off most available funds from all services other than those required to maintain control. Prisons have become true human warehouses often highly crowded, violent, and cruel.

The Financial Cost of Imprisonment

We must first consider the costs and benefits of increased imprisonment rates and the burden on our economy. The financial cost is the easiest to estimate. Most people are aware that prisons are expensive to build and operate. Few, however, understand just how expensive. Indeed, previous estimates routinely cited by public officials have dramatically underestimated the amounts of money spent on housing prisoners and building new prisons.

Prison Operating Costs   Since 1991, the amount of money required to operate the nation's prisons (excluding the massive jail system) has grown from $18.1 billion to $35 billion by 2005 and is projected to reach $40 billion by 2011.[2] To determine the costs per inmate per day or year, prison administrators typically calculate operating costs by dividing their annual budget by the average daily prison population. Using this crude method, the daily costs are estimated at $66, or about $24,000 per year. There is wide variation among the states, with some reporting operational costs of over $44,000 and others under $14,000 per year.

The most expensive prison systems tend to be relatively small and are in states that are more affluent, have lower crime rates and lower incarceration rates, and have organized labor. The states with prisons of this type are Massachusetts ($43,026), New York ($42,202), Rhode Island ($44,864), and Alaska ($42,082). The least expensive prison systems are located in the south and tend to be in states that are less affluent, have high crime rates and high incarceration rates, and have a lack of organized labor. These prisoner systems, which house predominantly black inmates, are in Alabama ($13,019), Louisiana ($13,009), Mississippi ($13,428), and Texas ($14,622).

However, this accounting practice is misleading and produces patently low estimates of the true costs of imprisonment. For example, agency budgets may exclude contracted services for food, education, medical and mental health care, legal services, and transportation provided by other governmental agencies. According to two early studies these additional expenses increased the official operating costs by 20 to 25 percent.

An independent audit of the Indiana prison system found that actual expenditures were one-third higher than those reported by the agency.[3] Besides these "hidden" direct expenditures, other costs are rarely included in such calculations. To name only a few: the state loses taxes that could be paid by many of the imprisoned, pays more welfare to their families, and maintains spacious prison grounds that are exempt from state and local real estate taxation. In a 1977 New York study reported by the National Council on Crime and Delinquency and conducted by Coopers and Lybrand, these indirect costs increased the total amount of money spent per prisoner by 25 percent.[4] Because the current figure of $24,000 per prisoner per year does not include these indirect costs, the true annual expenditure probably exceeds $45,000 per prisoner. This would increase the estimated total prison expenditure from $35 billion to $45 billion.

Construction Costs   The other enormous cost is prison construction. Just as prisons vary dramatically in their "mission," construction (and operating) costs vary dramatically. Prisons are enclosed, "total" institutions in which prisoners are not only housed but also guarded, fed, clothed, and worked. They also receive some schooling and medical and psychological treatment. These needs require—in addition to cell blocks or dormitories—infirmaries, classrooms, laundries, offices, maintenance shops, boiler rooms, and kitchens.

But these costs are just part of the costs associated with building a new prison. First, the prison construction often needs to be financed. Instead of using current tax revenues to pay directly for this construction, however, the state does what most citizens do when they buy a house—that is, they borrow money that must be paid back over several decades. The borrowing is done by selling bonds or using other financing instruments that may double or triple the original figure, depending on the prevailing interest rates. One such financing scheme is known as lease revenue bonds. These bonds are also known as Certificates of Participation or COPs). Such bonds do not require voter approval and thus are hidden from public scrutiny. In Florida, a 2010 report found that since 1995, the state had issued about $850 million in bonds to finance the state's massive prison construction program. As of 2010, the state taxpayers owed $727 million on these bonds and will pay approximately another $1 billion in interest and principal payments. Other states that have used COPs and/or lease revenue bonds are Texas, California, Alaska, New York and Michigan. California recently issued $5 billion lease revenue bonds in an effort to construct 32,000 prison beds at a total cost of $156,000 per cell. That effort is lagging and is experiencing significant cost over-runs which is driving some costs per cell to exceed $300,000 per cell constructed.[5]

Second, there are other costs associated with the construction costs themselves. These include architectural and legal fees, project management fees, prison equipment, and site improvement costs for removing existing structures and hazardous waste materials, and for landscaping. Third, prison construction costs are further increased by errors in original bids by contractors and cost overruns caused by delays in construction, which seem to be the rule rather than the exception. Because of these almost predictable overruns, prison construction projects typically have "contingency fees" set aside to cover such expenses.

The Million Dollar Cell   It is obvious that states will spend a lot more than $25,000 per year to house a prisoner and to build a cell in which he or she can live. But just how much more? In a study conducted for the U.S. Department of Justice, estimates were made on the costs of operating and constructing new prison beds for the District of Columbia. Table 10-1 uses the assumptions made in that study to develop the likely costs of a typical prison cell. At the time of the study (1997) the estimated construction cost was $50,000 per cell and COPs interest rates were over 7 percent. Since then construction costs have increased but interest rates have declined to about 4 percent or 5 percent. Table 10-1 provides an estimate that is current to

Table 10-1 The Million-Dollar Cell Typical Thirty-Year Life Cycle Costs
of a Prison Bed

Cost Item	Costs
I. Construction Costs	
A. Direct construction costs	$75,000
B. Twenty-year debt service costs at 4.50 percent per year	$37,500
C. Project management at 4 percent of construction costs	$3,000
D. Legal fees/testing and inspection at 2 percent of construction costs	$1,500
E. Architectural and engineering fees at 8 percent of construction costs	$6,000
F. Fixtures and equipment at 6 percent of construction costs	$4,500
G. Project contingencies at 5 percent of construction costs	$3,750
H. Site improvements at 8 percent of construction costs	$6,000
II. Total Construction and Debt Service Costs (Items A through H)	**$137,250**
III. Operating Costs	
Direct operating costs	$25,000
External indirect administrative support at 25 percent of direct operating costs	$6,250
IV. Total Operating Costs Per Year	**$31,250**
V. Thirty-Year Operating Costs	**$937,500**
VI. Total Costs for One Prison Bed at 2010 Costs	**$1,074,750**

SOURCE: Based on Austin et al., *District of Columbia Department of Corrections Long-Term Options Study* (Washington, DC: National Institute of Corrections, U.S. Department of Justice, January 31, 1997).

2010 with an average construction cost of $75,000 and a lease revenue interest rate of 4.5 percent. The results show that in total, a state will likely spend over $1 million in operating and construction costs over the projected thirty-year life cycle of that prison bed. The vast majority of those costs will be operating costs.[6]

THE "INCARCERATION REDUCES CRIME" DEBATE

Perhaps the single most cited justification for having a massive prison system is that it has a major impact on crime. Thus, the most hotly debated topic today is whether the imprisonment binge has actually reduced crime rates. Those who are largely responsible for this state of affairs—elected officials who have harangued on the street crime issue and passed laws resulting in more punitive sentencing policies, judges who have delivered more and longer prison terms, and government criminal justice functionaries who have supported the punitive trend in criminal policies—promised that the great expansion of prison populations would reduce crime in our society.

Figure 10-1 repeats the chart shown in Chapter 1, which showed crime rates and incarceration rates from 1933 through 2009. As the chart indicates, prior to 1965, there were relatively low crime and incarceration rates. Thereafter, both

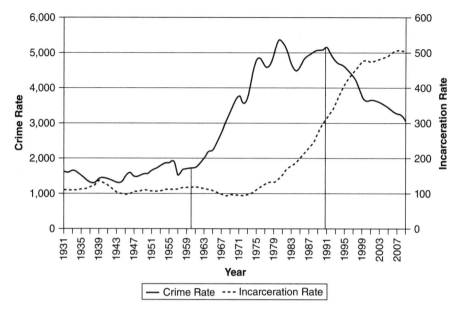

FIGURE 10-1 Comparison of U.S. Crime and Incarceration Rates 1931–2009

measures have steadily grown but not in tandem. Only since 1995 have crime rates begun their steady decline while incarceration rates have continued to increase. Reported crime rates have dropped significantly and are now near the levels that existed in the 1960s when the incarceration rate was one-fifth of what it is today. And, as we have noted throughout the book, the increase in the prison population is not due to more people being sentenced to prison but due to prisoners serving longer sentences.

Does the chart in Figure 10-1 prove or disprove the arguments for the "incarceration reduces crime" equation? In this section, we will review the scientific basis that has been offered by criminologists in support of the imprisonment binge. In making our assessment, we maintain that there are two basic requirements for their argument to hold. First, there must be a steady and consistent association over time between incarceration rates and crime rates. Where departures exist from the basic relationship, they must be reported and explained. Second, changes in other factors known to be associated with crime rates must be controlled for or, at least, acknowledged. Failure to meet either of these two requirements would be sufficient reason to reject the pro-incarceration position.

The Argument in Favor of "Incarceration Reduces Crime"

The pro-incarceration advocates have a very simplistic two-variable equation—as incarceration goes up, crime rates must go down. To provide the scientific basis for this argument, in the 1980s and 1990s, the U.S. Department of Justice played a key role in both articulating this proposition as a reasonable policy and funding a number of studies to demonstrate the causal relationship between imprisonment and crime. Beginning in the late 1980s, several key officials (none of whom were trained in criminology, economics, or statistics) in President George Herbert Bush's administration's department of justice launched a major information campaign to solidify the scientific basis for supporting incarceration as the best means for reducing crime by making the following statement:

> Statisticians and criminal justice researchers have consistently found that falling crime rates are associated with rising imprisonment rates, and rising crime rates are associated with falling imprisonment rates.[7]

President George Herbert Bush's attorney general William Barr restated this position, arguing that the country had a "clear choice" of either building more prisons or tolerating higher violent crime rates. This view implied that increasing the government's capacity to imprison is the single most effective strategy for reducing crime. Barr listed twenty-four steps the government should take to reduce violent crime, including "truth in sentencing" that requires inmates to serve the full amount of their sentences, increased use of mandatory minimum prison sentences, relaxation of evidentiary rules to increase conviction rates, greater use of the death penalty, and higher numbers of police officers.[8]

Similarly, President William Jefferson Clinton, after suffering a major setback in the 1994 midterm elections, purposely embraced a number of federal crime fighting initiatives to neutralize the Republican Party's reputation for being tough on crime. Specifically, he pushed for federal funds to hire 100,000 police officers and to encourage states to adopt "truth in sentencing" laws. Known as the 1994 Crime Bill, it was eventually adopted in 1996 by the Republican-controlled Congress The "truth in sentencing laws" required inmates convicted of violent crimes to serve 85 percent of their sentences. States that adopted these laws were rewarded with federal funds to help pay for the construction of more prison beds. Clearly, both political parties had decided that we need to get even tougher with criminals.

Looking back at Figure 10-1, the "incarceration reduces crime" advocates believed their thesis had been validated. Although there are some inconsistencies over time, the basic pattern remained: as incarceration rates have increased, crime rates have declined although not in a linear manner. These trends led a major U.S. Justice Department spokesperson to claim that violent crime will decline even more if more persons are imprisoned.

> No one knows for sure what the 1990s will bring. But my guess, based on the lessons learned over the past three decades, is this: If imprisonment rates continue to rise, overall violent crime rates will not increase and could actually fall in the 1990s. A big "if," of course, is whether imprisonment rates will continue their steady upward climb.[9]

The Argument Against "Incarceration Reduces Crime"

The major flaw in the "incarceration reduces crime" policy is its simplistic nature. For some reason, imprisonment advocates have completely rejected or ignored the long and rich history of criminology that has shown that many other social forces, in addition to the response of the criminal justice system, affect crime rates. It would be hard to find any credible social scientist or reasonable person who would agree that the rate of crime in any society is the sole product of the number of citizens that have been incarcerated. Even the public, when asked what they thought was the most effective way to reduce crime, has consistently said that "attacking social and economic problems" was the best choice (60%) versus "improving law enforcement and more prisons" (only 30%).[10]

Rather, crime is the product of a very complex set of individual, social, economic, political, and even random circumstances. The pro-incarceration advocates are asking the American people to exclude all other known factors associated with crime and to put all of their crime-fighting eggs in the incarceration basket. We believe, however, that a more careful examination of all available information demonstrates major inconsistencies in their argument and lends greater support to the conclusion that more imprisonment has little to do with crime rates.

Inconsistencies in the "Incarceration Leads to Lower Crime Rate" National Trend

A more careful, year-by-year analysis of the same UCR data cited by the justice department shows that the nation's overall crime rates have had relative periods of stabilization in all four decades, usually during the initial part of the decade (1960 to 1962, 1970 to 1973, 1975 to 1978, 1980 to 1984, and 1990 to 1994), despite increases in the use of imprisonment (Figure 10-1). For the imprisonment theory to be valid, these countervailing trends either should not have occurred or should somehow be explained by the imprisonment theory. If there was a direct causal relationship between imprisonment and crime rates, stabilization in crime rates during these time periods should not have taken place.

The UCR is one of two ways that the government tracks crime rates. The other, the National Crime Victimization Survey (NCVS), was established in 1973 in recognition of the fact that the UCR had major biases in the way crime was counted. The NCVS is often considered a more accurate and complete picture of crime in the United States, as it is based on interviews of household members.[11] According to the NCVS, the pattern of changes in crime rates is very different. As shown in Figure 10-2, NCVS shows no increases in property crimes from 1973 to 1980. Similarly, NCVS shows no increase in violent crimes between 1973 and 1993, unlike the UCR data that showed a steady increase over the same time period. So, using department of justice data, there is contradictory evidence of a 1970s crime epidemic, which was the major rationale for expanding the use of imprisonment.[12] Regardless of which measuring method is used, there was no large drop in the incarceration rate before crime rates began to increase after 1963. While there are a variety of theories as to why crime rates rose from 1964 to 1974, the cause was not a large drop in prison populations, which remained fairly stable until 1973.[13] Prison populations began increasing

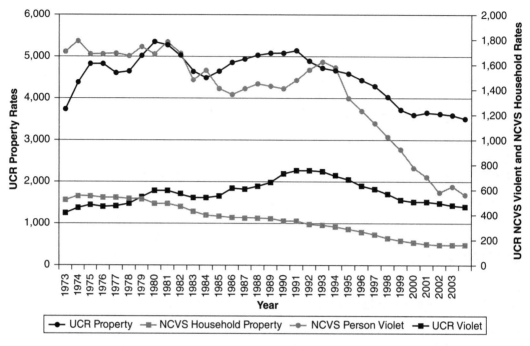

FIGURE 10-2 UCR and NCVS Crime Rate Comparisons 1973–2005

only *after* crime rates had already stabilized or, according to the crime victimization surveys, had already begun to decline.

Lower Incarceration Means Lower Crime Rates

There are significant variations among the states with respect to their crime and incarceration rate trends. As shown in Figure 10-3, there is a strong positive correlation between crime rates and incarceration rates. In general, states with *higher* rates of imprisonment tend to have *higher* crime rates, and, conversely, states with *lower* incarceration rates tend to have *lower* crime rates. A comparison strongly indicates that the massive increases in incarceration failed to produce any reduction in crime rates. If incarceration rates were the principal driver of crime rates, the opposite result would occur—states with the *higher* incarceration rates would have the *lower* crime rates.

Inconsistencies Among Selected States Over Time

If we were to pick three states to use in testing the imprisonment theory, California, New York, and Texas would be the obvious choices. As shown in Table 10-2, both California and Texas are the nation's leaders in increasing prison populations. In 1992, then attorney general William Barr believed that California should serve as a model for the rest of the country. In fact, he was urging Texas to follow California's lead. "California quadrupled its prison

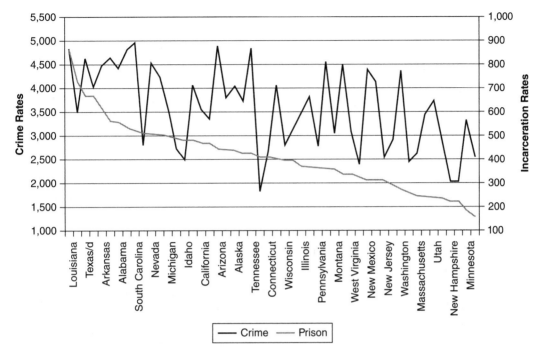

FIGURE 10-3 Crime and Incarceration Rates by State 2007

population during the 1980s and various forms of violent crimes fell by as much as 37 percent. But in Texas, which did not increase prison space, crime increased 29 percent in the decade."

Under then-Democratic Governor Ann Richards' leadership, Texas embraced Barr's advice and launched the largest prison construction program in the state's history. As shown in Table 10-2, both states continued to increase their imprisonment rates in the 1990s. California increased its imprisonment rates by over 50 percent, while Texas nearly tripled its rate. Both reported the same decline in crime rates (about 35%), just as they have fallen nationally. Not surprisingly, politicians in favor of imprisonment point to these two states as examples of how imprisonment reduces crime. However, if we add New York to the analysis we see how the greater "imprisonment lowers crime" thesis fails. New York has only slightly increased its prison population and imprisonment rates. Yet it has reported an even larger decrease in its crime rate. Furthermore, the overall crime rate is significantly lower in New York than in California and Texas despite its lower incarceration rate.

Inconsistencies Within States

The pro-incarceration argument also fails to explain why jurisdictions within a state that exercises very different sentencing policies report similar declines in crime rates. The most recent example of this situation was reported in Chapter 9 in the discussion of the effects of the "three strikes and you're out" law in California. There we saw that counties that largely ignored the "three strikes

Table 10-2 Comparisons Between Crime Rates and Incarceration Rates per 100,000, California, Texas, and New York, 1990–2008

Year	California		Texas		New York	
	Crime	Prison	Crime	Prison	Crime	Prison
1990	6,604	311	7,827	290	6,364	304
2000	3,740	453	4,956	730	3,100	383
2008	3,461	471	4,500	669	2,394	322
% Change	−48%	51%	−43%	+131%	−62%	+6%

and you're out" law had declines in the crime rates similar to those that had aggressively used the law to send more persons to lengthy prison terms.

Bad Math—The Numbers Do Not Add Up

There have been a number of criminologists and some major studies that have greatly contributed to the scientific basis for expanding the use of incarceration. Much of this "science" was grounded in a small number of studies that were funded by the U.S. Department of Justice in the 1970; they were conducted by the Rand Corporation and its leading researchers, Jan and Marcia Chaiken, Joan Petersilia, Peter Greenwood, and Alan Abrahamse. These studies consisted of having newly admitted prisoners self-report how many crimes they had committed prior to being incarcerated. Based on these survey results, the Rand researchers reported that a small number of prisoners admitted to having committed a very large number of crimes before they were incarcerated. Assuming they would continue to commit crimes at the same rate for an extended period of time, crime rates could be lowered by "selectively incapacitating" them. Lost in the discussion was the finding that most inmates sentenced to prison have very low or even nonexistent rates of criminal activity, suggesting that many prisoners pose little threat to public safety and need not be incarcerated. Nonetheless, policy makers were urged to adopt selective incapacitation sentencing strategies.[14]

A review by the National Academy of Sciences and Rand's own follow-up research later discovered that the selective incapacitation policy was incorrect for two reasons. The National Academy reanalysis of Rand's research found they had significantly overestimated the incapacitation effects of their proposed selective incapacitation policy. And then Rand itself found that its criteria for identifying high-risk inmates at the time of sentencing was invalid, but these findings did not deter others from arguing that incapacitation was a proven, cost-effective approach to fighting crime.

The first major effort to promote incapacitation was a report written by Edwin Zedlweski that was published with great fanfare by the U.S. Department of Justice, National Institute of Justice (NIJ), in 1987.[15] Zedlweski argued that by incarcerating high-rate offenders, as defined by the Rand studies, crime would be significantly reduced and society would reap enormous economic benefits. Specifically, he stated that although one year of incarceration would cost $25,000, society would avert $430,000 in social costs. Most of these averted costs were to be realized by assuming that each incarcerated offender would have committed 187 crimes per year that would have cost victims and society, in responding to crime, about $2,300 per crime.

In a related but later study, Mark Cohen and his colleagues tried to quantify the "true" costs of crime. The study, which was first published in 1988 and released in another version by the U.S. Department of Justice's NIJ in 1996, took the cost of crime one major step higher by adding the costs of "pain and suffering" to the cost-benefit equation. Remarkably, this piece of research claimed that the true cost of crime was actually $450 billion per year, with $345 billion being linked to so-called "quality of life" issues. These cost figures are well above the government's own estimates of $17.6 billion.[16]

These two studies have formed the basis for many politicians to argue that increased incarceration will significantly reduce crime and yet save money—in fact, hundreds of billions of dollars. Policies that served to reduce lengths of stay were criticized as "ineffective." Instead, "truth in sentencing," "three strikes and you're out," and other efforts to lengthen prison terms were advocated by many politicians who now had the scientific basis for their ideology. For example, John DiIulio, using this data, claimed that "prisons were a bargain"; and California's then-Governor Pete Wilson's chief economist promised that passing the "three strikes and you're out" legislation in 1994 would cause the crime rate in California to drop by 20 percent and save the state $55 billion.[17]

These studies have been roundly criticized largely because the numbers do not add up to what is well known regarding the number and cost of crimes. With respect to the number of crimes associated with incarcerated felons, Zimring and Hawkins have simply noted that, assuming the prevention of 187 crimes per offender was accurate and given the large increase in the prison population, crime would have been eliminated in the United States many years ago.[18] A pointed example of the unfulfilled promise of a crime-free California by 1982 developed by Zimring and Hawkins is shown in Figure 10-4. Clearly, something is very wrong with the assumption that the average number of crimes committed per year for sentenced inmates is so high.

With respect to the cost-benefit claim made by Cohen and colleagues, Austin as well as Zimring and Hawkins have pointed out the inappropriateness of using rarely awarded jury awards for "pain and suffering" for all crimes regardless of their relative pettiness.

> These estimates are applied to all crimes despite the fact that virtually none of them result in jury awards.... Even if one assumes that the $345 billion estimate of "quality of life" is accurate, what does it mean in real dollars? The answer is very little. The number is only a monetary symbol; it has nothing to do with real dollars, and has no economic significance.[19]

> The specific cost estimates are opportunistic, arbitrary, inconsistent, and too high. The schema lacks an articulated theory of either public or private cost. Moreover, Cohen's analysis reveals no relationship between its cost estimates and its conclusions about the cost-effectiveness of the investment in further crime control resources.[20]

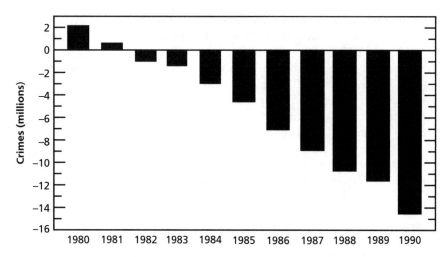

FIGURE 10-4 Hypothesized Crime Volume in California, Using 1980 Crimes, the Zedlewski Model of Incapacitation, and California Prison and Jail Trends
SOURCE: Zimring and Hawkins, *Incapacitation* (1995), p. 145.

Failure to Control for Other Factors Known to Be Associated with Crime Rates

All of the data presented here point to an inescapable conclusion: crime rates are much more the products of other aspects of our society rather than how many people we imprison. Here, we return to the themes articulated in Chapter 8 on rehabilitation: many factors other than incarceration rates are known to be linked to crime rates. In order for the "incarceration reduces crime" thesis to be valid, it must be shown that these other crime-related factors remained constant or were controlled in the analysis. But, as shown below, when these other factors are included, the relationship between crime and incarceration either diminishes or disappears.

Demographics   Since most crimes are committed by males between the ages of fifteen and twenty-four, as that population grows or subsides, one should expect associated fluctuations in crime rates. Before changes in crime rates can be attributed to changes in imprisonment rates, the influence of demographic changes must be considered.

Beginning in the early 1960s and throughout the 1970s—the exact period of the rise in crime rates—this age group grew in size. By 1980, the growth had peaked, and the size of this group began to decline—just as the crime rate also began to decline. An article by Darrell Steffensmeier and Miles Harer found that most of the decline in crime rates observed from 1979 through 1985 was the direct result of a declining "at-risk" population (young males age 15–24 years).[21]

The Economy and Other Socioeconomic Indicators   The 1990s also witnessed major improvements in a number of areas known to be related to crime rates. The unemployment rate in general declined from 6.2 percent of the work-eligible population in 1990 to 4.1 percent in 1999. There are also indications that the number of teenage births and those on public welfare rolls declined as well. And there were more indicators of social well-being that also pointed in a positive direction. Many of these indicators are reflective of the Linsky and Strauss study cited earlier. As these indicators continue to improve, we can expect further declines or at least stabilization in the crime rates.

The Bottom Line   More sophisticated studies of the relationship between crime and incarceration rates that incorporate demographic and other socioeconomic factors generally show a weak or nonexistent relationship. For example, a study of crime and incarceration rates from 1980 to 1991 in all fifty states and the District of Columbia shows that incarceration rates exploded during this period. The states that increased incarceration rates the least were just as likely to experience decreases in crime as those that increased them the most.[22] The study's authors pointed out that although San Francisco and Alameda counties in California *reduced* the number of individuals sentenced to state prison, their crime rates dropped as much if not more than those California counties that *increased* their prison commitments.

Other studies using multivariate analyses reach similar conclusions, finding "no consistent relationship between incarceration rates and crime rates"[23] and "no support for the 'more prisoners, less crime' thesis."[24] One study discovered an initial decrease in crime related to increases in rates of incarceration, but no decrease from further increases in incarceration.[25]

Probably the most-cited recent study on this matter was conducted by William Spelman, who argues that the crime rate today would be 25 percent higher were it not for the large increases in imprisonment from 1970 to 1990.[26] Assuming for the sake of discussion that this figure is correct, it is not a large effect, considering the enormous increase in imprisonment needed to achieve it. However, Spelman's estimate is probably too large. His analysis is based on national trends and does not explain why some states and counties that have lowered their incarceration rates experienced the same crime reductions as states that increased incarceration rates; his estimates of crime reductions rely on controversial data—prisoners' own claims about how much crime they had committed before incarceration. He further does not take into account the dramatic rise in the probation population, which is the largest segment of the total correctional system. More significantly, Spelman agrees that further investment in expanding the prison population will have little or no impact on crime rates.

VOODOO CRIMINOLOGY

The failure of the massive expansion of prison populations to accomplish the most important objective of incarceration—the reduction of crime—should come as no surprise because the idea that increased penalties will reduce crime is based on a simplistic and fallacious theory of criminal behavior. It starts with the idea that every person is an isolated, willful actor who makes completely rational decisions to maximize his or her pleasure and to minimize his or her pain. Consequently, individuals only commit crimes when they believe it will lead to more pleasure, gain, or satisfaction, and with minimal risk for pain or punishment. If penalties for being caught are small or nonexistent, then many persons who are not restrained by other factors (for example, strong conventional morals or the disapproval of close friends or family) will commit crimes—indeed, a lot of crimes. Only by increasing the certainty and severity of punishment, this thinking goes, will people "think twice" and be deterred.

The punishment/incapacitation/deterrence theory assumes that all individuals have access to the same conventional lifestyles for living out a law-abiding life. This is not true for most of the individuals who are caught up in our criminal justice system. For many, particularly young members of the inner-city under-class, the choice is not between conventional and illegal paths to the good life but between illegal and risky paths or no satisfaction at all. They are faced with a limited and depressing choice between a menial, dull, impoverished, undignified life at the bottom of the conventional heap or a life with some excitement, some monetary return, and a slim chance of larger financial rewards, albeit with great risks of being imprisoned, maimed, or even killed. Consequently, many "choose" crime despite the threat of imprisonment.

For many young males, especially African Americans and Hispanics, the threat of going to prison or jail is no threat at all but rather an expected or accepted part of life. Most minority males will be punished by the criminal justice system during their lifetimes. The federal government reports that an estimated 1 of every 20 persons (5%) can be expected to serve time in prison during their lifetime. The lifetime chances of a person going to prison are higher for men (9%) than for women (1%) and higher for blacks (16%) and Hispanics (9%) than for whites (2%). At current levels of incarceration, newborn black males in this country have a greater than 1 in 4 chance of going to prison during their lifetimes, while Hispanic males have a 1 in 6 chance and white males have a 1 in 23 chance of serving time. These numbers do not include the probabilities of being arrested, jailed, or placed in a juvenile detention system.[27]

Deterrence and punishment are effective only when the act of punishment actually worsens a person's lifestyle. For millions of males, imprisonment poses no such threat. As a young black convict put it when Claude Brown told him that his pre-prison life meant that there was a "60 percent chance he will be killed, permanently maimed, or end up doing a long bit in jail":

> "I see where you comin' from, Mr. Brown," he replied, "but you got things kind of turned around the wrong way. You see, all the things that you say could happen to me is dead on the money and that is why I can't lose. Look at it from my point of view for a minute. Let's say I go and get wiped [killed]. Then I ain't got no more needs, right? All my problems are solved. I don't need no more money, no more nothing, right? Okay, supposin' I get popped, shot in the spine and paralyzed for the rest of my life—that could happen playing football, you know. Then I won't need a whole lot of money because I won't be able to go no place and do nothin', right? So, I'll be on welfare, and the welfare check is all the money I'll need, right? Now

if I get busted and end up in the joint [prison] pullin' a dime and a nickel, like I am, then I don't have to worry about no bucks, no clothes. I get free rent and three squares a day. So you see, Mr. Brown, I really can't lose."[28]

AMERICA'S FARM SYSTEM FOR CRIMINALS

We have a less deterministic view of human nature. Most people who engage in crime do so not as isolated individuals, but as participants (as we all are) in various social organizations, groups, or "social systems," each of which has its own rules and values. Some groups in our society (often because of subjection to reduced circumstances, such as poverty, idleness, and incarceration over an extended period of time) develop preferences for deviant lifestyles. For example, young males who were abused as children, dropped out of school, lived in poverty, abused drugs, and served many juvenile jail and prison sentences have become immersed in deviant values and are distanced from any set of conventional values. They are most satisfied when engaging in specialized deviant practices related to their unique culture—wild partying involving drug use and sex along with extremely risky behavior involving extreme displays of machismo.[29]

Since crime is not the sole product of individual motives, efforts, especially by the state, to punish the individual without addressing the social forces that produced that individual will fail. Individuals do not decide to sell drugs, purchase drugs, or set up single-proprietor operations on their own. Most street crime involves groups, organizations, and networks. Drug dealers are persons who have been involved in groups and networks of people who use drugs, have connections, and know or are dealers. The same is true of gangbangers, hustlers, and thieves.

In effect, America has created a lower-class culture designed to produce new cohorts of street criminals each generation. Similar to organized sports, most of these criminal operations have major leagues, minor leagues, and a bench. Children come up through the ranks, learn the game, and finally move into the starting lineup once they reach their adolescent years. When they are temporarily or permanently removed (that is, arrested, imprisoned, or killed), they are replaced by others from the bench to continue the game. When the bench is depleted, someone comes up from the minors. Much as in professional and college sports, the span of their career is short, with most of their active crime years taking place between the ages of fifteen and twenty-four. Our impoverished inner-city neighborhoods (or what is left of them as neighborhoods) have almost unlimited reserves milling about who are kept out of the starting lineup by managers and first-string players. As soon as the police arrest the "kingpin" drug dealer, the leaders of a gang, or some of the top pimps or hustlers, new recruits move in to take over these positions.

This characterization of criminal operations also explains why the "War on Drugs," which has been going on for two decades, has failed. During the 1980s, the government spent billions of tax dollars and arrested millions for drug possession or drug trafficking. Regularly, the media reported that a new large-scale drug operation and some kingpin drug dealers had been caught. Drugs continued to be at least as available as they were before the new arrests, however, as "new" kingpins quickly and often violently replaced the recently departed leaders.

The Guiding Philosophy of Proportionality of Punishment for Reversing the Imprisonment Binge

Reversing the imprisonment binge is possible but will require a redefinition and an acceptance, by the public, of the primary objectives of the correctional system. In particular, it will be necessary to reduce the various amounts of punishment now being handed out by the criminal justice system, which takes the form of imprisonment and community supervision.

There is now a growing consensus that many punishments are not proportionate to the crimes being committed. This disproportional level of punishment fuels the prison population and produces widespread injustice. A growing body of research shows that the burgeoning use of incarceration generates racial and social inequality. Moreover, it damages children, families, and communities, with limited impact on the original objective: public safety.

Table 10-3 illustrates the vast disparity between the economic losses associated with four common crimes and the amount spent to incarcerate the offenders. For example, the median loss associated with a robbery reported to the police is $100. The typical prison sentence for robbery in the United States is 97 months, or about eight years, of which the typical time served is 55 months. Together with the time spent in jail pretrial, the average robbery offender is incarcerated for 60 months at a total cost of approximately $113,000.

Another example of the disproportional level of punishment is the widespread use of state imprisonment for technical probation and parole violators. These are behaviors for which persons can only be incarcerated in a state or federal prison system if they are on probation or parole status. This is not to

Table 10-3 Economic Loss to Victims and Costs of Incarceration

Type of Crime	Median Victim Loss	Prison Sentence (in mos)	Pretrial Time (in mos)	Prison Time Served (in mos)	Total Time (in mos)	Incarceration Costs*
Robbery	$100	97	5	55	60	$115,000
Burglary	$280	69	5	30	35	$64,100
Larceny Theft	$100	43	5	19	24	$42,200
Auto Theft	$2,500	41	5	19	22	$42,200
Drug Possession	$0	55	5	19	24	$46,000

*Incarceration costs are based on an average annual incarceration cost of $23,000.

SOURCES: Rennison, C. & Rand, M. (2003). *Criminal Victimization, 2002.* Washington, DC: Bureau of Justice Statistics; Bureau of Justice Statistics National Corrections Reporting System. Accessed on December 28, 2008, at http://www.ojpus doj.gov/bjs/dtdata.htm#ncrp.

diminish the problem of noncompliance with imposed conditions of probation or parole supervision. Nevertheless, it raises the question of why we rely on many months or years of imprisonment for behaviors that by any definition are not dangerous or even criminal. One of Tonry and Morris's key recommendations was to develop proportionate sanctions that are *"between prison and probation."*[30] Such intermediate punishments should help people understand and take responsibility for the harm they cause, as well as mandate that lawbreakers make amends to victims and the communities that they damage.[31]

Along these lines, the general principle that would have to be adopted by the courts would be that imprisonment should be reserved for people who inflict the greatest harms. More precisely, these are the crimes of murder, manslaughter, robbery, assault, rape, child abuse, and kidnapping. This is not to say that people who commit these crimes must all be sentenced to prison. There are varying degrees of harm associated with these offenses. The National Crime Victimization Survey, for example, shows that the majority of robberies and assaults result in little physical and financial harm to victims, and many people convicted of these crimes are now being placed on probation.

Probation, fines, short jail sentences, and restitution would be punishments largely reserved for those who have caused little financial, psychological, or physical harm, but whose actions are nevertheless blameworthy. Specifically, these would be for people who have committed and continue to commit property, public disorder, drug, DUI, corporate, and related financial crimes.[32] The use of such non-prison sanctions would also be applied to people who continually and habitually fail to comply with the conditions of probation or parole.

Finally, the current fiscal crisis at state and federal levels has convinced policy makers that excessive criminal justice and penal policies are no longer affordable. Such fiscal pressures are only likely to escalate in the face of a U.S. recession. Thus, state and local governments are faced with the reality that they will need to reduce their criminal justice and correctional costs whether they want to or not.

Length of Stay and Recidivism Rates   Perhaps one of the strongest arguments for lowering the length of imprisonment, and thus the prison population, as shown in the U.S. Department of Justice recidivism studies for 1994 releases (California dominates the results by virtue of its large numbers) is the lack of a relationship between how long persons are incarcerated and recidivism rates (see Table 10-4).

Although the recidivism rates appear to decline slightly, those declines are not statistically significant, except for people who serve more than 24 months, and that reduction in recidivism may be due to the maturation of the prisoner; older prisoners have lower recidivism rates. When this study is replicated and controlled for age and other related factors, there is no statistically significant difference in recidivism rates by length of stay.

A recent summary assessment of twelve early release studies by the National Council on Crime and Delinquency found that all of the studies reported that early released inmates had the same or lower recidivism rates compared to those who were not early releases. Further, the state crime rates either declined or

Table 10-4 Three-Year Follow-Up Rate of Rearrests of State Prisoners Released in 1994 by Time Served in Prison

Time Served	3-Year Rearrest Rates
6 months or less	66.0 percent
7 to 12 months	64.8 percent
13 to 18 months	64.2 percent
19 to 24 months	65.4 percent
25 to 30 months	68.3 percent
31 to 36 months	62.6 percent
3 to 60 months	63.2 percent
61 months or more	54.0 percent

SOURCE: Bureau of Justice Statistics, *Prison Statistics*. Available: http://www.ojp.usdoj.gov/bjs/prisons.htm. Accessed August 1, 2006.

remained the same during the period that the early release program or policy was in effect.[33]

One of the reasons that lowering or increasing the length of stay, or LOS, has little, if any, impact on aggregate crime rates is because released prisoners constitute a small proportion of the pool of people being arrested. There have been two BJS reports and several state studies showing that the percent of crime, or more precisely, arrests, that can be attributed to released prisoners is quite low. BJS estimates that about 5 percent of the arrests that occurred over a three-year period could be attributed to prisoners released in a given year (see Table 10-5). Similar estimates have been made in Texas, Michigan, Illinois, and California. This body of research shows that shorter periods of incarceration do not aggravate crime rates and that the stream of some 700,000 prison releases each year has a minimal impact on arrest and crime rates.

A Blueprint for Reducing Correctional Populations

Just how does one begin the daunting and politically difficult task of lowering the correctional populations? The good news is that the necessary reforms have been adopted in many states either currently or in the past. So, the

Table 10-5 Percent of Arrests Attributed to Released Prisoners

Arrests in Seven States	Number	Percent
Total Arrests from 1994 to 1997	2,994,868	100 percent
Total Arrests of Prisoners Released from 1994 to 1997	140,543	5 percent
Total Arrests of Prisoners for Violent Crimes	36,000	1 percent

SOURCE: Bureau of Justice Statistics. (June 2002). *Recidivism of Prisoners Released in 1994* (Special Report, NCJ 193427). Washington, DC: U.S. Department of Justice.

means for making the desired reductions are available. It should also be noted that these changes are neither radical nor take a long time to implement. As will be shown in this section, what is required are relatively modest changes in current practices. This is because relatively small adjustments in the key decision points will have a large cumulative effect over a relatively short period of time.

A good starting point is to observe that currently there are places where lower incarceration rates exist. In 1988, the state and federal incarceration rate was approximately 250 per 100,000 population and reached 509 in 2008.[34] But there is a tremendous amount of variation in the states' incarceration and crime rates, with a low of 133 per 100,000 in Maine to a high of 858 in Louisiana. Thus, for most states and the federal government, returning to the 1988 incarceration rate will be a long-term process involving systemic policy and legislative changes in law enforcement, prosecutorial practices, sentencing, and correctional policy. If the goal is to reduce not only the state and federal prison populations, but also the attending probation, parole, and jail populations, then other reforms will be required.

So, the shift toward a less punitive and proportional system of penalties need not be a gradual one. A deliberate and well-thought-out strategy to reestablish a new equilibrium for these policies will be required. Yet for *all* states, localities, and the federal government, there is an immediate need to initiate a structured and gradual shift away from current practices and trends.

The reduction in the correctional system must also address crime rates and public safety. Because there is a positive relationship between crime and incarceration rates, any strategy to reduce incarceration rates must, at the same time, seek to lower crime rates. But, one should also note that today's crime rates mirror the rates in the early 1970s or earlier, when the incarceration rates hovered at 100 per 100,000 population. If we were to apply that crime-to-incarceration rate standard to 2007, the nation's state and federal prison populations would be approximately only 300,000 prisoners. But even today, the lowest state incarceration rate, in Maine, is well above the 100 per 100,000 incarceration rate, thus showing the difficulty in lowering our national threshold for incarceration.

So, to lower the overall incarceration rate will not be one path, but rather fifty-one paths for the state and federal governments. It will require fifty-one strategies, each tailored to fit the policy circumstances of the government in question, to return these systems to a more normal level. In this regard, some states have a great deal more work to do than others.

In the analysis that follows, a series of crucial pressure points that have a substantial impact on the size of the prison, jail, probation, and parole populations are identified. Using the most current national data, simulations of how adjustments in these pressure points will prompt change in the targeted population will be presented. These simulations are based on current national data, which have been disaggregated by admission type and offense group. In essence, it reflects a micro-simulation model that allows various assumptions to be made. The status quo simulation, modeling the current prison population, is shown in Table 10-6. Because the national data reflect each state's own policy and sentencing structure, each state will have to engage in its own policy analysis of these pressure points to see which changes, when enacted, will provide the most rapid return to a desired level of punishment. The key reforms that will have to be implemented are as follows:

1. Reduce length of stay for sentenced prisoners
2. Divert technical parole violators from prison and reduce their length of stay
3. Divert technical probation violators from prison and reduce their length of stay
4. Divert persons convicted of victimless crimes from prison
5. Reduce length of stay for persons placed on probation
6. Reduce length of stay for persons placed on parole
7. Reduce probation revocation rates
8. Reduce parole revocation rates
9. Greater use of fines, restitution, and community service in lieu of probation

1. Reduce the Length of Stay for Sentenced Prisoners The most direct and significant reform that states and the federal government can undertake that would have an immediate and significant impact is to lower the current length of

Table 10-6 Current Admission and Length of Stay for State Prison Admissions

State Prison Admissions	Current Admissions and Length of Stay in Months		
	Admits	**LOS**	**Prisoners**
Total Admissions	684,656	30	1,401,605
New Court Admissions	351,510		860,321
Violent	91,393	49	373,186
Property	101,938	23	195,381
Drug	112,483	23	215,593
Public Disorder	45,696	20	76,161
Technical Probation Violators	143,792		351,931
Violent	37,386	49	152,659
Property	41,700	23	79,924
Drug	46,013	23	88,192
Public Disorder	18,693	20	31,155
Technical Parole Violators	189,354	12	189,354
U.S. Population		303,000,000	
State Incarceration Rate		463	

SOURCE: Bureau of Justice Statistics. Corrections Reporting Program and Prisoners 2005.

stay. As shown in Table 10-7, if the states as a whole were to return to the LOS that existed in 1988, the current state prison population would eventually decline by about 400,000 prisoners. How long a person remains incarcerated is based on the sentencing structure of that state and often complex sentence calculation rules that can apply. But in general, states can be separated into the two basic categories of determinate and indeterminate sentencing structures. The former is a minority of states, estimated at fifteen, but it does include several major states, such as California, Washington, Arizona, Illinois, Indiana, Ohio, Virginia, and Florida, to name a few, along with the Federal Bureau of Prisons. In these states, prisoners are released once they have completed a certain proportion of their imposed sentence, less any good time they may be allowed to accumulate.

For these determinate states, legislative reform will be required to either ease current sentence ranges, lower truth-in-sentencing and other restrictions on the proportion of time to serve, or allow good time credits for program completion or other forms of satisfactory behavior. In the indeterminate states, a parole eligibility date is set based on a percentage of the sentence imposed, plus any good time the prisoner may be allowed to receive. In some states, like Michigan, the parole eligibility date cannot be adjusted by good-time credits. Or in some states like Louisiana, there are many restrictions on who is eligible for parole

Table 10-7 Current Trends versus 1988 Lengths of Stay

State Prison Admissions	Current LOS and Admissions			1988 Length of Stay In Months		
	Admits	LOS	Prisoners	Admits	LOS	Prisoners
Total	684,656		1,401,605	684,656		1,037,930
New Court Admissions	351,510		860,321	351,510		602,225
Violent	91,393	49	373,186	91,393	34	261,231
Property	101,938	23	195,381	101,938	16	136,767
Drug	112,483	23	215,593	112,483	16	150,915
Public Disorder	45,696	20	76,161	45,696	14	53,312
Technical Probation Violators	143,792		351,931	143,792		246,351
Violent	37,386	49	152,659	37,386	34	106,861
Property	41,700	23	79,924	41,700	16	55,947
Drug	46,013	23	88,192	46,013	16	61,735
Public Disorder	18,693	20	31,155	18,693	14	21,808
Technical Parole Violators	189,354	12	189,354	189,354	12	189,354
U.S. Population	303,000,000			303,000,000		
State Incarceration Rate	463			296		

consideration, based on the type of crime the prisoner is convicted of and/or the prisoner's prior record.

In these states, increasing what are referred to as the "parole grant rates" would serve to lower the prison populations, especially in those states that have low grant rates. These are states where the grant rates are below 40 percent, meaning that most prisoners are not being paroled at either their initial or subsequent parole hearings. There may also be the need to reform other aspects of the parole hearing that are delaying the actual release. For example, some parole boards rely upon a decision called "delayed release," where the prisoner is granted parole, but must remain in prison until a program is completed.

So, to lower the length of stay in a specific state will require a tailored strategy in that state. But, in general, all states will have to repeal some aspects of their current sentencing laws and replace them with less punitive sanctions. The only exceptions to this requirement are the states with parole boards and discretionary release powers.

2. Divert Technical Parole Violators and Reduce Their Length of Stay The second major reform would serve to greatly restrict the extent to which technical parole violators can be reincarcerated and the length of that reincarceration. Nationally, an estimated 250,000 prison admissions are parole violators. Some proportion of that group are parolees who have been convicted of a new felony and have a new or additional sentence to serve. The remainders are people who have violated the terms of their parole supervision, but have not been convicted of a new crime. Importantly, the technical violator can represent a situation in which the parolee has been arrested for a crime, but the prosecutor declines to proceed with the case(s). In such situations, the revocation and subsequent reincarceration is viewed as sufficient punishment so that prosecution is not warranted.

The other aspect of the parole revocation decision is how long a person will remain incarcerated before being rereleased. Because so many people are being revoked each year and their period of reimprisonment is quite lengthy, this decision by the parole board can have a substantial impact on the prison population.

The extent to which parolees are returned to prison varies substantially among the states. The two extremes are Washington state and California. The former prohibits by statute the readmission of a parole violator to prison (they can be held in local jails for up to sixty days), while California has over 90,000 parolee revocations each year—almost 1 out of every 2.5 parole violations occur in California. But the California technical violator spends only an average of three months in custody before being rereleased. This compares with other states where the technical violator remains in custody for 1 to 2 years. Often the time spent on parole, prior to the revocation, is not credited toward the "time served" calculation, meaning that the prisoner must complete all of the remaining time on his or her sentence.

The simulation shown in Table 10-8 assumes that the number of technical parole violations would be reduced by 80 percent and the remaining violators would be successfully prosecuted and receive new prison terms. Those who are violated would receive a short period of imprisonment that generally would not exceed ninety days.

3. Divert Technical Probation Violators and Reduce Their Length of Stay   Similar to the technical parole violators, a large proportion of the new court commitment stream consists of persons who were originally sentenced to probation, but have failed the terms of probation and technically their prison term is suspended. The revocations, like the technical parole violators, are people who have not been convicted of a new felony but may have been arrested for a new crime. In most cases these are people who have multiple violations that range from positive drug tests, failure to pay supervision fees, failure to report, or have failure in a treatment program.

Estimates from some states suggest that about one-third of the new court commitments are such cases and that they serve about two years once they are admitted to prison. Often the time spent on probation prior to the revocation is not credited toward the sentence. The simulation, also shown in Table 10-8, assumed that about 30 percent of the technical probation violators would be diverted. Those who are not diverted will serve the same lower time in prison as the other new court commitments.

Collectively, these first three reforms target the state prison population and would reduce the current prison population by about 600,000 inmates.

Table 10-8 Current Trends versus 1988 LOS, and Diverted Parole and Probation Violators

State Prison Admissions	Current Length of Stay and Admissions			1988 LOS Plus Diverted Probation & Parole Violators		
	Admits	LOS	Prisoners	Admits	LOS	Prisoners
Total	684,656		1,401,605	502,954		803,948
New Court Admissions	351,510		860,321	351,510	21	602,225
Violent	91,393	49	373,186	91,393	34	261,231
Property	101,938	23	195,381	101,938	16	136,767
Drug	112,483	23	215,593	112,483	16	150,915
Public Disorder	45,696	20	76,161	45,696	14	53,312
Technical Probation Violators	143,792		351,931	104,105	21	189,889
Violent	37,386	49	152,659	33,647	34	96,175
Property	41,700	23	79,924	31,275	16	41,960
Drug	46,013	23	88,192	34,510	16	46,301
Public Disorder	18,693	20	31,155	4,673	14	5,452
Technical Parole Violators	189,354	12	189,354	47,339	3	11,835
U.S. Population	303,000,000			303,000,000		
State Incarceration Rate	463			265		

4. Divert Persons Convicted of Victimless Crimes from Prison This reform recognizes that many people are now arrested for what is referred to as victimless crimes, such as drug possession, drug sales, disorderly conduct, drunkenness, drunk driving, prostitution, curfew, vagrancy, loitering, gambling, and a wide variety of motor vehicle violations. They are being incarcerated in our jails or being placed on years of probation. Once placed on probation, some of these people are likely to be sent to prison as a probation violator for continuing such behavior as failing to pay their probation supervision fees, not maintaining employment, not attending treatment, or for many other noncriminal acts.

Such recommendations do not mean that "victimless" crimes do not often have significant consequences—not only for the safety of the persons themselves, but also their families and the surrounding communities. Further, these cases can be more complicated in that such persons may have another current conviction for a property or violent crime, are wanted for such crimes by other jurisdictions, or have extensive prior records for property and violent crimes.

Table 10-9 shows the historical trends in the number of state prisoners who are incarcerated on any given day, by the primary crime they have been convicted of. It should be noted that for probation and parole technical violators, the primary charge is the one they were originally sentenced for and not the technical violation itself.

From a historical perspective, the proportion of prisoners incarcerated on any given day for violent crime has fluctuated, but remains relatively unchanged. The major shift has been in the percentages and the number of persons convicted for property, drug, and public disorder crimes that has increased by about 500,000 inmates since 1980. However, the proportion of state prisoners incarcerated for property crimes has declined from 30 percent to 19 percent, while the proportion of prisoners sentenced for drug offenses, both sales and possession, has increased from 6 percent to 20 percent. Public disorder crimes are a relatively small percentage of the total prisoner population, but it has doubled from 4 percent to 8 percent.

One must also look at the federal prison population that has grown faster than any other prison system. Unlike the state prison population, the BOP population did not begin to escalate until the early part of 1980, and only after the Federal Sentencing Guidelines were adopted. These guidelines mandated longer sentences for drug crimes and further mandated that people would be required to serve 85 percent of their imposed sentences. In essence, the BOP has become the dumping ground for drug offenders who are involved, in one way or another, in a federal prosecution for the possession, sale, or conspiracy to sell large amounts of marijuana, cocaine, and other illegal drugs. The 2007 BOP population now exceeds 200,000 people, of whom 107,000 (54 percent) are incarcerated for drug crimes. If one adds the number of state prisoners convicted of drug (253,300) and public disorder (98,700) crimes and the BOP immigration prisoners (about 20,000), the grand total of people convicted of victimless crimes approaches 478,000.

Diverting some portion of these people from state or federal prisons could have a significant impact, but it would also cut into the reductions achieved by

Table 10-9 Persons in State Prisons by Primary Offense

Year	Violent	Property	Drug	Public Order	Total	%Violent	% Property	% Drug	% Public Order
1980	173,300	89,300	19,000	12,400	294,000	59%	30%	6%	4%
1981	193,300	100,500	21,700	14,600	330,100	59%	30%	7%	4%
1982	215,300	114,400	25,300	17,800	372,800	58%	31%	7%	5%
1983	214,600	127,100	26,600	24,400	392,700	55%	32%	7%	6%
1984	227,300	133,100	31,700	21,900	414,000	55%	32%	8%	5%
1985	246,200	140,100	38,900	23,000	448,200	55%	31%	9%	5%
1986	258,600	150,200	45,400	28,800	483,000	54%	31%	9%	6%
1987	271,300	155,500	57,900	31,300	516,000	53%	30%	11%	6%
1988	282,700	161,600	79,100	35,000	558,400	51%	29%	14%	6%
1989	293,900	172,700	120,100	39,500	626,200	47%	28%	19%	6%
1990	313,600	173,700	148,600	45,500	681,400	46%	25%	22%	7%
1991	339,500	180,700	155,200	49,500	724,900	47%	25%	21%	7%
1992	369,100	181,600	168,100	56,300	775,100	48%	23%	22%	7%
1993	393,500	189,600	177,000	64,000	824,100	48%	23%	21%	8%
1994	425,700	207,000	193,500	74,400	900,600	47%	23%	21%	8%
1995	459,600	226,600	212,800	86,500	985,500	47%	23%	22%	9%
1996	484,800	231,700	216,900	96,000	1,029,400	47%	23%	21%	9%
1997	507,800	236,400	222,100	106,200	1,072,500	47%	22%	21%	10%
1998	545,200	242,900	236,800	113,900	1,138,800	48%	21%	21%	10%
1999	570,000	245,000	251,200	120,600	1,186,800	48%	21%	21%	10%
2000	589,100	238,500	251,100	124,600	1,203,300	49%	20%	21%	10%
2001	596,100	233,000	246,100	129,900	1,205,100	49%	19%	20%	11%
2002	624,900	253,000	265,000	87,500	1,230,400	51%	21%	22%	7%
2003	650,400	262,000	250,900	86,400	1,249,700	52%	21%	20%	7%
2004	663,700	265,600	249,400	88,900	1,267,600	52%	21%	20%	7%
2005	687,700	248,900	253,300	98,700	1,288,600	53%	19%	20%	8%

SOURCE: Bureau of Justice Statistics. *Correctional Populations in the United States, 1997; Prisoners in 2005.*

Table 10-10 Current State Trends versus All Recommended Reforms

State Prison Admissions	Current Length of Stay and Admissions			All Reforms Plus Diversion of Victimless Crimes		
	Admits	**LOS**	**Prisoners**	**Admits**	**LOS**	**Prisoners**
Total	684,656		1,401,605	418,109		731,077
New Court Admissions	351,510		860,321	311,965	21	551,168
Violent	91,393	49	373,186	91,393	34	261,231
Property	101,938	23	195,381	101,938	16	136,767
Drug	112,483	23	215,593	84,362	16	113,186
Public Disorder	45,696	20	76,161	34,272	14	39,984
Technical Probation Violators	143,792		351,931	94,310	21	176,950
Violent	37,386	49	152,659	33,647	34	96,175
Property	41,700	23	79,924	31,275	16	41,960
Drug	46,013	23	88,192	25,883	16	34,726
Public Disorder	18,693	20	31,155	3,505	14	4,089
Technical Parole Violators	189,354	12	189,354	11,835	3	2,959
U.S. Population	303,000,000			303,000,000		
State Incarceration Rate	463			241		

recommendations 1 through 3, since the prisoners are represented in those estimates. For purposes of this chapter, it is assumed that approximately 25 percent of the current stream of drug and public disorder prisoners would be diverted to probation in lieu of prison.

Table 10-10 summarizes the overall effects of these four major reforms on state prison systems. In total, the state prison population would drop about 50 percent. This decline would not happen all at once. It would depend on such questions as whether new laws were retroactive or applied only to newly sentenced prisoners, and the adoption of new sentencing, parole, and probation policies.

The remaining five reforms, as listed below, are all designed to lower the large probation and parole populations that are essential to accommodate the transfer of prisoners to either the probation (diversion) or parole (reduced LOS):

Reduce Length of Stay for Persons Placed on Probation

Reduce Length of Stay for Persons Placed on Parole

Reduce Probation Revocation Rates

Reduce Parole Revocation Rates

Greater Use of Fines, Restitution, and Community Service in Lieu of Probation

Similar to the data on prison lengths of stay, there is little, if any, evidence that extending or reducing the period of probation or parole supervision has any impact on recidivism. A number of studies in California revealed that (1) there was no relationship between the time on supervision and parole success, and (2) there is no difference between people placed on parole versus people with no parole supervision on recidivism rates.[35] Probation or parole supervision failure is most likely to occur within the first twelve months of supervision; thereafter, supervision is more of a nuisance than a means for assisting people after prison or preventing them from committing another crime.

A 2005 Urban Institute study, among others, revealed that individuals released with no parole supervision return to prison at a significantly lower rate than those released on parole.[36] Nevada has been experimenting with this policy shift, as it has produced positive results. The basic tool is allowing probationers and parolees to earn "good time" credits for each month of satisfactory behavior on supervision. For parolees, the "successful" termination rate has increased from 60 percent to about 85 percent. Since the practice was adopted for probationers, the success termination rate increased from 53 percent to 63 percent. Washington state has adopted a policy where low-risk parolees received no supervision.

On the use of fines, restitution, and community service, these penalties (especially fines) are frequently used today but rarely as the *sole sanction*. Related to current practices, people are often required to attend and pay for their treatment and the costs of their probation supervision. This reform would alter these practices and eliminate probation as a sanction for many property, public disorder, and drug possession crimes—especially marijuana. Hillsman noted twenty years ago that Western European countries differ from the United States in their use of fines as the sole sanction for a wide array of crimes.[37] Table 10-11 summarizes the likely effects of these reforms. The largest decline would occur by lowering the period of supervision by about one-third. Further reductions would be achieved by reducing the placement of people on probation or parole by 25 percent. In the case of probation, these people would receive other sanctions (fines, restitution, and community service). For people released from prison, the requirement of additional supervision would not be required, but based on risk or the nature of the crime.

Table 10-12 produces the grand totals for all correctional populations including the federal prison system and the jails. Modest reductions in the nation's jail population are noted based on what appears to be a growing trend in a reduced arrest rate, which fuels jail bookings. One would expect additional savings in the jail bookings as fewer probationers and parolees are violated and are required to remain in jail until they receive their revocation hearings. The federal prison systems would decline as the 85 percent truth-in-sentencing laws are relaxed, and a greater use of probation would be implemented. With these two additions, the 50 percent correctional population reduction is achieved.

All of the reforms are "evidence-based" in that they have been shown to be effective in reducing correctional populations without adversely impacting crime or recidivism rates. Indeed, a strong case can be made that with the billions of dollars that would be saved each year by the states, public safety would be greatly

Table 10-11 Estimated Impact on Parole and Probation Populations of Reducing the Length of Time on Supervision

Population	Current LOS and Admissions			New LOS - Only			Plus Diverted Probationer/ Parolees		
	Admits	LOS	Population	Admits	LOS	Population	Admits	LOS	Population
Probation	2,362,100	21	4,190,896	2,362,100	14	2,755,783	1,771,575	14	2,066,838
Parole	512,800	17	710,065	512,800	10	427,333	384,600	10	320,500
Totals	2,874,900		4,900,961	2,874,900		3,183,117	2,156,175		2,387,338

Table 10-12 Summary of the Eight Recommendations' Impact on Correctional Populations

Correctional Populations	Current Policies	New LOS	New LOS and Diversions	Plus Diverted "Victimless" Crimes	% Change
Grand Totals	7,496,425	5,126,628	4,071,866	3,842,879	−49%
State Prisons	1,398,698	1,037,930	803,948	731,077	−48%
Federal Prisons	199,618	125,000	100,000	100,000	−50%
Probation	4,293,163	2,755,783	2,066,838	2,066,838	−52%
Parole	824,365	427,333	320,500	320,500	−61%
Local Jails	780,581	780,581	780,581	624,465	−20%

enhanced by investing those funds in those communities that each year produce the vast majority of admissions to the correctional systems.

In terms of timing, these reductions would occur gradually over time. Much would depend on how they are implemented and the need for new legislation to reverse or modify current laws. But assuming that such reforms could be implemented within twelve to twenty-four months, the trajectory of the population reductions would be as represented in Figure 10-5.

The Future

It has been forty years (1969) since a decline in the nation's prison population has been reported. At that time the nation was busy fighting the Vietnam War and drafting hundreds of thousands of young males to serve in the military. In 1969, our crime rate was 3,680 per 100,000 population and our incarceration rate was 97 per 100,000. Today the crime rate is 3,667 (the same as 1969), but our incarceration rate is about five times higher at 508 per 100,000.

The most recent report by the Bureau of Justice Statistics reported a decline in the nation's prison population for 2009. More signficantly, BJS noted that twenty states recorded declines in their prison populations. The list of states with declining prison populations and the size of the decreases is likely to

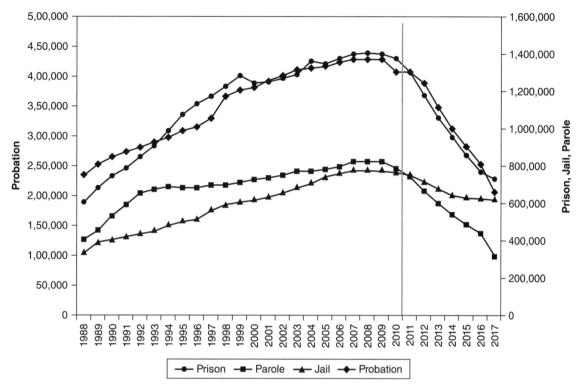

FIGURE 10-5 Past and Projected Declines in Correctional Populations 1988–2017

grow. Fueled by the soaring costs of corrections and a stagnant economy, policy makers are searching for ways to lower their investments in corrections. The question no longer is *can* we reduce prison and other correctional populations but *how best* can this be achieved while keeping the record, low-crime rates at their current levels?

Mathematically, the only way to lower correctional populations is to reduce the number or admissions and the lengths of stay in prison or under probation and parole. It is highly unlikely that such a reduction can be achieved by reducing recidivism rates that have remained unchanged for at least twenty-five years and as correctional systems struggle to keep what meager programs they now fund. Rather, the solution lies in simply returning to the same sentencing and correctional policies that existed a few decades ago when our crime rate was what it is today.

Overcoming Our Vindictive Society   Crime has incurred another profound cost: the increase of general vindictiveness in our society. Historically, Americans (as compared to Europeans and Japanese, for example) have been highly individualistic, which means, for one thing, that they are prone to blaming individuals for their actions. In America, according to the dominant ideology, everyone is responsible for his or her acts, and every act is accomplished by a willful actor.

Consequently, every undesirable, harmful, "bad" act is the work of a blameful actor. This belief has resulted in our being the most litigious people in the world and has given us the world's largest legal profession. It has also led us to criminalize more and more behavior and to demand more and more legal action against those who break laws. Today, many Americans want someone blamed and punished for every transgression and inconvenience they experience.

Social science should have taught us that all human behavior is only partially a matter of free will and that persons are only partially responsible for their deeds. Everyone's actions are always somewhat influenced or dominated by factors not of one's own making and beyond one's personal control (with economic situation being the most influential and obvious).

Moreover, seeking vengeance is a pursuit that brings more frustration than satisfaction. It has not only been an obstacle in solving many social problems and in developing cooperative, communal attitudes (the lack of which is one important cause of the crime problem), but it is in itself a producer of excessive amounts of anxiety and frustration. Ultimately, vindictiveness erects barriers between people, isolates them, and prevents them from constructing the cooperative, communal social organizations that are so necessary for a meaningful, satisfying human existence. Ironically, it is just these social structures that contain the true solution to our crime problem.

The Crime Problem as a Diversion   Our tendency toward vindictiveness is greatly nurtured by the media, politicians, and other public figures who have persistently harangued on the crime issue. They do this largely because the crime issue is seductive. It is seductive to politicians because they can divert attention away from larger and more pressing problems, such as the economy and pollution, whose solutions would require unpopular sacrifices, particularly for them and other more affluent segments of the society. Street crime is seductive to the media because it fits their preferred "sound bite" format of small bits of sensational material. Likewise, it is deeply seductive to the public, who, though they fear crime, possess, at the same time, deep fascination for it.

It's About Time   We must turn away from the excessive use of prisons. The current size of the entire correctional system is consuming large amounts of tax money that are being diverted from essential public services, such as education, child care, mental health, and medical services—the very services that will have a far greater impact on reducing crime than will building more prisons. As we continue to imprison millions of people under intolerably cruel and dangerous conditions, we will accumulate a growing number of ex-convicts who are more or less psychologically and socially crippled and excluded from conventional society, posing a continuing nuisance and threat to others. We will severely damage some of our more cherished humanitarian values, which are corroded by our excessive focus on blame and vengeance. And we will further divide our society into the white affluent classes and a poor nonwhite underclass, many of whom will be convicts and ex-convicts. In effect, we are gradually putting our own apartheid into place.

We believe that the current system can be dramatically reduced without jeopardizing public safety. But how should we accomplish a turnaround of this magnitude? First, we must recognize that crime can only be, at best, marginally reduced by escalating the use of imprisonment. If we are to truly reduce crime rates, we as a society must embark on a decade-long strategy that reverses the social and economic trends of the previous decade. In particular, we must jettison the overly expensive and ineffective criminal justice approach and redirect our energies on the next generation of youth, who already are at risk for becoming the next generation of criminals.

The "crime reduction" reforms we have in mind have little to do with criminal justice reform. Rather, these reforms would serve to reduce poverty, single-parent families headed by females, teenage pregnancies and abortions, welfare dependency, unemployment, high drop-out rates, drug abuse, and inadequate health care. These are the social indicators that have proven to be predictive of high crime rates.

The programs and policies that will work—such as better prenatal health care for pregnant mothers, better health care for children to protect them against life-threatening illnesses, Head Start, Job Corps, and Enterprise Zones—have been well documented and may well be contributing to the current decline in crime.[38] But we also need a level of commitment from our major corporate leaders to reduce the flight of jobs, especially the so-called blue-collar and industrial jobs, from this country to Third World nations where cheap labor can be exploited for profits but at tremendous cost to this country.

So how do we go about cutting our losses? We begin by reducing the prison population as outlined in this chapter and reallocating those "savings" to prevention programs that target at-risk youth and their families.

Humanize Our Prisons   Whether or not we make any progress toward rational sentencing policies and succeed in dramatically reducing our prison populations, we must confront another issue. Our prisons are, at best, warehouses where prisoners stagnate and are rendered less and less capable of coping with outside society or, at worst, cruel and dangerous maxiprisons where prisoners are damaged and suffer severely. As a civilized people, we must not tolerate this.

The consequences to our society of supporting or even tolerating inhumane prisons are varied and profound. There is the obvious consequence of having to receive back into our society released prisoners who have been critically damaged by their imprisonment. Less obvious is that the general society itself is polluted by the mistreatment of its prisoners. In the first place, guards and other staff persons who must work in the inhumane prison environment are contaminated by it, as are their families and the townsfolk near the prison. It is virtually impossible to be part of or witness to the systematic mistreatment of other human beings without experiencing some deleterious effects. More generally, support for an inhumane prison system requires that citizens embrace the simplistic concept that prisoners are less worthy beings who deserve their extreme punishment. This belief, which is advanced by unscrupulous and self-serving politicians for their self-gain, rests on and then in turn, in a looping process, promotes invidi-ousness, hate, fear, and other emotions that are inimical to the functioning of a cohesive, orderly, beneficent society.

Prisons where prisoners are systematically treated as less than human; denied dignity, basic human rights, and life necessities; and are physically and mentally mistreated are festering sores that poison the entire society. The state does not have to make prisons into country clubs or "molly-coddle" felons to treat prisoners humanely. Prisons are inherently punitive and can operate effi-ciently and effectively while treating prisoners in a manner consistent with the minimum standards and rights for prisoners that have been formulated by many private and public bodies.[39] Many of these were proposed in the late 1960s and early 1970s, when considerable concern and effort to reform the prison system were manifest. Some have been realized in many prison systems. But many have not; at present, most people who decide or influence prison policy completely ignore prisoners' rights and welfare. The courts, particularly the U.S. Supreme Court, after almost completely ignoring the plight of prisoners (the "hands-off" policy), began ruling in the early 1960s on issues regarding prisoners' rights, cruel and unusual punishment, and due process. However, after the mid 1970s, the Supreme Court effectively returned to the hands-off policy.[40]

Given the anti–prison reform climate, we believe that presenting an argu-ment in support of a full prisoners' rights agenda would be futile at this time. However, several features of a system of incarceration should be acceptable to anyone interested in accomplishing the prison's dominate goals—punishment and incapacitation—and not engaging in unnecessary and counterproductive punitive practices. These are as follows:

1. *No cruel and unusual punishment.* Prison overcrowding, the adoption of control practices in reaction to prison violence, and the lack of concern on the part of the public have resulted in an increase in extremely punitive policies and practices. These include denial of adequate medical services, the excessive use of physical punishment in the management of prisoners, and housing pris-oners in extremely punitive arrangements, all of which, when delivered maliciously, have been ruled in violation of the Eighth Amendment of the Constitution.

2. *Safety.* Prisoners should be able to avoid being attacked, raped, and mur-dered, and in other ways being preyed on by other prisoners and staff. Effective strategies, such as adequate surveillance, voluntary access to safe living areas within prison systems, housing prisoners in small units, and single celling should be introduced.

3. *Health.* Prisoners should have access to the resources and services required to maintain their physical and mental health. These include access to medical and psychiatric services, an adequate diet, and recreation.[41] It also means that they should not be subjected to incarceration regimens that are physically and mentally deleterious, such as extended periods of isolation and a restriction on mobility.[42]

4. *Rehabilitation.* As suggested earlier, there has been considerable disagreement on whether rehabilitative programs, as they have been practiced, have been effective in reducing recidivism. However, it appears obvious to us and certainly consistent with a rational system of punishment that prisoners should have access to programs that, according to their and appropriate experts' judgment, improve their chances to adjust to life after prison. This approach would include education, vocational training, and a wide variety of treatment programs that have been experimented with in the past or will be created in the future.

5. *Reentry assistance.* Given the large number of inmates being released and the high rate of parole violations, it will be increasingly important to start building supportive reentry programs for these inmates. Most inmates receive little if any preparation for their release or assistance in the three areas they require help the most: employment, residence, and family support. Certainly it makes little sense to simply dump inmates out of prison with no more than $20 to $50 and expect them to make it on the outside as an ex-convict with few, if any, marketable or social skills. Community-based programs operated in particular by nonprofit organizations are needed to help facilitate the reentry process.

This is a minimum list of features that would serve as a foundation for a humane and rational system of incarceration. Many other characteristics should be introduced to achieve a truly effective and humane system.[43] But these listed features are crucial. Without them we will continue to deliver excessive and irrational punishment to our prisoners and dump them back out into the "streets," damaged and handicapped, ready to descend into the growing urban pit called the "underclass" or to be recycled once again through our jail and prison systems.

NOTES

1. Peter Elikann, *SuperPredators: The Demonization of Our Children* (New York: Insight Books, Plenum Publishing, 1999).

2. JFA Institute, *Public Safety, Public Spending: Forecasting America's Prison Population 2007–2011* (Washington, DC: PEW Charitable Trusts, 2007), p. 21.

3. D. McDonald, *The Price of Punishment* (Boulder, CO: Westview, 1989).

4. Carl Loeb, "The Cost of Jailing in New York City," *Crime and Delinquency* (October 1978): 446–452.

5. Collins Center and Florida TaxWatch. *A Billion Dollars and Growing: Why Prison Bonding is Tougher on Florida Taxpayers Than on Crime.* (Tallahassee, Florida, April 2011). Mac Taylor. *Status Report. Implementing AB 900's Prison Construction and Rehabilitation Initiatives.* (Sacramento, CA: Legislative Analyst Office, May 14, 2009).

6. James Austin, Darlene Grant, David Bogard, and Curtiss Pulitzer, *District of Columbia Department of Corrections Long-Term Options Study* (Washington, DC: U.S. Department of Justice, National Institute of Corrections, January 31, 1997).

7. Steven D. Dillingham, *Remarks: The Attorney General's Summit on Law*

Enforcement Responses to Violent Crime: Public Safety in the Nineties (Washington, DC: Bureau of Justice Statistics, March 4–5, 1991).

8. William Barr, *Combating Violent Crime: 24 Recommendations to Strengthen Criminal Justice* (Washington, DC: U.S. Department of Justice, Office of the Attorney General, July 22, 1992).

9. Ibid.

10. The Gallop Organization, Inc. *The Gallup Poll,* www.galloppoll.com (August 2, 2007)

11. Crime in the United States is measured by two different methods. The first is the Uniform Crime Reports (UCR) that includes all crimes reported to the police and tabulated by the FBI. The UCR only captures a limited number of crimes (homicide, rape, aggravated assault, robbery, burglary, larceny theft, and motor vehicle theft). A second method involves annual surveys conducted by the Census Bureau of persons living in households to determine how many households have been victimized by one of seven crimes (rape, robbery, assault, personal theft, household theft, burglary, and motor vehicle theft) each year. This crime reporting system, known as the National Crime Victim Survey, or NCVS, began in 1973. The NCVS does not include crimes against businesses (shoplifting, commercial burglaries), drug crimes, homicides, or crimes against children under the age of twelve. Furthermore, the NCVS tends to record a large number of trivial crimes that are ordinarily not reported to the police. The UCR, unlike the NCVS, does include homicides, crimes committed against businesses or commercial properties, and crimes committed against children under the age of twelve and those not living in households. For a review of the methodological merits of the UCR and NCVS, see Darrell Steffensmeier and Miles Harer, "Did Crime Rise or Fall During the Reagan Presidency?" *Journal of Research in Crime and Delinquency* 28, 3(1991): 330–359

12. Criminologists debate the sources of the discrepancy between the growth in violent crime shown in UCR data and the decline shown by the NCVS. The U.S. Department of Justice has suggested that victims were more likely to report crimes to the police, and law enforcement agencies improved their recording and reporting systems. If these explanations are correct, these changes in reporting created the illusion of a growing crime problem when there actually was none. Also note that the NCVS property rate is based on the number of households, which is lower than the number of persons.

13. As the NCVS was started in 1973, it cannot be used to determine if—or how much—crime rates increased between 1964 and 1973. Most criminologists agree, however, that there was an increase and that some of the increase was due to demographics—the large numbers of baby boomers passing through their high crime-committing years. People aged fifteen to twenty-four commit a substantial proportion of index crimes. The persons in the baby-boom cohort started reaching age fifteen in 1964 and began turning forty around 1990. But demographics cannot explain all of the increase.

14. Richard B. Abell, "Beyond Willie Horton: The Battle of the Prison Bulge," *Policy Review* (Winter 1989): 32–35; William P. Barr, "Speech to California District Attorney's Association," *Federal Sentencing Reporter* 4, 6 (1992): 345–346; John DiIulio and Anne Morrison Piehl, "Does Prison Pay? The Stormy National Debate over the Cost-Effectiveness of Imprisonment," *The Brookings Review* (Fall 1998): 28–35.

15. Edwin W. Zedlweski, *Making Confinement Decisions* (Washington, DC: National Institute of Justice, 1987).

16. Mark A. Cohen, "Pain, Suffering, and Jury Awards: A Study of the Cost of Crime to Victims," *Law and Society Review* 22, 3(1988): 537–555; Ted R. Miller, Mark A. Cohen, and Brian Wiersema, *Victim Costs and Consequences. Research Report* (Washington, DC: U.S. Department of Justice, National Institute of Justice, 1996); *Criminal Victimization in the United States, 1992* (Washington,

DC: U.S. Department of Justice, Bureau of Justice Statistics, 1994), Table 91.

17. Phillip J. Romero, *How Incarcerating More Felons Will Benefit California's Economy* (Sacramento: California Governor's Office of Planning and Research, March 31, 1994).

18. Franklin E. Zimring and Gordon Hawkins, "The New Mathematics of Imprisonment," *Crime and Delinquency* 34 (1988): 425–436.

19. Zimring and Hawkins, *Incapacitation: Penal Confinement and the Restraint of Crime*, p. 138.

20. James Austin, "Are Prisons Really a Bargain?" *Spectrum* (1996): 10.

21. Darrell Steffensmeier and Miles Harer, "Did Crime Rise or Fall During the Reagan Presidency?" *Journal of Research in Crime and Delinquency* 28, 3 (1991): 330–359.

22. Jenni Gainsborough and Marc Mauer, *Diminishing Returns: Crime and Decarceration in the 1990's.* (Washington, DC. The Sentencing Project).

23. Michael Lynch, "Beating a Dead Horse: Is There any Basic Empirical Evidence of the Deterrent Effect of Imprisonment," *Crime, Law and Social Change* 31, 4 (1999): 361. Lynch examined data on U.S. crime and imprisonment trends from 1972 through 1993.

24. Tomislav V. Kocandizic and Lynne M. Vieraitis, "The Effect of County-Level Prison Population Growth on Crime Rates," *Criminology & Public Policy*, 5, 2 (May 2006): 234. The authors examined the effect of incarceration on crime rates in different Florida counties.

25. Raymond Liedka, Anne Morrison Piehl, Bert Useem, and Raymond V. Leidka, "The Crime-Control Effect of Incarceration: Does Scale Matter?" *Criminology & Public Policy*, 5, 2 (May 2006): 245–276. This study analyzed the data on crime rates and incarceration rates for all fifty states and the District of Columbia in the period from 1972 to 2000. The authors believe that whatever gains were achieved in the dramatic rise in imprisonment that began in the 1970s there was a diminishing effect over time.

26. William Spelman, "The Limited Importance of Prison Expansion," in *The Crime Drop in America*, ed. Alfred Blumstein, revised edition, (New York: Cambridge University Press, 2006), pp. 97–129. Spelman based this estimate on the amount of crime recently incarcerated felons *told* interviewers they had committed the year before their arrest. Spelman then assumed that incarcerating and incapacitating those individuals averted the same amount of crime he assumed would be committed subsequently.

27. Bureau of Justice Assistance, "Lifetime Likelihood of Going to State or Federal Prison" (Washington, DC: U.S. Government Printing Office, March 1997).

28. Claude Brown, "Manchild 1984," *This World* (September 23, 1984): 7–8.

29. Jack Katz, in a study of street criminals, found that the excitement of criminal behavior was one of the strong attractions it holds for many offenders. See *Seductions in Crime* (New York: Basic Books, 1990). In a much earlier study, Joan Moore documents the culture of urban Chicanos in Los Angeles and how their involvement in gangs inevitably leads to drugs, arrests, and prison. See *Homeboys: Gangs, Drugs and Prison in the Barrios of Los Angeles* (Philadelphia: Temple University Press, 1978).

30. M. Tonry and N. Morris, *Between Prison and Probation: Intermediate Punishments in a Rational Sentencing Structure* (New York: Oxford University Press, 1988).

31. These punishments may include restitution to victims through apology and paid compensation, restitution to communities through work, and active participation in treatment programs. On the issue of treatment and rehabilitation, research shows that such programs are most effective when targeted at "high risk" people who voluntarily enter such programs. Thus, mandating participation in such programs, especially for people who may not require such services, is counterproductive.

32. People who commit so-called "white collar" crime should pay massive restitution, do extensive community service, and possibly serve house arrest. In short,

they should pay their victims and the community (rather than the taxpayers paying to house them in expensive prisons).

33. C. Guzman, B. Krisberg, and C. Tsukida, (January 2008). *Accelerated Release: A Literature Review*. Oakland, CA: National Council on Crime and Delinquency.

34. http://www.ojp.usdoj.gov/bjs/pub/pdf/pim08st.pdf.

35. D. Star, *Summary Parole: A Six and Twelve Month Follow-Up Evaluation* (Sacramento: Research Unit, California Department of Corrections, 1979); P. G. Jackson, *Bay Area Parole Project*. 1978, Report to the California Department of the Youth Authority. Mimeographed; D. R. Jaman, L. A. Bennett, and J. E. Berecochea, *Early Discharge from Parole: Policy, Practice and Outcome*, Research Report No. 51. (Sacramento: California Department of Sacramento Corrections 1974).

36. A. L. Solomon, V. Kachnowski, and A. Bhati, "Does Parole Work? Analyzing the Impact of Post-Prison Supervision on Re-Arrest Outcomes." (Washington, DC: Urban Institute, 2005).

37. S. Hillsman, (1990). "Fines and Day Fines," in M. Tonry and N. Morris (eds.), *Crime and Justice: A Review of Research*, Vol. 12 (Chicago, Illinois: University of Chicago Press, 1990), pp. 49–98

38. Lisbeth Schorr and Daniel Schorr, *Within Our Reach* (New York: Anchor Books, 1990), for an exhaustive list of such programs and policies.

39. As early as 1955 at Geneva, the United Nations Congress on the Prevention of Crime and the Treatment of Prisoners adopted a set of Standard Minimum Rules for the Treatment of Prisoners. See *Human Rights: A Compilation of International Instruments* (United Nations publication, Sales No. E.88.XIV 1), section G.

40. Jack E. Call, "The Supreme Court and Prisoners' Rights," *Federal Probation* (March 1995): 36–46, for a discussion of the Court's shift in prisoners' rights matters.

41. *Madrid v. Gomez*, 889 F. Supp. 1149 (N.D. Cal. 1995).

42. See *Madrid v. Gomez*. The federal district court of northern California ruled that treatment of prisoners at Pelican Bay SHU (segregated housing unit) was cruel and unusual in these regards. In the opinion delivered by the Federal District Court regarding the conditions of confinement in the SHU at Pelican Bay, the court found that "many, if not most, inmates in the SHU experience some degree of psychological trauma in reaction to their extreme social isolation and the severely restricted environmental stimulation in the SHU."

43. Working Party for the American Friends Service Committee, *The Struggle for Justice* (New York: Hill & Wang, 1971) pp. 168–169. This group, consisting of persons with a variety of experiences with prison systems, produced one of the best-thought-out lists of these reforms. It remains today an excellent guide for the future.

Index

Note: f indicated figure; t indicates table